I0820530

Far Calls

Far Calls

On Omens, Slips & Epiphanies

Daniel Heller-Roazen

ZONE BOOKS · NEW YORK

2025

ZONE BOOKS
633 Vanderbilt Street
Brooklyn, NY 11218

Printed in the United States of America.
Distributed by Princeton University Press,
Princeton, New Jersey, and Woodstock, United Kingdom

Library of Congress Cataloging-in-Publication Data

Names: Heller-Roazen, Daniel, author.
Title: Far calls : on omens, slips, and epiphanies / Daniel Heller-Roazen.
Description: New York : Zone Books, 2025. | Includes bibliographical references and index. | Summary: "Moving from the divinatory rituals of the ancient world to Freud and Lacan, from Homer and Augustine to Edgar Allan Poe and Mallarmé, the Surrealists, Yeats, and Proust, Far Calls explores the persistent power of sonorous coincidence and the varieties of reading that it incites" —Provided by publisher.
Identifiers: LCCN 2024058173 (print) | LCCN 2024058174 (ebook) | ISBN 9781945861048 (hardcover) | ISBN 9781945861055 (ebook)
Subjects: LCSH: Listening in literature. | Divination in literature.
Classification: LCC PN56.L539 H45 2025 (print) | LCC PN56.L539 (ebook) | DDC 809—dc23/eng/20250311
LC record available at https://lccn.loc.gov/2024058173
LC ebook record available at https://lccn.loc.gov/2024058174

Contents

CHAPTER ONE

The Interval

The act of speaking implies an act of hearing—another's or one's own. Between these two events, however, there is an interval, which is perceptible in several forms. It may consist of a gap in time that is due to the process of articulation; it may appear as a lag in cognition that lasts as long as it takes for what has been said to acquire sense and consequence. It is tempting to dismiss such transient phenomena as accidents of articulation and comprehension. The truth is that they attest to a precious possibility. When speaking and hearing imply each other without being coincident, what is said can be heard otherwise than as it was intended. There is a chance, then, for language to prove itself more than an instrument to an end and for it to exceed "communication," defined as the transmission of information by means of a code, a context, and a contact from an addresser to an addressee.[1] When what has been uttered must be apprehended part by part, when it runs the risk of being heard solely in part, and when it may therefore be understood too soon as well as also too late, meanings shift. Senses accrue and are effaced. Diverse, conflicting, and even contradictory phrases and propositions become audible. The saying itself, in its shifting relation to understanding, becomes an event.

What appears in such circumstances may well appear to be no more than a minor perturbation in the course of discourse. Yet the membrane that separates articulation from comprehension can also allow a truth to sound. Its sign can appear in many guises. It may seem to be incontrovertible or to be concealed, yet susceptible to identification by means of intuition or a technique of decipherment. It can be the fruit of a concerted effort to listen or to listen in, to hear or to overhear, if not to eavesdrop, but it can also be the unintended effect of a momentary distraction or the result of concentration on some unrelated matter. It can be audible in a fleeting resemblance: an echo or a pun by which a syllable, word, or phrase suggests several meanings at once. It may be sealed in a slip or parapraxis in the Freudian sense, in which an apparent blunder of the tongue or ear turns out to be the index of a thought that can assume no other shape. Evidently or subtly, such events all interrupt the orderly exchange of intentions. They give respite from communication: a pause for breath in which explicit statement and oblique suggestion, word and omen, can scarcely be told apart.

Whether such moments are understood as accidents or as the effects of a hidden cause, they imply the variety of event known as "coincidences," which can be neither foretold nor repeated and in which distinct series of causation seem suddenly to cross. Those who have dared to consider such happenings as objects worthy of study in themselves compose a company of interpreters at once motley and distinguished. In various settings and for the most dissimilar of reasons, prophets, priests, and rabbis, poets and philosophers, linguists, psychiatrists and psychoanalysts, novelists and filmmakers have all suggested that in the hazards of speaking and hearing, misspeaking and overhearing, there are indications that can be gleaned by no other means. To catch and read them, they have also held, arts of inference and elucidation are required.

Those arts have an exceedingly long history. One might even argue that they stretch beyond the records of the past, being identifiable with a practice that is attested across the world: "divination," as it is called in the traditions that understand themselves in vocabularies marked by the terminology of the ancient Romans. Cicero, who is the first author to employ the Latin word *divinatio*, defines it as the anticipation of what seems to occur by accident: "the prediction and presentiment of those things which are thought to occur by chance" (*earum rerum, quae fortuitae putantur, praedictio atque praesensio*).[2] Cicero presents *divinatio* as the Roman equivalent of a Greek expression, *mantikē*, which, as he well knew, also admitted of other understandings. Sextus Empiricus, a century or two after Cicero, presents it as "a theoretical and interpretative knowledge of the signs sent by gods to men" (*epistēmē theōrētikē kai exēgētikē tōn hypo theōn anthrōpois didomenōn sēmeiōn*).[3] The Hippocratic treatise *On Regimen* offers a fuller account:

> Divination is like this: By the visible it knows the invisible, and by the present it knows the future, and by dead things it gains knowledge of the living, and it becomes aware from things that have no awareness. The person who knows it is always correct, while the person who does not sometimes is and sometimes is not. In this way it imitates human life and human nature [*physin anthrōpou kai bion tauta mimeitai*].[4]

"Divination" in that broadly Hippocratic sense has been studied from almost innumerable perspectives, in research informed by anthropology, sociology, political science, philosophy, and religious studies.[5] In scholarship on the cultures of the ancient Mediterranean, mantic theory and practice has been the object of at least three critical approaches. One line of inquiry has taken it to involve the field of apparently supernatural causation all too summarily dubbed "magic." A second mode of analysis understands it as involving forms of inferential reasoning that in their outline, if not in all their contents, illustrate or anticipate the methods of modern science. A third approach understands divination as a crucial element in collective social and political practices.

Each of these three scholarly paths has proven fertile, and none has been exhausted. Yet there are also other means by which to grasp practices of divination and the forms of reasoning that they have involved. In an extraordinarily wide-ranging essay first published in 1979, Carlo Ginzburg presented mantic procedures as among the oldest examples of an epistemological model that he called the "conjectural paradigm."[6] According to his account, divination consists in a detection by means of clues that is close in kind to the forms of reason informing such disparate practices as hunting, medicine, criminology, art-historical authentication, and psychoanalysis. Focusing on ancient Greek texts, Peter Struck, by contrast, argued in an original 2016 book that divination is best understood as involving "surplus knowledge," which is extracted from "messages" from the world that "add up, sometimes in uncanny ways, to more than the sum of their parts," constituting what is known today as "intuition."[7]

In a few brief texts composed in 1932 and 1933, Walter Benjamin proposed an elusive, yet far-reaching account of such an intuition that he rooted in an ability that he called "the mimetic faculty." "Nature produces similarities [*Ähnlichkeiten*]," he declared, introducing his "doctrine of the similar," adding, "one need only think of mimicry." Human beings, as he went on to state, "possess the highest capacity for producing similarities." Because of "the once powerful compulsion to become similar and to behave mimetically," they perceive resemblances, and "there is perhaps not a single higher power" of the mind in which such an apprehension does not "play a decisive role." That a "mimetic faculty" enables the human perception of likenesses among things that share a common form is obvious enough. More striking and more perplexing is the claim that the same power enables human beings to grasp similarity of a subtler kind: "nonsensuous resemblance" (*unsinnliche Ähnlichkeit*). The meaning of that term is far from clear. It appears to signify a likeness between things that do not or that no longer share a "sensuous" (*sinnlich*) property, such as a shape, form, feature, or set of traits. Benjamin gave several examples of practices consisting in the detection of such "nonsensuous resemblances." He alluded to games and make-believe, in which children and adults imitate human and inhuman objects and processes. He mentioned dance, which Stéphane Mallarmé and Paul Valéry, in works that he read with care, cast as an art by which human beings become "everything" and "nothing."[8] Above all, Benjamin evoked divination, both archaic and modern, his preferred examples being the interpretation of the motions of celestial bodies in astrology, the extraction of a sense from handwriting in graphology, and the study of the viscera of sacrificial animals in extispicy.

All such procedures, for Benjamin, involve the perception of nonsensuous similarities. To employ his term of choice, they are therefore practices of "reading." Today, that activity is commonly understood to involve the coordination of a graphic sign, such as a letter or a character, with a sound, word, or idea according to a convention. Benjamin proposed a different account, in which the habits of children and adults and the practices of earlier and later stages of humanity converge. "The schoolboy reads his ABC book, and the astrologer reads the future in the stars. In the first sentence, reading is not separated out into its components. Quite the opposite in the second case, though, which clarifies the process at both its levels: the astrologer reads the constellation from the stars in the sky; simultaneously, he reads the future or fate from it."[9] Moved by the "compulsion to become similar and to behave mimetically," readers, whether children or astrologers, grasp correspondences between orders that share no stable likeness: orders such as script and speech or the constellation and a present, past, or future moment. In such practices of putting into relation the unalike, a "nonsensuous resemblance" is grasped in the perception of a fugitive event. "The perception of similarity is in every case bound to a flashing up," Benjamin wrote, stressing its transience. "It flits past. It may be won again, but it cannot truly be held fast as can other perceptions."[10] Reading is in this sense a productive practice, which implies at once the identification of units such as letters in media in which they are inapparent, the ordering of such units in a sequence, and a consequent act of inference. Far from corresponding to a given script, reading, then, is what enables writing. Benjamin found the formula for such a generative process in a phrase of Hugo von Hoffmannsthal's that he cited more than once: "reading what was never written" (*lesen, was nie geschrieben wurde*). It is "the oldest reading": "reading prior to all languages, from entrails, the stars, or dances."[11]

The ancient Romans were familiar with a saying that sets out the conditions of such reading in the perception of unwritten language. The saying is a dictum that in its verbless syntax yokes together two words of a resemblant sound: *nomen omen*. The meaning of the proverb is at first glance clear. It states that the name (*nomen*) is a portent or a presage (*omen*). The second term of the phrase, one might comment, is implicit in the first, just as the Latin *omen* lurks within the word *nomen*. According to the grammar of the ancient language and the logical ambiguities that mark assertions of identity, however, the proverb also suggests an inverse thesis: *omen nomen*, "the portent or the presage is a name." The two sentences concord in suggesting that the unexpectedly revelatory signs that the Romans called "omens" (*omina*) are discernible not only in such obviously portentous phenomena as constellations, striking natural occurrences, and the enigmatic morphology of living bodies. Presages are also to be found in the field of names, which is speech.

Yet when exactly might words and portents, *nomina* and *omina*, converge or coincide? The answer that is proposed in the pages of this book is that it happens in the gap that separates utterance from understanding, in moments of hesitation and confusion, when speaking cannot be distinguished from misspeaking, when hearing fades into unanticipated mishearing or overhearing, and when seemingly clear statements suddenly show themselves to contain riddles to which guesses alone are adequate. At such points, language runs off the rails of its "communicative function." If only for an instant and if only in the most particular and least repeatable of situations, signs are susceptible to divination, defined as a "reading of what was never written."

Such a coming to legibility implies a model of linguistic activity that is in several respects unusual, if not unique. Here, what is at issue is not the articulation envisaged by the Augustinian and the Cartesian traditions, by which thinking beings clarify their own representations to themselves through a sonorous or silent chain of reasoning. Yet the conditions of the disclosure of the *nomen-omen* (or *omen-nomen*) are also irreducible to conversation as it is generally conceived, in which several people in one place and at one time address each other. When a portent momentarily "flashes up" in a word, a phrase, or the silences that punctuate it, one or many speakers may be present, but the paradigms of the monologue and the dialogue are inadequate. To define such occurrences, one requires another model: that of reading the unwritten.

Those who catch an unanticipated sense in a scrap of discourse can be intimately, even intensely touched by it. Yet they grasp immediately that the striking sign hails from elsewhere. Should they themselves have spoken the word or phrase that astonishes them, they will be aware that they did not distinctly intend to do so; otherwise, they will hardly have been surprised by it. Should the revelatory expression, by contrast, sound from the mouth of another individual, hearers will likewise understand that it was not ostensibly addressed to them or that its speaker did not mean to utter it as they have inadvertently—rightly or wrongly—received it. Perceiving an omen in a passing word, catching a presage in a fragment of circumstantial talk, the diviner deciphers something that no one has spelled out, like the astrologer grasping fate in the constellation or the graphologist reconstructing character from a series of immobile marks.

How to do so, according to what rules and principles, and to what effects, are questions that can be treated adequately only case by case, through a reconstitution of the diverse ritual, literary, psychological, and philosophical uses to which the seeming accidents of speech have been put. Such an endeavor requires that one entertain the possibility that the mishaps of communication may be more than they appear to be. Such a supposition may of course prove to be unfounded, and it cannot be granted in advance that the interpretations that it enables explain more than misunderstandings. Yet there is also no certainty that unanticipated coincidences in the emission and the reception of discourse are but senseless stumbles. It may be that that in concentrating on the fleeting interval that ties and disjoins hearing from speaking and in attending to what comes to pass in it, one may catch sight of a thing rarer than error: truth readable in the unexpected, be it necessity or chance.

CHAPTER TWO

Hermes at Dusk

Hermes, "bringer of dreams, night-watcher, and gate-lurker" (*hēgētor' oneirōn, nuktos opōpētēra, pulēdokon*) begins life out of sight, in the shadows of the cave where his mother, Maia, the most modest of goddesses, "shunned the company of the blessed gods."[1] He who will become the "immortals' coursing messenger" is the last-born of the twelve Olympians. At the time of his birth, the mighty children of the Titan Kronos, Hestia, Zeus, Poseidon, Hera, and Demeter, have revealed themselves; their progeny, Apollo, Artemis, Ares, Aphrodite, Hephaestus, and Athena, are all familiar to humanity. Each of these divinities is understood to prevail over certain domains of individual and collective life; each is therefore accorded ritual forms of worship and sacrifice. Born into a world in which titles and honors have been "divided and distributed," Hermes faces a new predicament.[2] How will he establish himself? "Resourceful and cunning" (*polyptropos kai haimulomētis*), he loses no time in finding a solution. It consists in a new practice. Hermes takes what he encounters, removes it from its setting, and refashions it. Often, he then puts it into circulation in a disguised or altered form that few have the skill to recognize.

One might call Hermes's practice robbery or, more euphemistically, exchange. One can also conceive of it as a technique of divine appropriation whose traces become discernible to mortals in the events and objects that the Greeks called *hermaia*: "gifts of Hermes," "unexpected bouts of luck," "godsends," "windfalls."[3] Nowhere do such happenings play more crucial roles than in the oldest surviving account of the god's youth, the archaic "Hymn to Hermes" that tradition attributes to Homer. Unexpected occurrences are woven into the fabric of this account of the god's birth and first actions, a "chronometrical theogony" in which every event is accorded a precise moment in a tightly defined sequence.[4] The poem recounts how Hermes, springing "from his mother's immortal legs," "jumps up," advancing to the place with which he would henceforth be most associated: the threshold. There, in front of his mother's cave, he sees a tortoise "grazing on the lush grass." "Here's a portent of good fortune for me! I will not slight this!"[5] the young god exclaims. The animal has "fallen into" (*antebolēsen*) Hermes's path, and without a moment's hesitation, the infant grasps the sudden occurrence as a *symbolon*: a "sign" or "token" and, more literally, a "falling together" and "encounter of two things" that possesses the value of an "omen."[6]

Hermes salutes the animal in flattering terms, admiring its "blotchy shell." He suggests that there is much to be gained from its passing across the threshold of the cave. As is quickly clear, the truth of his claim holds above all for the god. The tortoise, mute and immobile at the entrance, has no time to respond. "'Better to be in the house; it is dangerous outside,'" Hermes tells the animal, "'For you will be a check against baleful visitation while you live, and if you die, then you may be a beautiful singer.'" With arms outstretched, the newborn deity picks up the tortoise and goes back inside the dwelling, "carrying the lovely plaything."[7] It meets a swift death at his hands. Hermes scrapes out the body of the animal, cuts reed stalks, and fastens them to its shell, stretches an ox hide over the stalks, attaches to it two arms, a crossbar and "seven sheep-gut strings to sound in concord."[8] From the carapace, Hermes invents the lyre.[9]

As scholars have observed, the god's first fabrication consists in a sequence of acts of removal, displacement, and reversal. The body of the animal moves from the mountains to the home, from outside to inside, passing from the silence of life into song in death, even as its once-convex shell assumes the concave position against which strings will sound.[10] Joined to various other objects presumably lying about in Maia's cave — reeds, an ox hide, sheep guts — the remains of the tortoise furnish the frame for a divine *bricolage*.[11] Hermes immediately exhibits its power. "He tried it out with a plectrum in a tuned scale," the poet recounts, "and it rang out impressively under his hand." The god proceeded to sing "of Zeus son of Kronos and fair-shod Maia," their love, their union, and their sole child.[12] Hermes sings, in short, of himself. He "declares his own renowned lineage,"[13] anticipating the hymn that will contain that song.[14] It is the "birth of *epos*"[15] within *epos*, from a lucky find.

Yet even as he sings, the god ponders other projects. Although divine, he has not yet attained the indifference with respect to food that characterizes the mature Greek gods. As the Homeric hymn puts it in no uncertain terms, the immortal child "craves meat."[16] On the evening of his first day, as "the sun was dripping below the earth towards Ocean with his horses and chariot," Hermes therefore sets aside his lyre and leaves the cave in search of Apollo's cattle. The poem presents the god's subsequent motions in measured steps. It is nightfall when Hermes leaves Mount Cyllene for Pieria, the "shadowy mountain" beneath Olympus, where Apollo's kine is grazing. At midnight, having driven the herd to the river Alpheios, the godly child kindles a fire and slaughters two of the curly-horned cows, cutting the carcasses, roasting them, spreading out their hides to dry, and dividing the meat into twelve portions. Hermes appears to enact a sacrifice: anticipation or imitation of the sacred rites that mortals would offer to the twelve Olympians, among whom Hermes, son of Zeus and Maia, is implicitly included.[17] As day breaks, he returns stealthily to the place of his birth, on the border of Arcadia and Achaia: "Zeus's courser Hermes twisted sideways and slipped in through the latch-hole of the mansion like an autumn mist. Heading straight through the cave he reached the rich sanctum, treading softly, making no noise as on a floor; and speedily glorious Hermes had gone to his cradle."[18]

By this point, Hermes has absconded with the property of Apollo and destroyed it in part, but it would be an oversight to consider his deeds to be no more than theft. They consist less in taking what belongs to another than in drawing it away and transferring it elsewhere with such cunning as to be almost undetectable. As Jenny Strauss Clay remarks, in his taking of the kine, "Hermes adopts three different devices to conceal the direction of his theft. First, he drives the cattle on a zigzag path, avoiding the normal roads (*planodias d'ēlaune* [75]; *odoiporiēn aleeinōn* [85]); then, he turns them around, so that their tracks are reversed (*antia poiēsas hoplas* [77]); and finally, he disguises his own tracks by tying branches to his feet (*hypo possin edēsato sandala* [83])."[19] Searching for his cattle, Apollo cannot make sense of the complex markings that remain of their movement: "Heavens," he exclaims, gazing on the many tracks, "this is an extraordinary thing [*mega thauma*] that I see!"[20] Hermes has concealed the "sign" (*sēma*) of his sacrifice, driving the remaining cows into a dark cavern. Dominique Jaillard comments that "Apollo, the diviner, the solver of riddles, understands (*egnō*) that the robber of the herd is his newborn younger brother only when he perceives and interprets (*enoei*) a complementary sign, which is itself 'independent' of Hermes' acts and deeds: a bird that is flying through the sky."[21] In a "propitious moment," the god glimpses hides stretched out to dry on a rock; he thus infers that two of his cattle have been killed.[22]

On the next day of his life, Hermes must face his enraged brother, who has found his way to Maia's cave, demanding explanations from her young son.

> When the son of Zeus and Maia saw that it was the far-shooter Apollo angry about his cattle, he burrowed down into his fragrant swaddling cloth; as a mash of log embers is concealed under the wood ash, so Hermes curled himself up on seeing the Far-shooter, and compressed his head and arms and legs into a little space, just like a fresh-bathed baby inviting sweet sleep, though wide awake, in reality, keeping his lyre under his armpit.[23]

Apollo demands an answer. Hermes, feigning ignorance and innocence, makes a striking gesture: he "pushes his hands up by his ears," or, according to another rendition, "with both hands, pushes up the covering around his shoulders to his ears," even as he protests and claims that he has done no wrong.[24] Ultimately, Hermes admits to the deeds he has committed. Yet he avoids paying the price of his actions by resorting an ingenious proposition of exchange. He presents his brother with the instrument that he fashioned from the tortoise that he met. Apollo marvels at the lyre, accepts it, and gives Hermes his remaining cattle in return.

Yet the young god is still not satisfied, and in the last section of the Homeric hymn, he asks for more. The text is difficult to interpret.[25] It is clear, however, that Hermes begs his brother to grant him a share in the power of divination (*tēn manteiēn*).[26] Apollo refuses, declaring himself the sole god to know "Zeus' intricate intent."[27] The end of the hymn, however, does not find Hermes empty-handed. Apollo puts in his brother's charge "certain august maidens, sisters, adorned with swift wings," explaining, "they are three in number, their heads are dusted with white barley meal, and they dwell down in a hollow of Parnassus. They are sources of separate prophecy, which I practiced when still a child tending my cattle."[28]

The identity of these three "august maidens" is obscure and has been the subject of considerable commentary.[29] Yet certain characteristics of their "separate prophecy" may nonetheless be distinguished. Theirs is a form of divination of which it appears that "Zeus takes no account."[30] This is perhaps why Apollo may freely remit it to his acquisitive sibling. One might also deduce that it concerns matters of meagre importance in which the god of Delphi, having reached maturity, has little interest.[31] Most important is doubtless that in being disjoined from the will of Zeus, the proleptic speech of these maidens eludes any strict necessity. Apollo declares that when the three Parnassians "speed on after consuming honey, they are favorable and will tell the truth [*alētheiēn agoreuein*], but if they are turned away from the sweet food of the gods, then they are misled [*pseudeontai dēpeitai*], agitating among themselves."[32] The divinatory power over which Hermes will hold sway may lead, therefore, to the false no less than to the true.

Well after the period in which the hymn was composed and first recited, Hermes is associated with practices of conjecture and the uncertain interpretation of the future. The messenger god is the divinity who presides, in particular, over decision processes involving drawing by lots and throwing dice.[33] There are also indications that in the "lucky events" named after Hermes, *hermaia*, the people of antiquity discerned *symbola*: coincidences, significant happenings, tokens, and augurs. At times, the "gifts of Hermes" acquired an oracular force. A precious example is to be found in the *Geography* of Pausanias, the voyager of the second century AD. Discussing the settlements and monuments of Achaia, this author recalls seeing, in the middle of the marketplace of Pharae, near Patras, "an image of Hermes, made of stone and bearded":

> Standing right on the earth, it is of square shape, and of no great size. On it is an inscription, saying that it was dedicated by Simylus the Messenian. It is called Hermes of the Market, and by it is established an oracle. In front of the image is placed a hearth, which also is of stone, and to the hearth bronze lamps are fastened with lead. Coming at eventide, the inquirer of the god, having burnt incense upon the hearth, fills the lamps with oil and lights them, puts on the altar on the right of the image a local coin, called a "copper," and asks in the ear of the god the particular question he wishes to put to him. After that he stops his ears and leaves the market-place. On coming outside he takes his hands from his ears, and whatever voice he hears he considers oracular.[34]

This passage constitutes the sole surviving account of a shrine belonging to Hermes.[35] Yet that circumstance is but the first of its distinctions. It is striking that for the operation of this oracle, details of setting—timing as well as placement—are crucial. The rite is to be accomplished at dusk, in the moment when night begins to fall, and Hermes, divinity of the passage, transition, and threshold, is at his apogee. Movement through space is also embedded in the conditions that prompt the god's action and that determine the reception of his gift. The inquirer is to come, to perform the ritual deeds, to murmur his question into the stony ears of the divinity, and to go. It is in the motion from the inside of the market to its outside — and from the covering of his ears to their uncovering — that the divine answer will arrive.[36] The omen will be revealed at the point where the worshipper and the sudden sound cross paths.

Hermes of the Market exemplifies a practice of divination by a curious means for which the ancient Greek language had a name: *klēdōn. Klēdones* are "presages or omens contained in words," words that are less heard than overheard, being perceived by chance or accident. In a secondary and tertiary sense, *klēdones* are "rumours," "tidings," "callings" or "invocations."[37] Accordingly, inference by *klēdōn* or, to employ the modern term of art, "kledonomancy," is "the acceptance of the fatal word or of the spoken omen":[38] the unexpected perception of an utterance understood as prophetic.[39] Auguste Bouché-Leclercq offered the first modern account of the phenomenon in 1879 in his four-volume *History of Divination in Antiquity*. He explains:

> What is at issue is human speech employed by Providence as an enigmatic sign, sometimes with a meaning that is far removed from the natural meaning of words. To designate the sole source of kledonomancy, one must give up the search for technical terms. There is no designation for supernatural speech that cannot also be used to designate human speech; and, moreover, the word *klēdōn*, which one might wish to reserve for spontaneous discourse, can also point by extension to the divine voice or, in the language of the late Empire, the invocation of a demon.[40]

Pausanias himself alludes to two other oracles of such a "kledonomantic" variety, one in Egypt, the other in Smryna.[41] Scholars have found evidence of a third example, a statue from Pitane, in Asia Minor, bearing the inscription "Kledonic [*Klēdonios*] Hermes."[42] Before Pausanias, however, there is no textual record of a shrine to such a god. Earlier examples of divination by seemingly chance acts of hearing differ from the Achaian oracle that he describes. Herodotus's *Histories* are in this respect instructive. In book 9 of his chronicles, the Spartan king Leutychides arrives on the island of Samos, where a man beseeches him to join his people in their revolt against the Persians, "delivering the Greeks from slavery and driving the barbarians away."[43] "As the Samian stranger was pleading so earnestly," Herodotus writes, "Leutychides asked him (whether it was that he desired to know for the sake of a *klēdōn*, or through some happy chance of a god [*eite klēdonos heineken thelōn pythesthai eite kai kata syntykhiēn theou poieuntos*]), 'Samian stranger, what is your name?'" The answer resolves the question: "'Hegesistratos,' he replied," uttering a name that, in Greek, can be etymologically analyzed as "Army Commander" (*Hēgēsi-stratou*). To hazard a transposition into English, it is, in other words, as if the king just learned that he was speaking to a man named "Victor." "Leutychides cut short whatever else Hegesistratus had begun to say and cried: 'I accept the omen of Hegesistratos [*dekomai ton oiōnon Hēgēsistratou*], Samian stranger; now see to it that before you sail from here you and those who are with you pledge that the Samians will be our zealous allies.'"[44]

The exchange is remarkable for the conditions of its interruption. The attempt at persuasion ends abruptly for reasons that neither of the speakers in the dialogue anticipated. The Samian succeeds in winning the case that he pleads, but not for the reasons for which he argued. Conversely, the Spartan assents to the request that has been advanced not due to a sentence that has been asserted, but due to the resonances of a name that happens to have been uttered. In an instant, Leutychides catches hold of a portent in a part of speech, a portent that was not intended by its speaker. Meaning to identify his name, the Samian unwittingly gives the king a reason to consent to his demand. With his decisive judgment—"I accept the omen of Hegesistratos"—the monarch submits himself to the greater force of the *symbolon*. It is a coincidence of syllables in a certain situation and at a certain time. He declares his reverence for a sonorous contingency: the audible superposition of different words.

The contrast between such divination and the oracles associated with Apollo is sharp. In the exchange between Leuchytades and Hegesistratos, mortals are alone. No hieratic intermediary stands between human beings and gods; priests and priestesses, seers, prophets and prophetesses are lacking. Zeus and his "intricate intent" are absent from the discussion, if not indifferent to its outcome. The truth is neither sung nor declaimed; rather, it is unexpectedly heard in the instant of its speaking. To this degree, one might compare the king's sudden catching of the *klēdōn* in the *Histories* to the act by which, according to Pausanias, the visitor to Pharae in Achaia takes hold of the first sound that he hears upon stepping out of the market. In both cases, speech, in Bouché-Leclercq's terms, is "employed as an enigmatic sign"; words are perceived in unanticipated senses and accepted as "prophetic."

Yet the differences between the two "kledonomancies" are significant. Relating that the Spartan king asked his interlocutor for his name, the Greek historian admits to an uncertainty: he cannot say whether or not Leutychides "desired to know for the sake of a presage [*klēdonos heineken*]." Herodotus suggests that in the dialogue between Leutychides and Hegesistratos, the perception of the *klēdōn* may have occurred by accident. Although the "ominous" response may have been solicited by the king, it may also have been a chance happening or a stroke of luck. By contrast, in the shrine at Pharae, the event belongs to the domain of ritual practice. In the visit to Hermes of the Market, every step taken, every gesture performed, has a single end: to draw out a portent from a throng of seemingly random sounds.

It is remarkable that in both Herodotus and Pausanias, the *klēdōn* becomes perceptible only once discursive segments are disjoined from dialogue. In the exchange evoked by Herodotus, the appearance of the omen briefly interrupts the discussion between the Spartan and the Samian. Speech then takes on an unexpected valence; the speaker says a thing he did not intend to state, identifying himself as "Army Commander," even as the hearer finds himself before a signification that he cannot refer to his interlocutor's intention. The ritual evoked by Pausanias loosens the practice of hearing more drastically from participation in conversation. In stepping out of the market of Pharae and uncovering his ears, the inquirer to the god is to listen for a signal without partaking in any verbal exchange. He absents himself from the event of discourse even as he strives to grasp hold of a sign. He does not lay claim to the role of the speaker, nor does he presume to be himself directly addressed. He is, in short, neither *I* nor *you*. Mute, he merely strains to hear.

In this sense, the visitor who honors the Hermes of Pharae leaves the shrine in the image of his god. At the end of his ritual itinerary, he becomes a "gate-lurker." Covering and uncovering his ears, he has prepared himself to encounter a sonorous event as precious as it is elusive. Hermes, known in Athens as the "Whisperer" (*Psythuros*), will give him a signal on the threshold of the audible.[45] To assume that such a signal must be a phrase or word would be to presume too much. The geographer is more prudent. "On coming outside" the market, Pausanias specifies, the visitor to the shrine "takes his hands from his ears, and whatever voice he hears he considers oracular." That "voice" (*phōnē*) could be some spoken discourse, but it could also be a thing far less distinct. "The term *phōnē* is here compatible with any *noise* that is significant because of being perceived in adequate conditions."[46] What matters in this case is not the meaning of an utterance, but the sense that sounds accrue when perceived from a particular perspective and at a certain moment. As night falls, the divinity of the path, of gods "the friendliest and most generous of all towards human beings,"[47] offers a mortal the chance to catch hold of an augur in its sounding. Wrenched from conversation or snatched from the sound world, the found voice is the answer to the question that Hermes alone has heard.

CHAPTER THREE

The Summons

Calls resound in almost every instance of discourse: between those who know each other and those who have yet to be acquainted, among adults as well as children. They stretch from simple signals and vocal gestures to the most articulate of demands, from the automatism of the exclamation to the ritual forms of the prayer and the hymn. One might adopt several methods in studying their structure. One possibility is to take the call to be a dialogic element, definable with respect to the conditions that determine the exchanges between speakers and hearers. Proceeding on the basis of that hypothesis would require establishing the circumstances of conversations in which calls are made. Participants, their various relations, and their discernible intentions would then all need to be defined. They would form the settings in which invocations occurred. A different possibility would be to follow a more minimal program, abstaining from any assumption about the dialogic nature of the call. The task, then, would be to conceive of a calling, so to speak, in itself, as the event in which an invocation comes to pass.

That it is possible to isolate a summons irreducible to any single speaker's will is suggested by the fact that languages contain nouns signifying nothing but the act of "calling," "invoking," and "demanding," nouns such as the classical Greek word *klēdōn*. Dictionaries suggest that it possesses three senses: "omen or presage contained in a word or sound"; "rumor, tidings, and report"; and "a calling on, invocation."[1] Yet in its construction, the term betrays a simpler nature. As Pierre Chantraine noted in a seminal 1933 study of Greek morphology, *klēdōn* is the action noun that corresponds to the verb *kaleō or kalō*, "to call or summon," "invite," "invoke," and "demand." More exactly, *klēdōn* belongs to a class of substantives formed through the addition to the verbal theme of a suffix in /d/, followed by a nasal, such as /n/. *Lēthedōn*, "forgetting," derives in the same way from *lēthō*, a form of *lanthanō* and *lanthanomai*, "to forget," just as *lampēdōn*, "shining," is constructed on the basis of *lampō*, "to give light, shine, beam," and *khairēdōn*, "rejoicing," is linked to *khairō*, "to rejoice, take pleasure in, enjoy." In its structure, *klēdōn* likewise points to a complete action: the event of a calling.[2]

It is worth trying to refer the word's three dictionary definitions to this fact. Once one grasps *klēdōn* as the action noun of *kaleō*, the meaning of "calling on, invocation" is self-evident. That the term may denote "rumor, tidings, and report" can also be derived from this sense; all three meanings are graspable as the contents of an "invocation." More difficult is the relation that an "omen or presage contained in a word or sound" might bear to "calling, summoning; inviting; invoking; demanding." What links the augur to the summons? The linguistic evidence suggests a curious idea: in the movement by which one person calls to another, something other than a speaker's intention and knowledge is discernible, something attainable solely through the special practice of inference that is divination. Beyond their explicit reference to persons, in other words, calls contain portents. Conversely, the notion of the "omen or presage contained in a word or sound" seems to be derivable from a certain notion of address. Attempting to articulate the relation of *kaleō* to *klēdōn*, one might conclude that no matter the awareness of the speaker, wherever a summons takes place, there is material for divination. One could add, symmetrically, that when hidden presages are detected in discourse, they are the effects of callings, demands, and invocations.

To venture further, it is necessary to assemble and examine the textual evidence, which consists of *klēdones* in Greek sources: utterances that are either identified by this term or that, although never named as such, illustrate the senses of the word *klēdōn*. The first occurrences of the expression are to be found in the earliest stratum of ancient poetry. In book 18 of the *Odyssey*, the son of Laertes has returned from the war and his wanderings to his native Ithaca. To avoid detection by the suitors who occupy his palace, he has disguised himself as a beggar. He is shunted aside by one Arnaios or Iros, a vagabond who refuses to share with him the provisions that the suitors at the court accord the indigent. Odysseus and Iros quickly come to blows. Aided by Athena, the hero is victorious. At the conclusion of their skirmish, Odysseus drags the bleeding Iros by the foot through to the porch, where he props him up "against the courtyard wall." Returning inside, Odysseus is greeted by the suitors who, "laughing sweetly" at the spectacle of the fight, congratulate him on his exploit. Without having any inkling of the identity of the man to whom they speak, they wish him well in his future undertakings:

> May Zeus, stranger, and all the other immortals give you
> what you want most of all and what is dear to your spirit,
> for having stopped the wandering of this greedy creature
> in our neighborhood.[3]

Summoning the greatest of the gods to hear their prayer, the suitors say more than they mean.[4] Zeus is to grant the "stranger" what he wishes; yet since what he most desires is to rid his house of the guests, the speakers of these lines make themselves into the unwitting petitioners of their own downfall. The augur in their words is not lost on the man of many wiles. In silence, he catches the sense that the suitors do not intend. "So they spoke," the bard relates, "and great Odysseus was pleased at the omen" (*hōs ar' ephan, khairen de kleēdoni dios Odusseus*).[5] The hero rejoices in the *klēdōn* because of the clear blessing that it holds for him and because of the hidden malediction that it contains for its speakers. Their incapacity to grasp the meaning of their words may be a propitious sign that despite their number and their apparent strength, the suitors are weak before the intelligence of Odysseus.

Confronted by a truth spoken without a speaker's intention or awareness, the ancient Greeks would often draw an inference: in the *klēdōn*, they surmised, a more than human voice sounds in the mouths of mortals. Herodotus evokes this idea in recounting the exchange between the Spartan king and the Samian, in which the king's request for his interlocutor's name expresses either his wish for a *klēdōn* or "some happy chance of a god."[6] It seems that, whether anticipated or unexpected, the man's answer is an "omen or presage contained in a word or sound" because it suggests a divine power. Describing the Achaian shrine to Hermes in Pharae, Pausanias, for his part, indicates that the *klēdōn* that sounds in the word or noise heard by the worshiper is a sign sent by the god. What the visitor hears on the edge of the market may well be the acoustical effect of an ordinary event. Yet for such a *phōnē*, "voice or noise," to count as divinatory, it must be grasped as an occurrence also attributable to the youngest of the Olympians.

The archaic epic poem that Aristotle calls the *Little Iliad*, which survives today in a fragmentary form, contains a striking example of the perception of such presages. The setting is a dispute that occurs outside the narrative limits of the "greater" *Iliad*, after the death of Achilles, between Ajax and Odysseus. Both Achaean warriors lay claim to the armor of the fallen hero. To resolve the conflict, Nestor counsels the men to remit themselves to the will of the gods insofar as it can be gleaned through overhearing. In the words of the scholiast who relates the scene, Nestor "advised the Greeks to send some men to below the Trojans' wall to eavesdrop concerning the bravery of the heroes in question [*ōtakoustēsontas peri tēs andreias tōn proeirēmenōn hērōōn*]." When the Achaeans reach their destination, they hide and make out the voices of two

Trojan girls who are arguing about the merits of the Greek fighters. One praises the son of Telamon: "Ajax, after all, lifted up the warrior son of Peleus and carried him outside of the fighting, but noble Odysseus would not." Her claim is countered by the words of her companion. She defends the king of Ithaca, ending the debate: "What did you say? How can you be so wrong?" The words are spoken, as the scholiast relates, "by providence of Athena" (*Athēnas pronoiai*), Odysseus's protectress.[7] The text does not identify them as a *klēdōn*, yet they constitute a perfect illustration of an "omen or presage contained in a word or sound." In a mortal voice, a divine judgment suddenly becomes audible to those who listen for it.

At the center of the *Oresteia*, Aeschylus constructs a scene in which a god's message unexpectedly speaks through a human voice to no less momentous effect. To measure its force, one must recall one of the features of early Greek drama. Tragedy, as Aristotle writes in the *Poetics*, "came to be from an improvisatory beginning," increasing "little by little" before attaining its "nature." Aeschylus played a major role in that process, being the one who "diminished the role of the chorus, provided for speech to take the leading part," and—in a crucial innovation—raised the number of speaking performers onstage from one to two.[8] These accomplishments are clearly visible in the *Oresteia*, even where Aeschylus seems to complicate or undo them. In the *Agamemnon*, the first play in the trilogy, Clytemnestra, after years of waiting, greets her husband upon his return from Troy. Feigning joy in welcoming him to the palace of Argos, she kills him brutally on the evening of his arrival. In the play that follows it, the *Libation Bearers*, her son Orestes appears in Argos in the company of his friend Pylades to avenge his father. At the climax of the play, mother and son confront each other onstage. Orestes has killed Clytemnestra's consort, Aegisthus, as she learns. When Orestes proceeds to threaten his mother with his sword, she bares her breast and recalls to him the bond that unites them:

Oh take pity, child, before this breast
where many a time, a drowsing baby, you would feed
and with soft gums sucked in the milk that made you strong.[9]

Not all the details in the staging of this scene can be clearly reconstructed.[10] That the dialogue occurs between Orestes and Clytemnestra, however, is certain; they are the two whose speech constitutes the dramatic action. Yet when challenged by his mother's cry for mercy, Orestes suddenly turns to his faithful companion in one line: "What shall I do, Pylades? Be shamed to kill my mother?"[11] Pylades may have stepped onto the scene moments before, or he may have been present, although resolutely mute, up to this point. Orestes's questions are in any case unexpected. Yet soon the dramatic frame is profoundly shaken. Since, according to the conventions of early tragedy, no more than two actors speak onstage at once, the audience would not have expected Orestes's words to elicit any response. Now, however, an unprecedented event occurs.

In three lines, Pylades answers, reminding Orestes that he swore by the god Apollo to avenge his murdered father:

What then becomes thereafter of the oracles
declared by Loxias at Pytho? What of sworn oaths?
Count all men hateful to you rather than the gods.[12]

Orestes immediately accepts that order: "I judge that you win. Your advice is good."[13] He turns back to his mother, reaffirms his intention, and at the end of the scene, commits matricide beyond the viewers' eyes. That fateful deed appears as the immediate consequence of Pylades's words. As Karl Otfried Müller was perhaps the first to note, here, Pylades "serves as a kind of stand-in for Apollo."[14] His is, Bernard Knox notes, "the voice of Apollo himself; these three lines seal Clytemnestra's death warrant."[15] Sarah Nooter adds that the shock produced by the voice is "compounded by the brevity of his speaking role: after just one fleeting utterance, he is again silent."[16] Put in the mouth of an actor playing a mortal expressing a higher power's command, the lines in which Pylades invokes "Loxias at Pytho" are an event. They break into the dialogue between Orestes and Clytemnestra, precipitating action. Unanticipated, they are the god's word.

That outburst is one of many utterances in the *Oresteia* in which words sound onstage from a source that simultaneously demands and resists identification. The Aeschylean *klēdōn* may be named or unnamed, unmistakable or uncertain, effective or merely virtual. In at least one case, it is thwarted, to disastrous consequence. Yet the characters onstage are everywhere aware of the consequences of calls and summons. From play to play, in the most diverse of circumstances, dramatic persons draw attention to the supreme force that words can exert even when uttered in conditions removed from prophecy.

The action of the trilogy opens in *Agamemnon* with a watchman who insists on the power of what is said, even as he hints at the implications of the unsaid:

> May the king come home, and I
> Take up within this hand the hand I love. The rest
> I leave to silence; for an ox stands huge upon
> My tongue. . . .[17]

Once Agamemnon has returned and the chorus has asked after those who are still missing, a herald makes of the avoidance of unpropitious words a principle: "It is not well to stain the blessing of this day / With speech of evil weight."[18] As John J. Peradotto observes, however, "he has already done so, albeit unwittingly." Earlier in the play, Clytemnestra suggested that while at war, the Argive army might have desecrated sanctuaries, thereby provoking divine wrath; and in his discourse, the herald affirms that Agamemnon's men committed that sacrilege in Troy.[19]

The shadow of the *klēdōn* as omen, presage, rumor, and calling pervades the discourse of the tragic sequence. In the *Agamemnon*, Clytemnestra, presenting the difficulties of her position in studied terms, laments her susceptibility to the "rumors" of her husband's demise:

> It is an evil and a thing of terror when a wife
> Sits in the house forlorn with no man by, and hears
> Rumors that like a fever die to break again. . . .[20]

Some ten lines later, she again evokes what she has heard, "cruel rumors" that kept her long awake: accounts of Agamemnon wounded more than once, killed, or else close to death, as she puts it once, "cut full of gashes like a fishing net." Both times, the Greek word for "rumors" that she employs is the plural *klēdones*.[21] To the chorus, Clytemnestra seems to be relating tidings that she wishes were untrue; to the spectator, however, her words leave little doubt as to the violence that she will commit. David Raeburn and Oliver Thomas comment that "Clytemnestra is inventing rumors about Agamemnon's extreme suffering, in the knowledge that by stating them she is ominously spelling his actual death."[22] She will murder Agamemnon precisely in a net, declaring to the chorus: "As fishermen cast their huge circling nets, I spread / deadly abundance of rich robes, and caught him fast."[23] Agamemnon, in his language, also seems to anticipate the circumstances of his death, unknowingly, yet no less ineluctably. When his wife first greets him, she bids him to step onto a red carpet leading into the palace. He demurs: "Footmats and embroideries are different; their very names say it."[24] He fears the rumors that may be spread about the arrogance with which he will have trod upon the richly colored carpet. The "very names" to which he alludes are *klēdones*. As he appears to intuit, they will become a crucial element in the retelling of his death.[25]

There is a further aspect to the *klēdōn* that pertains essentially to Aeschylean drama, where verbal exchange, as Aristotle notes, plays the "leading part." Wherever omens are disclosed in being heard by chance in discourse, they bring about semantic changes that trouble or overturn a speaker's intentions. Whether or not they are expressly meant is of little consequence; what matters in each case is that someone detect them and explicitly affirm them. In his 1913 *Greek Divination*, W. R. Halliday presented the conditions of such kledonomancy as follows:

> (1) the spoken word may produce an effect, not irrespective of its meaning, but other than the meaning or intention of the person who carelessly utters them; (2) the act of acceptance makes them irrevocable, and that in the sense which best accords with the interest of the person who accepts them. Indeed, it is almost not too much to say that he forces his own meaning on the omen.[26]

The augur in such cases lies concealed in speech; it awaits the hearer, who discloses it in putting it in the service of an unexpected end. "Words, once uttered, can be rearranged, reinterpreted, and accepted by another in their new meaning so as to function as an irrevocable omen, which not only predicts future events, but actually has the power to effect what it predicts," Froma I. Zeitlin writes, referring to Aeschylus's *Seven against Thebes*. "For everyone can speak more truly than he knows and his own words may prophesy against him without his knowledge, the only protection of one's utterance being euphemism or silence."[27]

In the *Oresteia*, the clearest example of a *klēdōn* of this variety is to be found at the close of the *Agamemnon*, where Aegisthus, before being killed by Orestes, faces the challenge of the Argive chorus. Responding to their call that every man "clap fist upon his ready sword," he retorts, "I as well am ready-handed; I am not afraid of death" (*alla kagō mēn prokōpos ouk anainomai thanein*). The chorus leader perceives those words as an omen that is both favorable for the city and inauspicious for its speaker: "Death you said and death it shall be; so I take up the word of fate" (*dekhomenois legeis thanein se. tēn tukhēn d'hairoumetha*).[28] Responding to Aegisthus's utterance, the member of the chorus fastens onto the word "death" (*thanein*); he takes it to be a presage by which the ruler has announced his imminent end. With his words, Aegisthus meant, of course, to distance himself from that eventuality. In the interval between articulation and perception, however, what is said undergoes an irreparable change. "The perversion of the meaning which was intended by the original speaker is part of the regular procedure for making use of *klēdones* of this kind," as Eduard Fraenkel notes.[29]

This exchange is fraught with difficulties, the first of which is textual. The assignment of the lines is itself a matter of dispute. The manuscripts refer the claim to be "ready-handed" and willing to face death to the chorus leader, rather than to Aegisthus, as do many modern editions. If one follows that attribution, it is Aegisthus who catches and affirms the presage.[30] It seems that anyone on the Aeschylean stage is capable of unwittingly uttering a portent or divining one. Peradotto raises a further question. Where the spoken word appears as not only signifying, but also efficacious, it can play one of two roles with respect to dramatic action. "It may be an index of what is happening or will happen, or it may actually precipitate events. In practice, these two aspects are not often easy to distinguish. . . . Does Aegisthus's *ouk anainomai thanein* ['I am not afraid of death'] become an omen for the Argive elders because it merely signals death, or because it will actually cause his death? It is hard to say."[31] What is certain is that in tragedy, spoken augurs exert effects on the dimension in which all characters move. Omens sound less in single acts of speech than in the uncertain movements of their emission and reception.

One set of *klēdones* in the *Oresteia*, however, is unique. It belongs to the scene whose memory determines the course of events in the *Agamemnon* and, by extension, the *Libation Bearers* and the *Eumenides*.[32] Ten years before the action of the first play, the Argive king and his men set sail for Ilium. To assure his fleet favorable winds, Agamemnon committed a deed of "unequaled violence."[33] "Sacrilegious, utterly infidel," the Atreid dared to offer up his daughter to the gods.[34] In its first ode, the chorus recalls this scene, evoking terrible details: the "stainless maiden," likened to a goat, was bound and led to the altar, her saffron mantle against the ground, her eyes "arrows of pity," "lovely as in a painted scene." "What happened next," the chorus leader says, "I saw not, neither speak of it."[35] That omission protects against the effects that the reference to the corrupted ritual would entail. A proper name is also carefully withheld: "During their long and detailed description of the binding of Iphigenia for sacrifice in the parodos, the girl's name is not once mentioned, almost as if to do so would hasten the retribution that must come from her murder."[36]

The chorus relates how, in directing the most impious of rituals, Agamemnon took pains to exclude the possibility of unpropitious speech. Iphigenia was gagged on the altar on which she was put to death. The king ordered his servants

to hold back with a guard
on her mouth, like a lovely prow,
a voice, inauspicious for the house,
by the force of its silencing strength.[37]

Commenting on these lines, Paul Mazon wrote that "what Agamemnon fears is not the remorse or shame that Iphigenia's voice might elicit in him but a greater danger, that of the *imprecation* hurled by the victim against her murderer. Once released, the formula of malediction works by itself, 'walking unhesitatingly toward its goal without failure' (*Seven against Thebes*, 840). No one can stop it; even the one who sets it in motion cannot call it back."[38] Any "sound" (*phthongos*) made by the maiden might have endangered the house of Atreus.[39] Yet only a few lines before evoking "the force of silencing [or 'speechless,' *aunaudōi*] strength," the chorus names an extraordinary summons, a phenomenon that is at once sonorous and yet also mute. They evoke the cries or "supplications" that Iphigenia, had she had her voice, would have made:

Her supplications and her cries of father
Were nothing, nor the child's lamentation
To kings passioned for battle.[40]

Those unspoken "supplications and cries of father" are, in Greek, *klēdones patrōious*. Their translation raises questions. They might also be rendered as "cries of 'Father!'"[41] They are a silent calling of which the Argives preserve a memory.

In the following play, Iphigenia's surviving siblings, Orestes and Electra, seem obscurely to allude to these *klēdones*, even as they twist the form in which the chorus of the *Agamemnon* evoked them. At the start of the *Libation Bearers*, Agamemnon is deceased. Electra, performing funeral rites over her father's tomb, meets Orestes, who has returned with Pylades to Argos. Brother and sister pray that the killing of Agamemnon may be avenged. Electra calls out to the dead:

> Hear one more cry, father, from me. It is the last.
> Your nestlings huddle suppliant at your tomb: look forth
> And pity them, female with the male strain alike.[42]

The following lines are also of contested assignation.[43] Either Electra or Orestes suggests that Agamemnon will outlive himself through their survival: "for when / a man dies, children are the *klēdones* of his salvation / afterward" (*paides gar andri klēdones sōtērioi / thanonti*).[44] The lines are arresting in themselves, but they are no less striking in their relation to those evoked by the chorus in the *Agamemnon*. For Iphigenia, *klēdones* were or would have been calls of the victim to the butcher in the moment of execution; for Electra or for Orestes, they are, by contrast, the summons of the surviving. The *klēdones* are for the same father, albeit in opposing ways.

Later in the play, Orestes takes a further step, evoking a *klēdōn* that will outlast him while he lives in exile. By that point Aegisthus, who rules Argos with Clytemnestra, has appeared onstage. He has heard news of Orestes's death, but he doubts its truth; he declares, therefore, that he will interrogate the bearer of the tidings. He wants to know if the messenger witnessed the death himself or relates some "blind rumor," literally, an "indistinct" or "dim" *klēdōn* (*amauras klēdonos*).[45] Orestes soon announces himself, dispelling the hearsay. Too late, Aegisthus learns that Orestes lives and has returned to avenge his father. Later in the play, after he has killed both Aegisthus and Clytemnestra, Orestes prepares to follow Apollo's command to leave his city and journey to the Pytho's sanctuary at Delphi. Orestes tells those whom he forsakes that in his homeland, a "calling" will henceforth survive him: "I go, an outcast wanderer from this land, and leave / behind, in life, in death, the *klēdōn* of what I did."[46] That *klēdōn* is also "name," "rumor" and "renown."[47]

The Greek verbal omen can take on several forms. In one configuration, as in book 18 of the *Odyssey* or in the *Little Iliad*, it consists in the unexpected sounding of a divine intention in the voice of a mortal being. In another arrangement, as in many of the exchanges among speakers in the *Oresteia*, the *klēdōn* is discernible in the sudden modification of the meaning of what has been said, a modification that to be noted and affirmed need not require a god's direct intervention. Yet there is also a third possibility, which concerns a different event: that by which some fragment of human discourse reaches a divine faculty of perception.

That the classical gods are susceptible to sonorous invocations is certain. The deities of ancient Greece are *theoi epēkooi*, "hearing divinities," and the efficacy of prayer depends on the gods' receptivity to speech.[48] When Sarpedon invokes Apollo in book 16 of the *Iliad*, for example, he begins by recalling that no matter his location, the lord of Delphi can perceive his words:

> Hear me, my lord. You are somewhere in the rich Lykian countryside
> Or here in Troy, and wherever you are you can listen
> To a man in pain, as now this pain has descended on me. . . .[49]

The bard confirms that his words were heeded: "So he spoke in prayer," the poem continues, after Sarpedon ends his address, "and Phoibos Apollo heard him."[50] Silvia Montiglio suggests that such details illustrate a principle. In Greek antiquity,

> all rituals call for prayers, and all prayers call for fully audible voices. From Homeric epic down to tragic poetry the words meaning "prayer" most emphasize the sonorous quality of the utterance. . . . A prayer is an attempt to hit the ears of the gods, that they may "listen." Thus the relationship between man and god in prayer is envisaged as a relationship between a sender and a recipient of sounds. It is a relationship with a remote deity, which only a resonant voice can hope to bring near.[51]

Yet in the divine perception of a *klēdōn*, no less than in the mortal one, nothing about "the relationship between a sender and a recipient" can be taken to be certain. The crucial and crucially enigmatic example occurs close to the beginning of the last tragedy of the *Oresteia*. The first setting of the *Eumenides* is Delphi, where Orestes seeks refuge from Clytemnestra's ghost and the archaic goddesses known as the Erynes or Furies who pursue him, demanding retribution for his act of matricide, appearing before the spectators in a "theatrical event which defies all description."[52] Apollo tries to protect the man, but he cannot quell the Furies' wrath. He therefore evokes another god, the sole divinity capable of deciding on Orestes' guilt or innocence: "Pallas divine shall review the pleadings of this case."[53] Apollo directs Orestes to supplicate the goddess in her citadel: "Kneel there, and clasp the ancient idol in your arms, / and there we shall find those who will judge this case."[54] Orestes assents. The next and final scene is set on the Acropolis of Athens before the statue of Athena, where Orestes calls out: "My lady Athena, it is at Loxias' behest, / I come. . . ."[55] There the Furies quickly follow him; they threaten him anew, reciting a spell to "bind him in."[56] When they conclude their song, Pallas Athena steps onto the stage. On the distant plains of Troy, she perceived a *klēdōn*, as she declares in her first words: "From far away I heard the outcry of your call [*prosōthen exēkousa klēdonos boēn*] / It was beside Scamandrus. . . ."[57]

That gods should be receptive to *klēdones* is a circumstance neither obvious in itself nor granted by all scholars. It is striking that in his illuminating study of "cledonomancy in the *Oresteia*," Peradotto focuses on the first two plays in the trilogy, showing how the language of the *Agamemnon* and the *Libation Bearers* reflects a constant awareness of the force of *klēdones*. Hence the "tortuous indirection" and "repression" of speech, as with the fears that the watchman dares not express, or its violent "suppression," as in the cries that Iphigenia could not emit. "By contrast, the *Eumenides* concentrates upon the secular, civilizing efficacy of language," he writes, and since its speakers are mainly gods, "cledonomancy has no part."[58] That the course of violence is halted in the last play is beyond doubt. Through reasoned discourse, deliberation, and an appeal to the judges of Attica, Athena definitively resolves the conflict of the Furies and Orestes, as Apollo wished. She both appeases the ancient goddesses and cleanses Agamemnon's son of the stain of any crime. Yet the reconciliation comes to pass solely because of the goddess's perception of a *klēdōn*—and perhaps even because she has herself engaged in act of kledonomancy.

Athena's opening line raises several questions, not least that of its referent. When she states, "I heard the outcry of your call [*klēdōn*]," to which call is she pointing? It has been observed that if she is indicating the supplication that Orestes utters immediately before her appearance, her usage is "slightly unusual," since *klēdōn* "does not usually mean 'prayer.'"[59] In his commentary, Fraenkel therefore proposes that one give the word a special meaning in this line and in the passage of the *Agamemnon* where Iphigenia's *klēdones* are evoked: "*klēdōn* in the sense of 'cry, appeal' seems to occur only here."[60] Resolving the difficulty of diction by recourse to the hypothesis of an almost unique sense is in principle unsatisfying. Yet even if one accepts Fraenkel's gloss, a question about the organization of the action remains. Between the point when Orestes finishes his prayer to Athena and the moment when she appears onstage, almost a hundred lines are recited. They are those in which the Furies strive to subdue Orestes through their song. Their words raise a difficulty for the reading of Athena's appearance as a response to

Orestes. Scholars observe that where ancient Greek tragedy features supplicants, the usual procedure is for the one supplicated to appear immediately after the supplication; only then does the pursuer step onto the scene. The *Eumendies*, however, does not respect that sequence, and if Athena has been summoned by Orestes, her appearance is inexplicably belated.[61]

In a persuasive essay, Robert R. Rabel proposes a solution to these puzzles. Arguing against Fraenkel, he suggests that Athena employs the word *klēdōn* in exactly the sense in which it was known to Homer and Herodotus. When she mentions having heard a *klēdōn*, the goddess then refers to an "omen" or "presage contained in a chance utterance," her usage furnishing "the only significant occasion in which to see cledonomancy in operation in the third play of the *Oresteia*."[62] In this interpretation, Athena has engaged in the same art of divination by verbal presage of which the *Agamemnon* and the *Libation Bearers* furnish numerous examples. She has perceived utterances that she accepts as prophetic on condition of twisting and transforming them, "forcing" her own meanings, according to Halliday's terms, onto the words that she hears. This interpretation has the advantage of recovering a logical clarity in the dramatic action. When she evokes her perception of a *klēdōn*, Athena then alludes not to Orestes's distant prayer, but to the song of the Furies that has just been uttered. In it, the goddess catches words that she implacably turns against the raging deities.

Several passages in the binding spell may have furnished Athena with material for her kledonomancy. First, there is the statement by which the ancient immortals, addressing Orestes, name Pallas Athena, declaring: "Neither Apollo nor Athena's strength [*sthenos*] can win / you free. . . ."[63] Rabel observes that although the apparent meaning of these lines is "'neither Apollo nor Athena can save you,'" the wording suggests a different sense: "The boast is framed in just the sort of careless ambiguity that can easily be made to rebound against the speaker. . . . Though *sthenos* [strength] must fail, the way is left open for other approaches that do not entail the use of force."[64] If one accepts this reading, the Furies, despite themselves, announce Athena's resolution of the confrontation by deliberation, voting, and judgment, rather than by force.

Next there are the shocking terms with which the Furies threaten to consume Orestes even while he lives: "You are consecrate to me and fattened for my feast, / and you shall feed me while you live [*kai zōn me daiseis oude pros bōmōi sphageis*]."[65] In their evocation of a sacrificial slaughter (*sphazō*), the chorus associates its ambitions with the violently sacrilegious practices of the Atreides to which Athena will put an end. When they accept the Olympian's terms, the Furies agree to be honored not by violent feasts, but by peaceful "offerings for children and the marriage rite."[66] Finally, there is a portent concealed in the Furies' evocation of their own might. "We are stern, / nor can men's pleadings bend us," they sing, specifying literally that they are "hard for mortals to appease" or "hard for mortals to persuade" (*dusparēgoroi brotois*).[67] "This omen hints that the Furies, though implacable to mortals, may be responsive to divine persuasion."[68]

Such a reading dispels the obscurity of the *klēdōn* that Athena has perceived. At the same time, however, it raises a redoubtable question of theology, that of the gods' relationship to divination and the mutability of meaning. Kledonomancy, like all "mantic" practices, seems to be a human means of gleaning knowledge of what is otherwise inaccessible to mortal beings. Yet if the *klēdōn* plays a role in the *Eumenides*, its power stretches beyond the field of human discourse and awareness. The gods, too, appear to engage in acts of inference from verbal omens. Between the Furies, who are deathless, and Athena, the Olympian, words seem to travel along the same uncertain paths on which they pass when mortals speak, hear, and overhear each other. In every case, there is the promise—or the threat—that speakers can say more than they mean, that merely by being uttered and heard at a certain time and place, their discourse may do unexpected things and be turned against them. From god to mortal, from mortal to mortal, from mortal to god, and even among immortals, a truth may emerge, for better or for worse, in the space disjoining articulation from perception.

This is perhaps no more than a consequence of the common assumption that the gods are responsive to appeals and invocations, that they, too, speak and converse among themselves and on occasion enter into argument. The reasons for such related suppositions, of course, are all too evident. Were divinities ignorant of words and sentences and insensitive to cries and exhortations, they would lack the means to perceive and appreciate the rituals and sacrifices offered up to them. Yet the belief that immortals are speaking beings also entails a consequence that is less obvious. The gods must be vulnerable to the force of the evocation. They are exposed to a summons that exerts consequences that no speaking being can anticipate or control: a calling that exceeds the caller and the called. No matter the powers that may be ascribed to them, the gods, like those who worship them, cannot elude the power of such a summons. Knowingly or unwittingly, they are remitted to a dimension in which the unforeseen can befall any word or phrase — even its omission.

CHAPTER FOUR

Dawn in Ithaca

Prometheus, in the Greek tradition, is the god who brings fire to humankind. For betraying a divine secret to mortals, Zeus has the Titan fastened to a crag. It is difficult to forget how he then dispatches eagles there to eat the god's liver, before it grows back and is repeatedly consumed anew. Less well remembered is that the Promethean act is one of concealment as well as revelation. According to Hesiod, the first chronicler of these happenings, the theft constitutes a feat of guile. It is the second in a series of three instances of divine trickery. The first is that by which, at an almost immemorial moment in the history of the world, when immortals and mortals would soon be separated, Prometheus decides on the terms by which goods would be apportioned between them. He divides the body of a great ox with illusory craft: in one part, he hides the meat and innards under the animal's stomach; in the other, he buries the ox's dry bones under "gleaming fat." Prometheus gives Zeus the right to choose the share that he prefers, leaving the rest to human beings. Hesiod indicates that the "father of men and gods" sees through the subterfuge. Submitting to the game, however, he chooses the fat, becoming "enraged in his breast" when seeing that it is no more than a covering for the bones.[1] Henceforth, the gods will live by the smoke of sacrifice and the remains of burnings. Mortals will lay claim to the consecrated meat.

Hesiod relates that at a later point, after the theft of fire, Zeus exacts revenge on Prometheus and his beloved human beings. The sovereign immortal orders Hephaestus to fashion a semblance of a maiden after the image of the goddesses and to put "the voice and strength of a human into it"; he has Athena clothe and adorn it and Hermes breathe a "dog's mind" and "thievish character" into it. He then parades the prodigious construction before the other Olympians, in whom it inspires astonishment and admiration. "Wonder gripped the immortal gods when they saw the steep deception, intractable for human beings."[2] The invention is Pandora, whom Prometheus's careless brother, Epimetheus — failing to heed the Promethean warning never to accept gifts from Zeus — welcomes into his home. The mother of all women, Pandora would be the "beautiful evil thing" (*kalon kakon*) sent to human beings in retribution for the "good thing" that is fire.[3]

In the sequence of these divine deceptions, an order is discernible.[4] Setting the divided ox before the monarch of the gods, Prometheus succeeds in outwitting Zeus by means of a surface: the sheen of the fat conceals an empty depth. Sending Pandora into the homes of Epimetheus, Zeus, in turn, avenges himself through an artifice in which an attractive exterior conceals a harmful spirit. Between these two acts, Prometheus steals fire by an operation no less deceptive. It, too, pits a visible surface against an unseen cavity. To transmit fire to humanity, Prometheus conceals a spark of the divine flame in the plant known as the *narthex*, the giant fennel stalk.[5] "The stalk of the giant fennel was and is used for carrying fire from place to place," Martin L. West notes. "It is filled with a dry white pith in which the fire burns slowly without breaking through the hard outer rind."[6] While the bark of most living trees is dry when the interior is moist, the surface of the fennel stalk stays green even when, deracinated, it shelters a flame.[7] By his ingenious use of the narthex, Prometheus becomes not only the secret bringer of a good, but also the inventor of an ingenious technique for its conservation, as Pliny the Elder recalls in the catalogue of "Finders of Various Things" of his *Natural History*.[8]

Yet in the early Greek tragedy devoted to the Titan, which tradition assigns, rightly or wrongly, to Aeschylus, the theft of fire plays a remarkably minor role.[9] Appearing onstage in *Prometheus Bound*, the immortal dwells above all on his gift to humankind of *tekhnai*, "arts," "skills," or forms of "know-how." "You will marvel at the crafts and resources [*tekhnas te kai porous*] that I contrived," he tells the chorus.[10] He proceeds to explain that before he came to their assistance, mortals knew of no remedy for illness:

> When one of mankind fell sick
> There was no defense for him—neither healing food
> Nor drink nor unguent; for lack of cures they wasted,
> Until I showed them the blending of mild remedies
> With which they drive away all kinds of sickness.[11]

The god, however, offered mortals more than medicine. He also charted "the many ways of prophecy" (*pollous mantikēs*), making himself into the inventor of the arts of divination.[12]

In an extended discourse, Prometheus distinguishes among their varieties. He states that he was the one who showed human beings to grasp "the flight of hook-taloned birds" and to infer which is "in nature propitious / and which unlucky; what habits each species has, / what are their hates and loves and affiliations." Augury in the strict sense—the extraction of portents, that is, from the movements of birds—was his gift. He also taught the principles and practice of extispicy, divination through the study of animal organs and intestines, introducing mortals to the

> the smoothness of the entrails
> and what color the bile should have to please the gods
> and the dappled symmetry of the liver lobe.

Reminding the chorus of the act by which he first outwitted Zeus, allowing for the ritual communication between human beings and gods that is reenacted in sacrifice, the Titan notes that it was he who "burned the thigh bones wrapped in fat / and the long shank bone." He thereby enabled human beings to see portentous signs in the flicker of the flame and the movements of smoke in offerings.[13]

Such practices all involve the identification of a sense in apparent accidents. Imparting skill in augury, extispicy, and rules for the inference of meaning from fire and smoke, Prometheus showed that in the apparently unpredictable occurrence of natural phenomena, there are signals to note and consequences to deduce. Yet the Titan also instructed mortals on the art of culling meanings from their own actions. He taught humankind to be attentive to coincidences in their deeds: to grasp "the significance of road encounters" (*enodious te sumbolous*), or, in another rendition of that phrase, to decipher "symbols [*symbola*] in chance meetings."[14] Prometheus also offered instruction on the part of dreaming that "comes truly real"; he made himself, in other words, the father of oneiromancy. Finally, the tragic Titan lays claim to the invention of kledonomancy. He claims authorship of the divinatory practice by which words and noises perceived by chance are grasped as signs of unexpected meanings: "For mankind, I gave sense / to ominous cries, hard of interpretation." These "ominous cries" are in Greek *klēdonas duskritous*, obscure "sounds," "callings," or "evocations," or in Herbert Weir Smyth's translation, "voices baffling interpretation," or, according to Thoreau, "omens hard to be determined."[15]

A century and a half after the age in which *Prometheus Bound* was composed and performed, Aristotle proposes a doctrine of *tekhnē*, "art," "skill," or "craft." According to his *Nicomachean Ethics*, *tekhnē* is a "habit" enabling production. In his words, it is a "state concerned with making, involving a true course of reasoning."[16] Aristotle thus distinguishes the know-how implicit in fabrication from the discursive knowledge that he calls *epistēmē*, which informs demonstrative science. Whereas *epistēmē* concerns the necessary and the eternal, which by definition cannot be otherwise than it is, *tekhnē* involves the contingent, which can both be and not be. To illustrate his thesis, Aristotle cites a line by the poet Agathon: "Art loves chance, and chance loves art." The sounds of those words echo their sense, for in Greek, "art" (*tekhnē*) and "chance" (*tykhē*) are similar in form, suggesting the chiasmus of the original, *tekhnē tukhēn esterxe kai tukhē tekhnēn*.[17] Although the Titan of *Prometheus Bound* evokes no formal epistemology, he indicates that the "crafts and resources" to which he introduced humanity may be of such a kind. From medicine to the varieties of divination, the skills in which Prometheus initiates mortals bear on what is neither eternal nor necessary. His arts elude the certainty of the deductive sciences. Mastery in the Promethean *tekhnai* involves conjecture and the practice of a subtle intelligence. From the skill in treating illness to the knowledge drawn from the motions of birds and flames, sounds and crossings, the Titan's arts "love chance." They govern the drawing of sense from passing signs and shifting circumstances.

The hero of the *Odyssey* is an expert in such practices of contingent inference, being "the most Promethean of all Homer's heroes," as Karl Kerényi names him.[18] After the long war in Troy and his perilous journey back to his island kingdom, Odysseus recovers his land because he knows how to discern and interpret the signs that the gods strew along his path. By the time he comes ashore on Ithaca, to be sure, he has also received precious counsel from the dead. During his journey to the house of Hades, Odysseus meets Agamemnon, who tells him how, returning to his own palace after the voyage back from Ilium, he died at the hands of Aigisthos and Clytemnestra, cut down, with Cassandra and his companions, like an "ox at his manger."[19] Despite his keen awareness of the differences separating Clytemnestra and Penelope, Agamemnon advises Odysseus that to survive when he returns to Ithaca, he must adopt a different course of action: "When you bring your ship in to your own dear country, do it / secretly, not in the open. There is no trusting in women."[20]

Odysseus does as he recommends, his homecoming becoming the inverted image of Agamemnon's. The son of Laertes arrives alone. His companions have perished on the return, either due to their lack of judgment or his own poor leadership, if not both.

Agamemnon, in command of his men and vessels, directs his ships back to Argos. Odysseus, by contrast, reaches his homeland thanks to the assistance of people unmentioned in the *Iliad*. The Phaiakians convey him in their wondrous vessels from their own most distant island to his native shores. When they reach Ithaca, Odysseus is asleep. He does not awaken when they arrive, nor does he stir as the Phaiakians set him gently in the sand.[21]

When he at last opens his eyes, he is bewildered. It is not only that after twenty years, he may have forgotten something of his homeland. Athena has also "poured a mist" around him, disguising Ithaca to him. At first it seems that Odysseus may assume the mask that he donned in Phaiakia. There, according to the "strict reciprocity between seeing and being seen," he was most surely concealed before all others when he failed to gaze upon them, following Athena's explicit command to him "not to look any human being in the face."[22] On Ithaca, however, the goddess soon dispels his confusion, telling him where he has awakened and how she has brought him there. Now Athena promises that to enable him to rid his home of the suitors who occupy it, she will disguise him to all those whom he meets.

Such a strategy is hardly novel in the *Odyssey*, the "man of many ways" being no stranger to disguise. Not only does Odysseus conceal his identity by withholding or altering his name; he is also known in the epic to modify his appearance. Earlier in the poem, having returned to her native Sparta and her first husband, Menelaus, Helen recalls this practice of self-concealment to Telemachus, who is searching for "news" or "tidings" (*klēdones*) of his father.[23] Encouraging him in his inquiry, she evokes Odysseus's exploits, lingering on an episode that exemplifies his cunning. During the war, Odysseus once transformed himself to infiltrate the enemy citadel, flagellating himself "with degrading strokes" and putting a "worthless sheet about his shoulders" to resemble a servant: "So he crept into the wide-wayed city of men he was fighting, / disguising himself in the likeness of somebody else, a beggar."[24] All but Helen were deceived by his craft.[25] On the first morning of his return to Ithaca, Athena accomplishes what Odysseus then contrived to do. To allow him to reach the palace unobserved and destroy "the overmastering suitors," the goddess changes him. She withers his flesh, ruins his hair, gives him "the skin of an ancient / old man," and clothes him in a "vile rag and a tunic, / tattered, squalid, blackened with foul smoke."[26] Newly undetectable, he can then enter and win back his country.

Half of the *Odyssey* concerns the period in which the divinely altered Odysseus, long a missing person, makes himself secretly present on his native island, arranging the conditions in which he will drive the suitors from his house, if not kill them there. Yet the action quickens in book 19. Distinct series of communication become perceptible, echo each other, and overlap. Suddenly, the most diverse of mortal and immortal beings in the Homeric universe are drawn into unexpected relations. Chains of communication cross each other to unprecedented effect. Signs sent by the deathless gods are registered by mortal faculties of perception; human prayers reach the gods to whom they are addressed; and unintended, yet decisive messages move, openly and in secret, among mortals. In each of these conveyances of wishes and intentions, a sender and a receiver are readily identifiable. Yet in every case, a further figure is also observable. It is the reader, called into being in the instant of interpretation.

On the evening before the battle in which Odysseus at last confronts and vanquishes the suitors, Penelope inaugurates the extended ending of the narrative. She commands her faithful servant, Eurykleia, to wash the feet of her guest, whom the audience knows to be Odysseus. Bending down before the man's leg, the old nurse catches sight of the present sign of the past that is his scar. Immediately, she recognizes the one to whom she tended long ago.[27] Overjoyed, she seeks to impart her discovery to her lady, yet the potential communication is thwarted: "Penelope was not able to look that way, or perceive him, / since Athene turned aside her perception."[28] At the same moment, Odysseus keeps the woman from declaring her discovery.

The revelation having been twice impeded, Penelope gleans nothing of what her husband and servant know. Yet with perfect symmetry, she proceeds to inform her companions of something of which they are unaware. Addressing to her guest, she enjoins him to decipher a vision that she alone has seen:

> Come, listen to a dream of mine and interpret it for me.
> I have twenty geese here about the house, and they feed on
> grains of wheat from the water trough. I love to watch them.
> But a great eagle with crooked beak came down from the mountain,
> and broke the necks of them all and killed them. So the whole twenty
> lay dead about the house, but he soared high in the bright air.
> Then I began to weep—that was in my dream—and cried out
> aloud, and around me gathered the fair-haired Achaian women
> as I cried out sorrowing for my geese killed by the eagle.
> But he came back again and perched on the jut of the gabled
> roof. He now had a human voice and spoke aloud to me:
> "Do not fear, O daughter of far-famed Ikarios.
> This is no dream, but a blessing real as day. You will see it
> done. The geese are the suitors, and I, the eagle, have been
> a bird of portent, but now I am your own husband, come home,
> and I shall inflict shameless destruction on all the suitors."[29]

Challenging him to comment on her vision, Penelope begs the visitor to practice two of the "crafts and resources" to which the god of *Prometheus Bound* lays claim, augury and oneiromancy. Odysseus is to draw sense from birds and from a dream, the first being, in the "redundant form of divination" that is Penelope's vision, contained in the second, as "an omen within an omen."[30] Yet the guest is himself also in a position of formal "redundancy," in that Penelope's dream includes not only omens, but also an interpretation and an interpreter.[31] Before he can respond, Odysseus learns that he has in effect already spoken. Penelope has woven her most desired reader into the text that he is to read. As Struck wryly notes, "when Penelope asks the beggar to be the dream's interpreter, she is asking the beggar to be the eagle, and she asking him to be Odysseus. No wonder he doesn't have much to add."[32] Yet he nonetheless answers her. With consummate cunning, he simultaneously renounces and affirms his capacity to respond:

> Lady, it is impossible to read this dream and avoid it
> by turning another way, since Odysseus himself has told you
> its meaning, how it will end.[33]

It is the beginning of a sequence of coincidences in which the threshold separating sleep from waking plays a crucial role as husband and wife, guided by the gods, pass in and out of consciousness, in speech and silence, drawing close to each other. Penelope leaves the beggar to "go back up to her shining chamber," where she weeps for Odysseus until Athena casts "sweet slumber over her eyelids."[34] At the same time, Odysseus lies down, but is kept awake by thoughts of the evil that he means to inflict on the suitors. The goddess who relieved Penelope of her worries now appears before her agitated husband, reassuring him of the future and causing him, too, to sleep. The narrator suggests that just as Odysseus falls asleep, Penelope rises:

> When the sleep had caught him, a relaxing sleep, slipping
> the cares from his mind, at that time his virtuous wife wakened
> in turn, and cried, sitting up in her soft bed.[35]

Despairing, Penelope utters a prayer of dejection. She begs Artemis to take her life, so that, entering the shadow kingdom of Hades, she may be reunited with her lost husband. Whether the goddess hears her is left unsaid. What is certain, however, is that her words are overheard by mortal ears. After relating her plea, the bard specifies: "Great Odysseus was aware of her voice crying [*tēs d'ara klaiousēs opa suntheto*]."[36] In a "surprising and unique description," the epic poem sets before its audience a "hypnopompic phenomenon," in Graham Reed's terms, which is typical "of the transitional state between sleep and waking": "Into Odysseus's consciousness suddenly enters a vivid image, or fantasy, of an eagerly desired goal that is growing close."[37] The bard renders what the hero, in his indistinct awareness, perceives. It is a prophetic vision of a near future: "He pondered then [*mermērize d'epeita*], and it seemed to him in his mind [*kata thymon*] that now / Penelope was standing by his head, and she had recognized him already."[38]

When he regains full consciousness, Odysseus utters a prayer of his own. His is a plea to Zeus for auspicious signs:

> He rolled together the blanket and fleece, where he had been sleeping,
> and laid them down by the chair in the hall, and taking the ox-hide
> out, laid it down, and prayed to Zeus, with his hands lifted:
> "Father Zeus, if willingly you gods led me over
> wet and dry to my land, after giving too much affliction,
> let one of the waking people send me an omen from inside
> the house; and let Zeus also show me an outside portent."[39]

Odysseus demands a double presage, a spoken "omen" (*phēmēn*) from inside the house and a "prodigy," "portent," or "omen" (*teras*) from outside it. His words reach their addressee: "So he spoke in prayer, and Zeus of the counsels heard him."[40] In response to the mortal's supplication, the god sends two signs. The first is acoustical without being linguistic: suddenly, thunder rolls from "high above the clouds." A second presage follows. It is separated from the first by an interval in both the telling and the tale. The second is a discursive "omen" incited by the natural sound. It is speech that, uttered in the silence of interrupted work, acquires a sense the speaker could never have intended.

Inside the house, the bard explains, there were twelve mill women "bending / to grind the wheat and the barley flour, men's marrow."[41] The weakest of them had not yet finished her work. When Odysseus prays and Zeus answers him, she alone is therefore awake. Even as the disguised hero rejoices at the thunder, she also perceives a divine signal. After Penelope and Odysseus, the nameless servant then supplicates the god:

> She stopped the mill and spoke aloud, a sign for her master:
> "Father Zeus, you who are lord of the gods and people,
> Now you have thundered loud from the starry sky, although
> There is no cloud. You show this forth, a portent for someone.
> Grant now also for wretched me this prayer that I make you.
> On this day let the suitors take, for the last and latest
> Time, their desirable feasting in the halls of Odysseus.
> For it is they who have broken my knees with heart-sore labor
> As I grind the meal for them. Let this be their final feasting."[42]

Now, after the milling woman has heard the sign for which Odysseus begged Zeus, Odysseus, in a striking inversion, gleans a meaning concealed in the servant's wish. It is inscribed in the timing of its utterance. He hears an augur at a propitious moment. Omens cross each other, simultaneously heard and overheard. They are addressed to certain persons, yet also intercepted in the movement of their passage, being at once private and shared.

Odysseus catches the sign that sounds in the words that he perceives: "So she spoke, and great Odysseus welcomed the ominous speech and the / thunder of Zeus."[43] More literally, Odysseus "rejoices" (*khairen*) in the *klēdōn* and in the thunder that announces it. In the *Essay on the Life and Poetry of Homer* that tradition attributes to Plutarch, this line appears as the exemplary passage in which the word *klēdōn* figures in Homeric poetry meaning "omen."[44] Perceiving the milling woman's words from within the palace, Odysseus knows them to be divinely inspired not merely due to their content but also due to the circumstances in which he grasps them. For him, as for the bard, her prayer immediately follows his; it is at once the echo of and acquiescence to his own supplication. The milling woman, to be sure, addressed the god, but the *klēdōn* occurs when speech is driven off its intended course toward a hearer that the speaker did not anticipate. In an instant, Odysseus, outside the dialogic relation, exults on catching what was not said to him.

Now the hero is certain that the gods will support him. Challenged to draw sense from a dream and from the movement of birds, to interpret chance occurrences and "obscure cries," Odysseus proves his command of the Titan's "crafts and resources." Yet in this scene, the man of many ways also shows himself to be intensely Promethean in another sense. Beyond the individual arts of divination, there is a further knowledge that he possesses. Confronted by a sequence of events, he knows not only how to discern signals, but also how to link them, making of them an articulated sequence from which he draws a sense. In a word: he knows how to read.

In the tragedy devoted to him, Prometheus claims that this skill, too, is a gift that he bestowed freely on humankind. Before introducing medicine and the prophetic arts, the Titan recalls the circumstances in which he first intervened in the lives of mortals. As he tells the chorus, there was a time when human beings "saw without seeing" (*blepontes eblepon matēn*): they "had eyes but saw / to no purpose; they had ears but did not hear."[45] They "muddled everything haphazardly."[46] They lived "beneath the earth like swarming ants, / in sunless caves," knowing nothing of the seasons. Prometheus allowed them to overcome that lamentable condition by showing them how to note "the rising of the stars," telling apart the four seasons. He invented "number for them, preeminent among all skills," and he revealed to them "the combining of letters" (*grammatōn te syntheseis*).[47]

The last is the most peculiar item in the Titan's catalogue of benefactions.[48] That Prometheus should appear in the play as the initiator of astronomy as well as arithmetic illustrates his commitment to enabling mortals to improve themselves. Yet what sense can be given to the god's claim that it was he who first showed mortals to "join" or "combine letters"? The syntax of the Greek sentences in which the statement is embedded raises difficulties of its own. Two interpretations are attested in the manuscript tradition.

According to one, which is often followed in modern translations, Prometheus suggests that he revealed the

> combining of written letters as a means
> of remembering all things, the Muses' mother,
> skilled in craft.[49]

The knowledge of the joining of letters would then be "the memory of all things" (*mnēmēn hapantōn*) and "Muse-mothering worker" (*mousomētor' erganēn*), that is, Mnemosyne herself. According to a second reading, however, Prometheus would have granted several distinct gifts. More exactly, he would have bestowed knowledge in three domains: "number . . . and letters, and the memory of all things, mother of the Muses at work."[50] It is striking that in both cases, "letters" or *grammata* do not appear to be of divine origin. What the Titan revealed to mortals are less distinct units than their *synthesis*: their "joining" or "combining."

What might such a linking be? To answer the question, one must resolve a prior problem, that of the nature of the *grammata* to which Prometheus alludes. One may take them as "letters" in the modern sense, that is, minimal signs of writing. That supposition, however, runs up against a lexical difficulty. In a number of Greek philosophical sources, the *gramma* is a unit of sound and little more. It may but need not be inscribed.[51] Plato's Socrates alludes in this sense in the *Protagoras* to the practice of teaching children *grammata* that can correspond either to what is "written" (*ta gegrammena*) or to what is merely "vocal" or "oral" (*tēn phōnēn*).[52] In *De interpretatione*, Aristotle likewise suggests that letters, the elements of articulated speech, may be orally perceptible rather than written down.[53] Callias, the fifth-century author of a representation of the Greek alphabet known as the *grammatikē theōria*, similarly presents *grammata* and *stoikheia* as of a double nature: either oral or written.[54] Considering these passages in a study of the Promethean gift of the "joining of letters," Filippo Ferlauto argues that it would be an error to take the *grammata* in *Prometheus Bound* as strictly "written signs." According to his interpretation, the Titan lays claim to having revealed to human beings "'combinations of orally articulated letters,' 'orally articulated syllables,' that is, articulations of language."[55]

If one grants such a reading, the Titan's subsequent claims acquire a new sense. The knowledge of "articulations of language" sustains "memory, mother of the Muses," by comprehending the forms by which sounds and syllables are joined in poetry. The Promethean benefaction, in other words, enables the mastery of the very patterned language in which it is embedded, assuring the art of meter. Yet it also entails consequences that exceed poetic composition and transmission. Imparting the knowledge of the linking of *grammata*, the god initiates mortals into a practice of discerning unimagined sequences in discourse: combinations of units that, while nearly indetectable in themselves, are ceaselessly combined in the flow of speech. These units are the elements now known as "phonemes." In the languages of the ancients, they are called "letters" (*grammata*, *stoikheia*, and *litterae*). According to the recurrent definition of the Greek and Roman grammarians, letters are the "smallest parts of the voice" (*merē tēs phonēs*, *partes minimae vocis*), which possess no meaning in themselves and yet make up whole words and phrases.[56] The perception of such elements in speech is the condition of all phonetic writing. Discourse can be transcribed sound by sound only once it has been grasped as consisting of the conjunctions of such particles.

To have bestowed on mortals a knowledge of the linking of letters is therefore to have enabled the parsing of speech that is reading—even in the absence of a particular writing system or the possession of a script. That contribution, however, can be variously interpreted, "reading" lending itself to several understandings. In a first sense, it implies the analysis of discourse into its most minimal phonetic sequences. "Grammar," as it would one day be called, would be a Promethean invention. Yet the Titan's gift may also be understood in a less familiar and more far-reaching way. Revealing the "combinations of letters," the god may have taught humankind an art of reading that precedes the study of language: "the oldest reading" in Walter Benjamin's sense. From "entrails, the stars, or dances," such a practice of decryption infers sense from passing circumstance, placing things apparently unrelated among themselves in unexpected correspondences.[57] That reading is divination, a skill in which resourceful Odysseus excels. With eyes that see and ears that hear "to a purpose," he takes note of happenings. In waking as in sleep, he discerns a series that he is the first to interpret. Sensitive to events and portents, attentive to words that sound otherwise than as their speakers intend them, Odysseus brings his project to completion when, "rejoicing in the *klēdōn*," he begins to read, undetected and unbound.

CHAPTER FIVE

Crassus at the Crossing

In the winter of 55 BCE, Marcus Licinius Crassus, member of the First Triumvirate of Rome, arrived in Brindisium in Apulia. The *Lex Tribonia* had been passed, and Crassus, once reputed the wealthiest man in Rome, had been appointed proconsul of Syria. That position would enable him to embark on a major military expedition. With tens of thousands of Roman troops at his command, he planned to attack the Parthian Empire, which had its seat in Persia and controlled a territory stretching from central Asia to the Levant and Anatolia.[1] Before he could board the ship that would carry him from the shores of Apulia, however, Crassus had to pass by people near the harbor. There were his soldiers; there may have been travelers. If tradition is to be believed, there were also merchants selling vegetables and fruit, some of whom were indicating their wares. In the clamor to be heard at the port, one voice in particular was audible. It was repeating *Cauneas, Cauneas!*

In the language of the ancient Romans, *Cauneas* is a plural adjective deriving from a place name, *Cauno*, which refers to a city in Caria, Asia Minor, so well reputed for its figs as to have determined the modern botanical designation of the fig-tree subspecies as *Ficus carica*. Any speaker of classical Latin would have immediately grasped that at a market, a shout of *Cauneas, Cauneas*, was a sign of figs for sale, even if the syntax of the exclamation, being elliptical in form, could be interpreted in several ways. It is possible that the interjection was a truncated form of a sentence uttered by a speaker about himself, such as *ficus vendo Cauneas*, "I am selling Caunian figs." It might also have been the abbreviation of an injunction to passers-by, such as *Emite ficus Cauneas*, "Buy Caunian figs!"

It is likely that as he prepared to set sail, Marcus Licinius Crassus had little time for syntax or for fruit. His military project had met with fierce opposition in Rome. Some citizens had objected vehemently to the prospect of an attack on the Parthian Empire, with which Rome had had a longstanding peace. It had not been easy to overcome their opposition. When the law enabling the war had at last been passed, Crassus prepared for his departure according to the traditional form. Donning the commander's purple *paludamentum*, he performed the solemn rites of *profectio*. Even then, however, controversies continued. The tribune Gaius Ateius Capito alleged that while Crassus made his sacrifices, *dirae*, the most disastrous of portents, could be seen.[2] Crassus himself took no heed of them. Benefiting from the support of his two great allies, Pompeius and Caesar, he promptly set forth for Brindisium. Arriving in Apulia, he was sixty years of age, "a city politician who had held and sought no military command since he crushed the slave revolt of Spartacus as proprietor in 71, sixteen years earlier."[3] He stood before a difficult undertaking. It is possible that, absorbed by questions of strategy and tactics, he failed to reflect on the sounds around him, especially ones that would have reached his ears from local fruit sellers. Had he done so, however, he might have noted that by a curious coincidence, the name of the Carian delicacy, *Cauneas*, was in his language indistinguishable in sound from a warning: *Caue ne eas*, "Beware of going!"[4]

If the exclamation was advice rather than a claim to sell figs, it was sound, and Crassus should have taken it, for by all accounts, his expedition would be a disaster. The republic was to be defeated, thirty-thousand Roman troops were to be lost, and Crassus himself was to die at the battle of Carrhae, in Mesopotamia, in 53 BCE, his corpse being infamously defiled by the Parthians.[5]

With the distance of some two thousand years, one can only speculate, of course, about the conditions of the utterance of the phrase *Cauneas, Cauneas* in his vicinity. Did Crassus understand that an imperative, *Caue ne eas*, lay concealed in the apparently trivial naming of the Mediterranean fruit? Did he perceive the homophony of the two exclamations, *Cauneas* and *Caue ne eas*, if only for an instant, and set aside the possibility that it was a command since, such an order ran counter to his plans? Or, preoccupied with other matters, did Crassus pass by the speaker unaware of having been in the presence of anything but idle chatter?

It is Cicero who raises these questions in the work in which he first employs the term *divinatio*, root of the modern term "divination." A member of the Roman College of Augurs, Cicero himself had expertise in the identification and interpretation of signs sent by gods to mortals. In his dialogue, however, he explores ancient mantic practices from a critical perspective. It is here that with a philosopher's care for terminological detail, he defines divination as "the prediction and presentiment of those things which are thought to occur by chance" (*earum rerum, quae fortuitae putantur, praedictio atque praesensio*).[6] He investigates its varieties, its uses and its abuses, in two steps. In a first book, he has Quintus Tullius Cicero, his younger brother, set forth a series of arguments in support of the means of "prediction and presentiment" known to the Romans. In a second book, the author himself responds as a character in his dialogue, sometimes case by case, casting doubt on the legitimacy of these practices, despite their alleged antiquity.[7]

In passing, Cicero entertains the hypothesis that the cry of *Cauneas, Cauneas* perceived near the port of Brindisium may have been a monition sent by some god to the commander. "Let us say, if you will," Cicero concedes, "that *Cauneas, Cauneas* was a warning to Crassus to bid him '*Beware of going*,' and that if he had obeyed the omen, he would not have perished." Yet no sooner does Cicero evoke that possibility than he dismisses it. He draws out the absurd consequences that it would entail: "If we are going to accept chance utterances of this kind as omens, we had better look out when we stumble, break a shoestring, or sneeze!"[8]

In his treatment of divination, Cicero distinguishes between two procedures. Adopting what appears to have been a Stoic framework familiar to such Hellenistic thinkers as Posidonius, the Roman author divides the field of prophetic activities into the technical and the inspired. "The first," as he explains, "is dependent on art [*artis*], the other on nature [*naturae*]."[9] One source for that opposition can be traced to the Platonic dialogues, which contain an abbreviated account of one of those two kinds of foretelling. Plato presents inspired foresight (*mantikēs entheou kai alēthous*) as the result of a divine inspiration or "enthusiasm." Deriving the name "divination" (*mantikē*) from *mania*, "madness," Socrates explains that in becoming capable of foreseeing, diviners are possessed by a god, being dispossessed of their own reason.[10] When priests and priestess utter the words of a divinity or when gods appear in dreams and reveal what is to come, a holy "mania" is at work. It is what would later be called "natural divination." By contrast, "artificial divination" (*divinatio artificialis* or *tekhnikos*) follows from the application of a technique to an ordinary situation or occurrence. In the Graeco-Roman world, the flight of birds, the coloration of animal intestines, and the positions of heavenly bodies might all be subjected to such arts, yielding findings about the present, past, or future. "Natural divination," from this perspective, is spontaneous and immediate, being "without skill" and "without instruction," *atekhnos* and *adidaktos*, while "artificial divination" rests on knowledge, being *entekhnos* and *tekhnikē*.[11] As Auguste Bouché-Leclercq writes in his classical presentation of the sources, natural divination is "*internal*, *subjective,* or *intuitive*"; artificial divination, by contrast, is "inductive, *reasoned*, *conjectured*, or even *external*, and *objective*."[12]

Whether that distinction renders a generally held ancient conception and whether it applies to all Greek and Roman divinatory customs are open questions.[13] What is certain is that it scarcely does justice to the exclamation that Crassus may have perceived. Cicero nowhere indicates that the person who uttered the possibly portentous words *Cauneas, Cauneas*, was out of his mind, having been possessed by a god, and even if one grants that some divinity did move a man near the shore to shout the warning in the direction of the proconsul, what the speaker said in any case also had a meaning far removed from the discourse of priests, seers, and prophets, the crucial syllables being indistinguishable from talk of an ostensibly mundane kind. Whatever divination they contained was thus hardly "natural." Yet the happening appears also to have been irreducible to foretelling by "artifice." Unheeded, the repeated phrase was not subjected to any particular interpretation. One may even doubt whether the utterance was of such a kind as to be susceptible to analysis by a divinatory technique, such as augury or extispicy. Like most acts of speech, the shout was intimately bound to its conditions of enunciation in time and space. It was circumstantial, if not incidental, and by all appearances, it was banal.

In its structure, however, what Crassus heard or failed to hear nonetheless illustrates a particular variety of prophetic events, as Quintus Cicero, evoking several "well-known" examples, suggests. One such case involves an earlier Roman statesman, Lucius Aemilius Paulus. On the day that man was appointed consul to wage war against the Macedonian King Perseus, Paulus returned home to find his young daughter, Tertia, in tears. "What's matter, Tertia?" he asked her. "Why are you sad?" "Daddy," she responded, "Persa has died." "Persa," Quintus explains, was the name of the girl's beloved little dog. Her father immediately accepted the news as an unexpected verbal portent; in the resemblance of *Persa* and *Perseus*, he perceived a sign of the imminent defeat of his antagonist.[14] Another instance of such divination concerns Metellus's daughter, Caecilia, who wished to arrange a marriage for her sister's daughter. Lucius Flaccus, the high priest of Mars, related this happening to Quintus. Caecelia had gone with her niece to a small chapel. There, in accordance with tradition, she hoped to receive some hint from a god about the identity of her niece's future spouse. "As the young girl was standing and Caecilia was sitting and for a long time no sound was heard, the girl in her tiredness asked her aunt to let her sit in her place for a little while." Caecilia immediately responded: "'Yes, my girl, I give you my place.'" Her few words meant more than she could have known, "for she died soon after and the girl married the man to whom Caecilia had been married."[15]

Equivocation all too often prompts doubts and raises questions without furnishing any answers, yet Tertia's and Caecilia's words are trenchant as well as ambiguous, and their decisiveness is legible precisely in the multiplicity of their meanings. Each time, the speaker says what she intended to say yet also indicates something of which she could not have been aware. To the hearer who is capable of perceiving it in the moment of its sounding, a circumstantial remark becomes a prophetic word. It is then an example of a divination that defies the Ciceronian bipartition, being a "prediction and presentiment of those things which are thought to occur by chance" that is neither "natural" nor "artificial."

Such utterances may be taken as Roman instances of the calls that the ancient Greeks, from Homer to Herodotus, Aeschylus and Pausanias, called *klēdones*. That their memory survived in the Hellenistic age can be inferred from the works of Callimachus, poet, scholar, and fabled librarian of Alexandria. The first of his *Epigrams* recounts the unexpected conditions in which a "stranger from Atarneus" found a means to choose among the women he wished to marry. He consulted the sage Pittacus about the predicament in which he found himself: "Two marriages invite me. One lady is indeed my peer in wealth and lineage: the other is my superior. Which is better?" Raising "aloft his staff," "an old man's weapon," Pittacus referred him to some boys playing nearby, "spinning and whipping their swift tops in an open crossroads": "Look! Those over there shall tell thee all." "So the stranger stood by them," the poet relates. Watching their game, the man heard one boy issue a command to another: "drive your own line!" or "keep to your own!" (*tēn kata sauton ela*). "The stranger hearing this laid to heart the chance-heard remark of the boys [*paidōn klēdona sunthemenos*] and refrained from grasping at the wealthier house."[16]

Readers of the *Aeneid* may recall the scene in which a nobler man asks an oracle for assistance in deciding on an uncertainty of a related kind. King Latinus is seeking to learn to whom he would do best to promise the hand of his beloved daughter, Lavinia. When he consults the prophet of the god Faunus, who is his father, he receives a warning:

> Don't seek to marry your daughter within any Latin alliance,
> Son of my blood, don't trust in an easy and ready-made marriage!
> Sons-in-law will arrive from a foreign world and, with their blood,
> Raise our name to the stars![17]

Even as Rumor spreads the sound of those words throughout the countryside, the weary Trojans disembark and reach the mouth of the Tiber. Without any awareness of where they are, they unload the last of their provisions, making use of hardened bread as plates on which to devour the little they still possess. Hunger soon drives them to

> turn their teeth upon Ceres' wafer-thin trenchers
> And, with their hands and audacious jaws, break into the fateful
> Outer circle of bread, even take squared sections of starch-wheat.[18]

Then Aeneas's son, Iulus, exclaims, "Look, how we eat tables even!" (*Heus! Etiam mensas consumimus*). The poet observes that the phrase is said in passing and in jest (*adludens*), but his attentive father catches the portent that is expressed in it: Aeneas "snatches" the words even as they fall from the boy's mouth (*rapuit ex ore*).[19] Long before, Anchises, the hero's own father, had prophesied that the Trojans would have reached their final destination when, arriving at an unknown shore, they would "eat tables" (*consumere mensas*). When Aeneas hears Iulus's quip, he is "stunned by the show of divine will" (*stupefactus numine*). In an instant, he grasps that his son has named the moment that Anchises foresaw: "This was the hunger referred to, our very last trial that awaited, / Bringing a definite end to our exile."[20] The joke is the unexpected index of the truth and the medium by which the Trojans accomplish their fate.

For such unexpected revelations in speech, the Romans had a Latin word: "omens" (*omina*). Cicero draws attention to the term in a passage in which Quintus recalls an "observance" of the Pythagoreans: "It is not only the voices of the gods [or "utterances of the gods," *deorum voces*] that the Pythagoreans observe, but also those of men; they name them 'omens.'"[21] "Omens" are therefore voices under observation. Roman authors propose a suggestive etymology of the Latin term. In his treatise on the Latin language, Varro relates that *omen* derives from the name of "mouth" (*os*): "Because it was first uttered from *os* [*ex ore*], it is called *osmen*." *Osmen*, which is otherwise unattested in Latin, would in turn have given rise to *omen*.[22] In his treatise *On the Signification of Words*, Festus provides a similar account. He defines the omen as an "augur" performed on the basis of not birds, but "the mouth," being a simplified form of *oremen*: an "augury made by the mouth, rather than by means of birds" (*quod fit ore augurium, quod non avibus aliove modo fit*).[23] *Oremen*, which seems as conjectural a form as *osmen*, would thus have linked the omen to discourse. Not all the Latin evocations of *omina*, to be sure, conform to such accounts. Among Roman authors, *omen* can also refer to wondrous signs and events that involve no acts of speech.[24] Yet it has been argued that "in its origins, *omen* is indeed a verbal presage," and as François Guillaumont remarks, Cicero's usage accords with the claims of the grammarians. When he "employs *omen* in *De divinatione*, it almost always involves a presage furnished by human speech."[25]

Modern scholars have rarely accepted the Roman etymology of the word, preferring to put other explanations in its place. In their *Dictionary of Latin*, Charlton T. Lewis and Charles Short suggest that the term "perhaps" derives from *osmen*, which would be a form of *ausmen*, or "a thing heard" (from *audio*).[26] Several other accounts of the term's construction have been proposed. For some scholars, *omen* is traceable to the Greek *oiōnos*, "bird," and by association, "augur." Its origin might also lie in the hypothetical form **augsmen*, from *augeo*, "to augment." For still others, it is a compound built from the prefix **obs* or **ops* and the suffix *-men*, its meaning being then close to *ostentum*, "wonder, prodigy" and *monstrum* "miracle, portent."[27]

In 1962, Émile Benveniste intervened in the scholarly debate on the formation of the word. He proposed an innovative explanation that drew on a major accomplishment of the early twentieth century, the decipherment of the oldest known Indo-European language, Hittite, which had been written in cuneiform and used in Anatolia, as well as parts of the Levant and Mesopotamia, in the mid-second millennium BCE. "It seems to us that Hittite contains much more than has been drawn from it till now," Benveniste wagered in the preface to his book, *Hittite and Indo-European*. "We wish . . . to give at least an inkling of the ways in which Indo-European comparison can be enriched by it."[28] The first example of the "enrichment" that the archaic language offered comparative grammar concerned the name of the Roman verbal presage. "Until now nothing convincing has been proposed concerning *ōmen*," Benveniste wrote, dismissing the work of many predecessors with a single gesture. "The various etymologies that have been offered have been founded on arbitrary restitutions."[29]

Benveniste took the bipartite structure of the word *omen* to be indisputable. Given that *-men* is a standard Latin nominal suffix, the question becomes that of the origin of the word's theme, *ō*. It appears to be the root of a verb. But which one? Latin affords no clear answer. Hittite, by contrast, furnishes a key so patent that "the *ō* of *ōmen* does not even require reconstruction." Benveniste pointed out that "the ancient Latin *ō-* corresponds regularly to the Hittite verbal theme *hā-*, 'to believe; to hold to be true.'" From that circumstance, he drew a consequence: "*ōmen* can be literally interpreted as 'declaration of truth.'"[30] As Benveniste explained in his *Vocabulary of Indo-European Institutions*, "a chance word, uttered in decisive circumstances, may be accepted as *ōmen*, as a true presage, as the sign of destiny. It will be a word of good 'augur,' the announcer of fate. Several such examples are given in Cicero's *De divinatione*."[31]

The argument and the conclusion seem crystalline, yet they conceal a difficulty that follows from a defining feature of the Roman verbal portent. As Benveniste recalls, introducing the enigmatic Roman word, "in the Latin terminology of presages, *ōmen* designated a chance word that was susceptible of being transformed into a prediction if one *accepted* it as a real sign, if one took it explicitly as true and valid for the future; hence the expression *ōmen accipere* ['to accept the omen']."[32] Cicero's accounts of the matter are in this regard exemplary. Hearing Tertia announce the death of her dog, Lucius Paulus "embraced the girl more tightly," Quintus recalls, "and said, 'My daughter, I accept the omen'" (*'accipio,' inquit, 'mea filia, omen'*).[33] Livy evokes like formulae at several points in his chronicle of Rome. In the first book of his *History*, he thus recalls the period in which Evander lived in exile in the Peloponnese. Some shepherds had pointed him toward a stranger of "more than human stature and of a preternatural dignity of bearing." Hearing the man reveal his name, his parentage, and his country, Livy recounts, Evander exclaimed, "Hail, Hercules, son of Jupiter! You are he, of whom my mother, truthful interpreter of Heaven, foretold to me that you should be added to the number of the gods, and that an altar should be dedicated to you here which the nation one day to be the most powerful on earth should call the Greatest Altar and serve according to your right." Hercules "gave him his hand and replied that he accepted the omen [*accipere se omen*] and would himself assist the course of destiny by building and consecrating an altar."[34]

In Cicero and in Livy, as in analogous cases in Ovid, Tacitus, Pliny, and Virgil, a spoken augur is no sooner perceived than it becomes the object of an explicit assertion of "acceptance."[35] A crucial question about the "declaration of truth," however, then becomes difficult to avoid, even if Benveniste, preoccupied with etymology, refrains from raising it. The question is that of the identity of the subject of the "declaration." Is it the one who speaks the omen or the one who hears it and accepts it? Is it, in other words, the consul's daughter, who mourns for Persa, or her newly appointed father, who, listening attentively to her words, gleans the sign of the imminent death of Perseus? Evander, who restates a prophecy at a crucial moment, or Hercules, who pledges to fulfil it? Iulus, who jests, or Aeneas, who, listening carefully, solemnly concludes that a foretelling has been verified?

By virtue of the configuration that it presupposes, the omen implies two speaking positions, each of which is necessary for the act of divination, yet also insufficient on its own. Obviously, if no one speaks, the possibility of a verbal presage may be excluded. Yet if a "chance word" is by nature "susceptible of being transformed into a prediction" when "*accepted*" by another person "as a real sign," then one speaker alone is incapable of bringing about the mantic event. There must, each time, also be someone to acknowledge it. Cases where apparent verbal portents fail to be welcomed by those who hear them are instructive in this regard. "The Roman gave himself the right to accept or to refuse the omen," Jean Bayet writes.[36] A premonitory word could be met by an act of "refusal" on the part of the perceiver; in this case the Latin authors would write of *omen improbare* or *refutare*, "falsifying" or "refusing the omen." Possibly divine portents could be denied and disavowed. The Romans were also familiar with formulaic means of distancing unpropitious speech events. An unwelcome word could be the object of *exsecrari*, "cursing" or "profaning." It might prompt the action of "omen removing" that is literally denoted by the verb *abominari*, "to abominate."[37] In Rome, there was, Georges Dumézil writes, an entire "casuistry of escape clauses," which was as extensive as were the perils of inauspicious accidental signs.[38] According to Raymond Bloch, "any word of bad augur could be skillfully turned away from one's own person, pushed onto someone else, and sometimes sent back toward the very person who uttered it."[39] At the limit, unpropitious words might be rewritten by a hearer and, once transformed, put to new effect.

There were legendary precedents for such treatments of unwelcome words. One case involves the earliest history of Rome.[40] Ovid, Plutarch, and Arnobius all recount how Numa, the first of the Roman kings, sought to summon Jupiter, who had been inflicting lightning bolts on the Roman people for obscure reasons. Numa wished to call the god down from heaven and learn how the Romans might expiate the wrong for which they were being punished. When the king succeeded in evoking the divinity according to the correct ritual form, "eliciting" him from the sky, the god agreed to his request, promising to tell him what was needed to quell his rage. He spoke clearly and distinctly. Yet his words, in being received, underwent a change. In Ovid's telling, the god, appearing to Numa in answer to his prayer, demanded that a "head" be "cut off" (*caede caput*). The ruler responded that he and his people would obey while qualifying the command that they would follow: "We'll cut the head *of an onion*, dug up in my garden" (*caedenda est hortis eruta cepa meis*). Next, the god declared, as if to clarify his command: "Of a human being" (*hominis*). Numa again assented to the deity with an addition. He assured Jupiter that he would receive "*the hairs* of a human being" (*sumes capillos*). When, at last, the god explicitly ordered the Romans to give him "a life," Numa added, "of a fish" (*piscis*). Laughing, Jupiter consented: "See to it that by these things you will expiate my bolts!"[41] "Agreement was reached, and from then on Romans expiated lightning at the shrine of Jupiter Elicius with an onion, some human hairs and a fish."[42]

The fabled exchange has been read as offering a lesson in several aspects of Roman customs and conceptions. It suggests the limits of the legitimate demands that gods could make of their subjects, and it portrays the state of impassible tranquillity to which a pious mortal, in King Numa's image, might aspire.[43] Yet the tale also sheds light on the ancient awareness of the human ability to decide on the messages sent to them by their gods. The divine communication in that case is clear and direct, yet it may be read as a model for grasping more oblique signals. What held for presages that mortals "solicited" from immortals (*auspicia impetrita* or *impetrativa*) was also valid for signs that gods chose to "offer" without incitation (*auspicia oblativa*).[44] In each case, the decipherment of a Roman portent implied a crucial process of reception in which a divine command could emerge in the moment of interpretation.

It is worth pausing to consider the structure of such a reception. To interpret an omen is in each case to take account of two speakers and therefore to distinguish two moments: utterance and acquiescence, articulation and "acceptance." Yet in the Roman practice of divination by chance hearing, it is necessary to distinguish an order of logic, as well as of time. Both sequences unfold in two steps, but the pairs do not coincide. In the temporal occurrence of the event, the speaker of the portentous utterance must act prior to the one who perceives it. If, however, it is the hearer who takes the fortuitous pronouncement "explicitly as true and valid for the future" or not, it is he or she who first confers on it the status of being a portent. The "declaration of truth" that is the omen, then, exhibits a structure that defies chronology. In logic, it is the hearer who acts first, deciding on the nature of what has been said; the speaker of the presage is, by contrast, secondary. Words that have been uttered acquire an "ominous" character only when, after a delay, the one who has perceived them "snatches them" from their speaker, like Aeneas fastening onto Iulus's words. In accordance with a profoundly Roman insight into the fundamental role of the recipient, it is the perceiver who makes a phrase into a portent, interpreting it belatedly and otherwise than it was meant.

Hence the intractability of the question that Cicero puts before his readers in the apparently trivial example of Crassus passing through the port of Brindisium. The difficulty lies not in determining whether or not the three syllables of *Cauneas* or *Cau' ne eas* reached the proconsul's ears. That is a problem of physics and psychology, which is in principle solvable by empirical means, if not with the distance of centuries. The real issue concerns a subtler matter: the structural conditions of the sounding and the perception of an unexpected verbal presage. What does it take for a scrap of language to be charged with a sense unintended by a speaker and, in the event of speech, to reach some hearer as an unexpected truth? In the Roman omen and the discourse that the classical authors devote to its reception, that question becomes brightly discernible. Today, as in Cicero's time, it poses a challenge to the student of divination and the scholar of signs, portents, and interpretation. "Observing the voices of gods and men," as the Pythagoreans advised, is one way to respond to that challenge. It implies a method: attending both to what is said and to the event of its saying, examining the contents of utterances, in other words, and also the conditions in which they are believed to reveal truths otherwise inaudible. Taken as a program of historical inquiry, the way of such "observance" neither begins nor ends in Rome. It points in several directions, forward, past the age of Crassus, his immediate predecessors and successors, and backward, toward cultures older than Hellenic antiquity. In both senses, it leads to revelations in unexpected acoustical occurrences and to names, beliefs, and practices unknown in the Greek and Roman world.

CHAPTER SIX

Noise That Answers

Among premodern civilizations, none boasts theories of divination more extensive, more complex, or more influential than ancient Mesopotamia. The traditions of the Fertile Crescent are perhaps the distant sources of the oldest known mantic practices in European cultures, such as Etruria, where extispicy may have developed from Assyro-Babylonian models, and the Hellenistic world, where experts in divination were long associated with Mesopotamia, astrologers being called "Chaldeans" in homage to the Babylonian territory of Chaldea.[1] The earliest treatises on divination in ancient Mesopotamia antedate Greek and Roman literary history by more than a millennium, stretching back to the end of the seventeenth century BCE. Jean Bottéro notes that by that point, works in Akkadian on the reading of portents are "so numerous and so elaborate in their form, breadth, distribution, technical vocabulary, and in their procedures of analysis and exposition, with variants suggesting different theories and schools, that one must infer that they lie at the end of a long process . . . of written and oral tradition that leads us back well before the third millennium."[2] An indication of the enduring place of the study of omens in the civilization of Mesopotamia can be gleaned from the fact that more than half of the works in the library of King Ashurbanipal, the seventh-century Assyrian monarch who "aimed at collecting everything written in

Babylonia," were "devoted to divination and the consequent procedures to appease the gods."[3] In neighboring regions of the ancient Near East, Akkadian divination was "considered a major intellectual achievement," as A. Leo Oppenheim observes. The works that transmitted the principles and techniques of the Mesopotamian practices "were copied in Susa, the capital of Elam; in Nuzi; in Hattuša, the capital of the Hittites; and in such far-off places as Qatma and Hazor in Syria and Palestine."[4]

Oneiromancy is the type of ancient Near Eastern divination that is perhaps best known today. In Pharaonic Egypt, in particular, it attracted great attention. Yet in ancient Mesopotamia, the interpretation of dreams was but one branch of a vast field of theory and practice of reasoned inference. "The divinatory corpus explored all aspects of the universe," Marc Van De Mieroop explains, "its extent was unlimited."[5] For the peoples of Assyria, Bottéro writes, in similar terms, "*everything* in the world was divinatory, dreams like everything else."[6] "Divinatory," in such a setting, means "susceptible to interpretation," "interpretation" revealing messages from powers greater than humans. Oppenheim comments that in ancient Mesopotamia,

> divination represents a technique of communication with the supernatural forces that are supposed to shape the history of the individual as well as that of the group. It presupposes the belief that these powers are able and, at times, willing to communicate their intentions and that they are interested in the well-being of the individual or the group—in other words, that if evil is predicted or threatened, it can be averted through appropriate ways.[7]

Such communication might be inferred from natural events such as wind, thunder, and the motions of stars and planets. Yet portentous signs could also be discerned in processes that had been deliberately provoked. An individual might cast a set of lots, pour oil into water, or produce smoke from a censer. It was thought that a divinity would manipulate the lots, affect the spreading of the oil, or shape figures in the rising smoke. From such an occurrence, a prediction could then be extracted.

Mesopotamian divination treatises are catalogues of rules holding for such inferences. The oldest anthologies date to the end of the Old Babylonian epoch.[8] According to Sally Freedman, Mesopotamians viewed them "as scientific reference works." "The collections were edited and organized by being written on a number of clay tablets of specific content that succeeded each other in a certain order to form 'series.' The series were given titles, usually the first line of the first tablet in the series, and these titles were used for cataloging and reference purposes."[9] The treatise known as *Šumma Alu* is in this regard exemplary. Recorded in the seventh century on more than a hundred tablets, each of which contains some two hundred lines, it is thought to have developed over centuries. Today it is one of the largest surviving omen collections. It begins with the statement from whose first half the title of the series has been drawn: "If a city is set on a height [*Šumma Alu ina Mele Šakin*], living in that city will not be good."[10] The ensuing pronouncements are of the same form, as the next sentences indicate: "If a house's foundations are laid on the 16th day (of the month), that house will be abandoned"; "If water is spilled in the doorway of a man's house and (the spill) acquires a scute like a snake — release of evil"; "If a goatlike demon is seen in a man's house, that house will be dispersed."[11]

Such declarations exhibit a recurrent logical syntax in which two sentences are conjoined. The suggestion is that if a certain phenomenon is attested, an inference may be drawn. "A first phrase, a 'protasis,' as the grammarians say, is followed by a second: an 'apodosis.' Introduced by a hypothetical sign, *if, granted that* (in Akkadian, *šumma*), the protasis furnishes the detail introducing the object: it is the presage. The apodosis reveals the portion of the future that can be deduced from the presage; it is the prediction."[12] A "sign," each time, points to a "signified" according to a pattern that is implicit in the grammar of the omen. Francesca Rochberg notes that the divinatory pronouncements thereby illustrate a logical scheme that recalls the mode of reasoning on two statements, *P* and *Q*, that is familiar to the European philosophical tradition as *modus ponens*: "If *P*, then *Q*"; or "*P*, therefore *Q*."[13] However fantastical the circumstances that they evoke and whatever the religious uses to which they may have been put, the Mesopotamian omen anthologies consist of rules adhering to such logical form.

Confronted by the ancient divinatory treatises and their lists of correlated elements, scholars face an obvious question. According to what principles are protasis and apodosis joined? What, in other words, assures the passage from antecedent to consequent, *P* to *Q*? One answer that has been proposed is "circumstantial association." "Let us suppose that some memorable event (E) had been observed originally under a particular set of extraneous circumstances (C)," E. A. Speiser suggested. From their vision of the universe, he argued, the Mesopotamians excluded senseless coincidence, holding that there must be a reason for such a conjunction of happenings. Even if they did not understand it, the ancient Mesopotamians would therefore record the relation of *E* to *C*, before carefully filing away the record "for reference, not unlike our fingerprints." Then, whenever *C* would be observed in the future, *E* would be expected.[14] The "circumstances," consequently, would acquire the status of protasis, while the "event" would be the apodosis. "Once it was observed that a certain sign had been followed by a specific event," Hermann Hunger and David Pingree argued, advancing a like claim, it would be "considered known that the sign, whenever . . . observed again, will indicate the same future event."[15] The oracular rule would express a state of affairs and a confidence in the regularity of its recurrence.[16]

The explanation has the allure of simplicity, but it runs up against several notable difficulties. A first point is that the Mesopotamian divinatory proposition is hypothetical in syntax. Each time, it rests on a relation expressed by a crucial syncategorematic term: "if" (*šumma*). It does not point to a realized "circumstance" but rather to a possible occurrence. The oracle, in other words, consists in the reasoning that "*If x* occurs (or has occurred), (*then*) *y* will occur." "The grammar of the statement dictates that the verb of the protasis is in the preterit, '*x* occurs/occurred,' and that of the apodosis is in the present-future aspect, '*y* will occur.'"[17] The relation between the protasis and the apodosis is not one of direct causation. Rochberg remarks that the omen statement is thus best understood as a principle dictating that "*if x*, (expect also) *y*."[18] It is tempting to assume that a chronological relation is implicit in such reasoning, the protasis preceding the apodosis in time. Yet such a belief is belied by the fact that the antecedent can involve circumstances of a kind difficult to consider empirical, at least by contemporary standards. As an example, one need only recall the first lines of *Šummu Alu*: "If a goatlike demon is seen in a man's house. . . ." Yet there are further reasons to question the assumption that divinatory rules originate in attention to circumstances attested at a certain time.

Protasis and apodosis are often linked by evident patterns of analogy and similarity. "When reading through omen lists," Marc Van De Mieroop comments, "one sees a long chain of likenesses, which their authors saw as the key to truth."[19] In physiognomic omens, for example, "a short face means a short life, and its opposite, a long face, means a long life."[20] It seems that in extispicy, the disposition of animal entrails was understood to exhibit similar resemblances. "'If there are two abomasums," we read in a rule of inference from intestines, "'the (man's) wife will acquire a rival.'" "The association here is based on the subtle use made of the number 2," Ivan Starr notes, "two organs, two rival women in the man's house." A similar principle accounts for the following prediction: "'If the head of the 'station' is pointed (*zuqur*), elevation of (*nīš rēši*) the ruler.' The fact that the part of the liver is described in the protasis as 'pointed' suggests the idea of man's elevation to a higher status, involving divine favor, fame, success, and the like." Likewise, "'If the 'gate of the palace' is wide (*irtappiš*), (additional) income (*erbum*) will come (*irrub*) to the palace.' The primary association here seems to be between wideness (symbolizing prosperity) and income."[21]

In the relation of antecedent and consequent, further associations were also expressed. Mesopotamian diviners took linguistic resemblances as legitimate grounds for their inferences. "In many cases the relationship between protasis and apodosis is based on a play of words," Starr writes, offering several examples, "which can be multiplied manifold": "'If the 'station' is long (*arik*), the days of the ruler will be long (*irriku*)'; 'if the 'reinforcement' is thick (*ulluṣ*), rejoicing of (*ulluṣ libbi*) the army'; 'if there is a 'desire'-mark (*erištu*) in the head of the 'station,' request of (*erišti*) a great god; the god requests (*irriš*) regular offerings."[22] In *Ziqīqu*, a dream omen series, Rochberg relates, "a dream in which a man eats a raven (*arbu*) portends income (*irbu*) for that man. Similarly, a dream that presents fir wood (*mihru*) portents no rival (*māhiru*) for the dreamer."[23] Sensitivity to cuneiform signs, which were employed to notate both Akkadian and Sumerian, could also play a role in detecting associations at the basis of divinatory rules. In an extispicy omen, one finds following entry: "If the coils of the intestine look like the face of Huwawa (written logographically ^{d}ḪUM.ḪUM): it is the omen of the usurper king (*ḫammā'u*) who ruled all the lands." Rochberg comments: "Here the antecedent is related to the consequent by a word play based on the phonic echo of ḪUM.ḪUM in *ḫammā'u*, not by any empirical connection between intestines coiled that way and a usurpation."[24] "The diviner was a reader, and resemblances with cuneiform graphemes were very important in both extispicy and physiognomic omens," Van De Mieroop explains. Knowledge of the multiple ways in which cuneiform signs could be read was often required to interpret portents. Some diviners even went so far as to discern Mesopotamian graphemes in the shapes of living bodies: "There is a 57-line-long section in the physiognomic omen series *Alamdimmû* that identifies marks on the patient's forehands that look like cuneiform signs, some more complex than in extispicy."[25]

Yet the ancient Mesopotamian diviners not only inferred sense from the sounds of phrases and from the configurations of the cuneiform signs that they used to transcribe them. Scraps of discourse, in the Fertile Crescent, were also considered to be potentially portentous. The Assyro-Babylonian specialists in mantic arts taught that it was possible to draw consequences from words heard and overheard, without regard to the intentions of the speakers. When perceived in certain conditions, isolated utterances could then furnish diviners with grounds for inferences concerning "communication between the gods and man."[26] In the lexicon of divination, a name was reserved for such ominous soundings: *egirrû*. Attested in the Old Babylonian period, that term appears for the first time in the oldest known language transcribed in cuneiform, Sumerian, where it is inscribed on the Gudea cylinders, two terracotta structures believed to have been produced in the twenty-second century BCE.

A borrowing from the Sumerian *i/enim-ǧar(-ra)*, *egirrû* is an Akkadian expression whose literal meaning is "placed word."[27] It refers to an utterance that is generally "made by a human being" and that is "premonitory for those who hear it."[28] In an early study, Oppenheim sought to clarify the nature of this phenomenon by referring it to a notion in the field of Greek divination. The *klēdōn*, he wrote, "fits as exactly as one can reasonably expect all the contexts in which the Sumerian INIM.GAR and the derived Akkadian *(e)girrû* occur."[29] One might also evoke the *omen* as many early Roman authors understood it. In his account of Mesopotamian divinatory beliefs and practices, Bottéro, for his part, defined *egirrû* as "any noise whatsoever (perhaps with a preference for human speech) whose essential trait is its total independence from the will of the interested party, who perceived it in a completely fortuitous manner." He then added, "Insofar as it is an audible sound, it can be likened to that essential means of communication, even between gods and men, that is speech; and the fact that it is always unexpected and independent of the hearer draws it close to divine messages, which, even when requested, are absolutely free."[30] *Egirrû* appears to have eluded any systematic codification, for reasons all too easily understood.[31] Consisting of words, sounds, or noises perceived "in total independence from the will of the interested party," *egirrû* implies a field of sonorous material that can scarcely be delimited. As André Finet noted, "a descriptive protasis" is in this case "unimaginable."[32]

On the basis of an extensive study of the occurrences of *egirrû* in the Akkadian sources, Anne-Caroline Rendu-Loisel has concluded that in ancient Mesopotamia, attention to such "placed words" was a part of "daily life" and "common practice."[33] The traces of its presence in surviving divinatory treatises are suggestive. *Egirrû* plays a notable role in the ninety-fifth tablet of *Šumma Alu*, where it appears repeatedly in an extended sequence of related portents. The first divinatory inference concerns an individual engaged in an act of solitary piety: "If a man prays to his god," we read, "and an *egirrû* immediately answers him repeatedly: he will be granted his wish readily, for his god has heard his prayer." Next the tablets appear to envisage a similar situation in a temple: "If a man (is) on his knees, the silence of death reigns, and then it answers him: his god has heard his prayer; what he has asked will be granted to him."[34]

"Apart from the information concerning the form of private worship which these two omina contain," Oppenheim writes, "they also illustrate by their use of the verb *apālu* 'to answer' said of the *egirrû*, the specific mood of receptiveness which endows the *egirrû* with those premonitory implications that are the basis of its validity. The *egirrû* typically 'answers,' i.e. it comes as response to either a formulated query or one which remains in the subconscious."[35] As Rendu-Loisel has shown in remarkable detail, the Babylonian treatise offers several criteria for the interpretation of such respondent soundings. The setting and the timing of the acoustical phenomena are key. Where and how the "ominous" word is "placed" and when or how often it becomes audible are crucial factors for its interpretation. An *egirrû* that comes from inside a house or temple may bear a meaning decidedly different from one that comes from outside it. So, too, the tablets distinguish among the possible directions from which a portentous sound may reach the hearer: "front, rear, near or far."[36] Whether the *egirrû* arrives from a temple of a god or goddess, whether it comes from the sky or from the street, are significant distinctions. Arithmetical properties are also pertinent. What is heard once is to be understood otherwise than what is perceived two, three, four, or five times, and all those discretely recurrent acoustical phenomena are in turn to be distinguished from an *egirrû* that "responds regularly" to the asker. "Yet often in this list, the *egirrû*s that are heard are interpreted as *niphu*, 'ambiguous presages,' recalling the difficulty of regulating and systematizing a sound."[37]

Sensitivity to such phenomena appears to have been widespread in ancient Mesopotamia. If the divinatory treatises are to be believed, commoners and persons of noble birth alike could intercept such portentous sounds, both inside their dwellings and temples and also outside them. Yet the effects of *egirrû* were also thought to exceed the domain of human beings. Immortals, too, were held to be susceptible to the power of such "placed words." Oppenheim explains:

> The minor deities of the Mesopotamian pantheon, whose main function it was to act as intermediaries on behalf of the worshipper, are repeatedly asked to exercise their influence, with regard to the *egirrû*-phenomena possibility released by the prayers addressed to the chief deities. The typical situation at court: the supplicant approaching the king under the protection of an interceding courtier, is thus transferred to the level of the god-man relation. And exactly as the king is likely to be influenced in a favorable as well as in an unfavorable way by the wording of the demand, the deity is supposed to be liable to react to the *egirrû*-omina which the wording of the prayer may contain.[38]

Between those who catch such omens and those who emit them, a relation of transitivity obtains. "As man is ready and sometimes anxious to receive *egirrû*-omina, he can likewise be, unknowingly, the source, or better, the mouthpiece, of such utterances."[39] The Akkadian sources contain prayers for the elicitation of unexpectedly auspicious sounds. Yet they also contain rites for the avoidance of inauspicious words and phrases that speakers might utter by misfortune: "Grant me favourable *egirrû*—and when I (walk) on the street may my utterances (*qa-bu-ú-a*) be pleasant (add: for those who happen to hear them by chance)!"[40] Not only the hearer, but also the speaker are to be protected against the possibly pernicious effects of an ill-boding "placed word." Someone through whom a deity has communicated "*egirrû*-omina prognosticating evil events" is viewed as hateful and worthy of being shunned. The incantation series known as *Šurpu* alludes to such a person as "he (who) has eaten what is taboo in his town, he (who) has betrayed his town, he (who) has caused evil-portending *egirrû*-omina in his town (INIM. GAR URU-*šu ul-tam-mi-in*), he (who) has met a cursed man (*tamû*)."[41] The presage may become audible in what speaking beings hear, and it can also sound in something they themselves may say.

Among all the portentous happenings observed and recorded in ancient Mesopotamia, such a "means of communication between the gods and man" was perhaps the most transient. It could hardly have been more minute. An *egirrû* might consist of no more than a word or phrase. It could also become audible in something as fleeting and as indistinct as an animal's cry. Although the "placed word" is for the most part discursive, as the etymology of its name implies, the Akkadian divination treatises suggest that a panoply of nonverbal noises might fulfill its function. Birds, dogs, oxen, goats, rams, pigs, and donkeys, in certain circumstances, could produce the sonic material of this acoustical presage.[42] There appear to have been few or no limits to the sources from which such the *egirrû* could arise, as the ancient enumerations and classifications of its forms, in their extraordinary extension and often-baffling fragmentariness, attest. To have brought the manifold and mutable conditions of such portentous soundings into focus, laying bare the questions raised by fleeting words and noises demanding interpretation, was the accomplishment of the Mesopotamian priests and scribes. It is without known precedent, and it seems to have been without any single successor. Yet it was not to be lost on the other cultures of the ancient Near East.

CHAPTER SEVEN

A Lesser Prophesy

Among the many commandments given by the god of Israel to Moses in Leviticus, one seems to forbid all manner of divination. From the inside of the holy place that is the tabernacle, these words reach the prophet's ears, as recorded in Leviticus: "You shall not divine nor interpret omens" (*lo tenakhashu velo te'onenu*).[1] The first half of the prohibition involves the activity known in Biblical Hebrew as *nakhash*, "practicing divination, divining, observing of signs."[2] The second concerns *'anan*, "practicing soothsaying."[3] The observance of this commandment is to distinguish the Israelites from other peoples of antiquity, as a passage in Deuteronomy indicates: "When you come into the land that the LORD your God is about to give you, you shall not learn to do the abhorrent things of these nations." There follows an enumeration specifying the varieties of such "things," two of which clearly evoke the practices named in Leviticus:

> There shall not be found among you one who passes his son or his daughter through fire, a speller of charms, a soothsayer [*me'onen*], or a diviner [*menakhesh*] or a sorcerer, or a chanter of incantations or an inquirer of ghost or familiar spirit or one who seeks out the dead. For whosoever does these is the LORD's abhorrence, and because of these abhorrent things the LORD your God is about to dispossess them before you. You shall be wholehearted with the LORD your God.[4]

Implicitly, yet unmistakably, the Hebrew Bible thus formulates a judgment on many techniques of inference known to the civilization of ancient Mesopotamia, which preceded it and remained a major influence on it through the centuries of its composition. Yet it would be an error to conclude either that mantic practices are absent from Hebrew scripture or that the canonical sources of Judaism sources flatly deny their efficacy. Readers will recall that the Hebrew Bible contains incontrovertible instances of portents demanding to be interpreted. Practices of divination, in such cases, are more than merely licit; they are required, being the sole means for the conveyance of messages from God to the faithful. When the signs from the deity are correctly deciphered, the past is revealed, the present appears in a new light, and a way toward a promised future emerges clearly.

In Genesis, Abraham, Jacob, and Joseph all receive visions from God in dreams that disclose to them what is to come.[5] Oneiromancy, in such cases, possesses an indisputable value. Later in the Bible, the Israelites develop a means of establishing oracular judgments through the use of an instrument belonging to the high priest. Inside his garment (*ephod*), there was a breastplate (*khoshen*) containing a pouch. It held twelve stones bearing the names of the tribes as well as the "Urim and Thummim": gems or lots that priests would employ to reach a judgment about difficulties that could not otherwise be solved.[6] The Hebrew Bible also alludes, in diverse settings, to decisions made by the casting of a *goral* or "lot." Such practices all appear to illustrate the process known as cleromancy.[7] In addition to those special means of reaching knowledge of matters otherwise inaccessible to mortal cognition, the Hebrew Bible is familiar with other divinatory techniques whose status as licit or illicit is not always clear: practices involving a goblet, arrows, the inspection of animal livers, and astrology are all mentioned.[8]

Given the presence of divinatory procedures in the world of the early Israelites, and given that such practices are at times viewed as not only effective, but also permissible and even obligatory, the presence of a formal prohibition on the interpretation of omens in the Hebrew Bible requires explanation. The ban on divination appears to attest to an essential trait of the ancient Judaic religion. Forbidding *nakhash* and *'anan*, Leviticus programmatically excludes "artificial" means of determining what cannot directly be observed and inferred. Knowledge of the future, the present, and the past is instead to be secured by an inspired activity. Prophecy is to solve the difficulties on whose account other ancient peoples turned to mantic techniques. Recalling Greek and Roman terms, one might take prophecy to be a kind of "natural" divination, were the term "divination" not tainted in the Judaic tradition by a millennial history of polemics against the mantic arts.[9] That prophets in Israel are to take the place of other peoples' diviners is a point made explicitly in Deuteronomy: "These nations which you are about to dispossess heed soothsayers and spellers of charms, but you the LORD your God has not given such. A prophet like me from your midst, from your brothers, the LORD will raise up. Him shall you heed."[10]

In the Hebrew scripture, the clear distinction between prophecy and the mantic arts of such peoples as the Babylonians, however, cannot always be maintained. In at least one recurrent circumstance, the opposition between prophecy and divination becomes uncertain. That circumstance concerns unexpected events of speech and, more exactly, moments in which divine signs become discernible in what seem to be ordinary human utterances. In the world of the ancient Hebrews, as in that of the Mesopotamians, Greeks, and Romans, messages from the divine can be glimpsed in mortal discourse. If grasped at a propitious moment, such messages reveal tidings that no human being could know and that could not otherwise be ascertained.

The Hebrew Bible contains at least two cases of communication in such forms.[11] The first is to be found in 1 Samuel. Jonathan, faithful to his sovereign father, Saul, is battling the Philistines. He secretly leaves his father and his troops and, with a single attendant carrying his arms, approaches the pass that separates them from the Philistine garrison. As he and his companion are about to cross into the territory of their enemy, Jonathan remits himself to his god, exhorting his companion in the following terms: "Come, let us cross over to the garrison of these uncircumcised! Perhaps the LORD will act for us, for nothing holds the LORD back from rescue, whether by many or by few."[12] The divine "action" that Jonathan anticipates involves neither a wonder in the order of nature, such as those performed by God for Moses, nor a revelation through inspired speech, such as the ecstatic discourses of later prophets, not least Jonathan's father, Saul. When his attendant assents to his proposal, Jonathan explains his project. He means to incite the discourse of the Philistines and to extract a presage from the words with which they answer him. "Jonathan said, 'Look, we are about to cross over to them and we shall be exposed to them. If they say, 'Stand still until we get to you,' we shall stand where we are and not go up to them. And if thus they say, 'Come up to us,' we shall go up, for the LORD will have given them in our hand, and that shall be the sign for us [*vezeh-lanu ha'ot*]."[13]

Jonathan thus prepares the conditions for the reception of a "placed word" or *egirrû*, as the priests and scribes of ancient Mesopotamia might have put it. In Hellenic terms, the son of Saul anticipates the sounding of a *klēdōn*. Like Odysseus, he has entreated his god to grant him the favor of an omen become discernible in an unknown speaker's apparently incidental words. In this case, the circumstances of the mantic inference are sharply delimited. The trial, as Jonathan explains to his attendant, has only two possible outcomes. The Philistines will respond by one of two contrasting imperatives: "Stand still until we get to you" or "Come up to us."

The experiment goes as planned. "The two of them were exposed to the Philistine garrison, and the Philistines said, 'Look, Hebrews are coming out of the holes where they've been hiding.' And the men of the garrison spoke out to Jonathan and his armor bearer and said, 'Come up to us, and we'll teach you something!'"[14] Jonathan reads the "sign" (*'ot*) contained in their injunction, a sign that they, ignorant of the conditions of their speech, cannot guess. Without hesitation, he informs his attendant of the message from the deity that he thus perceives: "Come up behind me, for the LORD has given them into the hand of Israel."[15] Despite their greater number, the Philistines are swiftly defeated. That event incites marvels of human and natural kinds: "Terror shook the camp in the field and all the troops. The garrison and the raiding party were also shaken, and the earth trembled, and it became dire terror."[16]

In 1 Kings, words heard at a decisive moment prove otherwise portentous. Ben-Hadad of Damascus has laid siege to Samaria, the northern kingdom of Israel, and has been defeated. Retreating from his enemy, he flees, as the chronicler relates, into "an inner chamber" in the town of Aphek. Here, in contrast to the scene in 1 Samuel, it is a leader's nameless attendants who conceive of a method to elicit a salvific sign. They contrive to provoke a verbal presage that will ensure their survival. "His servants said to him, 'Look, pray, we have heard that the kings of Israel are merciful kings. Let us, pray, put sackcloth on our loins and ropes on our heads and go out to the king of Israel. Perhaps he will let us live.'" Without including his response, the text suggests that Ben-Hadad accepts their proposition. In the next scene that is related, the servants do as they have proposed. "They bound sackcloth on their loins and ropes on their heads and came to the king of Israel and said, 'Your servant Ben-Hadad has said, Let me, pray, live.'" Like the Philistines at the garrison, the king of Israel responds unhesitatingly, unaware that his words will mean more than he intends: "And he said, 'Is he still alive? He is my brother.'"

In that remark, the servants catch a precious portent: "The men divined and quickly caught the word from them [*yenakhashu vayemaharu vayakheltu hamimenu*], saying 'Yes, Ben-Hadad is your brother!'"[17] According to the diction of the Hebrew Bible, their "divining" is a form of *nakhash*, the practice expressly condemned in Leviticus and Deuteronomy. Here its power is both immediate and binding. Like Aeneas before the "jest" of his son Ascanius, the servants in the Hebrew chronicle seize an expression that falls from the speaker's mouth in the moment of its articulation. They take hold of the word "brother" (*akh*) even as the king utters it, repeating to the sovereign what he just has said to them. Their citation appears to be little more than echolalia, a confirmation of the last word that he has expressed. In the process of its reception and repetition, however, the king's response acquires a new sense. The servants of the vanquished leader make of it the guarantee that he renounces any right to punish his opponent. As Oppenheim remarks, "the king, realizing that words he had uttered had been put into his mouth by the Lord, that they have been a *klēdōn*, granted life to his defeated adversary."[18]

Both passages in the Hebrew Bible can also be read as instances of divination by *omina* in the sense given to the term by such Roman authors as Cicero and Varro. Each time, as Benveniste writes, an unexpected human utterance is "transformed into a true prediction" in being "accepted by another person as a real sign." Jonathan, the servants of Ben-Hadad, and the king of Israel are in this sense practitioners of "kledonomancy," as Halliday defines it in his *Greek Divination*. In different settings, they take in "the fatal word or the spoken omen."[19]

That there are not more such examples in the Jewish scriptures may be explained by the extraordinary importance that the Bible accords to prophecy. As long as the god of the Hebrews "raised up" men to act in his stead and to make his will known to them, there was little need for his servants to solicit divine signals in the passing utterances spoken by mortals to each other. Through his mouthpieces, the Lord revealed his will directly and with incontrovertible finality. In the sacred history of the Israelites, however, there was to come a time when the power of inspired discourse waned. It was first anticipated by the psalmist, who sings, "We do not see our emblems; there is no longer any prophet, and there is no one who knows how long."[20] The last prophets also announced its imminent occurrence. As Amos would relate, "The time is surely coming, says the Lord God, when I will send a famine on the land; not a famine of bread, or a thirst for water, but of hearing the words of the Lord."[21] Micah, his contemporary, evokes a coming darkness: "It shall be night with you, without vision, and darkness to you, without revelation. The sun shall go down upon the prophets, and the day shall be black over them."[22] Similar allusions to the cessation of prophecy can be found in apocryphal works, the Dead Sea Scrolls, Old Testament Pseudepigrapha, and the New Testament.[23] Multiple postbiblical Jewish sources also attest to it. In the first century of our era, Flavius Josephus mentions "the failure of the exact succession of the prophets," adding that "from Artaxerxes [who ruled from 464 to 424 BCE] to our own time, the complete history has been written but has not been deemed worthy of equal credit with the earlier records, because of the failure of the exact succession of the prophets."[24]

In the following centuries, the Rabbis of the Talmud also allude to the end of prophecy. Yet they teach that in the attenuation of the direct communication between the deity and human beings, a diminished medium of revelation persists. They call that medium *bat qol*, literally, the "daughter of the voice." "Since the death of the prophets Haggai, Zechariah, and Malachi," we thus read in a pronouncement in the Talmud and the Tosefta, prophetic inspiration has ceased: "the Holy Spirit departed from Israel. Yet they were still able to avail themselves of a *bat qol* [*hayu mishtameshin bevat qol*]."[25] The expression *bat qol* is often rendered as "heavenly voice." It is a late ancient locution, being unattested before the second or third century CE.[26] Medieval Jewish authors would explain its "daughterly" status by virtue of the fact that it names an acoustical phenomenon engendered by a primary sound: a periphrasis for "echo." Long ago, L. Blau showed that such an account is inadequate to the late ancient sources, where the term evokes a "reverberation" or a "hum."[27] In Rabbinic writings, moreover, *bat qol* refers to a revelatory sound, particularly when perceived in the absence of a visible body: a "voice heard behind the back," as one Talmudic text has it.[28]

In different cases, it emanates from various sources: heaven, Mount Horeb, the temple sanctuary, and other unidentified places. Distinctly, if mysteriously, it relates tidings on various matters: "factual information, evaluative statements, legal decisions, predictions of coming events, or counsels to individual courses of action."[29]

In some cases, the "daughter of the voice" becomes perceptible in the mouths of mortal speakers who seem devoid of any prophetic powers. Such people tend to be of too modest a status to be identified by name, and they appear to be unaware of the import of what they say. A passage of the Palestinian Talmud contains an instructive example of the concerted hearing of a "daughter of the voice" of this kind. "Rabbi Yonah and Rabbi Yose went up to visit Rabbi Aha, who was sick," we read. "They said, 'Let us follow the hearing of a *bat qol*.'" At that moment, "They heard the voice of a woman saying to her friend, 'Has the lamp been extinguished?'" Alluding to 2 Samuel 21:17, in which Samuel is presented as "the lamp of Israel," the unidentified woman's friend answered her, "The lamp of Israel will not be extinguished and shall not be extinguished." The Talmud leaves it to the reader to draw the conclusion implicit in that circumstantial remark, which Rabbis Yonah and Yose infer: Rabbi Aha, a light of Israel, is still alive.[30] In a manner that recalls the actions of Jonathan and the servants of Ben-Hadad, the Rabbis thus provoke the sounding of a portent that is embedded in apparently profane discourse. What they perceive is a message detached from the conditions of its utterance that its nameless speaker could not have intended. A true sign becomes audible in the echo of scripture.

It was Saul Lieberman who first noted the proximity of the "daughter of the voice" in such cases to the unexpectedly perceived words that the ancient Greeks counted among the objects of their mantic practices. In his 1950 book, *Hellenism in Jewish Palestine: Studies in the Literary Transmission, Beliefs and Manners of Palestine in the 1st Century B.C.E.–4th Century C.E.*, Lieberman dismissed the medieval accounts of the *bat qol* as "reverberation, sound, echo." "From the earlier sources," he wrote, "it is obvious that *Bath Kol* very often means simply *vox*, *verbum*, a voice or word heard without seeing the person who uttered it." On the basis of passages such as the one involving Rabbis Yonah and Yose's consultation of a *bat qol*, Lieberman also offered a second account of the expression. In many cases, the "daughter of the voice" is "a word heard from a person who was not conscious of the import of his saying." Or, as Liberman specified, evoking Greek words: "the *Bath Kol* is nothing but *phēmē* or *klēdōn*."[31]

Two decades later, David Sperling deepened Lieberman's argument by drawing on the ancient Mesopotamian divinatory traditions that informed the culture of Rabbinic Judaism. Citing Oppenheim's study of the *egirrû* as a Mesopotamian counterpart to the Greek *klēdōn*, Sperling made what he called an "obvious inference": "the *egirrû* and the *bt qwl* are related phenomena."[32] Several features, he argued, unite the ancient Mesopotamian and Judaic presages. In their designations, both contain a reference to speech, the *egirrû* being a "placed word," the *bat qol* being a "voice." Both also function as oracular responses to questions and solicitations. They may contain detailed information, but they may merely consist of affirmative or negative responses, "yes" or "no," to a single question, which can "repeated for emphasis." Furthermore, like the *egirrû*, the *bat qol* that is overheard in mortal speech is treated as divinely inspired, without, for that matter, being intended in its revelatory sense by its speaker: "the fact that the statement is purely accidental in no way detracts from the effect which it can have in the real world."[33] Sperling also showed that the varieties of *egirrû* identified in Akkadian sources are well illustrated by a subset of the extant examples of the Rabbinic *bat qol*. As evidence of a final "point of contact" between the two phenomena, he evoked the "evaluative functions" that both discursive portents accomplish; in the Judaic tradition, as in Mesopotamia, such signs contain judgments on the "merits and demerits of individuals."[34]

Yet in their evocations of the "daughter of the voice" lodged in human discourse in ways their speakers themselves cannot anticipate, late antique Judaic sources constitute more than merely Judaic version of the Sumerian *i/enim-ǧar(-ra)*, the Akkadian *egirrû*, Greek *klēdones*, or Roman *omina*. The Rabbinic corpus also grants a new theological status to the appearance of such signs. In stating that with "the death of the prophets Haggai, Zechariah, and Malachi, the Holy Spirit departed from Israel," even as a *bat qol* became perceptible, Judaic sources suggest that when divinely authorized messages become audible in the words of speakers unaware of what they are truly saying, a change in the form of revelation is observable. Prophetic power has departed from Israel while enduring in the form of a "minor survival."[35]

To bring such a persistence into focus, one might recall a Talmudic statement on dreams and their consequences, a statement made long after the ages of Jacob, Joseph, and Daniel, the great masters of classical Judaic oneiromancy. "Rabbi Yohanan said: 'One who awakened in the morning and a verse immediately falls in his mouth: it is a minor prophecy" (*hishkim venafal pasuq letokh pio — harei zeh nevuah qetana*).[36] That judgment does not bear directly on the *bat qol*. Yet the occurrence to which Rabbi Yohanan gives the name "minor prophecy" consists of an event discernible in a number of passages involving the "daughter of the voice," an event that would become increasingly important in both Judaism and Christianity: ominous citation.

Repeatedly, the Rabbis glean truths in hearing verses unexpectedly recited out of context.[37] Rabbis Yohanan and Shimon b. Laqiš, in the Palestinian Talmud, thus resolve to consult a *bat qol* before undertaking a voyage to visit Samuel of Nehardea, the head of the Rabbinic academy in Babylonia. "'Let us act in accordance with a *bat qol*,'" they said. "They passed by the school. They heard the voice of a child: 'And Samuel died' (1 Sam. 28:3). And they marked the hour, and this is how it was for him."[38] The child spoke more truly than he could have known, for when he named the decease of Samuel, king of Israel, Samuel of Nehardea, his late-born Rabbinic homonym in Babylonia, also died. The same Talmudic passage contains a further example of verses that, uttered in isolation, were to prove portentous. When Bar Qappara entered a town, we read, he injured his finger. At the same time, he heard a child's voice reciting a line from Exodus: "If he came by himself, he shall go out by himself" (21:3). Bar Qappara concluded that the injury, which came by itself, would go out by itself and that he himself would suffer no further harm. "And this is how it was for him."[39]

Among the Rabbis, Lieberman writes, the "procedure of consulting the verses casually uttered by children in the synagogue" was frequent.[40] Such "consultation" could take two forms. Sometimes it consisted in inference from biblical passages spontaneously uttered by children, as in the example of the Rabbis who unexpectedly learned of the death of Samuel of Nehardea. Sometimes it consisted in inference from biblical citations that the Rabbis themselves would solicit.[41] In some cases, to resolve an uncertainty, Rabbis asked children to recite the biblical passages that they had just learned. The verses would contain the solutions to the questions at hand.[42] Tractate Chagiga of the Babylonian Talmud contains an account of how Rabbi Meir once apprehended the heretical Rabbi Elisha ben Abuyah, euphemistically known as "Aḥer" or "the Other One," after he violated the sabbath laws. Rabbi Meir brought Aḥer into the study hall, where he faced the divine judgment implicitly contained in lines recited by children. Asked to repeat before Aḥer the last verse he has studied, a child uttered a prophet's words: "'There is no peace, said the Lord, concerning the wicked'" (Isaiah 48:22). Rabbi Meir

> brought him to another study hall. Aḥer said to a child: recite your verse to me. He recited to him: "For though you wash with niter, and take for you much soap, yet your iniquity is marked before Me" (Jer. 2:22). Rabbi Meir brought him to another study hall. Aḥer said to a child: Recite your verse to me. He recited to him: "And you, spoiled one, what are you doing, that you clothe yourself with scarlet, that you deck yourself with ornaments of gold, that you enlarge your eyes with paint? In vain you make yourself fair" (Jer. 4:30).[43]

As the speech of the prophets is referred to contemporary circumstances, God's judgments become audible.

The belief in the revelatory power of isolated verses belongs to an epoch in which the holy sources of Judaism undergo a major change. In the period leading to Rabbinic age, the parts of the Bible pass from being the objects of oral transmission to being portions of a written text. Toward the end of the second century BCE, the unknown Jewish author of the Hellenistic *Letter to Aristeas* becomes the earliest known writer "to call the Torah 'holy' (*hagnos*, *theios*)." He presents the Ptolemaic king of Egypt as bowing "in adoration seven times in front of the first Torah scroll in Greek."[44] In the same period, the first book of Maccabees describes a practice of which no earlier written traces have been found. The Judaic chronicle recounts how, when threatened by the Seleucid king Antiochus IV and his attempt to Hellenize the practices of the Temple of Jerusalem, the Jewish community turned for assistance to a scroll: "They opened [unrolled] the book of the Law to inquire into those matters about which gentiles consulted the likeness of their idols" (*kai exepetasan to biblion tou nomou peri ōn exēreunōn ta ethnē ta homoiōmata tōn eidōlōn autōn*).[45] Such an action suggests that writing and its elements, by this point, had become the objects of a particular practice of inference. As Pieter W. van der Horst notes, "in the same way in which the Gentiles by various means of divination tried to receive a verdict from their gods about the outcome of their enterprises, the Jews opened the Torah scroll at random in the hope that the first line their eyes hit upon would instruct them about what God had in store for them or expected them to do."[46] The second book of Maccabees contains a scene that illustrates such a practice. Judas the Maccabee "cast a glance into the Holy Book" (*paranagnous tēn hieran biblon*) and, happening on the phrase, "the help of God" (*theou boētheias*), understands it constitutes a portent: there will be divine support for his military resistance against a Seleucid general.[47] The chronicle verifies his interpretation.

By the Hellenistic age, the selection of biblical verses takes on an intensely literary form. It appears as the fortuitous reading of a single segment of the holy text. "Bibliomancy," divination by the use of books, becomes a recurrent practice in later Judaism as in Christianity. Certain Rabbinic pronouncements on scripture could be read as justifying it. "Turn it over and turn it over, for everything is in it" (*hafoch bah vahafoch bah, dechola' vah*), Rabbi Ben Bag-Bag is reported to have taught.[48] It had long been known that when in difficulty, non-Jews "consult[ed] the likeness of their idols" in the fervent hope that, in propitious conditions, some divine answer would reach them by auspicious means. By late antiquity, however, Jews made equally circumstantial inquiries of their holy writ, seeking thereby to elicit a clear indication about the troubling situations in which they found themselves. In ancient Achaia, the idol of Hermes dispatched an acoustical answer to the one who, following the correct ritual form, made inquiries of it in the market of Pharae. Centuries later, Jews would believe that the books of Moses, the prophets, and the later writings held the sacred power to resolve the most immediate of difficulties. Reading by chance unlocked it.

The historical irony implicit in such a development is difficult not to observe. Over the course of centuries and by means of the vagaries of tradition and innovation, inheritance and borrowing, the diverse corpus of poetry, chronicle, and law that had expressly forbidden divination became its essential instrument. The Hebrew Bible itself was transformed into the means of a mantic process. However Mosaic its origins and however Israelite its early legacy, by the Hellenistic period, the books of revelation came to be viewed by Jewish authors as playing a role that, while licit, was analogous to that of idols, as the author of 1 Maccabees makes clear. Scripture gathered within itself the powers of the summons, the omen, and portentous noise. Holy writ would therefore lend itself to readings that were not only liturgical, but also occasional. It would offer a window onto the transient as well as the everlasting, the present moment no less than universal history. After diversely archaic hums and reverberations, multiple oracular voices and their "daughters," the Bible's phrases could then be perceived anew at the crucial moment. They would remedy the "thirst . . . for the hearing of the words of the Lord." In a night without vision, in a darkness without revelation, prophecy, attenuated yet persistent, would glimmer in scraps and bits of inscribed matter. To perceive such a divine signal, it sufficed to know how and when to pick up the holy book and how and when to set it down again.

CHAPTER EIGHT

In the Garden

In the spring of the year 386, Augustine was a teacher of rhetoric in Milan. Initiated in his infancy into the religion of his mother, he had long been "marked by the sign of the cross."[1] Only recently, however, had he begun to return to the Christianity of his earliest childhood, becoming a "catechumen in the Catholic Church," as he recalls in book 8 of the *Confessions*.[2] By that point in the itinerary of his spiritual development, he was no longer uncertain in matters of philosophy or theology. He had renounced the doctrines of the Manicheans, devoting his attention wholly to "the books of the Platonists" and scripture. Nonetheless, as he avows to his god, he found himself in a state of grave difficulty: "All doubt had been taken from me that there is indestructible substance from which comes all substance. My desire was not to be more certain of you but to be more stable in you. But in my temporal life everything was in a state of uncertainty, and my heart needed to be purified from the old leaven."[3] He had yet to undergo the profound "turning" toward the divine that is known in Latin as *conversio*.

Seeking counsel, Augustine paid a visit to Simplicianus, the bishop of the city. To the initiate's account of his difficulties and the incomplete remedies that he had found for them, Simplicianus responded by recounting an episode from the life of Marius Victorinus, eminent Platonist, scholar, and translator from Greek to Latin.

There was a time, he explains, when Victorinus had confided to Simplicianus that he was a Christian, yet would not venture into a church, despite his friend's repeated urgings. As Augustine explains in his paraphrase, Victorinus feared "to offend" his acquaintances, "proud devil-worshipers." "He thought that from the height of Babylonish dignity, as if from the cedars of Lebanon which the Lord had not yet broken, the full weight of their hostility would land on him." Yet one day, the study of the Bible worked a change on him. "Suddenly and unexpectedly, he said to Simplicianus (as he told me): 'Let us go to the Church, I want to become a Christian.'" Soon Victorinus was baptized, "that he might be reborn." Thus he became a faithful servant of the Lord.[4]

The tale of Marius Victorinus was an encouragement to Augustine, yet it did not relieve him of his subjection to worldly appetites and the turmoil that they entailed. "I was still bound down to the earth," he observes, continuing to address God. "I was refusing to become your soldier, and I was as afraid of being rid of all my burdens as I ought to have been at the prospect of carrying them."[5] Even when in the company of his closest companions, Augustine suffered in solitude, acutely aware of his removal from the divine. He recounts how, one day, he was alone in his house with his friend Alypius, a man from Thagaste in North Africa, like him, who had previously been his student in rhetoric. Suddenly, Ponticianus, their countryman, appeared at their door. That unanticipated circumstance was followed by another. "By chance," Augustine relates, their guest "noticed a book on top of a gaming table which lay before us." "He picked it up, opened it, and discovered, much to his astonishment, that it was the apostle Paul."[6]

Ponticianus, "a Christian and a baptized believer," understood immediately that he was in the presence of two people who shared his faith. The three began to discuss holy matters. Learning that neither Augustine nor Alypius knew of "Antony the Egyptian monk," Ponticianus spoke to them of his life and deeds. Athanasius of Alexandria had made them known in a recent biography, which

Evagrius of Antioch had translated into Latin some fifteen years before the time of their conversation.[7] Ponticianus also relayed to them an experience of his own. As Augustine and Alypius listened "in rapt silence," he told them how, while a member of the Roman civil service some years earlier, he had found himself in Trier. The emperor having been "detained by a circus spectacle in the forenoon," Ponticianus and three of his colleagues had taken a walk in the gardens adjacent to the city's walls. They had separated into two pairs, one man walking with Ponticianus, the others setting off in a different direction.

On their stroll, Ponticianus relates, his colleagues happened upon a "certain house" inhabited by people "poor in spirit" who lived in anticipation of the kingdom of God. Inside the building, the visitors noticed a book. It was Athanasius's *Life of Antony*. They picked it up and read—to momentous effect. As soon as one of his colleagues began to make out the sentences of the codex, Ponticianus recounts, "he was amazed and set on fire." "During his reading, he began to think of taking up this way of life and of leaving his secular post in the civil service," dedicating himself to Christian worship: "Suddenly he was filled with holy love and sobering shame."[8] He confided his experience to his companion before returning his eyes to the page, and as he read on, "he experienced a conversion inwardly [*mutabatur intus*]," even as his mind gradually "rid itself of the world."[9] Moved by his words and by his calling, his friend chose to join him in his new vocation. Hearing of their decision, Ponticianus adds, their betrotheds, too, followed them, devoting themselves to God.

In this portion of the *Confessions*, coincidence follows coincidence. After the unanticipated event that is Ponticianus's visit to Augustine and Alypius, there is his unlikely sighting and reading of the book on their gaming table that contains the writings of St. Paul. That sequence prompts the telling of an unexpected visit to a garden, his colleagues' subsequent stumbling upon a house, and their unanticipated finding of a book about a holy man within its walls. One Christian work, opened as if by accident, incites the narrative of another. Each time, the act of reading transforms the reader. Aligned, the circumstances converge toward Augustine, yet at this point in the narrative of his repentance, he is still painfully at odds with himself. Unlike the holy men of the house near Trier, unlike Ponticianus's former companions, perhaps unlike Ponticianus himself, he believes, yet he is still dissatisfied. While Ponticianus recounts his experience, Augustine therefore turns his attention back to himself. "I looked and was appalled, but there was no way of escaping from myself."[10] Once Ponticianus finishes his tale and departs, Augustine puts a series of pressing questions to Alypius: "'What is wrong with us? What is this that you have heard? Uneducated people are rising up and capturing heaven, and we with our high culture without any heart—see where we roll in the mud of flesh and blood. Is it because they are ahead of us that we are ashamed to follow? Do we feel no shame at making not even an attempt to follow?"[11]

Then, as if striving to adhere the model set by Ponticianus and his colleagues, Augustine leaves his friend and goes outside. "The tumult of my heart took me out into the garden where no one could interfere with the burning struggle with myself in which I was engaged, until the matter could be settled."[12] Alypius quickly follows him, "step after step." "Although he was present," Augustine recalls, "I felt no intrusion on my solitude." Despairing, Augustine gives himself over to the gestures that "men make when they want to achieve something and lack the strength, either because they lack the actual limbs or because their limbs are fettered with chains or weak with sickness or in some way hindered."[13] He tears his hair, strikes his forehead, intertwines his fingers, and clasps his knee. Those movements are the regular effects of his will. "The mind commands the body," as he comments, "and is instantly obeyed." Yet when it strives to exert itself upon itself, the spirit encounters resistance of another kind: "mind commands, I say, that it should will, and would not give the command if it did not will, yet does not perform what it commands." The effect is lacking. Augustine infers that in such cases, the will, too, must be missing: "The strength of the command lies in the strength of the will, and the degree to which the command is not performed lies in the degree to which the will is not engaged.... So the will that commands is incomplete, and therefore what it commands does not happen."[14]

Powerlessness draws Augustine into a condition of more extreme distress. "From a hidden depth a profound self-examination had dredged up a heap of all my misery," he recounts. "That precipitated a vast storm bearing a massive downpour of tears."[15] Next he withdraws further from Alypius, "to ensure that even his presence put no inhibitions on me." "I threw myself down somehow under a certain fig-tree, and let my tears flow freely."[16] He begins to pose repeated questions in prayer: "'How long, O Lord, How long, Lord, will you be angry to the uttermost...' 'How long, how long is it to be?'"[17]

What happens next was to remain forever imprinted on Augustine's memory. The extended interrogation incites an unimagined response. A sign reaches him from his vicinity. "As I was saying this and weeping in the bitter agony of my heart," he writes, "suddenly I heard a voice from the nearby house chanting as if it might be a boy or a girl (I do not know), saying and repeating over and over again 'Pick up and read, pick up and read'" (*Dicebam haec et flebam amarissima contritione cordis mei, et ecce audio vocem de vicina domo cum cantu dicentis et crebro repetentis, quasi pueri an puellae, nescio: "tolle lege, tolle lege"*).[18] Augustine says no more of the origin of his perception. It is, he writes, a *vox*, which may be rendered by either "voice" or "sound." He limits himself to offering an account of his immediate impressions. It seemed to him that the speaker of the phrase might be a boy or a girl, adding that he did not know: *quasi puer an puella, nescio.* Given the tone and rhythm in which the words "pick up and read" were repeatedly uttered, he wondered whether he had had overheard a chant of some kind. "I began to think intently of whether there might be some sort of children's game in which such a chant is used," he writes. But he responds in the negative: "I could not remember having heard of one."[19]

Whatever its source and whatever its setting, the insistent phrase produces an immediate effect. "At once my countenance changed," Augustine recalls, "I checked the flood of tears and stood up."[20] As he confides to the reader, he spontaneously referred the event to a moment in the life of an exemplary Christian of whom he learned through two related accidents: the unexpected visit of his friend Ponticianus and Ponticianus's friends' unanticipated discovery of the *Life of Antony* near Trier. Augustine explains, "I had heard how Antony happened to be present at the gospel reading, and took it as an admonition addressed to himself when the words were read: 'Go, sell all you have, give to the poor, and you shall have treasure in heaven; and come, follow me.'" For the Egyptian, that biblical line was an *oraculum*, as Augustine goes on to note: "By such an inspired utterance [*tali oraculi*] Antony was immediately 'converted to you.'"[21]

The portent plays an important role in Athanasius's hagiography. The *Life* opens with an account of Antony's Christian upbringing and his pious youth. The Egyptian finds his calling when, one day, aged eighteen, he is deep in reflection on "how the Apostles left everything and followed the Savior, and also how the people in Acts sold what they had and laid it at the feet of the Apostles for distribution among the needy, and what great hope is laid up in Heaven for such as these." As "those thoughts were in his mind," the young man enters a church. "And so it happened," Athanasius relates, "that the Gospel was being read at that moment and he heard the passage in which the Lord says to the rich man: 'If thou wilt be perfect, go sell all that thou hast, and give it to the poor; and come, follow me and thou shalt have treasure in Heaven.'" Antony understands that those words are a command to him: "As though God had put him in the mind of the saints and as though the reading had been directed especially at him, Antony immediately left the church and gave to the townspeople the property he had from his forebears."[22]

Like Antony, Augustine grasps a message from God in words that he hears unexpectedly, but the differences between the circumstances of their two acts of inference are significant. Antony's unanticipated "oracle" consists in a scriptural citation that is read aloud to an assembly as he enters the house of God. For him, there is no mystery concerning the person of the reader or the identity and meaning of what has been read. When Augustine, by contrast, perceives his salvific sign under the fig tree, the speaker is unseen; Augustine alone catches the phrase without fully grasping either the source or the sense of what has strikes his ears. Confronted with its insistent repetition and its suggestion of an alliteration, if not a stutter (*tol-le-le-ge*), Augustine can only wonder whether the words are meant in earnest or as a game. Antony, like the Rabbis before him, seizes on a message in a fortuitously heard portion of the holy book. Augustine accomplishes a stranger feat: he perceives a sign from God in a fragment of unknown discourse.

His experience of the *tolle lege* is a Christian counterpart of the Greek *klēdōn* and the Roman *omen*, the Babylonian *egirrû* and the Judaic *bat qol*. It is a summons that, uttered by an unseen body, sounds at an unexpected yet crucial moment, reaching its hearer as a reply to questions that he put to his god in solitude. Referring the event to the *Life of Antony*, Augustine discerns in the Latin phrase an order destined for him alone: "I interpreted it solely as a divine command to me to open the book and read the first chapter I might find" (*nihil aliud interpretans divinitus mihi iuberi nisi ut aperirem codicem et legerem quod primum caput invenissem*).[23]

"I hurried to the place where Alypius was sitting," Augustine continues. "There I had put down the book of the apostle when I got up. I seized it, opened it and in silence read the first passage on which my eyes lit: 'Not in riots and drunken parties, not in eroticism and indecencies, not in strife and rivalry, but put on the Lord Jesus Christ and make no provision for the flesh in its lusts.'"[24] That commerce with the book suffices: "I neither wished nor needed to read further," he remarks. "At once, with the last words of this sentence, it was as if a light of relief from all anxiety had flooded into my heart. All the shadows of doubt were dispelled." After years of uncertainties and unfulfilled longings, Augustine is converted. In the narrative of the *Confessions*, he soon abandons his work as a teacher, retiring "as a salesman of words in the markets of rhetoric." He resolves henceforth to devote himself entirely to God and to a life of service in the Catholic Church. Yet in the immediate aftermath of his experience in the garden, Augustine is not alone. Alypius, by his side, has a share in the oracular event. Picking up the codex of St. Paul after him, Alypius reads the passage that follows the one on which Augustine's eyes fell. Alypius, too, is thereby "given confidence." "Without the agony of hesitation," Augustine relates, "he joined me in making a good resolution and affirmation of intention."[25]

Today, the scene in the garden is perhaps the best-known moment in the thirteen books of the *Confessions*.[26] It is at once a decisive turning point in the narrative of the work and a repetition of events that determined his existence to that point. In his youth, Augustine entered into the life and doctrines of philosophy as an immediate consequence of reading Cicero's *Hortensius*.[27] Now, in the third and last of the three itineraries of struggling catechumens told in book 8 of the *Confessions*, after the examples of Victorinus and the friends of Pontiacianus, Augustine sets out on a new way, thanks to an unexpected encounter with a passage of the sacred book.[28] Divination by chance reading allows him to accede to the renunciation and the faith that he sought but could not reach as long as he relied solely on his will.

Augustine's name would long be tied to revelatory experiences prompted by unexpected encounters with Christian writing. The most illustrious stands at the threshold of modern European literature. In the famous letter that he sends Francesco Dionigi de Roberti of Borgo San Sepolcro on April 26, 1336, Petrarch relates how he succeeded in climbing the highest mountain in Provence, the "Windy Peak" or Mont Ventoux, with a single companion, his younger brother. At the summit, having reached a height from which he could see the Rhone River, "the mountains of the province of Lyons to the right and, to the left, the sea of Marseilles as well as the waves that break against Aigues Mortes," the Italian author decides to turn from worldly beauty to "higher spheres." He therefore takes out the volume of Augustine's *Confessions* that he brought with him, "a little book of the smallest size but full of infinite sweetness." "I opened it," he writes, "with the intention of reading whatever might occur to me first: nothing, indeed but pious and devout sentences could come to hand."[29]

Petrarch happens on a sentence in book 10: "And men go to admire the high mountains, the vast floods of the sea, the huge streams of the rivers, the circumference of the ocean, and the revolutions of the stars—and desert themselves."[30] Petrarch reads no farther. That his eyes should have fallen on such a page is for him no accident. "I could not imagine that this happened to me by chance: I was convinced that whatever I had read there was said to me and to nobody else."[31] Augustine's discourse becomes the conduit of a divine message that rewrites the theologian's experience almost a thousand years earlier in Milan. On the Provençal mountaintop, the *Confessions* act on Petrarch as the codex worked on Augustine. The church father's narrative takes the place of the apostle's admonition.[32] Both times, a book is read in part at the crucial moment; both times, the written word acquires a new sense and a new reference, being interpreted as addressed solely to the unanticipated reader.

In the fourth century AD, the practice of turning at a decisive moment to the reading of an unexpected portion of a holy work was long-standing and variegated. First attested in the Book of Maccabees, Jewish bibliomancy had not fallen out of use in the centuries leading to the age of Augustine. Christian scripture also suggested that the reciting of inspired speech could be the occasion for unanticipated disclosures, albeit in a form unknown to Jewish authors. In his Gospel, Luke recounts how Jesus entered the synagogue on the Sabbath, stepping up to read from the scroll of Hebrew scripture. He thus reads out the following verses by Isaiah:

> The Spirit of the Lord is on me,
> Because he has anointed me
> To proclaim good news to the poor.
> He has sent me to proclaim freedom for the prisoners
> and recovery of sight for the blind, to set the oppressed free,
> To proclaim the year of the Lord's favor.[33]

Reciting those lines, Jesus makes them his own. Unexpectedly, yet irrevocably, the reference of their first-person pronoun shifts: in the words "The Spirit of the Lord is on me," the "me" suddenly points to the living reader, who is the anointed one. It emerges that the ancient expectation was for none but him. "Jesus rolled up the scroll, gave it back to the attendant and sat down," the Evangelist continues. "The eyes of everyone in the synagogue were fastened on him. He began by saying to them, 'Today this scripture is fulfilled in your hearing.'"[34]

By late antiquity, pagan readers also practiced divination through the seemingly random selection of passages. The Greek and Roman poets' texts were their sacred works. "In some circles in late antiquity little distinction was made between the books of Homer or those of the Bible as far as their magical power was concerned," Pieter Willem Van der Horst writes.[35] The belief in the inspired poets led to several practices of bibliomancy. One involved handling lines by Homer and Vergil according to procedures that resembled those employed in Jewish and Christian sortition. Through the division of the epic poems into books and individual hexameters, a multitude of discrete elements was engendered. Each line, taken on its own, could be treated as a lot and drawn according to a random process. To resolve a theoretical or practical difficulty, it could suffice, then, to roll dice; from the numbers thrown, a passage could be identified and brought to bear on the pressing situation. The *Historia Augusta*, an anthology of biographies of the Roman emperors from the age of Augustine, contains the earliest reference to such an oracular consultation of lines of the *Aeneid*: a first example of the *Sortes Virgilianae*, or "Lots of Virgil."[36] Homer's poems had been put to a like use.

In many late ancient practices of sortition, children were considered those best suited to making the selection of the decisive lot. "A single 'boy' (*puer*) (or perhaps a virgin) would mix the *sortes* in a receptacle and then extract one among them," Pierre Courcelle explains. "It was generally believed that someone chaste would be particularly capable of guessing the future, because of either his young age or his moral purity."[37] Various rites in the ancient Mediterranean were motivated by the belief that the discourse of children furnished a sure means of divination. The reader will recall how, in their solicitation of the *bat qol*, the Jews attended to the biblical lines that the young might utter and how, in illustrating the verbal *omen*, Cicero also evoked a child's speech. In his treatise *On Divination*, he related how Tertia, Lucius Paulus's young daughter, once lamented that her beloved little dog, "Persa," had died and how, from that remark, the commander inferred that the defeat of his adversary, Perseus, was imminent.[38]

The Egyptians also revered the unexpected speech of the young. The most famous evidence concerns the oracle of the god Apis at the temple in Memphis. Numerous sources, from Lucan to Pausanias, Aelian, and Dio Chrysostom, draw attention to its importance.[39] The sacred precinct was surrounded by boys and girls who would play in the temple or follow the processions that departed from it. They would utter fateful words in passing: *klēdones* or *omina*, as Bouché-Leclercq writes, "from which Graeco-Roman divination knew so well how to draw sense."[40] Plutarch suggests that the rites of Apis testified to a common belief. "The Egyptians think that little children possess the power of prophecy," he reports in *Isis and Osiris*, "and they try to divine the future from the portents which they find in children's words, especially when children are playing about in holy places and crying out whatever chances to come into their minds."[41]

Augustine's opening of a holy book upon hearing words uttered by a childlike voice owes much to such customs. Yet the scene in the garden places the ancient mantic practices in an unprecedentedly complex configuration. On the day of his long-awaited conversion, Augustine gleans a truth by fortuitous reading, but he does so solely because of an event of unexpected hearing. The two events are linked, and any interpretation of the conversion must account for them both. József Balogh was perhaps the first to name the task in a 1926 essay, "Double *Kledon* in the *Tolle-Lege* Scene."[42] Yet matters are more complicated than such a title suggests. Between the first and second oracular events, the differences are striking. The initial occurrence is a case of kledonomancy, divination by the unanticipated acoustical perception of an incidental phrase. The subsequent event consists of sortition: the kind of cleromancy that is bibliomancy.[43] The differences extend further. While the first occurrence is auditory and reflective, the second is visual and reasoned. The apprehension of the *tolle lege* has as its conditions the production of a sound and the sensitivity of the ear, but the steps that lead Augustine toward the holy book depend on inference, decision, and the capacity to read.

Both moments are fundamental, and one may wager that had Augustine been exposed to only one of the two events, the *Confessions* would be a different book. Were the catechumen to have been moved by the verbal omen alone, his summons to a life of piety would have had a form homogenous with that of pagan practices, whether Near Eastern, Greek, or Roman. The scene in the garden would hardly have brought him closer to the church. Had his conversion instead followed purely from bibliomancy, his discipline and intuition would have led him to God; the reasoned exercise of an art would have enabled him to reach his aim without assistance from an external source. The theology of the *Confessions*, then, would have been proven false, for the human soul would not require God for its turn to piety. That the conversion happens in two distinct steps is therefore crucial. The catechumen is affected by a sonorous sign, which prepares him to discover a message buried in the pages of a book. Trusting to his hearing, which registers the chanting utterance of the words *tolle lege*, and to his memory, which tells him he has never heard the like of it before, Augustine infers that he must make out letters on a page.

The most enigmatic element in the sequence is the first. Augustine himself draws attention to the oddity of the repeated phrase *tolle lege*. Modern research confirms his suspicion, at least as far as forms of play are concerned: "the refrain *tolle-lege* does not figure in any ancient game known to us."[44] Scholars have advanced several hypotheses about its sources. The imperative appears in Greek in the *Life of Porphyrius of Gaza* by Augustine's Eastern contemporary, Mark the Deacon. When Empress Eudoxia presents the holy monk with her child in that work, he is moved to recount a dream. In his vision, he saw himself "in the house of the idols that is called the Marneion." There he heard a voice commanding: "Pick up, read [*labe, anagnōthi*]." Opening the holy writ, his eyes fell on the lines in which Christ entrusts the church to Peter.[45] Mark's *Life* is dated to 401, barely ten years after the writing of the *Confessions*.[46] It has been said that "in the eyes of the Orientals," Augustine was the most renowned of Latin churchmen.[47] Did his *Confessions* determine Mark's account of Porphyrius's vision? Or do the accounts of the imperative heard by Porphyrius and Augustine, in Greek and in Latin, allude to a common source? The dates alone are insufficient to settle the issue.

If it is granted that *tolle lege* is equivalent to *labe, anagnōthi*, there are several antecedents to the Augustinian imperative. Johannes Geffcken showed in 1934 that the command to "pick up and read" would have been familiar in Greek settings. At court and in deliberations on legal proceedings, several formulae of such a kind were recited: "pick up the book and read the law" (*anagnōthi ton nomon . . . labōn*), "read and pick [it] up," and "pick up and read" (*labe, anagnōthi*).[48] Similar phrases could also be found in the books of the philosophers. In the *Phaedo*, Socrates recounts that he "picked up and read" a work by Anaxagoras, without, however, being swayed by it.[49] Epicurus, for his part, is reported to have employed the watchword: "Pick up and learn" (*labe . . . kai gnōthe*).[50] Biblical precedents for the phrase also been adduced.[51] "In the Christian period, apologists and hagiographers also make use of a formula of this kind, sometimes to argue for the concordance between the Bible and a profane text, sometimes to justify the reading of heretics, sometimes to justify a claim about a scriptural verse."[52]

Yet whatever the traditions from which the *tolle lege* may have been drawn, the mode of its sounding in the *Confessions* is novel. The syntax with which Augustine introduces the repeated words into his narrative is remarkable. The *vox* is qualified with extreme hesitation: it is, he writes, "as if it might be a boy or a girl (I do not know)." The "as if it might be" (*quasi*) effects the most tenuous of identifications. At first glance, the adverbial modifier seems to bear on the naming of the presumptive speaker ("a boy or a girl"), but a finer analysis suggests that it holds for the entire phrase. Augustine perceives a sensible phenomenon that is "as if it might be" that of a speaking voice.

Courcelle has shown that in its syntax, the crucial sentence alludes to the opening of the fourteenth chapter of Revelation. In that passage, John of Patmos discerns a thing "as if it might be the voice of many waters and as if the voice of loud thunder" (in the African translation known to Augustine, *uocem de caelo quasi sonum multarum acquarum aut magni tonitrui*). It is, John continues, employing the same construction, "as if it might be the voice or sound of harpers playing on their harps" (*uox quam audiui quasi citharedorum citharizantium*).[53] The sounding "as if it might be a voice" in the two works suggests that Augustine's perception, like John's, is perhaps ideal, rather than sensible.[54] A detail in the textual tradition confirms that possibility. The standard modern editions of the *Confessions* present the sound that Augustine hears as emerging "from a nearby house" (*de vicina domo*). Yet the sixth-century *Sessorianus* manuscript, the oldest surviving copy of the work and the only one to predate the Carolingian period, reads otherwise: there, the sonorous phenomenon proceeds "from a divine house" (*de divina domo*).[55] The allusion may be to a church, but it is also conceivable that the evocation is of a celestial source, such as the one from which "the harpers playing on their harps" reach John's ears.

The history of the reception of the *tolle lege* in images and words bears witness to this ambiguity. At times the scene of the conversion is figured as Augustine would appear to present it. In a fifteenth-century fresco representing the scene by Benozzo Gozzoli, a house is visible in the background. Two youths stand to the right of the saint, who is absorbed in reading, while one youth points at him with his index finger (fig. 1).[56] "Although the adolescents seem to bear masculine clothes and do not appear to be playing, let alone chanting," Courcelle writes, "they probably represent the 'voice of the nearby house . . . as if of a boy or a girl, I do not know.'"[57] Yet among the early illustrations of the *Confessions*, such a rendition is exceptional. In most cases, the scene suggests that the sounding exceeded all worldly experience. In the stained-glass windows of the Erfurt Augustinian Monastery, which dates from the fourteenth century, the saint stands beneath a banderole that descends directly from heaven, inscribed with the distinctly written words *tolle lege, tolle lege* (fig. 2). In Ottaviano Nelli's fresco in Gubbio (as in Guariento di Arpo's destroyed fresco in Padua), angels convey the imperative to Augustine on the page of an open book. Depictions from Germany, Belgium, and France concord with these imaginings; they, too, omit any representation of children or the neighbor's house.[58] Many of the work's early modern readers, from Francis of Sales to Teresa of Ávila and Cornelius Jansen, have understood the *tolle lege* in ways consonant with such illustrations. St. Teresa thus "perceives the *tolle, lege* as an interior voice," adding that she, too, has heard it.[59] According to St. Francis de Sales, Augustine "believed he heard a boy or a girl," but in fact "it was angels singing music" (*c'estoyent les anges qui chantoyent en musique*).[60]

Figure 1. Benozzo Gozzoli, *Augustine Reading the Epistle from St. Paul* (1464–1465), Church of Sant' Agostino, Cappella del Coro, San Gimignano, scene 9: Augustine in the garden.

Figure 2. Augustinerkloster, Erfurt, *tolle lege* stained window, ca. 1300–1310, Pierre Courcelle, *Recherches sur les Confessions de saint Augustin* (Paris: E. de Boccard, 1968), p. 737, plate 2.

Such readings respond to a significant, if subtle, indication in the text. A page before evoking the "voice as if of a boy or a girl (I do not know which)," Augustine recalls how he had been briefly captivated by the vision of an allegorical personage. As he struggled to overcome his worldly inclinations, there appeared before him "Continence itself" in the form of the "the dignified and chaste Lady Continence, serene and cheerful without coquetry." She was surrounded by others: "There were large numbers of boys and girls [*ibi tot pueri et puellae*], a multitude of all ages, young adults and grave widows and elderly Virgins. In every one of them was Continence itself."[61] She smiled at him, "as if to say" (*quasi diceret*), "Are you incapable of doing what these men and women [or "boys and girls," *isti* and *istae*] have done? Do you think them capable of achieving this by their own resources and not by the Lord their God? Their Lord God gave me to them. Why are you relying on yourself, only to find yourself unreliable? Cast yourself upon him, do not be afraid."[62] In his subtle reading of the work, Courcelle takes that passage as introducing the indeterminate young person, *puer* or *puella*, whose "voice" is later evoked in the garden. Hence his forceful conclusion: "The boy or girl who repeats *tolle, lege* constitutes the continuation of the inner vision and has no material reality."[63]

That interpretation has the merit of responding to one the work's basic stylistic features. It is often difficult to identify who is speaking in the *Confessions*. The text begins with words of the psalmist, which are indistinguishable from Augustine's own; only after several sentences can the reader tell David's perspective from that of the penitent Christian author, past and present.[64] In the work's prose, the books of the Bible, the words of Augustine's acquaintances, family, and friends, and the sayings of his erstwhile teachers and adversaries are woven into a single fabric. Without the assistance of the modern edition, its diacritics and annotations, the reader hesitates to decide on the attribution of discourse. That Augustine himself was sensitive to inner voices is also clear. The opening of the *Soliloquies* is in this regard exemplary: "For many days I had been debating within myself many and diverse things, seeking constantly, and with anxiety, to find out my real self, my best good, and the veil to be avoided, when suddenly one—I know not, but eagerly strive to know, whether it were myself or another, within me or without—said to me . . . ."[65] In meditation, Augustine speaks alone, but in his solitude, he is many. He listens to his memories as he articulates his ideas. Often, he hears his own thoughts as if they were those of others.

Yet such a model holds for the conversion scene only to a certain point. In the *Soliloquies*, the realm of the speaker's interiority expands indefinitely, for the mortal soul is in dialogue with itself. In the crucial moment of the *Confessions*, by contrast, there is no explicit indication that the words that break into Augustine's consciousness belong to any aspect of his mind. The author specifies the elements of external, albeit vague circumstances: the "nearby" (or "divine") dwelling, the child's voice, and its curiously chanting quality. Courcelle's thesis that the *tolle lege* is a dream vision risks distorting the theologian's argument. In all matters pertaining to his turn toward God, Augustine insists on the limits of his intellectual capabilities. To attribute the summons to an inner sight may be to transgress those boundaries. It seems crucial that the words "pick up and read" sound from elsewhere. Whether the other place is a child's voice, an angel's song, or writing from the sky may be of secondary importance. What matters most is that the sign reaches him from a domain that eludes identification. Arriving at the critical moment, announcing an unexpected hope in the instant of his dejection, the Christian omen exceeds Augustine's powers of cognition and representation. Interrupting his reflections, it testifies to a coincidence auguring conversion.

That the scene should occur under the fig tree is suggestive in more ways than one with respect to both the narrative of the *Confessions* and Christian sacred history. In the trajectory of the author's development, the setting recalls and reverses the episode by the pear tree that plays a crucial role in book two, being the occasion of

Augustine's early fall into the most iniquitous of sins: the commission of wrong for its own sake. In the garden of his youth, Augustine became the cause of the act of evil that is unmotivated theft; in the garden of the fig tree, he becomes the recipient of the undeserved gift that is grace. In the first scene, he was lured to do wrong by his unnamed companions, who urged him to steal; in the second, never far from faithful Alypius, he is surprised by a childlike voice summoning him to a new life.[66] Considered in its mythographic significance, the location recalls an image of redemption in the prophets, even as it announces its accomplishment: "Everyone will sit under their own vine, / and under their own fig tree," Micah had foretold, "and no one will make them afraid, / for the Lord Almighty has spoken."[67] At the same time, the setting alludes to the Gospel of John. When Nathanael meets the man of Nazareth and asks him, "How do you know me?" Jesus replies, "I saw you while you were still under the fig-tree."[68] By those words, Nathanael is summoned, becoming the devoted follower of Jesus.

Like the man from Cana, Augustine is called in the garden by a single phrase, even if the sentence that he perceives eschews all reference to "I" or "you." Yet for the Latin writer, unlike Nathanael, the decisive sign is not heard, but overheard. Augustine is converted by the catching of words that may or may not have been addressed to him. That is the source of the originality of his call. Never before the *Confessions* did a fragment of discourse, perceived as if by accident, impress itself with such intensity and consequence on a single mind. Never before the *Confessions*, moreover, did the effects of a presage so overshadow the question of the conditions of its sensible attestation. The Augustinian *tolle lege* is at once profoundly life changing, incidental, and obscure. After the Greek *klēdōn* and the Roman *omen*, after the Mesopotamian *egirrû* and the "heavenly voices" to the *bat qol* of the Judaic tradition, Augustine's hearing of the child's command inaugurates a new experience of the unexpected word. Subsequent revelations in the vagaries of discourse will occur in the space opened by the *Confessions*. Increasingly, truths perceived in the coincidences of discourse will be at once contingent and necessary, keenly felt and obstinately resistant to analysis. They will be subjective, yet irreducible to any self. After Augustine, omens will sound in a solitude in which no one is alone, bringing tidings of an elsewhere that is more intimate and more disquieting than any region of the conscious mind.

CHAPTER NINE

The Knight Guesses

The scene of Antony of Egypt's conversion became a model for later saints. At different times and in various places, they heard words of scripture read aloud as they stepped into church, and what they perceived forever changed them. Cyprian of Antioch was the first of their order. According to a late fourth-century chronicler, when Cyprian renounced the demons that he long consulted and smashed the idols that he kept at home, he prayed for a sign of divine favor. Like Odysseus in book 20 of the *Odyssey*, he requested an augur from his god: "Lord, if I deserve to be called your perfect servant, let me hear an oracular word [*klēdonismos*] from the holy writings as I enter your house." Only moments later, crossing the threshold of a church, Cyprian perceived a line from the Psalms: "You have seen this, Lord, do not be silent. Do not be far from me."[1] He heard Isaiah, "Behold, my servant shall understand" (*idou, sunēsei ho pais mou*). There followed other passages read aloud from the Psalms, Isaiah, and Paul, beginning with the words, "My eyes prevented the dawn, that I might meditate upon your oracles."[2] At once Cyprian declared that he was no longer a mere catechumen in the church. By an act of listening, he had become a faithful servant of "the one who was crucified."[3]

Some two centuries later, the Byzantine writer John Moschus reported how Babylas, erstwhile mime of Cilician Tarsus, underwent a conversion that was no less dramatic. For a long a time, the author recounts, Babylas lived a "disorderly life" in the company of two concubines, Cometa and Nicosa, "performing deeds which were truly worthy of the demons who urged him on." He and his two companions passed from lust to continence in the instant that, walking by a church, they happened to hear a reading of Jesus's admonition: "Repent, the kingdom of heaven is at hand." The three took that command to be addressed to none but them, and they obeyed the oracle that sounded in the words that they distinguished. "The actor shut himself up in one of the towers of the walls of the city. The women sold their property and gave the proceeds to the poor; then they too received the monastic habit. After that they made a cell for themselves near the tower and shut themselves up in it."[4]

In the same period, Gregory of Tours composed his *History of the Franks*, in which reading coincidences play diverse roles. The chronicler relates how, before attempting to conquer the city of Tours, Clovis, a "great and extraordinary fighter" and a devout Christian, sent messengers to the Church of Saint Martin, asking the divinity to grant him an augur there: "'Lord God,' said he, 'if You are on my side and if You have decreed that this people of unbelievers, who have always been hostile to You, are to be delivered into my hands, deign to show a propitious sign as these men enter Saint Martin's Church, so that I may know that You will support your servant Clovis.'" The messengers did as their commander ordered. They made the journey to Tours, Gregory relates, and "as they entered the church, it happened that the precentor was just beginning to intone this antiphon: 'For thou hast girded me with strength unto the battle: thou hast subdued under me those that rose up against me. Thou hast given me the necks of mine enemies: that I might destroy them that hate me.'"[5] Giving thanks to God, the messengers returned to their king, bringing news of what they heard.

In a later passage of the *History*, it is churchmen who practice divination through the consultation of books. The priests of the bishop of Langres beg God to reveal to them the fate awaiting

Chramn, a rebellious Merovingian monarch. "They agreed among themselves that each should read at Mass whatever he found when he first opened the book." Three codices of the Prophets, the Book of the Apostle, and the Gospel are opened, and all announce the destruction that awaits Chramn.[6] Yet in the world of the early Merovingians, men of war, too, were expert in bibliomancy. Gregory reports that King Merovech, doubting pagan Frankish soothsayers, turned to chance reading to glean knowledge of the future that awaited him. Imitating the priests, he placed the Psalter, the Book of Kings, and the Gospels on Saint Martin's tomb, spent a night in prayer, and at dawn, opened each book. The first lines on which his eyes fell foretold his doom.[7]

That books were common instruments of divination in the early Middle Ages is suggested by the history of theology, in which bibliomantic practices appear regularly. For obvious reasons, Augustine did not exclude the possibility that inferences from the sudden opening of the Bible might be valid, but he hesitated to offer unconditional support for such procedures. "As to those who read futurity by taking at random a text from the pages of the Gospels," he explains in a letter, "although it is better that they should do this than go to consult demons, nevertheless it is, in my opinion, a censurable practice to bring divine oracles, which were intended to teach us concerning the higher life, to bear on secular affairs and the vanity of this life."[8] He suggests that when opened at random, Holy Writ may be taken as a source of inspiration, but solely with respect to sacred matters. Any attempt to make a divinatory use of the Bible for profane purposes is to be strictly condemned, being a technique of soothsaying. As Thomas Aquinas later specifies, explicitly evoking Augustine's authority, if "the divine oracles are brought to bear on earthly affairs [*ad terrena negotia convertantur*]," "sortition" (*sortitio*) is forbidden.[9]

In the Middle Ages, there were also other texts that might be consulted to obtain knowledge of matters inaccessible to deductive reason. One practice had a clear model in a custom known to the culture of ancient Asia Minor. Greek sources indicate that in conditions of uncertainty, dice could be employed to reach a decision. Five *astragaloi*, sheep knucklebones or their bronze, wood, or ivory imitations, would be rolled. The number that resulted from the throw would point to one of a set of fifty-six Greek oracular sentences. As early as the 460s, Christian theologians mention a work called *Sortes sanctorum*, "The Oracles of the Saints," which appears to have involved a similar practice.[10] These "Oracles" consisted of a sequence of Latin pronouncements of which one would be drawn in a ritual setting. After three days of fasting and the singing of a mass, three six-sided dice would be thrown. Like the play of knucklebones, they would yield one of numerous possibilities, thereby referring the user to one of the Latin oracular propositions. By the later Middle Ages, the ancient divinatory procedure had acquired the character of a Roman Christian rite.[11] According to the medieval authors who introduce them, the *Sortes sanctorum* are to be consulted in a state of piety, "with great humility, in prayer and tears" (*cum multa humilitate, orando et lachrymando*).[12]

Another practice consisted in the consultation of Christian scripture by means of a special alphabet. On the altar of a church, a holy book would be opened at random to a page. The reader would then attend to the letter with which the selection began. A divinatory abecedarium would provide the key to its sense. Such alphabets are transmitted in Greek, Latin, and medieval European vernaculars. First attested in the twelfth century, they were redacted and copied in the Middle Ages for some four hundred years. The oldest surviving example of such a key, the so-called "Royal Alphabet," which is preserved today in manuscripts in London and Paris, contains a preamble defining the conditions of its use. For knowledge of "any matter," one must "sing a psalm before the first step of the altar." God will make manifest the hidden matter through the medium of the letters of the book. When the psalter is opened, readers will learn for themselves the answers to what they seek. It suffices to gloss the initial. An extended guide lays out the meaning of each opening letter: "*A* signifies life or power. *B* signifies power among the people. *C* signifies the death of a man. *D* signifies disorder or death. *E* signifies exultation or joy. . . ."[13]

Yet in the later Middle Ages, omens also sound in less formal circumstances. In the absence of books and in the apparent ignorance of the arts of writing, overheard discourse yields messages no less irrevocable for being unexpected. The scenes of such unscripted revelations are committed not to Latin, but to new vernacular languages. In the verse and prose of romance, in particular, those lacking traditional authority become the sudden mouthpieces of the most decisive of revelations. In literary works, omens sound in the discourse of children, as in the traditions known to the ancient Mediterranean, yet also in far less familiar voices: in the words of young men ignorant of Christian doctrine, in the sudden exclamations of unidentified women, and in the pronouncements of fantastic creatures. Such disclosures are all, in Roman terms, *omina oblativa*, augurs "offered" without having been either solicited or anticipated. To those who catch them, they convey the most intimate of truths. At times, they even tell those who hear them of their own identity, disclosing their real but hitherto unknown names.

The first and perhaps most far-reaching example is that of Chrétien de Troyes' last, unfinished work, *Perceval: The Tale of the Grail*, which is dated to 1181–1191.[14] The action of this romance begins during springtime in a "Barren Forest" (*gaste forest*). A boy introduced as "the son of the widowed lady" rises in the morning, saddles his horse, and rides toward the forest, intending to survey the peasants sowing oats in his mother's fields. That the young man is ignorant of the arts of reading and writing may be inferred from the narrator's omission of any reference to his schooling. Yet the "son of the widowed lady" seems also to know little of speech. As quickly becomes evident, there is an entire class of nouns of which he is ignorant, even if he is sufficiently well informed to ask about them. Hearing five armed knights begin to approach him from a distance, he wonders at the "immense racket" (*molt grant noise*) that they make. He initially infers that they must be devils, yet when the riders appear before him, he decides, in astonishment, that they can only be angels.[15] Later, in a conversation with the men on horseback, he learns what kind of men they are. The first exchange in the romance consists of a lesson in the lexicon of chivalry: the youth acquires a knowledge of knights and the weapons that they bear. He is introduced to the spear, shield, and mail shirt—both the things and the signs that stand for them.[16]

Two of the fifteen surviving manuscripts suggest that the boy is deficient with respect to not only nouns, but also names. In an exchange that most modern editors take to be a scribal interpolation, one of the knights asks the youth, "By what name will I call you?" (*par quel non je t'apelerai?*). He receives a perplexing reply. "I'll tell you. I'm called Dear Son [*biaus filz*]." "Dear Son?" his interlocutor inquires, "Yes, but I'm sure you have yet another name [*ancores / un autre non*]." "Oh yes, I'm called Dear Brother [*biaus frere*]." When the knight insists on the point, indicating his certainty that the boy also has a "true name" (*droit non*), he acquiesces once again: "'Sir,' was the answer, 'I'll tell you, of course. I'm called Dear Master [*biaus sire*].'" "I'm hearing stranger things, by God," the knight responds, "the strangest I've ever heard—and I'll never hear any stranger!"[17]

"We are present at the clash of two worlds," Reto R. Bezzola notes. "The knight realizes that he is before something unprecedented: he imagines the three stages in the life of the child, 'dear son' of a devoted mother, then, for a young man, 'dear brother,' who enters the Christian community, finally, a young lord, 'dear master,' who is venerated by his valets and servants, perhaps without even knowing the reason for this respect."[18] The boy is himself a future knight who wishes to become like the riders whom he has met. It does not occur to him that in addition to being and becoming something, defined by a noun that holds for things of a common nature, he may also be and become someone, laying claim to a sign that refers to what renders him unique. He knows nothing of the name that he lacks. The romance respects the character's ignorance, and in the first half of the work, he is simply called "the boy" (*li vallés*).

Repeatedly, he receives instruction, yet he fails to learn or so profoundly distorts the lessons that he receives as to provoke disorder, if not disaster. When he tells his mother that he has happened to meet five knights and that he intends to set out for King Arthur's court to be knighted, she collapses in a swoon. Once awake and reconciled to his imminent departure, she informs him that he comes from a family of fallen knights. She speaks to him of his late father, who was "wounded between the legs" (*parmi les jambes navrez*), in circumstances and to effects that she does not reveal, his "whole body crippled" (*mehaigna del cors*). She tells him also of his two older brothers, both killed in combat soon after being knighted.[19] Seeing that he will not be dissuaded from his project to become like the riders, she says no more of their relations, resolving instead to impart to him a few principles of knighthood. "My son, let me teach you something," she begins. She explains that as a knight, his first obligation will be to ladies "in need, anywhere near or far," or to girls "in need of protection." To win honor, he must serve them. If he courts a lady, moreover, he is to do "nothing to displease her"; should she grant him a kiss, he must ask for nothing more, even if he receives from her such small items as a ring or purse for alms.[20]

No sooner does the young man ride off the following dawn than he sees a tent, "pitched near a beautiful meadow near / where a brook babbled from the ground."[21] Inside he finds a girl asleep. The scene is the occasion for him to implement the rules that his mother has given him, deforming them beyond repair. When the girl awakens on account of the loud stumbling of his horse, he greets her, explaining that he does so "as my mother taught me I should." Terrified, the girl begs him to leave. He approaches her and kisses her against her will:

Awkwardly (not knowing
Any better), the boy
Clasped her in his strong arms,
And lay full length above her.[22]

He stops kissing her only when he sees she is wearing a ring. He asks her for it, as he explains:

"And my mother told me," he said,
"You'd be wearing a precious ring,
And that's all you'd give me, nothing
Else. I'd like that ring."[23]

She refuses, but the boy takes hold of her hand and forces it open, removing the ring from her finger and putting in on his own. Satisfied with his visit to the tent, he bids her farewell. He is unmoved by the girl's demands that he return her precious belonging: "nothing she said, not a single word, touched his heart."[24]

Readers of the romance will recall how the boy soon reaches the court, where Arthur knights him. Defeating an opponent by unexpectedly brutal force, he obtains the armor and the weapons that he sought. He learns to wield them later, when he meets a "distinguished man in ermine" who offers him instruction in knighthood.[25] The elder figure teaches him how to hold his spear, to spur his horse, and to defend himself with his shield. He also imparts a lesson in rhetoric. At length, he commands the boy to be neither "too garrulous nor too gossipy" (*trop parlanz ne trop noveliers*):

"Whoever talks too much
Is sure to say something
That someone will find offensive.
Wise men declare, over
And over, 'too much talking
Is sinful. . . .'"[26]

When the young man acquiesces, certain that his master speaks truly, his words being, as he notes, the echo of his mother's, the "distinguished man" corrects him:

"Please, good brother," the nobleman
Said, "don't explain

That your mother told you this
Or that. I'm not offended,
Hearing such things. But others,
If you keep announcing the fact
(which is why I beg you never
To say it again!), are sure
To take you for an absolute fool."[27]

If he must evoke some authority, the man explains, it should be his:

"You can always say that the man
Who gave you your spur told you
These things, and taught you well."[28]

For the boy to be a knight, speech must be disjoined from the mother, and her figure, once effaced, replaced by that of the elder lord.[29]

The boy finds several occasions to apply the rules that he has been given. Received one evening by the lady of a ruined castle in a city destitute of provisions, he pledges to fight to defend her and her people from the depredations of their enemy. He succeeds, thereby proving himself worthy of the lady's love. Arriving at a second castle, he faces a challenge of a different kind. He has just left the lady's dwelling when he reaches a river where he can ride no further. He catches sight of a craft descending along the water. It is carrying two men, one of whom, seated, is baiting for "fish as small as a minnow." He greets them, asking if they know where he may lodge for the night. Without rising, the fisher invites him to his home. The boy follows his directions and reaches a marvelous construction: "From there to Beirut," the narrator remarks, "there was nothing lovelier or better built."[30] The man in the boat reveals himself to be the lord of the castle, "a handsome knight with grizzled hair," dressed in black. On entering the hall, the boy finds him reclining, "leaning on his elbow," hardly able to stand to greet him. He explains that he is too weak to rise.

In the company of his ailing host, the boy witnesses an extraordinary procession. A servant enters the bright hall carrying a white lance from whose tip blood miraculously drops. Two other servants follow, carrying golden candleholders worked with enamel. They are accompanied by a "beautiful girl, elegant, extremely well dressed," carrying a plate, or *graal*, that

glowed
with so great a light that the candles
suddenly seemed to grow dim,
like the moon and stars when the sun
appears in the sky.[31]

After her, another girl passes bearing a silver platter.

That the boy is struck by these circumstances is a fact on which the narrator repeatedly remarks. "The boy saw that wondrous sight," the reader learns. Yet he

kept himself from asking
What it might mean, for he'd never
Forgotten — as his master at arms
Warned him, over and over —
He was not to talk too much.[32]

Some hundred lines later, the reader learns that, as the grail passed before him,

the boy watched them, not daring
To ask why or to whom
This grail was meant to be served,
For his heart was always aware
Of his wise old master's warnings.[33]

At the end of the sumptuous dinner offered by his hosts, "the wonderful grail"

was carried back and forth,
But again the boy was silent,

Not asking to whom it was served.
And again it was thoughts of his master
Which kept him from speaking, for he never
Forgot how clearly he'd been warned
To beware of too much talking.[34]

By luck or by destiny, the young man is present at a miraculous happening. It is the event on whose account the work, the reader infers, is called *The Tale of the Grail.* Yet the narrator indicates that the boy is inadequate to the proceedings that he witnesses, for despite the marvels he beholds, he says nothing:

I fear his silence may hurt him,
For I've often heard it said
That talking too little can do
As much damage as talking too much.[35]

"Although he wishes to know," we read later in the scene, the boy

told himself he'd surely
Make some safe inquiry
Before he left; someone
Would tell him. He'd wait until morning,
When he was taking leave of the lord
Of this castle and all who served him.[36]

Yet when he awakes the next morning, he sees no one. The castle is deserted. Having done as the man who gave him his spur commanded, the boy has missed his chance.

After Chrétien de Troyes, the lacunary experiences of the "son of the widow" were to be rewritten, explicitly and implicitly, in almost all their details, including that of the anonymity in which the boy reaches maturity and knighthood. In *Li Bels Descouneüs* or *The Fair Unknown*, a romance of the thirteenth century, Renaud de Beaujeu presents the narrative of another unidentified young knight. Renaud's narrative opens with his arrival at King Arthur's court. As he removes his armor, it seems to all that they have never seen such a handsome youth.[37] Asked for his name (*non*), the stranger responds in the terms of the foolish hero of the *Tale of the Grail*. The young man can only evoke the words employed by his mother, although, as he adds, distinguishing himself from Chrétien's *vallés*, he is also aware of the existence of the appellation that he lacks. When pressed for his name, he answers, "Truly, I do not know; but I can tell you that my mother called me *Dear Son* [*Biel fils*], and I do not know if I have a father."[38] Even as he accepts the namelessness of his guest, Arthur confers a title on him:

> "I shall give him a name,
> Since neither he nor I know what his true name is.
> Because Nature has bestowed on him
> Such perfect beauty
> That she sees in him her own shining image,
> And because he does not know who he is,
> Let him be named the Fair Unknown [*li Biaus Descouneüs*];
> So shall all my knights call him."[39]

The king's words are immediately effective. The character is henceforth known by the name he gives, which becomes, by metonymy, the title of the work that tells his tale.

In the romance, the unknown knight's arrival at the court is followed by the appearance of a lovely maiden on a palfrey accompanied by a handsome dwarf. She greets the king on behalf of her lady, the daughter of King Gringras. She then puts to Arthur an onerous request: she begs him to grant her the protection of a knight capable of saving the princess from a state of "suffering and sorrow, overwhelmed by sadness." That knight must be the most valorous member of the entire court. He must be prepared to rescue her lady by accomplishing an unidentified feat that she names "the Fearsome Kiss" (*li Fier baiser*). The men of Arthur's court tremble before the idea of such a challenge. Without hesitation, the Fair Unknown, however, accepts it. He therefore departs with the maiden and her companion, and after many adventures reaches the castle, where he stands the test. Having defeated a host of antagonists, some gigantic in size, some marvelous in shape, he withstands the shattering of the palace windows and the darkness into which it is plunged after the extinction of its candles. He prays for courage before the danger that awaits him.

Suddenly, a cupboard opens, and the dragon known in Old French as a *wivre* or *guivre* steps out toward him, shining from its body "as much light / as a brightly lit candle":

It filled the hall
With the great light it gave off.
No one ever saw such a serpent:
Its mouth was red,
And spewed forth flames.
It was huge and hideous,
Wider across the middle
Than a wine-cask
It had big shining eyes
Like to great carbuncles.
It slithered down the cupboard
Until it reached the ground.
It was nine yards long
And its tail—no one ever saw a longer one—
Had three loops in it.
All the colors God created
Were in this serpent's tail;
Its underbelly seemed to be golden.
It advanced towards the knight,
Who crossed himself when he saw it.[40]

When the Fair Unknown puts his hand to his sword to unsheathe it, he sees the creature inclining his head, as if bowing down before him. He hesitates. Yet the serpent glides toward him. Again, he motions to his weapon, but once more it lowers itself "in a sign of friendship" (*semblant d'*[*a*]*misté mostra*).[41] It comes still closer. He draws his sword to strike its chest; but the serpent "gently" (*doucement*) bows again.[42]

The knight is captivated by the image of the creature's mouth:

> He looked at it, his attention fixed,
> without moving,
> and he marvelled greatly,
> at the mouth so red [*de la bouce qu'a si vermeille*]
> He was so absorbed by looking at it
> That he could not turn away.[43]

The serpentine being is at once animal and human. Its "mouth," in particular, is striking. As has been observed, *gole*, "muzzle," not *bouce*, "mouth," is the Old French word that would be expected for such a beast. Here the evocation of the serpent's face "could easily have been lifted without change from a standard portrayal of ideal beauty."[44] In *Lybeaus Disconus*, the Middle English adaptation of the Old French romance or its earlier sources, the creature is depicted as a "worme . . . with a womanes face."[45] The combatant is not fascinated by the dragon's red lips for long, for in the next instant, "the serpent darted toward him / and kissed him on the mouth."[46] The deed accomplished, the dragon retreats. The knight has thus submitted to the Fearsome Kiss. As the serpent begins to slide away, he raises his sword to strike it, but it stops and bows again in "a gesture of respect" (*sanblant d'umilité li fait*), and he renounces the attempt to wound it.[47] It retreats into the cupboard from which it came. Left alone, the knight sits down in the hall, which is once again absolutely dark.

As the Fair Unknown wonders what will come of the unexpected embrace, words are audible in the absence of any visible shape. The knight "heard a voice" (*une vois oïe*), the narrator recounts, "which told him clearly his origins and his lineage." It "cried aloud," although its tidings were for him alone. First the voice extols his matchless courage and endurance. Then it reveals his name:

King Arthur called you by the wrong name [*mal te nonma*]:
He called you the Fair Unknown,
But Guinglain is the name you were given at baptism.
I can tell you of your entire life.
My lord Gawain is your father,
And I shall also tell you who your mother is:
You are the son of Blanchemal the Fairy.[48]

In its bodiless utterance, the "voice" may recall the heavenly disclosures familiar to the Biblical traditions, from the Judaic *bat qol* to Christian angelic announcements. Yet the discourse that sounds in the palace hall is a phenomenon of medieval romance. Speaking in the first-person singular, it relates itself to a legendary character of Arthur's court: "Son of my lord Gawain! I knew quite well that no other knight would have such strength. . . ." The voice is feminine, as becomes apparent in the next scene. When its discourse ends, the exhausted knight falls asleep at the table. He awakes in the company of a maiden of unparalleled beauty. She is King Gringras's daughter, who was long condemned to a monstrous form by a malevolent enchantment. Guinglain's endurance of the Fearsome Kiss has allowed her to regain her human shape.

In the instant of its sounding, the voice, however, reveals almost nothing about itself. It speaks above all of the young knight, to whom it addresses itself. Declaring "King Arthur called you by the wrong name," the voice strips its addressee of his previous identity, bestowing on him a name, Guinglain, that he did not know. The subsequent chapters of the narrative faithfully respect the announcement. Once "the voice grew silent, having finished its discourse," the narrator informs his audience: "Henceforth I shall tell you / of Guinglain, the worthy knight." The romance of the *Fair Unknown* now becomes the tale of Guinglain. According to a structure first exhibited by Chrétien de Troyes's *Lancelot: The Knight of the Cart*, the work's title changes belatedly, in conformity with the altered name of its protagonist.[49]

In the same period in which Renaud de Beaujeu composes his romance, Wolfram von Eschenbach drafts the massive rewriting of Chrétien's *Tale of the Grail* in Middle High German that is *Parzival.* The German poet frames the childhood of the "son of the widow" by an extended account of his father's family. The narrative of the foolish boy is retold in such a way as to change and reorder the unfolding of his adventures. In Wolfram's version, the "son of a widow" has just left the astonished damsel in the tent when he happens on a girl seated before "a spur of rock." She is grieving for her beloved, who lies dead in her arms. The boy greets her, and expressing sympathy for her friend, pledges to avenge him. She accepts. Yet "before she would let him ride again," the narrator recounts, "she asked him for his name, declaring his looks bore the marks of God's own handiwork." As in the probably interpolated scene in Chrétien's poem, the boy evokes the terms of endearment that his mother used for him. In their German transcription, three Old French noun phrases are indistinguishable from a proper name: "'*Bon fîz, scher fîz, bêâ fîz*' [Good son, dear son, beautiful son]—that's what they used to call me, those who knew me at home.'"[50]

The self-identification prompts a series of acts of cognition and recognition. From his presentation of the terms by which those at home "knew" (*erkennet*) him, the maiden, we are told, "knew [*erkande*] his name." Addressing the audience of his work, the narrator then involves his readers in the process of identification: "Now hear him named by his true name so that you may know [*da ir wol müget erkennen*] who is lord of the story as he stands there talking with the girl." Familiar with the designation "Good son, dear son, beautiful son," or perhaps familiar with the quality of his voice, the girl immediately replies to him: "Upon my word, you are Parzival."[51] As in *Li Biaus Descouneüs*, a feminine voice thus reveals a truth that the narrator will confirm. The "boy" will henceforth be Parzival. He accedes to his identity in hearing his name uttered as the reply to an answer that he could not provide.[52]

Yet in the Old French work from which Wolfram departs, the scene is more bewildering in its structure and more far-reaching in its consequences. In the *Perceval* of Chrétien de Troyes, the *vallés* hears his name uttered immediately after he has missed the chance to pose a question about the bleeding lance and grail. On the same morning that he leaves the unexpectedly abandoned castle, he meets a weeping damsel who holds in her arms the remains of a decapitated knight. As in Wolfram's text, she says that he has just been killed. But then she expresses interest in the young knight's appearance. "But one thing I see, as you stand there, seems to me astonishing," she adds. There are no castles anywhere near the place of their meeting, yet she notes that the boy's horse has been "groomed and brushed, washed and combed," and he seems "to have spent a restful comfortable night on some soft, well-made bed."[53] When he explains that he has enjoyed the best lodgings he has known, she infers that he has been received at the "castle of the rich Fisher King." She then asks him about the palace of his host, the objects he has seen, and the words that he may—or may not—have uttered there:

"Did you see the spear that bled
 Without the presence of flesh
 or veins?" "Did I see it?
 Oh yes, by God, I did!"
"And did you ask why
 It was bleeding?" "I said not a word."
"In the name of God, believe me,
 You made a mistake. That was wrong."[54]

The worst fault, however, concerns the grail. When the boy avows that he saw it, that he watched it carried from room to room behind servants carrying candleholders and before a girl carrying "a small silver platter," and when, furthermore, he admits that he did not ask "any of these people / where they were going with these things," she exclaims, "Oh Lord, that's even worse!"[55]

The weeping damsel then puts a question to the foolish boy. It is an echo of the query posed to him by the knights at the start of some versions of the romance: "My friend," she asks, "what is your name?" (*comant avez vos nom, amis?*).[56] The *vallés* answers, even as the narrator comments on his act:

And then, not knowing his name,
He guessed, and said
He was Perceval from Wales,
Not knowing if he spoke the truth,
But he did, though he did not know it.

Et cil qui son non ne savoit
Devine et dist que il avoit
Perchevax li Galois a non,
Ne ne set s'il dist voir ou non;
Mais il dist voir et si nel sot.[57]

The boy's tenuous apprehension of his own name appears in the text as a "guess." More exactly, it is an act of intuition by divination. "He who did not know his name," the Old French literally reads, "divines [*devine*] and says that his name is Perceval of Wales." He finds out who he was in the instant of this unreflective performance. The word that he utters, *Perceval*, has been subject to repeated analysis and decryption in the Middle Ages and the twentieth century as *Perce-val*, "valley-piercing," or "*perce a val*," "pierce through," as a name formed on the basis of *perdre*, "to lose," or *percevoir*, "to perceive," as an echo of his uncle's name *Pelles* or that of the common noun *père*, "father."[58] That the character's access to his own designation is barred is suggested by the rhyming of "name" and "no" ("*Perchevax li Galois a* non / *Ne ne set s'il dist voir ou* non"). It is explicitly and repeatedly stated by the narrator, who relates that the boy "spoke truly" or "spoke the truth" (*dist voir*), without, however, knowing it.

The strangeness of this happening has often been noted, and

modern critics have not hesitated to judge it "awkward," "absurd" or "inept."[59] Wolfram, for his part, has the boy learn his name from the grieving damsel. His revision thus resolves the difficulty by eliminating it. Yet the copyists of Chrétien's romance were committed to the author's rendition of the event, however peculiar it may seem today. Only one of the fifteen manuscripts presents an alternative to the boy's "guessing" or "divining," relating that instead he suddenly "said" (*dist*) his name.[60]

The question is therefore unavoidable: How could the boy "divine" a name that he did not know? Several answers have been proposed. One scholar interprets *deviner* as meaning "recounting."[61] Another proposes that one take the word as signifying "recalling, remembering."[62] In both cases, the boy would then have suddenly called to mind a thing that he had forgotten, even if the conditions of his act would remain a mystery. The context, however, excludes such glosses; the narrator states that the boy does not know (*ne savoit*) the name that he speaks aloud. Moreover, such interpretations are irreconcilable with the Old French lexicon. As Wendelin Foerster and Hermann Breuer indicate, *deviner* means "to guess, hazard, conjecture," or, as Tobler-Lommatzsch's dictionary establishes, "to presume" and "express as an intuition."[63]

Without contesting these facts, some readers have sought to explain the event of the boy's act by other means. Jean Frappier suggested that the passage alludes to the Celtic sources of the grail legend, in which the initiation into a mystery takes the form of the revelation of a proper name.[64] Bezzola claimed that in representing the boy's discovery of his name, Chrétien means to render the decisive point at which the character "glimpses the depth of his personality."[65] Such interpretations are certainly admissible. Yet they may be faulted for distracting attention from what is most extraordinary in this scene. Some three thousand lines into the romance, the audience learns of the identity of the "boy" in the very moment that he himself somehow stumbles upon it, although "he did not know it." As in the *Fair Unknown*, the narrator accepts the finding:

from this point onward, the "boy" becomes "Perceval," and the *Tale of the Grail* becomes the romance of *Perceval*.

Tajiro Amazawa has rightly wondered about the conditions of the "divining" and, more exactly, about the exact subject of the guess. Is it the speaker, who does not know the truth of what he says, or the unnamed damsel, who elicits his words before responding to them?[66] In the exchange, it she who speaks with certainty when he names himself:

> Hearing this the girl
> Rose and faced him, and spoke
> As if in anger, "You've just
> Changed your name, my friend" [*Tes nons est changiés, biax amis*].
> "Really?" "You're Perceval
> The Unhappy, the Miserable, the Unfortunate!
> Ah, how unlucky you are,
> For had you asked those questions,
> You could have completely cured
> The good king of all his wounds:
> He would have been entirely
> Whole, and ruled as he should.
> How much good you could have done!"[67]

Soon revealed as Perceval's cousin, the damsel is not merely the witness to his act of veridiction. She is also the guarantor of its authenticity.[68] One might argue that she is its *auctor*, in the etymological sense of the word, for she effects the "increase" (*augere*) by which his saying becomes a valid deed. Yet in the moment that she confirms the boy's words, she changes their sense. Perceval accedes to his name in its alteration and as the consequence of his fault.

Foolish and also prescient, innocent and yet blameworthy, Perceval is a figure without precedent in the history of diviners. Like Antony of Egypt or Babylas the Mime, he is surprised by the sound of words spoken at the crucial moment. Like them, he is transformed by what he hears in the instant that he listens. The differences between the settings of such revelations, however, are evident. Whereas the saints are converted in perceiving sentences of scripture read aloud in a public place, Perceval, in the presence of an unknown maiden, discovers his name in a landscape without orients. Far from priests and congregations, codices, and ecclesiastical constructions, he happens on a truth that, while solicited, results from no technique. Unlike the German Parzival, the *vallés* does not learn his name in hearing his speech interpreted by another. Unlike Guinglain in *The Fair Unknown*, he does not come to know his identity in listening to an otherworldly voice. In Chrétien de Troyes, a *klēdōn* overcomes the speaker not from without, as in antiquity and in earlier and later medieval culture, but from within. Alterity, in this case, inheres in the discourse of the speaker, who becomes the diviner of his own words.

That the sudden revelation is uttered and perceived by one and the same speaking subject constitutes the great novelty of this guessing scene. Here, for the first time, the diviner attends to an unexpected truth that sounds in words that he himself has uttered. Yet the scene is more complex than such a summary would suggest. For what is gleaned as if by chance is both true and susceptible to mutation. Even as the boy's single *non* is revealed, his *sornon* appears to undergo a change.[69] As the boy learns from his knowledgeable interlocutor, having been "Perceval the Welshman" (*Percevax li Galois*), he has now become "Perceval the Unhappy, the Unfortunate" (*Perchevax li chaitis . . . Perchevax maleüros*).

Readers can only wonder as to when that alteration was accomplished. The apparent suggestion is that the modification results from the boy's failure to pose a question in the castle of the grail. Yet it is surely important that the change comes to light solely when he utters his own name. Speech and silence seem to converge toward a single consequence, which is the effacement of "the Welshman" (*li Galois*). At a first level of interpretation, that title is an index of the boy's place of birth. But that identity is also, as Frappier argued, the mark of his "foolishness," "if one recalls that

Galois pejoratively also means 'fool' [*sot*], as Chrétien has one of the knights say, upon meeting the *vallés* in the forest: 'My lord, believe me, / The Welsh can't help it / They're all born like that. / Crazy as cows in a pasture.'"[70]

Long ignorant and repeatedly lacking in judgment, Perceval, however, ends by acceding to a far stranger folly. Having left unuttered the magic words that would have healed the feeble monarch, having erred not by "too much talking," but by the no less consequential fault of "talking too little," the young knight happens to make himself into the subject of an unprecedented feat of self-discovery in self-loss. Without any discernible awareness of what he accomplishes, he commits an act of divination concerning his own speaking nature: his identity as the bearer of a name. He gleans it exactly as he learns of the extraordinary things that he alone has been granted the chance to see. Each time, he is belated. When he hears that the shining plate in the castle of the Fisher King was "the grail," he has lost any means of approaching it. In the same way, when he grasps the sign by which he is distinct from every other "good son," "good brother," and "good master," it eludes him, altered in the moment of its utterance. In ignorance or in madness, in innocence or in sin, Perceval thus falls short of the great adventure of which he is to be the hero. Not only before, but also after the sounding of the oracle, he remains, unlike all holy men, in want of understanding. His true guess is a riddle that no one solves.

CHAPTER TEN

Of Proverbs

The thirteenth-century law code known as *Las Siete Partidas*, which tradition attributes to King Alfonso X the Wise of Castille and Leon, concludes with an account of the varieties of crime and the principles of punishment. After a brief treatment of the conditions of legitimate accusation and denunciation, the seventh and last *partida* turns to one of the "most serious and odious" of crimes, treason, "the vilest and worst offense in the heart of man."[1] There follows a discussion of murder and homicide, the tarnishing of honor, acts of violence, robbery, larceny, and the destruction of property. Offenses involving fraud, swindling, and sins and acts of a sexual nature are treated next. The following section bears on those guilty of deceit by more recondite means: "diviners, fortune-tellers, soothsayers, wizards, and buffoons." "Men naturally desire to ascertain coming events, and because some of them attempt this by numerous methods, they are guilty of sin and induce many others to do wrong," Title 23 begins:

> Wherefore, since in the preceding Title we treated of Procurers, who cause men and women to sin in many ways; we desire to treat here of these persons, who are very injurious to a country. We shall show what divination means; how many kinds there are; who can accuse parties who are guilty of it; before whom such an offense can be prosecuted; and what penalty those deserve who attempt to practice it as they should not do.[2]

The king's code defines divination (*adivinanza*) as the "assuming of the power of God in order to find out things which are to come." According to the *Partidas*, it is of two kinds. The first is "that which is accomplished by means of astronomy, which is one of the seven liberal arts." The rules of that activity are derivable from the observation of heavenly bodies and the books of Ptolemy and other learned authors. When "practiced by those who are masters and understand it thoroughly," such divination is a licit activity. By contrast, the second variety is in all cases forbidden. "Fortune-tellers, soothsayers, and magicians" are its expositors. They strive to grasp "omens" or "augurs" (*agüeros*) in diverse phenomena, which range from the flight of birds to sneezes, lots, crystals, mirrors, and swords. Alfonso declares that those who would look into the future by such means are "wicked and deceitful persons" (*hombres dañosos y engañadores*). Since "great evils result to the country from their acts," he banishes "imposters of this kind and all others like them" from the dominions subject to his authority. He also condemns those who would protect them in their homes: "We forbid anyone to dare to entertain them in their houses or conceal them."[3] Exile is the consequence for the infraction of such rules.

In the enumeration of the "augurs" by means of which "fortune-tellers, soothsayers and magicians" contrive to usurp the power of God, there is one that is unlike the others. Neither natural nor artificial, it pertains to language alone. Its substance is discourse, consisting, as the code has it, in "words, which are called 'proverbs'" (*palabras, a las que llaman proverbios*). In that allusion to a detail of terminology, *Las Siete Partidas* draws attention to a striking locution. "Proverbs" appear as the name of a variety of discourse from which portents may be inferred. From a strictly historical perspective, the usage is remarkable. The Castilian term *proverbio* derives from its Latin cognate, *proverbium*, whose classical meanings, like those of the corresponding English word "proverb," are "old saying," "maxim," and "adage."[4] In the Latin rhetorical tradition, the *proverbium* is often treated as equivalent to *auctoritas*. A memorable phrase or sentence stating a general truth, it can be cited and evoked in various circumstances.[5] From the passage in the code on the forbidden arts of divination, however, it appears that Alfonso X was familiar with the word *proverbio* in a different sense. One of a set of transient phenomena including the flight of birds, human bodily movements, and transient shapes visible on certain surfaces, the *proverbio* of Title 23 is not a *dictum* that is recalled, but an ordinary phrase that announces what is to come. It is of the family of the *klēdōn* and the *omen*.

The "proverb" in the sense of Alfonso X outlived the end of the Middle Ages. By the seventeenth century, it had become indistinguishable from the event known in early modern Spanish as *arfil* or *alfil*. Those two related terms derive from the Arabic *al-fa'al*, a word of unknown origin and etymology that is attested from an early date in the Arabic lexicon, definable as "the equivalent of *phēmē*, *klēdōn* and *sēmēion*, with all the varieties that it contains."[6] As late as the eighteenth century, the Castilian *Diccionario de autoridades*, which was published between 1726 and 1739, is still familiar with the *alfil* as "what is commonly called *proverbio* by women, which is in truth an augur and a guilty and sinful superstition [*agüero y superstición culpable y pecaminosa*]." The dictionary entry for the word explains: "It consists in the belief that certain words casually heard on certain evenings of the year, particularly St. John's Eve, are oracles [*oráculos*] announcing the lucky or unlucky future of the one who hears them."[7] As the authors of the *Diccionario* note, such a usage was recorded as early as 1494, when the Humanist Antonio de Nebrija, in his *Spanish-Latin Dictionary*, defined the *alfil* as the equivalent to *Toledano agüero* and the Latin *omen*.[8]

In 1540, the Spanish theologian and mathematician Pedro Ciruelo publishes a *Reproval of Superstitions and Sorceries* in which he evokes the *proverbio* and the *alfil*, without, however, deigning to mention either phenomenon by name. Ciruelo proposes a threefold classification of alleged "augurs." The first is that discerned in the sounds and motions of birds and animals. The second consists in the "purely natural movements" of the human body, such as coughing or sneezing. The third and last of common portents is also the "vainest" of the three: "what in Latin is called *Omen*." "It is divining [or "guessing," *adeuinar*] by sayings or deeds that other people do for another purpose; the diviners apply it to something else." Ciruelo gives two examples of the practice. When a man, concentrating on his own business and uncertain of how to continue, suddenly notices someone passing by who utters a word or commits a deed "for some other purpose of his own" (*a otro proposito suyo*), the diviner will advise the reflecting man to act in accordance with that gesture, as if God or an angel had unexpectedly intervened to guide him in his deliberations. Likewise, when someone is arguing with someone else "for a most doubtful reason," wondering whether to cease in his struggle, and a stranger walking by happens to say, "better to continue," the diviner infers a solution: the arguer must pursue his fight.[9] Ciruelo denounces all such guesses as "vanity," "superstition," and "mortal sin." "Let anyone who does such things know this well," he declares: "he has made a secret pact through the inspiration of the devil."[10]

The care that Ciruelo takes to identify and condemn divination from such scraps of speech indicates that the attention to "proverbs" may have been widespread in his time, as the literature of early modern Spain also suggests. C. E. Aníbal notes that in the 1499 *Celestina*, also known as *The Tragicomedy of Calisto and Melibea*, it is to "an *alfil* or *toledano agüero* that reference is made by the Celestina (who may well have practiced her arts in Toledo as she hurries to seduce Melibea)."[11] In James Mabbe's 1631 English translation of the work, la Celestina avows: "All Divinations [*todos los agüeros*] are in my favour, and show themselves prospicious in my proceedings; or else I am no Body in this art, a meere bungler, an Idiot, an Asse.... The first word that I heard, passing along the street, was a love complaint."[12]

In Mateo Alemán's influential novel, *Guzmán de Alfarache*, whose parts appeared in 1599 and 1604, the *pícaro* imagines a woman finding her husband by such a habit. Without mentioning any technical terms, the protagonist conceives of a discourse in which he challenges such a lady to deny that she ever made "prayers" for *proverbios*. In John Mabbe's 1622 rendition of the novel *The Rogue*, Guzmán de Alfarache asks:

> "Is it not . . . true, that since thou hadst the use of reason (nay rather before thou hadst it, because thou yet wantest it) there was never yet any Midsommer night, or feast of St John, wherein, without sleeping (for they say, that sleep hindereth the vertue and operation of those, you know what I meane) thou betookst thy selfe to such a prayer, thou knowst well enough what one, but better it had beene for thee, that thou hadst not knowne it (being such a one as it is, and so much reproved) and without opening thy mouth, or speaking so much as one word (for they likewise say, that silence is another essential point of that prayer) thou shouldst stay waiting and looking for the first that should passe along by thee after midnight, to the end, that by what thou shouldst heare come from him, thou mightst accordingly judge of thy future marriage, & know him that should be thy husband?"[13]

Unexpected hearing also takes on an oracular role in early modern Spanish drama. In many of his works, the seventeenth-century playwright Antonio Mira de Amescua employs a "type of stage-trick" that Aníbal calls "heavenly voices" (*voces del cielo*). By means of such "voices," "words or phrases casually uttered by persons quite innocent of their dramatic significance" acquire the status of a "mysterious warning."[14] The speakers of the ominous words may be either seen or unseen by the one who hears them; what matters is that a scrap of discourse relays a message to the perceiver without having been intended in that sense by the speaker. In *La confusión de Ungria*, the villainous Vertilo thus "mistakes the window of a prison for that of a lady." Once he has climbed up to it, he has his servant below remove the ladder he has mounted, "only to realize, after the servant has left, that he has brought upon himself a just punishment for his wickedness."[15] His true situation dawns on him when he distractedly overhears three stable boys and an old man gambling below him. Although it seems he cannot make out their dialogue in all its details, their evocation of defeat in a game of chance draws his attention to his hopeless position: "He seems at last to have heard the noise of their talk, but has not caught their words, so that the *voces del cielo* are here much more subtle in their implied power of mysterious suggestion than in the plays where the protagonist actually hears and understands the voices. It is due to the fact that Vertilo . . . finally repents, realizing his guilt and the justness of his own punishment."[16]

In his comedies, Tirso de Molina sets similar scenes before his audience. In *La eleccíon por la virtud*, the protagonist perceives "a voice" belonging to an unseen speaker and recognizes the following words, which are obscurely addressed to him: "very often for a man, forecasts are the sign of some good future" (*prognósticos son / señal de algún buen future / muchas veces para un hombre*).[17] In such cases, Aníbal writes, characters fail to identify the human source of the words that they distinguish, yet not being superstitious, they "never really interpret them as omens": "They find these warnings physically inexplicable, and consequently suppose them to be a direct communication of a mysteriously angelic nature — Christian rather than pagan."[18] In Lope de Vega's plays, by contrast, those who encounter such "voices" seek out their sources without dispelling the mystery of their sounding. Declaring his love to Doña Ana in *La inocente sangre*, Don Juan thus hears a question and an answer uttered by someone he cannot see: "So early are you plucking the flower? / You will enjoy the fruit late" (*¿Tan temprano lleváis flor? / Tarde goazaréis del fruto*). When Don Juan admits his consternation before what he has just heard, Ana reassures him. She explains that it is only the gardener outside, addressing a tree. Yet when Don Juan "asks Ana to give him her word that she will marry him, the voice of the gardener is heard again": "I swear to you that, in your life, you will not see yourself with her." "The words are now intolerable to Don Juan," Sonia Jones comments, "and he rushes out to ask the gardener for an explanation. The gardener tells him that he was talking to an almond tree which had bloomed too early in the season and was therefore in danger of losing its first fruit to the frost."[19]

That a passing word might reveal a truth unknown to the speakers and unnoticed by the interlocutor was a possibility that did not escape the "ingenious gentleman Don Quijote." At the close of Miguel de Cervantes's novel, the perception of a *proverbio* plays a notable role. The knight has just returned to the region of his home in the company of Sancho Panza. As they are "about to enter the village," the narrator relates, on Sidi Hamid's authority, Don Quijote sees "two boys fighting, rolling around on the communal threshing floor." Suddenly, one says to the other, "Stop your nonsense, Pete; you'll never see her [or 'it'] as long as you live" (*No te canses, Periquillo, que no la has de ver en todas los días de tu vida*).[20] In that isolated admonition, the reference of the pronoun "her" or "it" is impossible to establish; neither the adventurers nor the reader can know to whom or to what it may point. Yet the knight immediately discerns in it a sign for him. Don Quijote turns to his squire: "Didn't you notice, my friend, what that boy said? 'You'll never see her again as long as you live'? 'So what?' replied Sancho. 'Who cares what this boy says?' 'Good Lord!' said Don Quijote. 'Don't you see how, if you apply that to my own longing, it means I'll never see Dulcinea again?'"[21] A master of the method condemned by Alfonso and decried by Ciruelo, the knight takes the incidental exclamation to be a message destined for him. He hears a "heavenly voice" that sounds from the boys' rolling on the ground.

"Sancho was about to reply," the reader learns, when he was interrupted by the sight of another unexpected event: "He stopped himself, seeing a hare come running across the field, pursued by a horde of hunters with greyhounds; terrified, the animal tried to hide, crouching under the donkey. It wasn't hard for Sancho to pick him up and present him to Don Quijote, who was muttering: '*Malum signum! Malum signum!* [A bad sign! A bad sign!] A hare comes running, with greyhounds coming after, so Dulcinea will not appear!"[22] Sancho refuses to grant that inference.

> "You're very strange, my lord," said Sancho. "Let's suppose this hare really is Dulcinea del Toboso, and these greyhounds chasing after her are the wicked magicians who turned her into a peasant girl. She runs, I pick her up and hand her over to your grace, and you hold her in your arms and her feel good—and what kind of bad sign is that? And what kind of bad augur can you find in those boys? [*¿qué mala señal ésta, ni qué mal agüero se puede tomar de acquí?*]."[23]

When the boys come over to see the hare, Sancho asks them about their argument. They dispel the obscurity of the pronoun "her" (or "it"), which referred anaphorically to a noun of the feminine gender. "The boy who'd said, 'You'll never see her [or 'it'] as long as you live' told him he'd taken a cricket cage [*una jaula de grillos*] from his friend, and didn't intend ever to give it [literally, 'her'] back."

Sancho proceeds to remit the cage to Don Quijote's hands. In exchange for "four quarters," the boys relinquish it to the squire. He passes it on it to his master, while reproaching him for his benighted beliefs:

> "Here you are, my lord: now these augurs of yours are smashed to pieces and all gone [*rompidos y desbaratados estos agüeros*]—and anyway, it seems to me, fool though I may be, these things have no more to do with what happens to us than last year's clouds. And unless I misremember, I've heard our priest say that good Christians and sensible people shouldn't pay any attention to foolishness like this, and even you yourself, your grace, told me the same thing, explaining that Christians who do believe in augurs [*agüeros*] are idiots."[24]

Before the unexpected circumstance, the knight has shown precisely the superstitious attitude denounced by Ciruelo. Don Quijote has identified two of the theologian's three varieties of "augurs" in the happenings, inferring sense from the movement of animals and meaning from words spoken to a purpose the speaker could not have intended.[25] In his words of admonition, Sancho represents the position of the church, as he himself affirms, if not also that of a disenchanted modern reason.

Yet hermeneutic caution is in order, as several interpreters have observed. “The length and the amount of detail in the incident are disproportionate to its importance on the plane of events,” E. C. Riley writes, noting that the description of the occurrences alone occupies a fifth of the entire chapter.[26] The incident is also remarkable in its setting and its timing, being “the final event on the road as Don Quixote and Sancho come home to their village for the last time.”[27] The two “bad signs” recall the two comic omens that marked the riders’ departure in the first volume of the novel, “the whinnying of Rocinante and the ‘suspiros’ of Sancho’s donkey.”[28] As a result of Sancho’s efforts to reconcile his lord with the senseless chance of circumstance, Don Quijote soon finds himself in a striking position. The scene recalls one of emblematic iconography in which each component is significant: seated on his horse at the threshold of the village, the knight holds a hare in one hand and a cricket cage in the other.[29] Confronted by the scene, the reader is challenged to “see deeper” than Sancho. One may infer, Otis H. Green writes, that “Don Quijote is being led and admonished by a genuine Voice from Heaven.”[30] Critics have agreed that the episode is of “decisive meaning” without reaching any interpretative consensus.[31] At the very least, however, the reader may conclude that the knight is not altogether mistaken. The *malum signum* is true. Don Quijote will never see Dulcinea, and his death is near.

In the Renaissance, it is not only in Spain that scraps of speech may bear tidings discernible by no other means. When Rabelais publishes book 3 of *The Life of Gargantua and Pantagruel* in 1543, he has the giant’s son enjoin his friend to practice an art that corresponds to the habits of the diviners of *proverbios*. To Panurge’s uncertainties about marriage, Pantagruel responds that in cases of doubt, grounds for decision may be drawn from the practice of bibliomancy. “Now, here’s something you might do if you see fit,” he advises the young Parisian cleric, “Bring me the works of Virgil and, opening them with your fingernail three times running, we’ll explore, by the verses whose numbers we agree on, the future lot of your marriage. For, as by Homeric lots a man has often come upon his destiny."[32] Pantagruel recalls the examples of ancient figures, from Socrates to Roman emperors, who drew counsel from fortuitously found Homeric and Virgilian lines. In the early modern French work, the two young men proceed to do as the ancients did. Yet when the passages on which they happen lend themselves to different and even contrary inferences, and Panurge declares that if Pantagruel obstinately refuses to grant him his reading, he will "appeal," his friend demurs: "'Appeal,' said Pantagruel, 'one never can against judgments decided by lot and Fortune, as our ancient jurists attest, and Baldus says so, L. *ult.* C. *de leg.* The reason is that Fortune recognizes no superior to whom one may appeal from her and her judgments.'"[33] The friends are obliged to turn to divination by another means, seeking solutions to the young man's predicament in his dreams.

In one enigmatic episode in the life of an early modern author, such diverse varieties of induction are inextricably combined. The fortuitous hearing of words, the random reading of books, and the interpretation of dreams then become inseparable. The author is the thinker commonly considered the founder of modern philosophy as he is depicted by Adrien Baillet in his *Life of Monsieur René Des Cartes*, which appeared in 1691, four decades after its subject's death. In the "Discourse on Method," Descartes himself relates how, starting in his early youth, he was granted the fortune of "fashioning from maxims and reflections" a new path, "a method by which, it seems to me, I have a way of adding progressively to my knowledge and raising it by degrees to the highest point that the limitations of my mind and the short span of life allotted to me will permit it to reach."[34]

The way that he cleared first became discernible to him when, as a young man, he was staying in a town in Germany. At the age of twenty-three, while a member of the army of the Catholic Elector Maximilian during the Thirty Years' War, Descartes was delayed, as he indicates in the "Discourse," somewhere in the vicinity of the north Bavarian border.[35] "As I was returning to the army from the coronation of the emperor," he recalls, "I was halted by the onset of winter in quarters where, having no diverting company and fortunately also no cares or emotional turmoil to trouble me, I spent the whole day shut up in a small room heated by a stove, in which I could converse with my own thoughts at leisure."[36] Descartes says little more about the circumstances of that sojourn, if not that it was in that same stove-heated chamber that he conceived the basis of a new science, which would advance knowledge and guide conduct.

Baillet dates the momentous day of discovery to November 10, 1619, on the basis of a "little notebook bound in parchment" that Descartes filled during this period with thoughts on mathematics, physics, and the powers of the mind.[37] On one of its pages, Descartes clearly indicated the beginning of a new section, inscribed with the title "Olympica" and the Latin words, "On November 10, full of enthusiasm [or 'divine inspiration'] and in the process of discovering the foundations of an admirable science [*mirabilis scientiae fundamenta*]. . . ."[38] Descartes had already resolved to make of "the pursuit of the love of Truth the sole occupation" of his life. Yet it was only on that autumn day, Baillet explains, that the thinker, having fallen prey to "disturbances" (*tourments*), became a visionary: "The search that he wanted to make agitated his mind violently. These disturbances augmented more and more, as he found himself caught in a continual contention in which he could find diversion neither in walking nor in human society. This so exhausted him that his brain took fire, and he fell into a sort of enthusiasm, which so affected his mind, already over-tired, that it left him in the condition to receive the impression of dreams and visions."[39] These the young Descartes transcribed into his notebook.

On November 10, 1619, "having gone to bed *completely filled with enthusiasm*," Baillet writes, setting out in cursive script the words from the notebook that are italicized here, "wholly preoccupied with thought *of having found that very day the foundation of the wonderful science*, he had three consecutive dreams in the same night, which he imagined could only have come only from on high."[40] In the first vision, he was "struck by the representation of ghosts" and struggled to walk along a street; feeling "a great weakness on his right side," he was obliged to "lean to his left side," being "buffeted by gusts that carried him off in a sort of whirlwind that spun him around three or four times on his left foot." He tried to seek refuge in a church, and after catching sight of an acquaintance, met a stranger who spoke to him of one Monsieur N., who "had something to give him," which Descartes imagined to be "a melon from a foreign land."[41] In the second dream, he heard "a sudden, loud noise, which he took for thunder. Terrified," Baillet continues, "he awoke at once. Having opened his eyes, he noticed many sparks of fire scattered around the room." Descartes reminded himself that he had "experienced this phenomenon on many other occasions." Attributing the brightness to the disturbance of his own eyes, he "reassured himself" about what he had seen. As his terrors faded, he then "fell asleep again quite calmly."[42]

In his next and last dream, Descartes was confronted by multiple contingencies of speech and script demanding interpretation. First "he found a book on his table without having any idea who had put it there."[43] Opening it, he read its title, *Dictionary*. In the next instant, he glimpsed a second book, "a collection of poems by different authors, titled *Corpus Poetarum* etc." Perusing the second book, "he chanced upon this verse: 'What path in life shall I follow?'" (*Quod vitae sectabor iter?*). Before reading further, a man appeared and gave him "a piece of poetry [*une pièce de vers*] that began with these words: 'Yes and No'" (*Est et Non*). Descartes replied that he knew the text and its author, Ausonius.[44] He proceeded to try to locate it in the book. As the *Dictionary* beside him mysteriously vanished and appeared again in inexplicably fragmentary form on the table, Descartes leafed through the poetry collection in search of the selected "piece." He could not find it. He assured the man that he knew another poem "that was still finer," which began with the words, "What path in life shall I follow?" When the man asked him for that work, the dreamer set out to find it. Yet as he began to consult the well-illustrated volume before him, he noticed that it was "not the same edition as the one he knew." Then, suddenly, the books and the man disappeared.[45]

The third dream is of unexpected encounters with words and letters. Individual lines are read and spoken. Selected like lots, they are drawn from the memory of the stranger and an unwieldy poetic anthology, which seems a pendant to the mysteriously changing volume titled *Dictionary*. Cleromancy is at play both in the act of stumbling on a poem in the book and in the event of being confronted by a "piece of poetry" recited orally. The dreamer's first encounter with the anthology causes his eyes to fall on one of many texts of which he makes out only a line ("What path in life shall I follow?"), while his brief conversation draws his attention toward a composition condensed by synecdoche in three words: "Yes and No." Both times, Descartes encounters words wrenched from their context. In each case, Ausonius, the Christian poet of the age of Augustine, is the author of the lines extracted from the poems of which they are a part. Unlike Panurge and Pantagruel, the young dreamer has rolled no dice to find himself before such scraps of ancient poetry, yet he grasps that he must submit himself to the same challenge from which the Rabelaisian students, in frustration, retreat: the dreaming Descartes strives to draw a meaning from the lines of verse on which he happens.

For Baillet, what is most "remarkable" in the three oneiric sequences is external to the events that compose them. It concerns the dreamer alone. Even as he saw himself in such strange circumstances, the biographer relates, Descartes never ceased to reason: "Wondering whether what he had seen was a dream or a vision, he not only decided it was a dream while he was still asleep but also interpreted it before he was fully awake."[46] The notebooks indicate that before waking, Descartes inferred the meaning of what he had seen. The *Dictionary* stood for "all the Sciences," while the anthology "represented in a particular and in a more distinct way the union of Philosophy and Wisdom."[47] In the words "Yes and No," Descartes discerned a citation from Pythagoras ("*nai kai ou*," as he wrote in the margin of his notebook) and an allusion to the "Truth and Falsehood in human understanding and the profane sciences." In the question, "What path in life shall I follow?" he detected a reference to the "uncertainty of what sort of life one should choose" and a representation of "the good advice of a wise person or even of Moral Theology."[48]

In the notebooks, "Descartes-the-interpreter" thus deciphered "Descartes-the-dreamer," as Jean-Luc Marion writes, "to suggest a sketch of some thoughts belonging to Descartes-the Philosopher." The most important of such "thoughts" is doubtless that of reason itself, to which the visionary incident bears witness. In its rendition of what was seen and interpreted in sleep, the notebook attests to a rational "thinking" (*cogitatio*) that is irreducible to the difference between sleep and waking.[49] Well before the formulation of the Cartesian philosophy, the dream sequence and its gloss thereby present a new model of that cognitive activity. They announce the faculty of representation that Descartes later defines, which Marion presents as a thinking that "begins when consciousness becomes indifferent to its affections, when it recuses itself as affective consciousness and affected consciousness, to admit evidence alone as a criterion."[50]

When an inventory of the philosopher's papers was drawn up in 1650, the year of his death, the "little notebook" was present. By the end of the seventeenth century, it could no longer be found. Baillet's *Life* would have been the sole surviving source for any knowledge of the philosopher's youthful dreams had it not been for a surprising sequence of events. In 1672, the Elector of Mainz sent Gottfried Wilhelm Leibniz, then aged twenty-six, on a diplomatic mission to Paris. There, he was granted access to the posthumous papers of both Blaise Pascal and Descartes. By a happy coincidence, the young Leibniz thus perused the "little notebook." He was sufficiently struck by its contents as to transcribe (or to have transcribed) "substantial excerpts" from its pages in 1676.[51] First published in the late nineteenth century by Louis-Alexander Foucher de Careil under the title "Cartesii cogitationes privatae," the Leibnizian transcription is a precious source for understanding Descartes's early work and for defining the aspects of the Cartesian project that most attracted the German thinker's attention.

Leibniz was keenly interested in the "wonderful science" that Descartes envisaged in 1619, but he seems to have had little curiosity about his three dreams. "The otherwise respectful note taker lost patience when the heroic rationalist 'deviated' from the record of his thinking to recount his dreaming," John R. Cole writes. "He or his scribe did no more than simply note the fact of the dreaming and one element from one dream."[52] The one dream in question was the third, and the "one element" that Leibniz retained was the line in the poetry anthology on which the dreamer's eyes happened to fall. "It was on the night of November 10 that I began to understand the foundation of the marvellous invention (*fundamentum inventi mirabilis*)," we read in the Leibnizian transcription of the notebook. There follows the single detail that Leibniz drew from the philosopher's report: "I had a dream during which I recited poem 7 from Ausonius, beginning thus: 'What path in life shall I follow?'"[53]

Those Latin words seem to have made a deep impression on Leibniz. Years later, he recalls them in the introduction to the "Remarks on the Summary of the Life of Mons. Des Cartes" that he contributed to his erstwhile teacher Christian Thomasius's 1693 *History of Wisdom and Foolishness*. "Descartes devoted his energies to study for a long time at the Jesuit school at La Flèche," Leibniz writes in the opening of his "Remarks," "and as a young man he decided to reform Philosophy after some dreams, and much thought on Ausonius's 'What path in life shall I follow?' [*quod vitae sectabor iter?*]."[54] Decades after his consultation of the Cartesian papers, when he was no longer writing about Descartes's life and thought, Leibniz still retained a keen memory of the late Latin poet's line. He quoted it again not once, but twice in a later work.

That work was the 1710 *Essays of Theodicy, The Goodness of God, the Freedom of Man, and the Origin of Evil.* Here Leibniz seeks to show that divine providence, while perfect, imposes no constraints on the exercise of the human will. In the preface to his book, he evokes the example of those difficult situations in which one is confronted by a

> question . . . that is somewhat thorny, as for instance when one asks oneself, "what path in life shall I follow?" [*quod vitae sectabor iter?*], what profession one must choose; when it is a question of a marriage being arranged, of a war being undertaken, of a battle being fought; for in these cases many will be inclined to evade the difficulty of consideration and abandon themselves to fate or to inclination, as if reason should not be employed except in easy cases.[55]

Leibniz acknowledges the "temptation" felt by many to attribute their decisions in such situations to such an obscure a force as "fate" or "destiny"; but he nonetheless argues that for reasons both moral and theological, one must resolutely affirm that even in such circumstances, the human will is free.

Yet Leibniz is also aware of the necessity of accounting for more complex cases. Sometimes human action appears to be unmistakably constrained by external factors, some of which may even be divine. The Bible furnishes a clear example of such a case: in the book of Exodus, as Moses pleads the case of the Israelites before the Egyptian ruler, God declares that he will "harden the heart of the Pharaoh" and proceeds to do so.[56] Leibniz explains the incident in the following terms:

> This hardening is not to be taken as meaning that God inspires men with a kind of anti-grace, that is, a kind of repugnance to good, or even an inclination towards evil. It is rather that God, having considered the sequence of things that he established, found it fitting, for superior reasons, to permit that Pharaoh, for example, should be in such *circumstances* as should increase his wickedness, and divine wisdom willed to derive a good from this evil.[57]

Leibniz concludes that in each case, the domain of free action is ultimately reducible to the concatenation of events: "It all often comes down to *Circumstances*, which form a part of the combination of things" (*Ainsi le tout revient souvent aux Circonstances, qui font une partie de l'enchaînement des choses*).[58]

To illustrate the nature and effects of such "circumstances," Leibniz draws another example from the life of Nicolas Steno (or Niels Steensen), whom he met in 1677.[59] "The good Steno, a Dane," as Leibniz introduces him, "who was titular Bishop of Titianopolis, Vicar Apostolic (as they say) of Hanover and the region around, when there was a Duke Regent of his religion," underwent a life-changing experience. Steno presumably recounted it to Leibniz, who included it in his work, albeit surely not in the terms in which he heard it. Steno "was a great anatomist and deeply versed in natural science," we read,

> but he unfortunately gave up research therein, and from being a great physicist he became a mediocre theologian. He would almost listen to nothing more about the marvels of Nature, and an express order from the Pope *in virtute sanctae obedientiae* was needed to extract from him the observations M. Thévenot asked of him. He told us then that what had greatly helped towards inducing him to place himself on the side of the Roman Church had been the voice of a lady in Florence, who had cried out to him from a window: "Go not on the side where you are about to go, sir, go on the other side." "That voice struck me," he told us, "because I was just meditating upon religion." This lady knew that he was seeking a man in the house where she was, and, when she saw him making his way to the other house, wished to point out where his friend's room was.[60]

Were one to apply Leibniz's exegetical remarks on Exodus to this incident, one might conclude that God "found it fitting, for superior reasons," to allow the Danish scientist to find himself in such circumstances as to be perverted from his scientific vocation, led astray by misguided care for a voice. The "lady in Florence" was speaking of the location of a friend whom she thought Steno was seeking, as he himself appears to have been the first to concede. Yet the onetime physicist took her words otherwise than they were meant, understanding them to be a heavenly message that he had heard by chance. Steno thus committed himself to the superstition denounced by Alfonso X and Ciruelo, grasping what he happened to perceive in a moment of reflection as the work of an angel, if not God. Discerning a divine sign in an incidental remark, Steno, raised a Protestant, crossed to "the other side," as he believed the inspired voice had advised him to do, and once a Catholic, he became the "mediocre theologian" whom Leibniz came to know only too well.

According to the *Theodicy*, however, the "combination of all things" may also imply events and consequences of a different nature and consequence. Steno's is not the sole example that the Leibnizian *Essays* provide of the catching of an augur in contingent speech. The reader learns that not only confusion, but also illumination may result when someone attends to unexpectedly heard scraps of discourse. "There are countless examples of small circumstances serving to convert or to pervert," Leibniz writes. He then reminds the reader how Augustine, long in doubt, at last found piety:

> Nothing is more widely known than the *Tolle, lege* ("Take and read") cry which St. Augustine heard in a neighboring house, when he was pondering on what side he should take among the Christians divided into sects, and saying to himself, "What path in life shall I follow?" (*Quod vitae sectabor iter?*). This brought him to open at random the book of the Holy Scriptures which he had before him, and to read what came before his eyes: and these were words which finally induced him to give up Manichaeism.[61]

While Steno fell into error by taking a voice that he perceived by chance to be an augur, Augustine rose from anguish to conviction in discerning a divine command in two words that he happened to perceive. Even as the Danish scientist lost his way in attending to a "voice," the church father was released from his doubts by listening to a "cry . . . in a neighboring house."

In recalling the events of the *Confessions* in the *Theodicy*, Leibniz surreptitiously evokes a modern experience of the fortuitously heard word. The reader will observe that into Augustine's account of his conversion, the German author has inserted a line drawn from the church father's contemporary, Ausonius, a line that Augustine does not cite: "What path in life shall I follow?" (*Quod vitae sectabor iter?*) "When Leibniz was writing these lines, his memory of Augustine's *Confessions* must have been somewhat hazy," Christopher Wild writes, "since he conflated them with his memory of reading Descartes's now lost account of his similarly dramatic conversion, one in which books also played a pivotal role."[62] The philosopher's "conflation" superimposes several readings: Augustine's encounters with the *tolle lege* and the page to which he then happens to open the book of Paul's letters; Descartes's "Olympian" vision, in which he chances upon the line in the found poetic anthology; and Leibniz's own various experiences of hearing Steno recount his groundless conversion, reading the *Confessions* by Augustine, and once transcribing the "little notebook" by Descartes. In the *Theodicy*, these diversely divinatory perceptions of speech are woven into the fabric of a single scene.

At its center is the Ausonian "piece of poetry": "What path in life shall I follow?" In its syntax, that phrase is distinct from the omen that Augustine hears. *Tolle lege*, "pick up and read," is an imperative of the second person singular, addressed to an unnamed hearer. By contrast, *Quod vitae sectabor iter?* is a question spoken in the first person. Had Augustine heard these words, he could only have uttered them himself, as Leibniz infers. In this sense, the scene in the garden as the *Theodicy* presents it is more intensely subjective than the one represented in the *Confessions*. Here, as in Chrétien's romance, the diviner is at once speaker and hearer. He interprets for himself the discourse that he happens to utter. Being summoned to a life of true Christianity, in distinction to "the good Steno, the Dane," Augustine would have heard speech internal to his mind, like the Cartesian dreamer. Ausonius's words would have been his own, just as they later became those of Descartes. They would have constituted an adage and an augur, announcing the sounding of *tolle lege*; they would have functioned as a *poverbium* in the ancient sense and as a *proverbio* in the medieval meaning familiar to Alfonso the Wise. Inserting the line into the rewritten scene of the conversion, Leibniz effectively devises a "circumstance" at once Augustinian, Cartesian, and his own.

From this incidental, if artificial, "part of the combination of all things," Leibniz draws the elements of an implicit theory of revelations in unexpectedly heard words. The modern philosopher, to be sure, is far from justifying any practice of divination. That he harbored a rational skepticism toward ancient mantic techniques is certain. Referring to "those who inhabited the earth before Christianity" in the preface to the *Theodicy*, he evokes "observances" that were "very often ridiculous and absurd." "The pagans had their superstitions: they boasted of miracles, everything with them was full of oracles, auguries, portents, divinations."[63] Yet in recalling the events by which Augustine overcame his agonies, Leibniz does not contest the force of the *tolle lege* that the saint heard. Nowhere does Leibniz exclude the possibility that a part of discourse perceived in passing and as if by chance might prove itself unexpectedly portentous.

In the *Theodicy*, Leibniz suggests a modern doctrine of augurs that is coherent with the principles of his philosophy. In seeking to demonstrate that divine knowledge and the free will are perfectly compatible, he ventures boldly into what he considered to be a "famous labyrinth where our reason often goes astray." Yet in the *Theodicy*, Leibniz also presents himself as the cartographer of a less familiar labyrinth that, as he noted, "exercises philosophers" among all people. It is what "consists in the discussion of continuity and of the indivisibles which appear to be the elements thereof, and where the consideration of the infinite must enter in."[64] To clear a path through that maze, offering a correct account of continuity, Leibniz posits the existence of things that none before him envisaged: beings that, while of a most minute quantity, are not equivalent to nothing. His preferred examples of such entities are infinitesimals in the "analysis" that he devised and "small perceptions" (*petites perceptions*) in his theory of the mind: sensations too faint to be felt in themselves that, when combined, exert a sensible force on our awareness.[65] Such beings, he repeatedly argues, must be posited in the study of nature as in the doctrine of the spirit, for only then may one account for the seamless passage between different states in nature and the mind.

As Leibniz explains in the preface to his *New Essays on Human Understanding*,

> nothing happens all at once; and it is one of my great and most demonstrated maxims that *nature makes no leaps.* This is what I called the Law of Continuity when I spoke of it in the first "News of the Republic of Letters," and the use of this Law is very considerable in physics. It stipulates that one always passes from the small to the large and back [by passing] through the intermediary, in degrees as in parts, and that a movement is never immediately born from rest, nor can be reduced to it, unless it is by a lesser movement, just as one has never finished tracing a line until one has finished tracing a shorter one, despite the fact that until now those who have stated the laws of movement have failed to notice this law, believing that, in a single moment, one body can receive a movement that is contrary to its preceding one.[66]

In his account of conversions and perversions in the lives of theologians, Leibniz holds fast to this "great maxim." He allows that even the most minute of circumstances, being a part of the "combination of all things," may play a role in a decisive change. The isolated word or phrase, the cry, and the "piece of poetry" can, for this reason, be portentous—for better and for worse.

The apparently opposed cases of Steno and Augustine furnish complementary illustrations of this argument. Each theologian takes a scrap of speech that he has happened to hear not as it was most likely intended by the speaker, but in another sense, according to which it announces a momentous change. Defying the code of Alfonso the Wise, each man, in short, apprehends a *proverbio*; each theologian hears an *alfil* where others might perceive mere accidents of discourse. One may reconstruct the reasons why Leibniz thus implicitly admits as valid an ancient practice that is all too easily dismissed as nothing but superstition. The "combination of events" implies an infinity of lesser happenings that, however minute they may be, nonetheless play roles in great occurrences. Such happenings can announce changes that are to come or that have begun without being clearly and distinctly perceived. The risk of error may lie not in attending to lesser occurrences, as many would assume, but in failing to grasp them adequately and, with false certainty, ruling out all portentous sounds.

The example of "the good Steno, the Dane" is a warning against that presumption. Yet the fall from the rank of "great physicist" to that of "mediocre theologian" in no way excludes illuminations such as that of the cry of *tolle lege*. In the world conceived by the author of the *Theodicy*, the two events are equally admissible. Noises, whether articulate or inarticulate, heard or ignored, obey a law that holds for every phenomenon, displaying universal properties. As Leibniz would explain a few years after his *Essays on the Goodness of God, the Freedom of Man, and the Origin of Evil*, the world that we are fortunate to know has been adjusted by the highest mind: "everything is ordered in things once and for all, with as much order and agreement as possible, since supreme wisdom and goodness can only act with perfect harmony: the present is pregnant with the future; the future can be read in the past; the distant is expressed in the proximate."[67]

Incidental voices illustrate that argument, however softly they may sound. From the Leibnizian standpoint, listening to them closely is therefore neither a sin nor a crime, as Alfonso X declares in *Las Siete Partidas*; nor is it a delusion and superstition, as countless early modern authorities, Ciruelo and Panza not least, maintain. The scene of Augustine's conversion, as it is rewritten in the *Theodicy*, suggests that attention to a passing cry may even be the work of a sharp and pious mind. Yet success in the inference from fortuitous perception is anything but assured. The existence of "countless examples of small circumstances" serving "to convert or to pervert" ensures that "bad signs," as Don Quixote observed, warn of danger. Their subtlety renders the risk of error almost ubiquitous. Careful not to lead his readers astray, wary of observances "very often ridiculous and absurd," Leibniz offers no single solution to that peril. If, however, one were to draw from his remarks on hearing and overhearing some indication of the path to follow, it might be to situate the event, however minor it may seem to be, "in the combination of things." When the present is seen to be "pregnant with the future," when small circumstances that are proximate express those that are distant, a subtle harmony becomes discernible, and there is a chance that a thing as fleeting as a line heard in a dream—whether it is one's own or another's—can be read.

CHAPTER ELEVEN

Lines and Sentences

In a brief narrative first published in 1811 in his *Treasure Chest*, Johann Peter Hebel sets before his audience a phrase that is heard repeatedly, yet each time as if by accident, and that bears an unexpected truth—for both the one who hears and fails to heed it and those who, later, discover his tale. The phrase constitutes the story's striking title, which is neither German nor Dutch, although the unadvised reader might take it to be both: "Kannitverstan."[1] That expression transcribes an entire Dutch sentence, which appears in the story as the reply to three different German questions. It is, in each of its occurrences, an expression of unmitigated incomprehension. In repetition and in retrospect, however, the phrase becomes the occasion of an oblique revelation. Its four syllables mark out the interval that separates an act of speech from its failure to be registered. In that gap, a modern literary *klēdōn* becomes distinctly audible.

The reworking of an anecdote first recounted in French and later rendered into Latin and German, as well as English, Hebel's work concerns a "young German" who had traveled to Amsterdam to learn his trade.[2] Having journeyed from his home in Swabia to "that great and rich city of commerce full of splendid houses, swaying ships and industrious people," the youth was "immediately struck by a large and handsome building whose like he had not yet seen all along the road from Duttlingen to Amsterdam." After some time spent absorbed in silent wonder, "he could not refrain from addressing a passer-by":

> "My good friend," he said, "could you tell me the name of the gentleman who owns this marvellous house with its window boxes full of tulips, daffodils and stocks?" But the man, who probably had more important things to do and who unfortunately understood as much German as the questioner Dutch, namely none at all, paused only to snap "Kannitverstan" before hurrying on. This was a Dutch word, or really three words, meaning "I can't understand you" [*ich kann Euch nicht verstehen*]. But our good fellow in foreign parts thought this was the name he wanted to know. "He must be a very rich man, this Herr Kannitverstan," he thought, and walked on.[3]

In the next scene, the curious German youth is at the harbor, before "row upon row of ships, masts after mast." "At first he wondered how he, with just two eyes, could possibly take in all these marvels, until after a while his gaze remained on one great ship which had arrived from the East Indies and was now unloading." After watching again in amazement "for some time," he "asked a man who was carrying a crate on his shoulder the name of the fortunate person for whom the sea brought all these goods ashore." The answer that he received was the echo of the one given earlier: "'Kannitverstan' was the reply. So now he thought, 'Aha, so that's how it is! It's no wonder. If the sea delivers a man these riches he can easily build such houses on this earth and put tulips in gilded pots at his windows!"[4] Comparing the grandeur of the imagined personage to his own modest condition, self-pity overcomes him. "His thoughts were sad indeed as he contemplated how poor a man he was among so many rich people in the world."[5]

At that moment, the youth turns a corner and chances upon a "great funeral procession." Once again, he stands and stares. Having watched the mourners pass before him, having gazed on the "four horses decked in black" drawing a hearse, "likewise draped in black," having observed the "long train of the deceased's friends and acquaintances" following behind them, "two by two, shrouded in black cloaks, silent," and accompanied by the sound of a bell tolling in the distance, the young man addresses the last member of the assembly. He puts to the Dutchman before him an indirect question, phrased as a tenuous description: "'That gentleman,' he said, 'for whom the bell tolls, must have been a good friend of yours, you walk behind so downcast and so deep in thought.' 'Kannitverstan,' came the reply.'"[6] At the sound of that utterance, the astonished Duttlinger is moved to tears. "'Poor Kannitverstan!'" he cries, "'What can all your riches bring you now? No more than my poverty will bring me one day: a shroud and a winding sheet; and all your lovely flowers a bunch of rosemary perhaps on your cold breast, or a sprig of rue.'" He follows the cortège to the graveside, where he is more deeply touched by the Dutch funeral oration "of which he understood not a word, than by many a sermon in German to which he paid little attention."[7]

For the narrator, these happenings compose an unusual yet unmistakable moral itinerary. By "the most curious of detours" (*auf dem seltsamesten Umwege*), "error" (*Irrthum*) leads "the good young German" "to the truth and to its recognition."[8] The storyteller indicates that the occurrences thereby contain a lesson for the reader: there is no limit to the daily opportunities, "in Emmendingen and Gundelfingen or in Amsterdam," to ponder "the transience of earthly things." Vanity is everywhere to be inferred, even when the reasoning that would appear to suggest it is, like the German man's intuitive deduction, without any solid foundation. The narrator observes that although the young Swabian never grasped what he failed to understand, he was profoundly marked by his experiences on his formative voyage outside his native land: "Whenever again he was inclined to feel depressed because so many people in the world were so rich and he so poor, he just remembered Herr Kannitverstan of Amsterdam, his great mansion, his ship laden with riches, and his narrow grave."[9]

Without contesting the doctrine that the narrator draws from the series of encounters that he relates, one may also offer another reading of the text. That it depicts a disordering of the conditions of communication is certain. In such circumstances, an ordinary utterance acquires a force that is almost oracular: one phrase, said three times, is portentous in being misunderstood. To draw out its implications, one must first attend to the circumstances of the verbal exchanges. The three dialogues appear to stage scenes of total and mutual incomprehension. As Paul Fleming notes, however, an asymmetry marks each conversation. All three passers-by are aware that they do not grasp what the German has asked them, while the young man believes that he has received the information that he requested.[10] In the conversation, the assertion of not understanding—"Kannitverstan!"—is therefore misconstrued. "The good young German" infers that his interlocutor has provided him with the name that he has sought, and he supposes that he has grasped what they have said to him. Each time, he is, of course, doubly mistaken.

In this series of occurrences, as in every genuine witticism, pun, or play of words, the confounding of linguistic levels of analysis plays a crucial role. A single sequence of signifying sounds is segmented in diverse and incompatible ways. As the narrator methodically explains to his reader, for the Dutchmen, "Kannitverstan" is a sentence composed of three lexical units: literally, "Can not understand." Yet for the young German, the response is not a proposition, but a proper name. Giving to his tale the one-word title, "Kannitverstan," the author sets the events before the reader from the Duttlinger's misguided perspective. Yet the logic of the comedy demands that several points of view be perceived. The first is that of the men of Amsterdam. Each time they utter the phrase "Kannitverstan," they refer to themselves; it is they, they mean, who, confronted by a question in a foreign tongue, "cannot understand." The German, however, draws a different interpretation, convinced that the utterance names the objects of his curiosity: the one who owns the "marvellous house," the one "for whom the sea brought all the goods ashore," and the one for whom, finally, "the bell tolls." In following the thwarted exchanges, the reader is prompted to draw still a further conclusion. "Kannitverstan," in this last glossing, seems to spiral back upon the benighted youth himself. He might well be designated by the almost nominal Dutch expression that is the title of the tale.[11]

In a work first published in 1845, Edgar Allan Poe presents his readers with a story of a single sentence at once simpler and more obscure. It, too, sounds at first by chance, before recurring, at first almost inaudibly, to unexpected consequence. The work is "The Imp of the Perverse," a text that in its inception seems an essay on "the faculties and impulses of the *prima mobilia* of the human soul."[12] Its author argues for the existence of a certain "propensity" that phrenologists and moralists have overlooked despite its being "a radical, primitive, irreducible sentiment": an "impulse" and "an innate and primitive principle of human action" that, "for want of a more characteristic term," may be called "*perverseness.*"[13] "It is not more incomprehensible than distinctive," the author explains, giving a first example, drawn from the field of rhetoric:

> There lives no man who at some period, has not been tormented, for example, by an earnest desire to tantalize a listener by circumlocution. The speaker is aware that he displeases; he has every intention to please; he is usually curt, precise, and clear; the most laconic and luminous language is struggling for utterance upon his tongue, it is only with difficulty that he restrains himself from giving it flow; he dreads and deprecates the anger of whom he addresses; yet, the thought strikes him, that by certain involutions and parentheses, this anger may be engendered. That simple thought is enough. The impulse increases to a wish, the wish to a desire, the desire to an uncontrollable longing, and the longing, (to the deep regret and mortification of the speaker, and in defiance of all consequences,) is indulged.[14]

The author offers several more illustrations of the ways in which "the wrong or error of any action" may play the role of "the one unconquerable *force* which impels us." When a certain task is to be accomplished by the next day, and "we are consumed with eagerness to commence the work," "we put it off till tomorrow." Then, however, it is too late. So, too, when "we stand on the brink of a precipice," "our first impulse is to shrink from the danger." Yet we are soon captivated by a different thought: "the idea of what would be our sensations during the sweeping precipitancy of a fall from such a height."[15] "If there be no friendly arm to check us, or if we fail in a sudden effort to prostrate ourselves backward from the abyss, we plunge, and are destroyed." Each time, "*perverseness*," as a "*mobile* without a motive," brings about the action that must be most carefully avoided.

Poe's author is not merely a theorist of that "propensity." He is himself, as he explains, "one of the many uncounted victims of the Imp of the Perverse."[16] He once devoted himself to the preparation of a crime that would be inscrutable to all. "For weeks, for months, I pondered upon the means of the murder," he relates. "I rejected a thousand schemes because their accomplishment involved a *chance* of detection." At last, "reading some French Memoirs," he found the perfect means for his deed. He learned that if poisoned, a candle can cause death. Then he contrived to set a lethal "wax-light" in the candlestick of a wealthy relation of whom he was the sole heir. The morning after the commission of that deed of secret substitution, the relation "was discovered dead in his bed, the Coroner's conclusive verdict being 'Death by the visitation of God.'"[17] The murderer proceeded to inherit the entire estate. Having "left no shadow of a clue by which it would be possible to convict, or even suspect" him of any crime, he found himself, as he recalls, in "absolute security." Nonetheless, he was soon vulnerable to the temptations of the "imp." At first, he felt merely a slight inclination to act against his better interest. Soon the unfathomable "propensity" increased. In the end, he could not refrain from committing the sole act that, as he knew, would ruin him: he confessed his crime. "They say that I spoke with a distinct enunciation, but with marked emphasis, and passionate hurry, as if in dread of interruption before concluding the brief, but pregnant sentences that consigned me to the hangman, and to hell."[18] The writer drafts those words on the evening before his execution.

In the narrative of "The Imp of the Perverse," a sentence sounds between perfect crime and perverse confession. Yet it is not immediately perceptible. Evoking the time that followed the commission of the murder, the author stresses his preliminary sense of security: "For a very long period of time, I was accustomed to revel in this sentiment. It afforded me more real delight than all the mere worldly advantages accruing from my sin." That feeling of safety, however, soon turned perversely into a "haunting and harassing thought":

> It harassed because it haunted. I could scarcely get rid of it for an instant. It is quite a common thing to be thus annoyed with the ringing in our ears, or rather in our memories, of the burthen of some ordinary song, or some unimpressive snatches from an opera. Nor will we be the less tormented if the song in itself be good, or the opera air meritorious. In this manner, at last, I would perpetually catch myself pondering upon my security, and repeating, in a low undertone, the phrase, "I am safe."[19]

What pursued the man was an unspoken line, the "snatch" of a train of thought that went unsaid. Distractedly, the narrator soon found himself reworking the "customary syllables" of the sentence "I am safe" into a more unsettling remark. "One day, while sauntering along the streets," the narrator articulated a frame for the three words: "In a fit of petulance, I remodelled them thus: — I am safe — I am safe — yes — if I be not fool enough to make open confession!"[20] The narrator thereby sought to curtail the force and the validity of the "haunting and harassing thought." "I am safe" holds, he then told himself, as long as he made no public avowal. Yet that limitation cleared the way for the path of his self-denunciation. Once he identified the sole condition of his "safety," "an icy chill" crept into his heart. His act of "casual self-suggestion" began to exert an increasing force to the point at which, feeling the approach of the "consummation" of his fate and wishing he could tear out his tongue, he ultimately ceded to "the spirit of the Perverse": "I experienced all the pangs of suffocation; I became blind, and deaf, and giddy; and then, some invisible fiend, I thought, struck me with his broad palm upon the back. The long imprisoned secret burst forth from my soul."[21]

In Poe's tale, unlike Hebel's, the decisive words are formed on the lips of the person who perceives them. Speaker and hearer share a single body, even if, in the intensely subjective confusion of the "harassed" and "haunted" mind, they are structurally irreducible to each other. One consequence of this circumstance is that when the first-person pronoun "I" is uttered, no ambiguity marks its reference. When the narrator hears the words "I am safe" spoken, he knows that they point to none but him. "Perverseness," however, not only impels the uttering of the predicative sentence. It also bears on its logical form, twisting it beyond repair. As Stanley Cavell remarks, in reasoning, "'I am safe—I am safe—yes—if I be not fool enough to make open confession,'" the narrator intuits that the proposition that torments him possesses an unusual property. The sentence "I am safe" is "true as long as it is not said; saying refutes it."[22] Silence alone would assure the correspondence between the murderer's idea of his own security and its reality. Once he has begun openly to assert that he is "safe," the value of his statement changes. As he is the first to sense, when uttered, the declaration implies that he is effectively in danger. The sentence, falsifying itself, becomes the presage of his end.

Two decades later, Mallarmé explored the sounding of a single "haunting and harassing" sentence in a briefer text of greater density and complexity. In 1857, Baudelaire had published a French translation of Poe's "Imp of the Perverse" as the first item in the collection of *New Extraordinary Tales*. Baudelaire titled the rendered story "The Demon of Perversity."[23] In 1864 or 1867, Mallarmé, alluding to that translation, composed a text that he included in his *Divagations* of 1891 under the title "The Demon of Analogy."[24] It is a prose narrative that, revolving around two fragmentary lines of verse, recounts a curiously minimal acoustical occurrence. The narrator of the text leaves his apartment "with the distinct sensation of a wing sliding along the strings of some instrument, languid and light." That feeling is "replaced" by the consciousness of "a voice." It was, we read,

> a voice that, with a downward intonation, pronounced the words: "The Penultimate is dead," in such a way that
>
> *The Penultimate*
>
> ended one line and
>
> *Is dead*
>
> floated free within the fateful pause, the signifying void, more uselessly in the absence of all signification.[25]

> une voix prononçant les mots sur un ton descendant: "La Penultième est morte," de façon que
>
> *La Pénultième*
>
> finit le vers et
>
> *Est morte*
>
> se détacha de la suspension fatidique plus inutilement en le vide de signification.[26]

Walking along the street, the narrator is captivated by a single syllable that, excised from the first line fragment, resounds in his mind: *nul*, "null" or "void," in which he perceives "the tight string of a forgotten musical instrument, which Memory had just revisited with its wing or its palm." Soon, he recalls, the sentence, "The Penultimate / Is dead . . . came back, a virtual reality, detached from any previous stroke of plumes or palms, heard henceforth only through the voice, until finally it articulated itself all alone, animated by its own personality."

"Tormented by the sound" of the lines that he hears, "harassed" by their incessant recurrence, the narrator resolves to allow "the sad words" "to wander" on his lips, even as he murmurs to himself "comfortingly, as if offering condolences, 'The Penultimate is dead, she is dead, really dead, the poor desperate Penultimate.'" His deliberations are cut short when, "aghast," he sees his hand reflected in a shop window "stroking something." He then grasps that he himself has somehow acquired "the voice (the original, which undoubtedly had been the only one)." As he raises his eyes to look more closely at the sight before him, an "irrefutable surnatural force" intervenes. He is consigned to a new "anguish": "I was standing before the shop of a lute seller who had antique musical instruments for sale hanging on his wall, and, underfoot, yellowed palm fronts and ancient birds' wings, half in shadow. Then I fled, strange person, probably condemned forever to wear mourning for the inexplicable Penultimate."[27]

Mallarmé's "Demon" is a response to Poe's "Imp," as has often been observed.[28] The correspondences between the two works are undeniable. Both consist of tales told in the first person in which a secret sealed in a sentence is painfully divulged. Each narrative sets onstage a consciousness in which apparently circumstantial scraps of speech resound in increasing distinctness, "haunting" and "harassing" the mind that most concertedly strives to elude them. Poe's narrator evokes "the ringing in our ears, or rather in our memories, of the burthen of some ordinary song, or some unimpressive snatches from an opera." In the first sentence of Mallarmé's text, the speaker of "The Demon of Analogy" alludes to such linguistic bits and pieces: "Have unknown words ever played about your lips, the haunting and accursed fragments of an absurd sentence?" (*Des paroles inconnues chantèrent-elles sur vos lèvres, lambeaux maudits d'une phrase absurde?*)[29] Poe's "unimpressive snatches" were rendered by Baudelaire as *lambeaux insignifiants*, that is, "senseless fragments," and *lambeaux* is precisely the word that Mallarmé's narrator uses for the parts of the phrase that pursue him.[30]

In "The Demon of Analogy," the constituents of the "accursed fragments" play subtle, yet systematic roles in the pages into which they are woven. When Mallarmé first published the text in 1871, he titled it after the first noun phrase of the enigmatic line: "La Pénultième." That word contains within it the seeds of many of the figures of the work, starting with its first syllable, which is subtly evocative. Not only is it identical in sound to the French word *peine*, "pain."[31] As Mallarmé, teacher of English, translator and reader of Poe well knew, the word part *pén-* (/pen/), although nonsignifying in French, is homophonous with the English word "pen," which signifies not only "writing instrument," but also "quill" and, by extension, "feather."[32] Scholars have pointed out that *penultième* also anagrammatically contains two other words that play recurrent roles in the poem: *plume*, "feather," and *aile*, "wing" (a word whose homophony with the pronoun *elle*, "her," Mallarmé systematically exploits).[33] "Feathers" and "wings" are closely related to each other in the unfolding of the occurrences narrated in the poem. Feathers are implicit in scene with which the work begins ("I went out of my apartment with the distinct sensation of the wing sliding along the strings of some instrument . . . "), and they appear again in the narrator's final vision of "yellowed palm fronts and ancient birds' wings, half in shadow."

Yet in the Mallarméan prose poem, the syntagma "La Penultième" also presages more. The musical instruments glimpsed at the end of the tale contain a subtle echo of its phonic shape. In being "hung," the palms fronts and bird wings are literally ***pen****dus*. In addition to being composed of the letters of *la penultième*, the French words "palms" and "feathers," moreover, are near anagrams of each other: *palme/plume*. All that separates them is a single vowel: the /a/ of *palme* as opposed to the /u/ of *plume*, which is also the phoneme in *nul*, the word in which the narrator hears the "the tight string of a forgotten musical instrument, which Memory had just revisited with its wing or its palm." Given the rules of versification in force in the nineteenth century, in the disposition of lines in which he perceives the "voice" reciting the "absurd phrase," the sound of the "void" that is *nul* falls in precisely the metrical position that is known as "the penultimate": "*La Pe**nul**tième / . . . Est morte.*"[34] As Bertrand Marchal argues, the pronouncement "The Penultimate is dead" can therefore be read as an "anthropomorphic translation" of a "linguistic proposition": "the penultimate syllable of *penultième* is *nul*."[35]

In Mallarme's account of the mind's haunting and harassing by two elliptical lines of verse, as in Poe's tale of the insistent return of the perverse sentence, hearer and speaker can hardly be distinguished. The "accursed fragments of an absurd phrase" that fascinate the narrator are the same "sad words" that "wander" over his own lips. Confronted by their sound, the narrator of "The Demon of Analogy" is as baffled as was the uncomprehending subject of "Kannitverstan." Unlike the Duttlinger, the author of the prose poem correctly segments the phrase that he hears, identifying the words that compose it. Yet he cannot establish its sense. Mallarmé's narrator is the first to observe that once extracted from some unknown poem and recited, the words of the two fragmentary lines seem to "float" in a "signifying void," "more uselessly in the absence of all signification."

"The Demon of Analogy" assigns a new function to such "snatches of song." The suggestive power exerted by the words "The Penultimate" extends beyond the two lines of verse. In the prose poem, the recurrent four-word sequence is a key to the entire work. The phrase "The Penultimate / Is dead" is not only, as the narrator repeatedly asserts, an expression of mourning. It is also prophetic. In the last sentences of the text, it shows itself retrospectively to have announced the events that were to come. In the reflection on the shop window, the narrator catches sight of the unexpected fulfilment of the discourse that he has repeatedly perceived. After the "downward intonation" of the unidentified voice that first pronounced the words "The Penultimate is dead," he glimpses the inverted image of his own hand descending in the suggestion of a caress, and after the "distinct sensation of the wing sliding along the strings of some instrument, languid and light," he has the clear and distinct perception of the luthier's instruments suspended over the "birds' wings." The end of the prose poem reveals itself to be the literal inversion of the opening citation, which announced it.

In its enigmatically broken lines, which precede the first unrhymed poetry in French by twenty years, "The Demon of Analogy" announces the "crisis" that Mallarmé later identifies.[36] The prose poem also prefigures the literary project of which his 1897 essay, "Crise de vers," offers the poet's mature formulation. Detached from the presumed poem of which the reader will know nothing, the obscurely versified sequence, "The Penultimate / Is dead . . . ," sounding as if by chance, yet resounding by necessity, announces the "work" that his late essay qualifies as "pure":

> The pure work implies the disappearance of the poet speaking, who yields the initiative to words, through the clash of their ordered inequalities; they light each other up through reciprocal reflections like a virtual swooping of fire across precious stones, replacing the primacy of the perceptible rhythm of respiration or the classic lyric breath, or the personal feeling driving the sentences
>
> *L'oeuvre pure implique la disparition élocutoire du poëte, qui cède l'initiative aux mots, par le heurt de leur inégalité mobilisés; ils s'allument de reflets réciproques comme une virtuelle traînée de feux sur les pierreries, remplaçant la respiration perceptible en l'ancien souffle lyrique ou la direction personnelle enthousiaste de la phrase.*[37]

In the vanishing of the poet's "voice," in the ceding of the writer's will to "the initiative of words," the poem becomes a mere suggestion: as "Un coup de dés" has it, a "simple insinuation."[38]

"The haunting and accursed fragments of an absurd sentence" sustain that insinuation, rendering it audible. Unprompted in their first appearance, yet ineluctable in their recurrence, they are the elements of a *klēdōn* that is distinct in form and effect from the variously recurrent phrases evoked by Hebel and Poe in the decades that precede it. The lines that continue to sound in the mind of the prose poem's narrator are scraps of speech that their speaker and hearer, despite their efforts, "cannot understand" and that, in their risible technicity and their near senselessness, incite a folly worthy of the promptings of Poe's Imp, of which they are perhaps the comical "perversion." Their repetition, however, prompts more than a play of incomprehension and belated insight. In enabling the perception of analogies between the acoustical and the visual, the earlier and the later, the heard and the glimpsed, the "sad words" that wander on the narrator's lips constitute a new presage. They are the commanding principle of the text into which they are woven, being the cause of its graphic, phonic, and figural patterning and the key to the sequence of minor happenings of which its slight narrative consists. Summoning the "irrefutable supernational force" that is the source of the two line fragments even as he unfolds their inexorable consequences, Mallarmé thus releases a new spirit—imp or demon, if not genius—into the field of literary composition: that of absolutely determining accident. It was soon to make itself felt again, not once, but repeatedly, in the company of poets.

CHAPTER TWELVE

Magic Dictations

In 1833, John Stuart Mill poses a question that he takes often to have been asked: "What is Poetry?"[1] He begins by setting aside the familiar yet faulty "answers which have been returned." First among them is the "wretched mockery of a definition" that "confounds poetry with metrical composition." Such a thesis cannot satisfy any "person possessed of the faculties to which poetry addresses itself." A second common error consists in taking poetry to consist of narrative.[2] Although they often overlap in fact, he concedes, a "radical distinction" separates their reception. A story captivates by the force of the "incidents" that it relates. Poetry moves for another reason: because it is "the delineation of the deeper and more secret workings of human emotion."[3] Yet even as he defines poetry as "the expression or utterance of feeling," Mill distinguishes it from another type of speech, which is "eloquence." Recalling accounts of poetry by two "poets and men of genius," Ebeneezer Elliott and a contemporary whom he does not name, Mill asserts that "eloquence, as well as poetry, is impassioned truth" and that "eloquence, as well as poetry, is thoughts coloured by the feelings."[4] Yet he proposes a novel criterion by which to oppose them.

The crucial difference is the one that separates hearing from overhearing. "If we may be excused the antithesis," Mill explains,

> we should say that eloquence is *heard*, poetry is *over*heard. Eloquence supposes an audience; the peculiarity of poetry appears to us to lie in the poet's utter unconsciousness of a listener. Poetry is feeling, confessing itself to itself in moments of solitude, and embodying itself in symbols, which are the nearest possible representations of the feeling in the exact shape in which it exists in the poet's mind. Eloquence is feeling pouring itself out to other minds, courting their sympathy, or endeavouring to influence their belief, or move them to passion or to action.[5]

That poetry is the variety of literature that most intensely renders an individual consciousness is a thesis often found in nineteenth-century writers. Hegel gives it its most illustrious philosophical articulation, arguing in his *Lectures on Aesthetics* that among all literary forms, lyric poetry satisfies the need "for self-expression and for the apprehension of the mind in its self-expression."[6] Yet Mill does more than maintain that poetry is the utterance of "feeling, confessing itself." As several influential twentieth-century theorists would observe, he includes in his definition of poetry the virtual, albeit qualified, presence of an audience.[7] For him, someone must be present at the poetic utterance without ever being named or addressed by it; otherwise, "the expression or utterance of feeling" becomes eloquence and loses itself. Mill thus posits a link between the poet, in whom feeling is "poured out," and the "other minds" who will receive it. Yet he assigns them distinct positions: while the poet accedes to poetry in a state of pure effusion, the audience only ever does so indirectly and at a certain removal.

Critics have contested the adequacy of Mill's pronouncements in several ways. Some have doubted that they correspond to the conditions of composition and reception of works such as those by William Wordsworth and Percy Bysshe Shelley, which Mill evokes. Others have suggested that Mill did not intend his doctrine to hold for any given poems; perhaps he sought to conceive of an ideal yet to be instantiated.[8] What seems certain, however, is that for Mill, the poetic audience perceives "the delineation of the deeper and more secret workings of human emotion" solely through an interval. Poets, by contrast, accede to those "workings" directly, in "moments of solitude."

Without referring to Mill or evoking the details of his doctrine, several twentieth-century writers would reject those claims. In various settings and for different reasons, modernist poets would understand themselves to be "*over*hearers." The interval between utterance and perception, for such poets, would become the condition of poetic composition itself. As a consequence, the literary work would be understood to be given in a distention between the spoken and the heard, prior to the presence of an audience. The presentation that Valéry offers of his practice is to this degree exemplary. Discussing the genesis of the poem in the "Poet's Notebook" that he publishes in 1928, but whose components date back to at least a decade earlier, he alludes to the experience of the "haunted and harassed" narrator of "The Demon of Analogy." What Mallarmé cast as an exceptional event of partial acoustical perception appears to Valéry as the paradigm of the compositional process. Discussing the inception of a work, he writes, "It may happen that the seed is no more than a word or a snatch of a sentence [*un lambeau d'une phrase*], a line that is searching and working to create a justification and thus to engender a context, a subject, a person." From that "subject" or "seed," "reflection" works to "restrict chance" and, with the aid of a "convention," to create a state of "waiting" (*une attente*).[9]

Valéry proceeds to define the poet as a being of anticipation, in which the faculties of speaking and hearing, while distinct, can hardly be told apart:

> The poet at work is thus a state of waiting. . . . *His ear speaks to him.*
>
> We await the unexpected word—which cannot be foreseen but only awaited. We are the first to hear it.
>
> *To hear?* But that is *to speak*. One only understands what has been heard if one has said it to oneself by means of some other cause.
>
> *To speak*—that is to hear.[10]

For Valéry, the poem reaches the poet from a distance that is without measure. The work comes into being in a subjective state that defies the opposition between passivity and activity. What the poet hears is a word "said to oneself," which is nonetheless perceived otherwise than as it was uttered. It is, in short, speech that is *over*heard. As early as 1918, an entry in the *Notebooks* sketches such an account of lyric creation. Valéry transcribed it in the "Literature" aphorisms that he publishes in 1929:

> In the poet:
> The ear speaks;
> The mouth listens;
> It is intelligence, wakefulness, which gives birth and dreams;
> It is sleep that sees clearly;
> It is the image and the phantasm that look,
> It is the lack and the gap that create.[11]

Poetry, as Valéry observes elsewhere, begins in an event of "speech to oneself" that is marked by "a *rupture*":[12] "The Voice . . . appears in the interval, in the rupture of consciousness."[13]

That a literary work might have its origin in the catching of a fragment of a phrase, be it one's own or another's, is a possibility that several poets after Mallarmé explored. Among them was André Breton, who for a time presented himself as Valéry's disciple.[14] Breton claimed that he had forged from the perception of scraps of discourse a new means for literary composition. In "The Mediums Enter," an essay that he publishes in the journal *Littérature* in 1922 and includes in *The Lost Steps* the same year, he recalls the circumstances in which he began to grant a special importance to unexpectedly heard phrases: "In 1919, my attention had been drawn to the more or less partial sentences that, in complete solitude, as I was falling asleep, became perceptible to my mind, without my being able to find anything that might have predetermined them. These sentences, which were syntactically correct and remarkably rich in images, struck me as poetic elements of the first rank." At first Breton limited himself to transcribing them. Yet soon, with Philippe Soupault, he embarked on a more ambitious project: "voluntarily to re-recreate . . . the state in which they took form."[15]

When they put their project into practice, Breton and Soupault found themselves assailed by enigmatic phrases heard at the threshold of consciousness. As Breton informs the reader, "sentences" and "images" occurred to them "for two months running, increasingly plentiful, soon following each other without pause and with such speed that *we had to resort to abbreviations* in order to get them on paper." The paper would be that of their 1920 volume of poetry in prose, *The Magnetic Fields*, a work that Breton presented in 1922 as "the first application" of a new method of attending to an obscure yet "self-sufficient murmur."[16] He explains,

> I have never lost my conviction that nothing said or done is worthwhile outside obedience to that magic *dictation*. That is the secret of the irresistible attraction that certain individuals exert on us, whose only interest is to have once made themselves the echo of what we are tempted to consider the universal consciousness—or, if you prefer, to have gathered (without necessarily grasping their meaning) a few words fallen from "the mouth of shadows."[17]

Breton employs like terms in the first *Manifesto of Surrealism*, which appeared in 1924. Evoking the path that he followed on his voyage "back to the source of poetic imagination,"[18] he recalls "the more or less partial sentences" that he sought to catch on the edge of falling asleep. His diligence led to a "poetic adventure," granting him entry into the domain of the "image." Citing Pierre Reverdy, Breton defines such a representation as a "pure creation of the mind," born not by "comparison," but by the "juxtaposition of two more or less distinct realities." Their dynamic interaction exhibits a rule: "The more the relationship between the two juxtaposed realities is distant and true, the stronger the image will be—the greater its emotional power and poetic reality."[19] Readers may remember the arresting line by Lautréamont that Breton quotes in his 1935 lecture, "The Surrealist Situation of the Object," "as beautiful as the fortuitous meeting of a sewing machine and an umbrella on an operating table." That construction was to be a model for the "procedure which has been used, modified, and systematized by the Surrealists, both painters and poets, as they went along," leading to "one surprise after another since its discovery."[20] Yet in 1924, in the first of his manifestoes, Breton makes clear that it was through the studied attention to an almost indistinct murmur that he found his way back to such a "pure creation." The surrealistic project began with the catching of a *klēdōn*.

Breton recalls the scene of that inaugural event. "One evening," he writes,

> before I fell asleep, I perceived, so clearly articulated that it was impossible to change a word, but nonetheless removed from the sound of any voice, a rather strange phrase which came to me without any apparent relationship to the events in which, my consciousness agrees, I was then involved, a phrase which seemed to me insistent, a phrase, if I may be so bold, *which was knocking at the window.* I took cursory note of it and prepared to move when its organic character caught my attention. Actually, this phrase astonished me: unfortunately I cannot remember it exactly, but it was something like: "There is a man cut in two by the window" [*Il y a un homme coupé en deux par la fenêtre*], but there could be no question of ambiguity, accompanied as it was by the faint visual image of a man walking cut half way up by a window perpendicular to the axis of his body.[21]

In its articulation, the "rather strange phrase" that Breton perceived recalls the "sad words" that resound in the mind of the narrator of "The Demon of Analogy."[22] Unlike "The Penultimate / Is dead," however, "There is a man cut in two by the window" is not only "astonishing," but also uncertain, Breton having been unable to "remember it exactly." As if by accident, the sentence he heard was composed of twelve metrical syllables, as is the alexandrine. One might wager that it is therefore more complete a unit than the phrase that Mallarmé's narrator perceived. Yet "There is a man cut in two by the window" is also imperceptible as verse. Syntactically sufficient unto itself, abstracted from any relation to pauses that might follow or precede it, it is indistinguishable from prose. One might wager that it is in this sense more minimal than the declaration of the defunct Penultimate.

Nonetheless, Breton insists, "this phrase astonished me." "I realized that I was dealing with an image of a fairly rare sort, and all I could think of was to incorporate it into my material for poetic composition."[23] There is in fact an echo of the sentence in a passage of *The Magnetic Fields*, as Suzanne Guerlac has observed.[24] It occurs in lines that Breton himself reputedly considered to compose the book's "most beautiful passage."[25] The chapter rendered in English as "Two-Way Mirror" evokes a "window that cuts into our flesh":

> The window that cuts into our flesh opens out onto our heart. There you see an immense lake where at noon golden-brown dragonflies fragrant as peonies come to rest. What is this great tree where animals go to look at each other? For centuries we've been pouring out things for it to drink. Its gullet is drier than straw and ash has immense sediments in it. We laugh too, but you must not look for long without a telescope. Everyone can pass by here in this bloody hallway where our sins are hung, delicious paintings though dominated by gray.[26]

When he evokes the unexpected phrase about the window in the *Manifesto*, Breton notes that its sounding was "accompanied" by a "faint visual image." Had he been a painter, he adds, the "visual representation" might have made a stronger impression on him.[27] A writer, he relegated his reflections on its pictorial structure to a note. Hal Foster has specified the novelties of the composition that it implies: "This image suggests neither a descriptive mirror nor a narrative window, the familiar paradigms of postmedieval art, but a fantasmatic window, a 'purely interior model' in which the subject is somehow split positionally—at once inside and outside the scene—and physically—'cut in two.'"[28]

What matters most to Breton is the role that the phrase "knocking, so to speak, at the window" plays in illustrating a new "mode of pure expression": "SURREALISM," as he writes, adapting a word coined by Guillaume Apollinaire.[29] Alluding in "The Mediums Enter" to the "friends" with whom he collaborated, Breton introduces that novel expression in "a precise sense": "This is how we have agreed to designate a certain psychic automatism that corresponds rather well to the dream state, a state that it is currently very hard to delimit."[30] In the first *Manifesto*, Breton proposes a similar definition of "Surrealism," adding that "this word had no currency before we came along": "Psychic automatism in its pure state by which one proposes to express — verbally, by means of the written word, or in any other matter — the actual functioning of thought. Dictated by thought, in the absence of any control exercised by reason, exempt from any aesthetic or moral concern."[31] The first example of such a dictation was the haunting sentence that, detached from any discernible context, entered Breton's mind on the threshold of sleep.

"Psychic automatism" is a technical expression that derives from the lexicon of late nineteenth-century medicine. In that body of scientific literature, it points to a physical or mental act committed in the absence of any clear awareness. Pierre Janet dubs it, for that reason, an "inferior form of human activity" in his 1889 study of experimental psychology, *Psychic Automatism.*[32] Breton maintains a different position. Identifying "automatism" with the "actual functioning of thought," he extols such "physical or mental acts" precisely because of their apparent independence from "the control of reason." Following Valéry, who characterizes the "poet at work" as in a "state of waiting" for an unforeseeable word, Breton positions the surrealist writer before a spontaneous dictation that reveals a hitherto occluded reality. The power of such a dictation is so great, he writes in "The Mediums Enter," that he long expected nothing else to afford a greater revelation.[33] The partial phrase that, "removed from the sound of any voice," sounded as he fell asleep, being "without any apparent relationship to the events in which . . . I was then involved," becomes a model of the source from which "poetic imagination" is to flow.

Breton defines that model in terms that he draws from experimental psychology. Long after studying medicine and working as a psychiatric nurse in his youth, Breton remains an avid reader of diverse psychological authors, from Jean-Martin Charcot and Ambroise-Auguste Liébeault to Janet, William James, and Sigmund Freud. He is particularly impressed by the spiritualist branch of nineteenth-century psychology, as Jean Starobinski has shown.[34] In his 1933 essay "The Automatic Message," Breton expresses his admiration for both F. W. H. Myers, a founder of the British Society for Psychical Research in 1883, and Théodore Flournoy, who famously alleged that his patient, Hélène Smith, had received "automatic" dictations in Sanskrit, Arabic, and an unknown Martian language.[35] Breton holds that such authors have been unjustly neglected. "Chronologically before Freud," they uncovered "an entirely new and most fascinating world," enabling the study of "the precise constitution of the subliminal."[36]

Yet even as he draws on works such as Myers's *Human Personality and Its Survival of Bodily Death*, Breton takes pains to express an unequivocal rejection of all forms of spiritualism. He holds that there is no "communication" between the living and the dead, and the belief in a realm of souls beyond human beings is no more than superstition. As a Marxist, Breton champions a materialistic transmission. His "magic," therefore, is irreducibly profane. "For Breton, dictation does not come from the dark and solemn realm that Myers locates beyond death and the material ether," Starobinski writes. "It arises from the burning heart of life."[37] Despite his repeated evocations of mediumistic occurrences, Breton consistently distinguishes "spiritism" from "Surrealism," opposing the "lamentable jesting" of the first to the serious artistic project of the second.[38] In 1933, he explains that, for surrealists, the scraps of overheard discourse from which works may arise are attributable to no source beyond the mind. "The question of the exteriority . . . of the 'voice,'" he states, "cannot even arise."[39]

In an interview given to André Parinaud in 1952, Breton lingers on this point: "Everything that belonged to the domain of spiritualism and that, since the nineteenth century, has laid claim to the better part of the fantastical was always considered by us with great suspicion." Breton's surrealist project is to isolate an "automatic" dimension at the origin of literary creation without reducing it to merely psychomotoric activities, as Janet argued, or identifying it with any spiritual source.

Whether such an undertaking can be accomplished in his terms is doubtful. Several questions may be put to the theorist of materialistic automatism. Breton's account of the reception of "voices" implies that there exist criteria by which a process may be defined as "spontaneous" rather than contrived. Yet are such criteria accessible to someone other than the artist? Can they ever be as rigorously nonsubjective as Breton asserts? One may add that the opposition to which Breton appeals in distinguishing the deliberate and the automatic seems all too simple, if not simplistic. As Jean-Louis Houdebine remarks, for Breton, the unconscious is confined to "its manifestation as *dreaming*."[40] It is telling, in this sense, that Breton shows little interest in slips and parapraxes. His indifference appears to bespeak an avoidance of the real Freudian contributions to psychology—if not a desire, as Lacan would put it, to "reestablish order" by insisting on the separation of what Freud had shown to be often indistinct: dreaming and waking life, visionary intuition and rational reflection.[41] To this degree, Breton is captivated by a "dream" that he does not identify, as Lacan also suggests: "The dream consists in thinking that we wake up. We spend our time dreaming; we do not only dream when we are asleep. The unconscious amounts precisely to the hypothesis that it is not only when we are asleep that we dream."[42] Even as he evokes "powers of the mind of a unique variety and of vast implications," Breton, committed to their purely "automatic" nature, restrains their scope. They remain, for him, "subliminal" and "preconscious."[43]

In the same period in which Breton takes dictation to be the key to the surrealist project, an Irish writer assigns to "automatic" speech a different and no less crucial role in composition. In January 1926, barely a year after the appearance of the *Manifesto of Surrealism*, William Butler Yeats publishes the first edition of *A Vision*, whose sources, as he indicates, stretch back to 1917–1920.[44] "Grave and playful, poetic and geometric, concrete and abstract," as its most recent editors have it, Yeats's late work is "at once a work of theoretical history, an esoteric philosophy, an aesthetic symbology, a psychological scheme, and a sacred book."[45] Its four parts contain diverse elements, in prose and verse, attributed to two fictional contemporaries, Owen Aherne and Michael Robartes, and to their two distant sources, "Giraldus," a sixteenth-century Latin writer of *The Mirror of Angels and Men*, and "Kusta ben Luka," a "Christian philosopher of the Court of Harun al-Rachid," author of a lost treatise, the adaptation (as Robartes indicates) of a distant Syriac source inspired by a desert djinn.

Only in the dedication to the 1926 edition of *A Vision* does Yeats allude in passing to the manner by which he came to relate such materials to his readership. Here the poet recalls a conviction that he long shared with his oldest friends. In their youth, they distinguished themselves from their contemporaries by their "belief that truth cannot be discovered but may be revealed, and that if a man do not lose faith, and if he go through certain preparations, revelation will find him at the fitting moment."[46] Yeats evokes two examples of such propitious instants. According to a "learned brass-founder" whom he once knew, there is a time every year that brings with it a sudden and unexpected disclosure. Likewise, for "others," whom he does not name, a "messenger" from a higher source may be encountered in particularly modern circumstances, "in a railway train let us say."[47] In the opening of the 1926 edition of *A Vision*, Yeats does not voice explicit support for the belief in such revelations. He concedes that they seem unsatisfying to "our intellects," which are, as he acknowledges, "after all very modern." Yet he adds that such impressions recall "certain forgotten methods of meditation" developed long ago "to suspend the will" so "that the mind became automatic, a possible vehicle for spiritual beings."[48]

The exact meaning of those terms comes sharply into focus in 1929, when Yeats published a "A Packet for Ezra Pound," an essay that he included as the first chapter of the revised and final edition of *A Vision* in 1937.[49] The "Packet" contains an extraordinarily detailed account of the process by which a single mind, in his formulation, can become "automatic." "On the afternoon of October 24th 1917, four days after my marriage," Yeats writes,

> my wife surprised me by attempting automatic writing. What came in disjointed sentences, in almost illegible writing, was so exciting, sometimes so profound, that I persuaded her to give an hour or two day after day to the unknown writer, and after some half-dozen such hours offered to spend what remained of life explaining and piecing together those scattered sentences. "No," was the answer, "we have come to give you metaphors for poetry."[50]

Yeats does not identify the speaker of that peremptory declaration. He notes merely that "when the automatic writing began," he and his wife, Georgie Hyde Lees, were in England, "in a hotel on the edge of Ashdown Forest." When they returned to Ireland, the transmissions from those who came to bring Yeats "metaphors for poetry" continued, "my wife bored and fatigued by the almost daily task, and I thinking and talking of little else." In early 1919, W. B. and G. H. Yeats received news about the form of the revelations that they were receiving: "The communicator of the moment—they were constantly changed—said they would soon change the method from the written to the spoken word as that would fatigue her less." The alteration occurred in the United States, where Yeats was on a lecture tour. More precisely, it happened in the setting to which he had alluded in the first edition of *A Vision*: "in a railway train," "somewhere in Southern California," as W. B. and Georgie traveled in "one of those little sleeping compartments." A few minutes after she fell asleep, Georgie "began to talk in her sleep, and from that on almost all communications came that way." Invisible "teachers" sounded from her voice, speaking not "out of her sleep but as if from above it, as though it were a tide on which they floated."[51]

Yeats soon learned to expect such circumstantial revelations, preparing to have "pencil and paper ready" should a call become audible. He grew attentive to the "strange phenomena" that accompanied "the automatic writing and the speech during sleep." One evening, as Yeats was about to tell Georgie Hyde Lees "some story of a Russian mystic," "a sudden flash of light" fell between them, announcing the imminence of a communication.[52] Presages of automatic disclosures were also given in other sensory modalities, not least sound. "There was much whistling, generally as a warning that some communicator would come when my wife was asleep." Before long, the "servants at the other end of the house were disturbed by a 'whistling ghost.'" Yeats recalls being obliged to beg the voices "to choose some other sign." They proceeded to send "smells": sweet odors, floral fragrances, but also astringent and occasionally "bad smells." At the same time, the bodiless beings whom Yeats calls "communicators" announced their presence by "the ringing of a little bell," a "burst of music in the middle of the night," even an unexpected fragment of speech, "sometimes a word, sometimes a whole sentence."[53] Occasionally the visitations were attested in visions. "Sometimes my wife saw apparitions: before the birth of our son a great black bird, persons in clothes of the late sixteenth century and of the late seventeenth. There were still stranger phenomena," Yeats adds, "that I prefer to remain silent about for the present because they seemed so incredible that they need a long story and much discussion."[54] All led directly to *A Vision*.

Such circumstances of writing are in several respects unprecedented in modern literature. In their structure, they far exceed haunting by a single voice, such as that evoked by Mallarmé in "The Demon of Analogy." They also defy the logic of the poetic "rupture" that for Valéry marks the "appearance of the Voice" in the "interval" that separates speaking from hearing. Even the model of the "rather strange" and soundless phrase that came to Breton "without any apparent relationship to the events" in which he was "involved" seems insufficient to the dramaturgy of *A Vision*. It sets onstage a cast of characters far more complex than the "man cut in two" that surrealistic automatism implies. On a first level, as Catherine E. Paul and Margaret Mills Harper note, *A Vision* "is the product of two Yeatses": "the poet and the young Englishwoman who took his surname when she married him in the autumn of 1917."[55] Yet according to the narrative that accompanies the second edition, those two are merely the witnesses and representatives of countless other speaking beings: messengers, "Controls," "Guides," "Spirits," and "Daimons" whose communications the two Yeatses committed to writing and made known to the world.

While the "psychic automatism" often evoked by Breton is spontaneous and in principle infallible, the Yeatsian dictations soon reveal themselves to be anything but assured. Several factors could distort and corrupt the words and letters that W. B. and Georgie received. Although reminiscent in their form of the Muses, the beings who revealed themselves to the poet and his wife were far from omniscient. "Mouth-pieces and trumpets," they introduced themselves as mere intermediaries.[56] "They seemed ignorant of our surroundings," Yeats writes. Aware of the discourse exchanged by the couple without always understanding it, the messengers could easily be led astray. "Once when they had given their signal in a restaurant they explained that because we had spoken of a garden they had thought we were in it."[57] The "communicators" appear also to have been apt to become confused about their own disclosures. "They once told me not to speak of any part of the system," Yeats relates, "because if I did the people I talked to would talk to other people, and the communicators would mistake that misunderstanding for their own thought."[58] Most surprisingly, the "communicators" who came to convey "metaphors for poetry" were not alone among their kind. There were also others, as he learned to his dismay.

The communicators warned Yeats of beings as malicious as they were beneficent. "Because they must, as they explained, soon finish, others whom they named Frustrators attempted to confuse us or waste time."[59] The poet gleaned little more: "Who these Frustrators were or why they acted so was never adequately explained."[60] Yet he had no doubt as to their effects on the texts that he is charged to prepare. "The automatic script would deteriorate, grow sentimental or confused, and when I pointed this out the communicator would say, 'From such and such an hour, on such and such a day, all is frustration.' I would spread out the script and he would cross all out back to the answer that began it, but had I not divined frustration he would have said nothing." Yeats recalls a particularly cruel act of deceit once committed at his expense. Six months before he finished receiving an elaborate "communication," it seemed to him that he perceived a clear command: "Do not write anything down, for when all is finished I will dictate a summary." The voice then continued "almost nightly for I think three months, and at last I said, 'Let me make notes, I cannot keep it all in my head.'" The communicator was startled: "He was disturbed to find that I had written nothing down, and when I told him of the voice, said it was frustration and that he could not summarise."[61]

It has been asserted that *A Vision* constitutes "the greatest of all Surrealist experiments."[62] The claim is suggestive but hardly holds in any exact sense. Yeats shared Breton's interest in the "experimental psychology" of the kind promoted by the Society of Psychical Research, Yeats himself being one of its members from 1913 to 1928.[63] Yet the two poets' epistemological and aesthetic assumptions could scarcely have been more distant. Breton looked to "psychic automatism" as a means of liberation from the constraints of what he called "disciplined thinking": from "the order of *logic* (the strictest rationalism, which ensures that nothing not stamped by its cares be accepted)," as he once explained, "from the order of *morals* (in the form of sexual and social taboos); finally, from the order of *taste*, upheld by the spurious conventions of the 'right tone,' which are perhaps the worst of all."[64] By contrast, Yeats deduced from his experience of automatic script and speech the existence of an anarchic multitude of speaking beings that revealed to him the most outlandish of poetics, histories, and cosmologies. Yet despite the differences separating their first principles and their instantiations, the surrealistic and the Yeatsian automatisms would in time converge.

In the second half of the twentieth century, a poet in the United States became the architect of an unexpected synthesis. Jack Spicer drew from the twin models of dictation to which Breton and Yeats appealed the elements of a single, original theory of poetic composition. By a curious coincidence, he presented it on the day on which W. B. Yeats would have turned one hundred, as Spicer himself noted in passing at the beginning of the lecture that he held in Vancouver on June 13, 1965. He began by telling his audience that over the course of the three "lecture/readings" that he would be giving, he would read some of his work and discuss "the problems that have to do with poets." He went on to state that the first among them in order of importance is "the problem of dictation." "Now, tonight is a rather interesting time to discuss poetic dictation," he declared, adding, "It's Yeats's birthday. . . . And Yeats is probably the first modern who took the idea of dictation seriously."[65] Alluding to "A Packet for Ezra Pound," Spicer recalled the experiences that W. B. Yeats and his wife had undergone while in California, even as he gave to them a precise, if fantastical, setting: "He was on a train back in, I guess it was 1918. The train was, oddly enough, going through San Bernardino to Los Angeles when his wife Georgie suddenly began to have trances, and spooks came to her."[66] Spicer imagined that Yeats initially assumed "Georgie was doing all of this to divert him" during the long and unpleasant ride "across the country on the Southern Pacific." "He finally decided he'd ask a question or two of the spooks as Georgie was in her trance. And he asked a rather good question. He said, 'What are you here for?' And the spooks replied, 'We're here to give metaphors for your poetry.'"[67]

In that claim, Spicer discerned a fundamental shift in the conception of the poetic event, "the first thing since Blake," in his words, "on the business of taking poetry as coming from the outside rather than from the inside." In contrast to the writers of the nineteenth century, who believed the poet to be "a beautiful machine which manufactured the current for itself, and did everything for itself"—a "machine," one may add, such as that by which "feeling confesses itself to itself in moments of solitude"—Yeats presented himself in a position of structural removal from his source: for the modern Irish poet, there was "something from the Outside coming in."[68] Spicer shares this view, while rejecting the idea that what "comes in" are "metaphors for poetry." To this degree, he sees himself as agreeing with "people as opposite in their own ways as, say, Eliot on the one hand and Duncan on the other." For a given poet, he explains, exteriority may assume various forms: "the subconscious," "the racial memory," or "the this or the that." Spicer dismisses the question of its exact identification, maintaining that "the source is unimportant."[69] He retains only the theses of exteriority and transmission at the origin of poetic composition: "something . . . comes from the Outside."

To bring that passage into focus, Spicer turns to what he calls "the analogy of the medium."[70] Yeats, as he recalls, evoked it at great length. Yet as Spicer and his audience were no less aware, a similar likeness also played a role in surrealism, an artistic movement that Spicer repeatedly mentions by name in his 1960 collection *The Heads of the Town Up to the Aether*.[71] In his lectures, Spicer alludes in particular to Jean Cocteau's 1950 film *Orphée*, in which the "analogy with the medium" takes on a specific technical form: it appears as a car radio. "Dictation" appears, then, as a modality of transmission. In the film, Orpheus, a contemporary poet, takes notes from a device over which mysterious signals are intermittently emitted. The automobile in question belongs to a princess who, following the sudden death of a poet named Cégeste, beckons to Orpheus to join her in her car. Once Orpheus climbs in, she issues a curt command to her chauffeur: "The radio!" The driver turns the radio knob. Static, a short-wave signal, and a Morse code sound. A voice then makes itself heard: "Silence moves faster when it's going backwards. Three times. Silence moves faster when it's going backward. Three times."[72]

It is the first of a series of transmissions that capture Orpheus's attention. The second is no less enigmatic. Like the phrases recorded by Breton, it consists in the insistent repetition of an image: "Just as one glass of water lights up the world . . . twice . . . . Listen carefully. Just one glass of water lights up the world. Twice . . . . Just one glass of water lights up the world."[73] Orpheus is immediately fascinated by the voice that sounds in such transmissions. He shuts himself up inside the car, even when it is stationary, leaning close to its radio, pen and paper in hand lest he miss the precious messages that it may relay. He is not discouraged by the apparent obscurity of "what comes in." "I repeat," he hears in the subsequent transmission: "2294 twice. 7777 twice. 3398 three times. I repeat. 2294 twice. 7777 twice. 3398 three times."[74] Later in the film, the viewer is granted a vision of the source of the broadcast. It is Cégeste, the dead poet, who sits at a table before a transmitter, turning its knobs, reciting his compositions into its microphone. "The black crepe of the little widows is a real sunshine meal. Twice. The black crepe of little widows is a real sunshine meal. Twice. I repeat. The black crepe of little widows. . . . "[75]

It is clear that such scenes of reading and listening are fantastical allegories of dictation. In the notes to his screenplay, Cocteau indicates that they provide an account of the origins of poetry, even as they illustrate a possibility of its distortion. Introducing the film, Cocteau writes, "The theme is inspiration. One should not say inspiration but rather expiration. What is called inspiration comes from us, from our night and not from the outside, from another, so to speak divine night. It is when Orpheus renounces his own message and willingly receives messages from the outside that everything is spoiled [*tout se gâte*]."[76] Yet Spicer, in knowledge or in ignorance, reads the film against its author's wish. He takes the radio transmissions to illustrate a theory of dictation stranger than any that Cocteau himself envisaged.

In *Orphée*, a living poet receives communications from a man who differs from him by being dead. In the account that Spicer proposes, "the Outside" is far less easily imagined. Developing his own metaphor, "just to be funny," Spicer identifies the source of poetry in the figure of an exteriority at once fantastical and contemporary: beings of the planet Mars, who do not know a poet's language—and who, one may also infer, do not know any human language. "Dictation" consequently takes on the structure of a visitation both extraterrestrial and infantile. As Spicer explains to his audience, "It's as if a Martian comes into a room with children's blocks with A, B, C, D, E which are in English and he tries to convey a message."[77] Likewise, Spicer reasons, the "Martians" take hold of the nonlinguistic "building blocks" with which the poet tends to work: "your memories, your language, all of these other things which are yours which they rearrange to try to say something they want to say."[78] Prompted to arrange the blocks in an unfamiliar and perhaps unintelligible sequence, the poet will be inclined to defy his source. Spicer imagines him objecting: "Oh no, Mr. Martian, it doesn't go this way. That spelling p-r-y-d-x-l doesn't make any sense in English at all. We'll change it around."[79] The comprehensible poem that results from such a rearrangement, then, will be syntactically and lexically correct as far as the poet's own language is concerned, but it will have distorted the unearthly text of which it was to have been the transcription. On account of the poet's sophisticated meddling, the final poem will have become the anagrammatic rearrangement of a Martian message.

Like Yeats, Spicer holds that what "comes in from the Outside" may be a communication. Yet unlike his forerunner, he doubts that what the poet takes down is intended for its writer. As he remarks in the discussion following his first lecture, "I don't think the messages are for the poet any more than a radio program is for the radio set."[80] In the most provocative moments of his lectures, Spicer goes so far as to indicate that what comes in from the Outside may in truth admit of no human addressee whatsoever. In his revision of the Yeatsian account of "spooks" and Cocteau's Orphic transmissions, Spicer suggests that through poetry, unknown "communicators" seek to reach other communicators of their own kind, the poet being no more than their medium. What is "automatic," from such a perspective, is the relay of a signifying sequence whose exact meaning the terrestrial receiver cannot know. "Just to make it even funnier," Spicer adds in the discussion following his lecture, "suppose Martians were trying to communicate. They couldn't really say '*pnixlz* on the *prazl*' and so forth and so on. They would have to use your own memories of what your things were rather than theirs."[81] Poetic dictation, then, would be the process by which some chain of meaningful units, such as words, figures, or numbers, attests to an unknown being—a "Martian"—in a pattern that only a fellow alien might decipher.

Such a supposition entails the extreme extenuation of the notion of "communication." The transmission from the Outside becomes a series as ciphered as an unknown code: "I repeat. 2294 twice. 8888 twice. 3398 three times. . . ." As if by means of a "spooky" intuition into the theory of the signifier that Jacques Lacan developed in the years in which Spicer held his lectures, in such a doctrine of dictation, "a signifier represents a subject for another signifier."[82] Poets are summoned to receive and to transmit a series of words, images, and memories whose sense they cannot grasp, their elements of articulation having values solely in a system of signs that eludes them. Recalling Valéry, one might say that in such circumstances, the ear speaks in a tongue that the mouth cannot interpret, but to which it must nonetheless attend.

Such is the unearthly response that Spicer proposes to the old question renewed by Mill: "What is Poetry?" It is tempting to discern in it an echo of an ancient understanding of the inspired bard, such as that presented in Plato's *Ion*.[83] That dialogue records the infelicitous exchange between Socrates and the professional reciter of Homeric verse known in classical Athens as a "rhapsode." With his customary irreverence, Socrates tells Ion in the dialogue that far from possessing any knowledge, a performer is as witless as a poet. The bard, the rhapsode, and the audience all share in a single "magnetic chain." Moved by the power of the Muse, they are inspired to the degree to which, touched by a divine force, they are "out of their right minds" (*ekphrōnes*).[84] Yet the resemblance between the Platonic and the Spicerian doctrines is deceptive. Spicer's poet is neither *aōidos* nor *rhapsōdos*, neither "poet" nor "reciter." He is more akin to Cocteau's Orpheus, seated mutely, if attentively, before the car radio. He is closer still to that sensitive "thing" by which Dante defined the poet of the "sweet new style": "a thing that, / when Love inspires, goes notating" (*un che, quando / Amor mi spira, vo notando*).[85] Yet in this resolutely postmodernist account of poetic "communication," inspiration is starkly depleted. For Spicer, no Muse stands behind the poet; even such lesser mythographic figures as Poe's imp and Mallarmé's demon fade from view. As a being into which a signal is transmitted, the poet becomes a radio, as Spicer suggests in a poem, "Sporting Life," while mentioning a difference: "radios don't develop scar-tissue."[86]

That metamorphosis is of consequence for the theory of poetry and the auditory dimension that it implies. Straining to receive and to relate the most inscrutable of dictations, poets appear in a new guise. They become constitutionally uncomprehending overhearers: the mediums of *klēdones* that they cannot gloss, if not at the risk of mistaking the signals that they receive, like children rearranging blocks meticulously ordered by mute, yet intentionally acting extraterrestrials. Once inscrutable Martians are put in the place of the "feeling" that Mill took to "confess itself to itself in moments of solitude," once utterly inhuman sources have usurped the roles of dead poets, spirits, communicators, and even "Frustrators," dictation is shorn of its traditional magic. Yet in the absence of deities and divinatory arts and in the lack of rituals other than those of profane practices of composition, something, Spicer suggests, still "comes in." Word or gibberish, a revelation or a distorted anagram, it is by necessity equivocal. Whether it is an omen, a slip, or an epiphany must therefore remain uncertain. If it comes from elsewhere, however, it can bear the unexpected, and if it surprises those who chance upon it, it may also challenge them to make sense of its fleeting presence, demanding to be heard.

CHAPTER THIRTEEN

The Inside of Stumbling

In one of the short texts that compose his 1928 book, *One-Way Street*, "Madame Ariane: Second Courtyard on the Left," Walter Benjamin suggests that omens occur with the frequency and regularity that mark the undular patterns known to modern natural science: "Portents, presentiments, signals pass day and night through our organism like wave impulses" (*Vorzeichen, Ahnungen, Signale gehen ja Tag und Nacht durch unsern Organismus wie Wellenstöße*).[1] Implicitly warning against the "Madame Ariane" of his text's title, Benjamin expresses doubts, however, as to the benefits to be gained from consulting self-styled experts in such matters. It is not that he judges their knowledge to be illusory, unreliable, or even merely limited. His claim is rather that the reliance on an interpreter diminishes the inquirer's own capacities. "He who asks fortune-tellers the future unwittingly forfeits an inner intimation of coming events that is a thousand times more exact than anything they may say," Benjamin writes. "He is impelled by inertia, rather than by curiosity, and nothing is more unlike the submissive apathy with which he hears his fate revealed than the alert dexterity with which the man of courage lays hands on the future. For presence of mind is an extract of the future, and precise awareness of the present moment is more decisive than foreknowledge of the most distant events."[2]

To consult a soothsayer, Benjamin suggests, is to put oneself in a position of expectation rather than to face the moment. It is to fail to act. Yet a less obvious antithesis also informs his discussion. Faced with the "portents, presentiments, signals" that "pass through our organism like wave impulses," there are two methods that may be adopted: "To interpret them or to use them: that is the question. The two are irreconcilable. Cowardice and apathy counsel the former, lucidity and freedom the latter." When we take a portent, a presentiment, or a signal as material to be "mediated by word or image," we forgo access its promise: "We read it. But now it is too late." Once "unlived life is handed over to cards, spirits, stars," it is alienated: "squandered, misused, and returned to us disfigured." What might have been encountered immediately in the motions of an agile body vanishes in decipherment. Interpretation comes at a price. "We do not go unpunished for cheating the body of its power to meet the fates on its own ground and triumph."[3]

Benjamin takes the people of distant ages to have been familiar with surer means of receiving portents. In "primitive epochs," presages were perceived in such a way that "the threatening future" made itself present in a "fulfilled now." From the archive of those distant times, Benjamin extracts a single example, which he presents as a "telepathic miracle." Several sources relate that after vowing to subjugate Carthage to Rome, Publius Cornelius Scipio reached the country's shores, disembarked, and suffered a mishap; he stumbled and fell to the ground. That slip might have counted as the most unpropitious of events. Even as he faltered, however, the commander spread his arms wide and cried out "the watchword of victory," *Teneo te, Terra Africana!*, "I hold you, African land!"[4] Without a moment's pause, without reflection and without advice from any reader in the sense of coincidence, Scipio thereby appropriated a portent and decided on its sense. He did so by exploiting an ambiguity of Latin vocabulary. In the classical language, the phrase *teneo te* means "I hold you or I grasp you," but by extension, it also signifies "I have you or I possess you."[5] With his exclamation, Scipio remarked upon the fact that stumbling, he had steadied himself by taking hold of the ground. At the same time, he affirmed the "wave impulse" that passed through him, transforming a portent of disaster into a propitious sign. Binding the event "bodily to the moment," Scipio made of himself "the factotum of his body."[6] He turned his slip into the augur of his victory.

That each instant may be charged with a mass of subtle signals is a thesis with which the most materialist of modern theorists of the mind would doubtless have agreed. At the opening of his 1901 *Psychopathology of Everyday Life*, Freud quotes two lines of Goethe's *Faust II* in which the magician remarks that insubstantial beings are everywhere perceptible: "So many ghostly beings haunt the air / That none can tell how to avoid them there" (*Nun ist die Luft von solchem Spuk so voll, / Daß niemand weiß, wie er ihn meiden soll*).[7] In this early book, Freud sets out to study the nature and effects of those ubiquitous apparitions, showing how, in daily life, even what seems the least of ordinary events may harbor a hidden meaning. At times, Freud argues, what would seem a chance occurrence is in truth the effect of necessity; coincidence can turn out, upon analysis, to be the result of law-bound processes. "Certain inadequacies of our psychic performance," Freud writes in his conclusion, "and certain actions performed apparently unintentionally prove, when the methods of psychoanalytic investigation are applied to them, to be well motivated and determined by factors of which the conscious mind is unaware."[8]

Among such seemingly random "actions" (*Verrichtungen*), Freud classes a diverse collection of imprecisions, bungled deeds, and misguided beliefs, or, as his extended subtitle has it, "Forgetfulness, Slips of the Tongue, Inadvertent Actions, Superstitions and Mistakes" (*Vergessen, Versprechen, Vergreifen, Aberglaube und Irrtum*). Among their number, Freud accords a particular importance to unanticipated events of discourse: words misspoken, matters misstated, and expressions that, despite a speaker's best intentions, come to be formulated in apparently misleading ways. Attending carefully to such linguistic mishaps, Freud develops a theory of the revelatory force of unanticipated words. His book, for this reason, may be read as a modern inquiry into augurs, *klēdones*, and variously ominous and propitious scraps of speech.

According to *The Psychopathology of Everyday Life*, three conditions must be satisfied for an apparent accident of speaking to constitute as a revelatory a slip, parapraxis, or, to evoke Freud's German term of preference, "faulty performance" (*Fehlleistung*). First, the seeming error needs to imply no more than a slight deviation from the domain of habit. Negatively stated, "it must not go beyond a certain point, a point that is established by our judgment and complies with our ideas of 'what is in the range of normality.'" Second, it must constitute "a brief and temporary disturbance." "We must have carried out the same action correctly before," Freud stipulates, "or believe ourselves capable of carrying it out more correctly at any time. If someone else corrects our slip, we must immediately acknowledge the justice of the correction and the malfunctioning of our own psyche." Finally, when the mistake is observed by those who make it, it must seem to them to no more than coincidence: "If we notice the slip at all, we must not recognize any motivation for it in ourselves; instead, we must be tempted to put it down to 'carelessness' or 'chance.'"[9] Minor, fleeting, and seemingly fortuitous, the Freudian mishap possesses the consistency proper to the discursive presages of earlier ages. Like the *klēdōn* and the *omen*, the *egirrû*, and the circumstantial *bat qol*, like "proverbs" and the fortuitous and portentous dicta of the Renaissance, the "faulty performances" on which Freud focuses his gaze are among the least substantial of discernible phenomena. Yet they all bear precious tidings that can be gleaned by no other means.

Some of the examples discussed in *The Psychopathology of Everyday Life* are still familiar today. There are the words of the erstwhile president of the Austrian Parliament when "he *opened* a session by announcing: 'Members of this House! I confirm the presence of such-and-such a number of gentlemen, and hereby declare this session *closed*.'"[10] There is the case of a Viennese psychoanalyst who systematically confused the names of two his patients from Trieste, Mr. Askoli and Mr. Peloni, although he knew which name belonged to which.[11] There is the patient who, mistaking one foreign phrase for another, claimed she only ever saw her uncle *in flagranti*, before adding, "What I meant to say was *en passant*."[12] There is the young man who addressed a lady in the street with the words: "If you will allow me, Fräulein, I would like to *begleit-digen* you," forging a hitherto unknown German expression by crossing the German verbs *begleiten*, "to accompany," and *beleidigen*, "to insult."[13] Freud also recalls how Dr. A. A. Brill of New York, the first English translator of his book, once assured one of his friends that he could treat a certain patient satisfactorily. "I believe in time I can remove all his symptoms by psycho-analysis," he declared, "because it is a durable case." He meant, of course, that it was "curable."[14] Freud argues that such "slips of the tongue" are far from reducible to simple accidents. When correctly analyzed, each reveals itself, rather, to be the result of a psychic process whose rules may be distinctly articulated.

Freud draws the examples of such mistakes from diverse sources, evoking the words and deeds of acquaintances, patients, colleagues, and followers. Yet in *The Psychopathology of Everyday Life*, his entire discussion of "faulty performance" begins with a chapter, "The Forgetting of Proper Names," that concerns an event to which he alone bears witness. That fact points to what may be considered the first novelty in the psychoanalytic inquiry into revelatory events of speaking. The presages of Greek poetry, the omens known to the Romans, and the fortuitously heard prophecies of the ancient Near East are all related, as a rule, by persons other than those who perceive them. The reader will recall that with Augustine, a change is detectable. The theologian perceives the presage of his conversion himself, and it is he who relates it to his readers. Centuries later, Chrétien sets before his audience a scene of a riddled revelation no less novel: without any apparent motivation, Perceval "guesses" or "divines" his real name as if by chance and immediately accepts it. Such diversely introspective modern persons as the

Cartesian dreamer, the haunted narrators of Poe and Mallarmé, Valéry, Breton, and Yeats are surprised by revelatory words and phrases formed on their own lips. Freud carries the interiorization of augurs to a more extreme point, even as he aims to account in scientific terms for seemingly accidental disclosures in speech.

For Freud, slips are at once objects of the new science that is psychoanalysis and empirical events that are discernible solely through a study of subjective experience. Evoking grammatical terms, one might therefore state that Freudian parapraxes cannot be adequately defined with reference to "third persons." To grasp them, it is necessary to attend to "first persons," examining the position of those who live through such seemingly fortuitous occurrences. In this regard, Freud implicitly breaks with a long-standing principle in scientific method that demands that the observer be and remain external to the matter under investigation. The psychoanalytic assumption is that the parapraxis is an event explicable solely from the perspective of the conscious and unconscious processes of a single being.

Yet the opening case discussed in *The Psychopathology of Everyday Life* is also instructive for a second reason. As the term *Fehlleistung* indicates, Freud's interest in verbal disclosures concerns acts that do not occur as they would appear to have been intended. In the book's opening example, the revelatory word is therefore not the one that is correctly uttered, but the one that, despite the speaker's wishes, remains unspoken even as its absence is intensely felt. That incident provides Freud with the paradigmatic case of "the forgetting of proper names" *(das Vergessen der Eigennamen)*, which illustrates several general principles. First, "the person concerned does not merely *forget*, but also *remembers incorrectly.* " Second, "as he tries to remember the names that elude him other names—*substitute names* [*Ersatznamen*]—come into his mind, and although they are immediately recognized as incorrect, they persist in forcing themselves upon him." Third, "the process that ought to lead to the correct reproduction of the name he is looking for has, so to speak, become *displaced* [*hat sich gleichsam* verschoben], thus leading to the incorrect substitute."[15] Finally, according to Freud's basic "presupposition" (*Voraussetzung*), such a "displacement" (*Verschiebung*), however disordered it may appear, is not a matter of "psychic arbitrariness" (*psychicher Willkür*). It follows regular paths.

The conditions of the first mishap evoked in *The Psychopathology of Everyday Life* are well known, but they must be recalled if the details of Freud's analysis are to be brought into focus. One day during the summer of 1898, Freud was traveling by carriage from "Ragusa in Dalmatia," now known as Dubrovnik in Croatia, to a nearby town in Bosnia and Herzegovina. He was in the company of a stranger, a lawyer from Berlin, with whom he began to speak. When the conversation turned to Italy and its sights, it occurred to Freud to ask his fellow traveler if he had ever been to Orvieto. Freud himself had visited the *duomo* of the Umbrian city the previous year, in September 1897, and had been deeply impressed by it. During the ride in 1898, Freud wondered aloud, as he wrote in his book, whether his interlocutor had been to Orvieto and "seen the famous frescoes of *** there."[16] Those elliptical asterisks mark the place of the proper name that Freud, on that day, to his astonishment and dismay, could not recall. The name "Signorelli" had suddenly escaped him and, despite his best efforts, he could not succeed in retrieving it.

Searching for the absent word, Freud recalls, "the names of two other painters, *Botticelli* and *Boltraffio*, sprang to mind, and were immediately and firmly rejected by my judgment as wrong." Such a judgment indicated that his apparent "forgetting" was in fact an "incorrect remembering," of which he was himself also dimly aware. Although he could not fully identify the name "Signorelli," Freud retained sufficient knowledge of the appellation to reject the two "substitute names" that appeared in its absence. Soon thereafter Freud had an occasion to observe further evidence of his partial, yet persistent grasp of the elusive word. When he learned the painter's name from "another source" a few days later, Freud "recognized it instantly and without hesitation." Such a spontaneous "recognition," he reasons, necessarily supposed a prior and enduring cognition. He concludes that it was only for a brief but painful moment that his access to the word was barred.

The analysis of the mishap became the subject of an article, "On the Psychical Mechanism of Forgetfulness," that Freud published in 1898 in the *Monatsschrift für Psychiatrie und Neurologie* a few months after returning from his voyage. In *The Psychopathology of Everyday Life*, Freud briefly recalls the findings that he presented in his essay. He begins by excluding the most obvious explanations for the disturbance. "The reason for my forgetting the name *Signorelli* is not to be sought in any special feature of the name itself, or in the psychological nature of the context in which it occurred." He was well acquainted with the name that escaped him—every bit as well acquainted as he was with the first "substitute name" (*Ersatzname*) that came to his mind when he failed to summon it, "Botticelli." Moreover, "Signorelli" was even more familiar to Freud than the second nominal replacement, "Boltraffio," that occurred to him once he set "Botticelli" aside. Neither the properties of the name "Signorelli" nor the conditions of its absence from the conversation with the stranger, therefore, sufficed to account for his transient confusion.

The happening could be explained only by returning to an earlier point in the carriage trip, this slip being an instance of a particular kind of perturbation: "a case of *disturbance of the new subject* [that is, the works in Orvieto] *by its predecessor*."[17] Before beginning to discuss Italy and its sights, Freud and his interlocutor had exchanged a few words on Bosnia and Herzegovina, where they found themselves. Freud related to the other gentleman something he had heard from a colleague "who practiced medicine among these people, and who said they usually show both complete confidence in their doctors and a total resignation to fate." When a physician tells this people that nothing can be done to treat a patient, they reply: "Sir [*Herr*], What can I say? I know that if he could have lived, then you would have saved him!"[18]

As he quoted that response, Freud thought of a second utterance that, in his mind, was "closely associated" with the first, but that he did not think it appropriate to divulge. "These Bosnian Turks set a very high value on sexual pleasure," he found himself remembering, "and if anything impairs their sexual faculties they fall into despair, a despair which is in curious contrast to their resignation in the face of death. One of my colleague's patients once said to him: 'Well, you know, Sir [*Herr*], without all that, life's not worth living.'"[19] No sooner had Freud thought of that line, however, than his attention wandered further from the conversation, continuing his "train of thought along those lines, lines that could have led to the subject of 'death and sexuality.'" Freud was at the time still suffering the "after-effect" of painful news that he had received during a brief visit to the town of Trafoi in South Tyrol. He explains, "A patient over whom I had taken a great deal of trouble had committed suicide because of an incurable sexual disorder."[20]

Those circumstances set the stage for the vanishing of the word "Signorelli," a vanishing that consisted only superficially in a disturbance of the faculty of memory. Freud's thesis is that in truth not forgetfulness, but rather "repression" (*Verdrängung*) lay at the source of the event. He explains,

> I . . . wanted to forget something; I had *repressed* something. What I wanted to forget was not in fact the name of the painter of the masterpiece in Orvieto, but the other subject, the one I did want to forget, contrived to associate itself with his name, so that my act of volition failed to find its target, and I *unintentionally* forgot one idea while I *intentionally* meant to forget the other [*ich* das eine wider Willen *vergaß, während ich* das andere mit Absicht *vergessen wollte*]. My aversion for remembering was directed against the content of one idea; my inability to remember emerged in another context.[21]

Freud draws the crucial evidence for that thesis from the two incorrect names, "Botticelli" and "Boltraffio," that came to his mind as he sought "Signorelli." More exactly, he finds his proof in the linguistic relations that unite the substitutes and that relate them to the true name that they fail to represent. Even as he struggled to conjure the word "Signorelli," Freud performed an unconscious operation on its phonetic form. He bisected it, breaking the first two syllables (*Signor-*) from the last (*-elli*). Freud retained *-elli* and discarded *Signor*. He therefore thought of "Botticelli." That erroneous name then suggested to him the second, "Boltraffio," which began with the same consonant and vowel. Freud notes that the phonetic sequence *Bo-* also alluded to the situation in which he found himself: *Bo-* echoed the sound at the start of the country name "Bosnia." At the same time, a different word and word part lay hidden in the train of association that led him from "Signorelli" to "Botticelli" and "Boltraffio." While the *Bo-* of "Bosnia" is voiced in both "Botticelli" and "Boltraffio," the corresponding element in "Herzegovina" remains unspoken. Its first syllable, *Her-*, is in sound identical with a German expression, *Herr*, "Sir." That is the term of address used for the physician in the two sayings that Freud was pondering, sayings that, combined, evoked "the subject of 'death and sexuality'": "Sir [*Herr*], What can I say?" and "Well, you know, Sir [*Herr*], without all that, life's not worth living!"

Yet Freud notes other associations in the sequence of words and word parts. In its German meaning, *Herr*, "Sir," corresponds to the Italian word *Signor*, which is the portion of "Signorelli" that he could not call to mind. Replacing "Signorelli" with "Botticelli," Freud thus tacitly suppressed the element of the first painter's name that was synonymous with the German "Sir" (*Herr*). In this way, he enabled the passage from "Signorelli" to "Botticelli" and "Boltraffio." Yet a particular phonetic detail in "Boltraffio" also seemed to him noteworthy. The "*-traffio*" of "Boltraffio" recalls "Trafoi," the name of the village where Freud had received the news of his patient's suicide. Moving from "Signorelli" to "Botticelli" and from "Botticelli" to "Boltraffio," Freud, for all these reasons, only seemed to associate Italian names randomly. In his inability to recall the first name that he sought, his mind followed a path of displacements and substitutions that pointed to the "subject of 'death and sexuality'" that he wished not to consider.

To exhibit the order that obtained in his apparent act of mental confusion, Freud reprints in his book a diagram that he devised for his 1898 article. The "schema," as he calls it, transcribes each of the words that played a role in his faulty performance, isolating their signifying segments and indicating the links that bind them (see figs. 3 and 4). From top to bottom, the reader passes from the names that he sought and spoke aloud ("Signorelli" — "Botticelli" — "Boltraffio"), to the immediate circumstance of their utterance ("Herzegovina" and "Bosnia"), and finally to the "repressed thoughts" that were obliquely expressed in their disorder, "Subject of Death and Sexuality." From bottom to top and from right to left, the reader moves from the representations that Freud unwittingly repressed to the words that he uttered. What appears in the diagram is thus the "very striking" (*sehr auffällig*) "manner of connection" (*Art der Verknüpfung*) between the sought name and the "repressed subject matter" (*verdrängtes Thema*). That "manner of connection" occurred "as if there had been a displacement of meaning through the linked names of 'Herzegovina and Bosnia,' but disregarding the sense and the acoustic demarcation of the syllables. In the process, therefore, the names are treated like the written characters of a sentence that is to be turned into a rebus or pictorial puzzle."[22]

Critics have noted that there are subtle differences between the presentation of the incident that Freud proposes in his 1898 paper and the study of it that he offers in the first chapter of *The Psychopathology of Everyday Life*.[23] There is also a third account of the happening that dates to an earlier point. It is contained in the letter that Freud sends Wilhelm Fließ on his return from his travels along the Adriatic coast on September 22, 1898. Its terms diverge slightly from both his two later accounts.[24] Despite their variations, however, the three Freudian treatments respect the same basic principles of analysis. Although Freud writes of "repressed thoughts" identifiable with the "content of an idea," what undergoes distortion

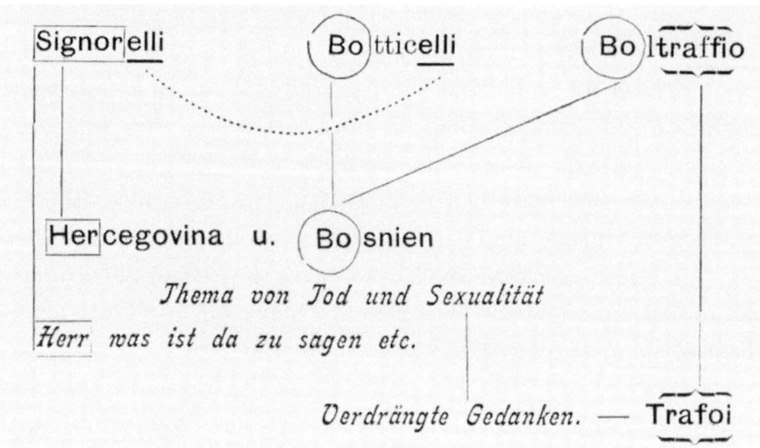

Figure 3. Freud, "Signorelli" diagram from "Zum psychischen Mechanismus der Vergesslichkeit" (1898).

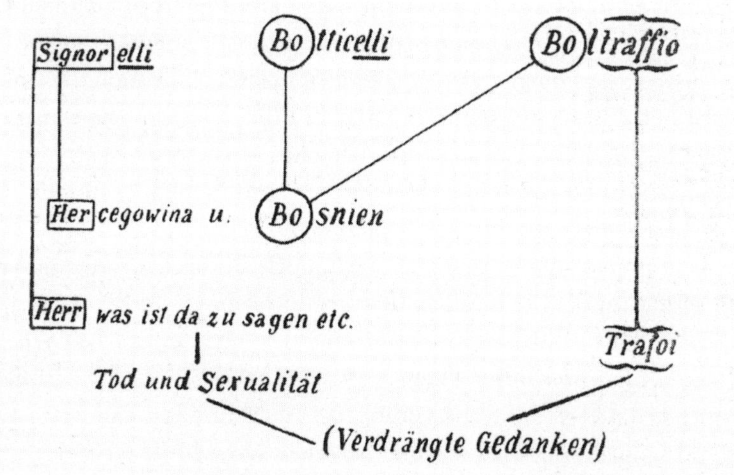

Figure 4. Freud, "Signorelli" diagram from *Zur Psychopathologie des Alltagsleben* (1901).

in his failure to remember is, in each case, one kind of word: a foreign name, that is, "Signorelli." Freud consistently treats that lexical unit, moreover, as consisting of more minimal grammatical elements: syllables, consonants, vowels, and letters. What appears at first glance as an act of faulty recollection shows itself, upon examination, to be a process in which those units are permuted according to discernible patterns.

Half a century after Freud, Jacques Lacan argued that those patterns illustrate the two fundamental varieties of linguistic relation identified by Roman Jakobson. Developing Saussure's science of language, Jakobson distinguished between "two basic modes of arrangement used in verbal behavior, *selection* and *combination*."[25] "Selection" supposes a relationship of substitution between terms, an example being the relationship linking one word (for example, "mistake") to another word of a like sense (such as "error"). In rhetorical usage, the principle of such "selection" is at work in the variety of replacement of one term by another commonly known as "metaphor." Its principle is similarity or synonymy. "Combination," by contrast, consists in the relationship of a word to those that precede and follow it. The rules of syntax to a large degree dictate the possibilities of such combination. In the field of rhetorical figures, such an association is illustrated by metonymy, where one term stands for another on the basis of some real connection. In the metonymic expression "a thousand sails," for instance, "sails" takes the place of "ships" because the first term points to an object that is linked to the second, sails being parts of ships.

In the volumes of his *Seminar* as in the essays of his *Écrits*, Lacan maintains that while knowing nothing of Jakobson's opposition or its Saussurean source, Freud proposes an analogous formal opposition between such types of relation. In *The Interpretation of Dreams*, Freud distinguishes between the unconscious process of "compression" or "condensation" (*Verdichtung*), on the one hand, and "displacement" (*Verschiebung*), on the other.[26] For Lacan, who comments on these terms in the vocabulary of structuralist linguistics, condensation "is the superimposed structure of signifiers in which metaphor finds its field"; it corresponds, in Freudian parlance, to Jakobsonian "selection." Displacement, by contrast, consists in the "transfer of signification that metonymy displays," being of the order of "association."[27] When Lacan argues that for Freud, "the unconscious is structured like a language," he means that in its characteristic formations, such as dreams, jokes, and slips, both types of relationship are discernible. As Lacan explains in *Seminar 5*, "the compositional laws of the unconscious . . . exactly match some of the most fundamental laws of the composition of discourse."[28]

Freud's analysis of the forgetting of "Signorelli" illustrates that "matching," for it suggests that in his faulty performance, disturbances of both selection and combination — in other words, both metaphor and metonymy, or condensation and displacement — are at work. The link between *Signor* and *Herr* is involves the order of "selection," *Signor* being the word in Italian that corresponds in meaning to *Herr*. At the same time, for Freud, the word part *Signor-* in the name "Signorelli" stands in a relation of obvious similarity to the *Her-* of "Herzegovina"; hence his unthinking substitution of the first for the second. In such cases, words replace each other on the basis of likeness. In the terms of *The Interpretation of Dreams*, a process of "condensation" is thus operative. Mechanisms of "displacement," however, are no less evident in Freud's attempts to summon the forgotten name. "Botticelli" is composed according to the form of "Signorelli," the link between them being the persistent part *-elli*. So, too, the last three syllables of "Boltraffio" suggest "Trafoi." Such associations illustrate the patterns of metonymy, in which words stand for each other on the basis of a real bond.[29]

Bringing linguistic categories to bear on Freud's theory, Lacan renewed a link between psychoanalysis and the science of language that Freud himself had established. In *The Psychopathology of Everyday Life*, Freud draws heavily on the work of an Austrian linguist, Rudolf Meringer, who, with a psychologist colleague, Karl Meyer, published a book in 1895 titled *Misspeaking and Misreading: A*

Psychologico-Linguistic Study.[30] As Freud notes, Meringer and Meyer marshalled copious evidence to show that to show that "language errors" (*Sprachfehler*) are of several kinds. In "reversals," the order of sequences is inverted. A speaker will say "Milo of Venus," meaning "Venus of Milo." In "anticipations," a word is misspoken in such a way as to resemble one uttered after it. Someone may say, "*Es war mir auf der Schwest . . . auf der Brust so schwer*," ("I felt it weigh heavily on my breast"), replacing *Brust* ("breast"), with the inexistent word *Schwest*, which suggests both *schwer* ("heavy") and *Schwester* ("sister"). In "echoes or resonances," different expressions are superimposed: someone will say, "*Ich fordere Sie auf, auf das Wohl unseres Chefs aufzustossen*" ("I will ask you to belch to the health of our leader"), replacing *anzustossen* ("to toast") with *aufzustossen* ("to belch"). "In "contaminations," phrases are erroneously merged: combining the sentence "*Er setzt sich einen Kopf auf*" ("He stands up on the back of his head"), meaning "he is headstrong," and "He gets up on his hind legs," someone may say, "*Er setzt sich auf den Hinterkopf*" ("He gets up on his hind head").[31]

Distinguishing such categories, Meringer and Meyer sought to establish the conditions in which errors of speaking and reading are made, defining rules for the occurrence of linguistic mistakes. That Freud took their research seriously may be inferred from his evocations of their typology and his repeated citations of their examples in his book. Yet he could not consider their psycholinguistic account of such mistakes to be exhaustive. As his analysis of the Signorelli incident suggests, for Freud, the parapraxis is, in each case, the result of a unique process of repression. Rules may well be discernible in the conditions in which words are misspoken or misread. Ultimately, however, the sense of an apparent mishap is identifiable solely with reference to the mind of the speaker.

The authors of *Misspeaking and Misreading* appear to have understood immediately that Freud was contesting the basis of their research, even if he treated it respectfully. In works published in 1908, 1911, and 1923, Meringer responded to the psychoanalyst in a different tone, dismissing Freud's book as "a scholarly bluff" (*ein wissenschaftlicher Bluff*).[32] Evoking the Signorelli case in his final appraisal, he raises many objections. He judges it highly improbable that the word *Herr* in the sentence that Freud did not utter ("Well, you know, Sir [*Herr*], without all that, life's not worth living!") could have been associated with the *Signor-* of "Signorelli" because in such a phrase, *Herr* "is an utterly irrelevant word, a vocative devoid of emphasis, a mere filler." Meringer takes the alleged link between *Herr* and "Herzegovina" to be even weaker, "absolutely implausible." Foreigners in the region might pronounce the country name by accenting the penultimate syllable, "Herzegovína." Locals would stress the last syllable, "Herzegoviná." In no case, however, would *Her-* stand out as a distinct syllable. And even if one were to grant Freud's argument, Meringer adds, the explanation would still be "impossible." "The two words *Herr* and *Herzegovina* were also present in the sentence that Freud did relate and that he did not pass over in silence ('*Sir*, what is there to say?'); therefore, if there had been any connection [of *Her-*] to *Signor, Signorelli*, those words would have contributed to facilitating the memory of the artist's name, not to blocking it."

Expressly foregoing Freudian "imagining" and "fantasizing" (*Phantasterei*), Meringer holds that a simpler fact explains the entire incident. He observes that the words "Signorelli," "Botticelli," and "Boltraffio" all consist of four syllables. That suffices to account for the confusion, especially if one also grants that such names belong to a category of words susceptible to being forgotten. Proper names stand outside regular linguistic groupings. For this reason, they are poorly "grounded in the mind." Meringer thus concludes that Freud has posed the entire problem incorrectly. "We should not be asking ourselves: *Why do we forget something?* But rather: *Why do we remember it?*"[33] Not only does Freud, according to Meringer, fail to offer an adequate account of the case with which he begins his book. He also mistakes its nature. What seems to Freud an incident in need of explanation is in fact the illustration of a rule. For

Meringer, recourse to a psychological cause is therefore superfluous and therefore may be set aside.

In the second half of the twentieth century, Meringer's argument against the Freudian analysis of the "psychopathology of everyday life" was to be pursued in further detail and with greater sophistication by Sebastiano Timpanaro. Like Meringer, Timpanaro was a specialist in the analysis of linguistic faults, but whereas Freud's contemporary took as his objects "misspeaking and misreading," Timpanaro, trained as a scholar of Greek and Roman manuscripts, drew the tools of his appraisal from philology. That scribal errors might be understood as the textual equivalents of "pathologies" was a fact that had been long granted by scholars of the discipline. As early as 1867, the French classicist Louis Havet published a *Textbook of Verbal Criticism* in which he defined his project as a scholarly treatment for "the pathology of texts."[34] Yet it was only with Timpanaro's 1974 book, *The Freudian Slip: Psychoanalysis and Textual Criticism*, that the convergence of Freudian theory and philology became brightly visible.

Timpanaro opened his study by noting that however different their aims and methods,

> psychoanalysts and textual critics have to a large extent studied the same phenomenon.... The task of the textual critic is to inquire into the origin of alterations undergone by a text in the course of its successive transcriptions, so as to be able to correct those errors persuasively or to establish which of two or more variants deriving from different sources is the original, or approximates most closely to it.[35]

Some textual "pathologies" result from scribal misunderstanding or a conscious wish to revise and improve the work being transcribed. As Timpanaro hastened to explain, however, a vast majority of inconsistencies in transcription and quotation are "errors due to distraction," errors "to which anyone transcribing or citing a text may be subject — whether scholar or lay man, mediaeval monk or modern typist or student."[36] Timpanaro anticipated an obvious objection: "a mistake made in copying a text that one has before one's eyes is very different from a mistake made in attempting to remember a word or phrase registered a long time before." Yet the customary conditions of transcription render that distinction less certain than might at first glance appear. "It has long been established that a copyist, whether ancient or modern, does not as a rule transcribe a text word for word, still less letter for letter . . . but reads a more or less lengthy section of it and then, without looking back at the original at each point, 'writes it down from memory.'" A copyist is then liable to commit slips of exactly the kind that attracted Freud's attention.

Just as Meringer and Meyer distinguished the varieties of speech and reading errors, Timpanaro classified writing mistakes into types. When a word has been substituted by another, "whose meaning is actually or apparently the same, but whose usage is more familiar to the copyist," the philologist speaks of "banalization."[37] Timpanaro also grants the textual equivalents of Meringer and Meyer's errors of "anticipation" while generalizing their scope. In errors influenced by "context," a writer distorts a detail of a passage under the influence of what follows or precedes it. Furthermore, there are blunders of "self-dictation": "Textual criticism teaches us that one of the most frequent categories of errors is a confusion between words of an equal number of syllables which are also connected by a marked phonic similarity, or even better, by assonance or rhyme."[38] "Polar errors," by contrast, involve the substitution of words of an antithetical meaning. "Haplography" and "haplology" consist in the uniting of double letters or sounds. When it seems that a copyist has jumped from one group of letters to an adjacent one on the basis of a similarity of sounds (mistaking, for instance, *teleologico* for *teologico*), philologists speak of a "leap from the same to the same" (*un saut du même au même*).[39] "Dipthography," finally, is the common error of improperly repeating certain sections of words or entire sequences of words.[40]

That such categories are well illustrated by the cases evoked by Freud is all too evident. Restricting oneself to the forgetting of the name "Signorelli," one may note the presence of several of the kinds of error known to philologists. Timpanaro remarks that the substitution of "Botticelli" for "Signorelli" seems an obvious case of "banalization," the author of *Spring* and *The Birth of Venus* being better-known to people of Freud's culture than the master of Orvieto.[41] For the purposes of argument, however, Timpanaro grants Freud his claim that the two Italian masters were equally well known to him. Timpanaro passes, then, to consider the second "substitute name." In moving from "Botticelli" to "Boltraffio," Freud replaces a well-known name with a lesser-known one, as Freud himself concedes. That substitution provides a perfect illustration of the "unsuccessful attempt at correction" that is known in textual scholarship as "disimprovement" or *Schlimmverbesserung*.[42] The emendation goes awry because Freud, like a copyist aware that he has made an error but unable to identify it, fails to locate the linguistic segment that stands in need of rectification. Taking his own mistake to have concerned the ending of "Botticelli" rather than its beginning, Freud crosses out the authentic portion of the word (*-elli*), even has he retains the corrupt one (*Bo-*). At the same time, like Meringer before him, Timpanaro also suggests that the entire incident admits of a simpler explanation: mistaking names of an equal number of syllables is an obvious case of faulty "self-dictation."[43]

In evoking such categories, Timpanaro adopts a clear method. He accounts for cases by referring them to rules that are by definition general. The philologist reasons that just as the utterances that are made in a certain language respect a certain grammar, the disturbances that can affect them also exhibit patterns. To analyze an error is to identify the type of confusion that it illustrates. Yet Timpanaro, like Meringer, also holds a second conviction that is no less consequential. It is the belief that when a condition for a mistake has been found, there is no need to search for any further "cause."

Freud's argument and method would oblige him to differ on

both counts. To those who aim to dissolve the particular mishap in a generality of a rule, he might respond that it is the individual occurrence that matters most: not what renders it an instance of a general phenomenon but what constitutes it as an irreducible event for a unique mind. Confronted by the second argument, he could respond by recalling a basic thesis in his theory of scientific explanation. To grant that there are conditions in which mistakes are made and to observe that one of such conditions is discernible where an error has been committed is not to "account" for that error unless one presumes that for each phenomenon, there is but a single explanation. That presumption, however, is one that Freud refuses to make.

Starting with the *Studies of Hysteria* that he publishes in 1895 with Josef Breuer, Freud evokes the principle of "causal overdetermination," which, following Wilhelm Wundt, he also dubs the "principle of the complication of causes."[44] "According to this principle," Adolf Grünbaum writes, "clinical phenomena are normally attributable to a conjunction and/or temporal succession of causes, each of which is only a partial cause, precisely because—at best—these causally relevant factors are only jointly rather than singly causally sufficient for the production of the given clinical phenomenon."[45] Defending himself from the linguists, Freud might recall that principle. He could grant Timpanaro all his points about his own act of forgetting. Nonetheless, the "principle of the complication of causes" entails that beyond any single general condition for his mistake, there may also be another cause. Freud himself would be the sole witness to it, being the only one to have experienced the slip and therefore to have been a position to attest to the fact that it was a significant event. He alone was aware of the name that escaped him, feeling both the distress occasioned by the momentary confusion and the relief that followed when he finally identified the term that had eluded him. No matter the general features that it may exhibit, the Freudian slip is, in its happening, each time singular. Like the Roman *omen*, its occurrence puts a unique question to a single individual.

The fact that *The Psychopathology of Everyday Life* opens with the forgetting of a proper name suggests that such an act is exemplary for verbal mishaps, but also for more. In the order of Freud's book, the momentary lapse announces screen memories, slips of the tongue and pen, inadvertent deeds, symptomatic acts, and combined mistakes. In the following chapters, Freud proceeds to argue that such events all involve disclosures whose seemingly casual form betrays the regular processes of displacement and substitution. Yet a fundamental difference separates such happenings in the modern mind from the oracular events known to earlier ages as *klēdones*, omens, or presages. It may be recalled that to convey an unexpected truth, a *klēdōn* needs be not only heard, but also extracted from its context, for it is only in being wrenched from its immediate setting that it conveys an unanticipated truth. The slip bears a different relation to the conditions of its utterance, being evidently at odds with the situation in which it comes to pass. In the carriage ride in Bosnia and Herzegovina, for example, neither "Botticelli" nor "Boltraffio" belonged to the series of words that Freud meant to utter. Both names were, as Freud immediately recognized, out of place. The misspoken word, the misplaced action, or the omitted deed all disturb the regular course of discourse and action according to such a form. The incongruity of such slips with respect to the conditions of their occurrence may be minimal and momentary. It nonetheless suffices to invest them with a special power. In short, while the *klēdōn* is a word that, to be oracular, must be withdrawn from the conditions of its occurrence, the Freudian slip implies a symmetrically opposed configuration: a context portentous in its undeniable disorder.

Yet there is more that is new in the psychoanalytic doctrine of sudden verbal disclosures. In according the perspective of the first person a crucial importance, in focusing with a new intensity on actions that go awry, in identifying the revelatory word where it fails to be uttered, Freud's theory accords unexpected speech events an unprecedented importance. Psychoanalysis puts such occurrences at the center of a new theory of revelatory phenomena. The contrast with earlier models is sharp. In ancient Greece, the *klēdōn* constitutes an unusual variety of portent whose interpretation eludes the general opposition between the "natural" and "technical" types of divination. Likewise, in Rome, the *omen* is a special presage, treated in passing by Cicero in his rewriting of the Greek bipartition in Latin terms. For the ancient Mesopotamians and Jews, acoustical presages constitute one of many circumstances from which conclusions may be drawn. In the medieval and modern periods, verbal presages continue to occupy such a stable, yet minor, if not marginal position. They are present in the depiction of mantic arts and revelations, yet they remain in the shadow of other portents. Even in surrealism, it is contingency rather than circumstantial discourse in itself that occupies center stage. If unexpectedly heard words attract attention in an author such as Breton, it is because they illustrate a general rule concerning "objective chance." Freud sets out on an untrodden path when he takes the apparent coincidences of discourse to illustrate the fundamental principles of mental life. Faulty linguistic performances, for him, indicate that where agents speak otherwise than they intend to do, an order holds. Words remain "well motivated and determined," the impression of chance being due to the fact that the major factors are ones of which "the mind is unaware." The parapraxis, in this sense, points to what Freud calls "determinism": the fully defined nature of mental life, in which accidents are illusory and all events "have their sense."[46]

From the slightest of deviations, from the most minimal of imprecisions, from even the seemingly blank event that is the encounter with an unsaid word, Freud thus infers a far-reaching consequence: where the psyche is concerned, there are no accidents. Yet he seeks to do more than to explain the mechanism by which "certain actions performed apparently unintentionally prove, when the methods of psychoanalytic investigation are applied to them, to be well motivated and determined by factors of which the conscious mind is unaware." Freud also aims to explain why such events in the past were taken to be significant. For this reason, despite the novelties of his analysis, he takes his own project also to be in a continuity with earlier practices. In certain passages of his writings, he even goes so far as to present the science of psychoanalysis as the modern form of an activity as old as human history: that of inferring sense from coincidence.

In the *Introductory Lectures on Psycho-Analysis* that he publishes in 1916–1917, Freud begins his presentation with an account of parapraxes, certain phenomena "which are very common and very familiar but which have been very little examined, and which, since they can be observed in any healthy person, have nothing to do with illnesses."[47] After begging his audience not to "under-estimate small indications," which can point to the track "of something bigger," he offers a survey of slips of the tongue in daily life and in literary works. He proceeds to argue that what seem to be "chance events" are "serious mental acts" arising from "the concurrent action—or perhaps rather, the mutually opposing action—of two different intentions" (*durch das Zusammenwirken—vielleicht besser: Gegeneinanderwirken zweier verschiedener Absichten*).[48] Proposing a new order of demonstration with respect to *The Psychopathology of Everyday Life*, Freud considers the forgetting of names and intentions before reaching "accumulated and combined parapraxes," "the finest flower of their kind," and bungled deeds.

Fifteen years after *The Psychopathology of Everyday Life*, Freud refrains from evoking his own faulty performances. By this point in his career, he is in possession of a vast archive of examples of apparently inscrutable mistakes that, upon study, disclose hidden meanings. He gives the following summary enumeration:

> A. Maeder tells of a lady who, on the eve of her wedding had forgotten to try on her wedding-dress and, to her dressmaker's despair, only remembered it late in the evening. He connects this forgetfulness with the fact that she was soon divorced from her husband.—I know a lady now divorced from her

> husband, who in managing her money affairs frequently signed documents in her maiden name, many years before she in fact resumed it.—I know of other women who have lost their wedding-rings during the honeymoon, and I know too that the history of their marriages has given a sense to the accident. And now here is one more glaring example, but with a happier ending. The story is told of a famous German chemist that his marriage did not take place, because he forgot the hour of his wedding and went to the laboratory instead of the to the church. He was wise enough to be satisfied with a single attempt and, at an advanced age, died unmarried.[49]

To the reader versed in ancient letters, such a collection of cases exhibits a familiar form. As Freud himself is the first to observe, it resembles nothing so much as a catalog of portents of the kind that Cicero might have offered in *On Divination*. "The idea may possibly have occurred to you," he wagers to his audience, "that in these examples, parapraxes have taken the place of the omens or auguries of the ancients [*daß in diesen Beispielen die Fehlleistungen an die Stelle der Omina oder Vorzeichen der Alten getreten sind*]. And indeed some omens were nothing else than parapraxes, as, for instance, when someone stumbled or fell down."[50] Psychoanalysis and the doctrine of divination thus converge: coincidence, augurs, and slips can hardly be told apart. Freudian theory and practice appear as scientific mantic arts.

Yet the inventor of psychoanalysis is too lucid a rationalist to assume that in all cases, modern science is opposable to the reflection implicit in religious or even superstitious practice. In the final chapter of *The Psychopathology of Everyday Life*, Freud makes clear that like "superstitious persons," he concedes that accidents can betray meanings. The "chance" (*Zufall*) that he considers to be "real," however, is external to the psyche. He expressly denies the basic operation of "superstition," which extends "a long way even into the most modern forms of religion" and which consists in "projecting psychology into the outside world." "I may believe in outer (real) chance," he asserts, "but not in fortuitous inner (psychic) contingency" (*ich glaube zwar an äußeren [realen] Zufall, aber nicht an innere [psychische] Zufälligkeit*).[51] Whereas superstitious people look outside themselves for means to understand what befalls them, Freud seeks a key within himself; whereas they "interpret chance" (*deutet den Zufall*) by means of external occurrences (*Geschehen*), Freud deduces it from thoughts (*Gedanken*). Yet Freud also concedes that in earlier periods, "superstition" had a role to play. "Superstition seems misplaced only in our modern, scientific but by no means complete view of the world," he grants. "As the world appeared to pre-scientific ages and peoples, superstition was legitimate and logical. Relatively speaking, the Roman who abandoned some important enterprise if he saw birds flying in the wrong formation was right; he was acting logically in line with his assumptions."[52]

Yet Freud also goes further. Not only may a practice such as augury be reasonably consistent with a premodern vision of the world. In some cases, the application of a divinatory technique yields insights that surpass the understanding of the people of the "scientific age." Freud explains, continuing with his example of "the Roman":

> If he abstained from the enterprise because he had stumbled on the threshold of his door (*un Romain retournerait* [a Roman would turn back], as they say), he was definitely superior to us unbelievers, and a better psychologist than we are, despite our current efforts. His stumbling showed him that some doubt existed, something in him was working against his enterprise, and its power could impair his own ability to carry out his intention just as he was on the point of performing it. One can be sure of success only if all mental forces are united in making for the desired aim.[53]

In its general outline, the possibility that Freud evokes is certainly intelligible. Psychoanalysis teaches that a "superstitious" attention to stumbling may be more rational than the enlightened dismissal of such accidents. In its detail, however, Freud's example is obscure. The citation of a French phrase in the German text—

"(*un Romain retournerait*, [a Roman would turn back], as they say)"—raises difficulties that the German and English editions of the text have failed to register. To what source is Freud alluding in his passing parenthetical allusion to what "they say"? Whose French words is he quoting? Who is the indefinite "Roman" who "would turn back," and what stumbling is at issue?

These questions appear to have eluded study, yet they may be resolved. Freud seems to be alluding to an episode in a book with which his readers may have been familiar, Walter Scott's 1827 *Life of Napoleon* as it was rendered into French in 1829. The incident involves the most audacious and the most disastrous of the emperor's military undertakings: the attempted conquest of Russia. In 1812, when the Grande Armée had drawn close to the river Niemen, Napoleon ordered the "overwhelming masses" of his soldiers to proceed from three positions. The King of Westphalia and his forces marched upon Grodno; the Viceroy of Italy advanced against Pilony; and the emperor and his men approached "a point called Nagaraiski, three leagues beyond Kowno," known today as Kaunas in Lithuania. The English text reads as follows: "When the head of Napoleon's columns reached the river which rolled silently along under cover of immense forests on the Russian side, he advanced in person to reconnoitre the banks, when his horse stumbled and threw him. 'A bad omen,' said a voice, but whether it was that of the emperor or one of his suite, could not be distinguished; 'a Roman would return.'"[54]

Scott's source may have been the much-read 1824 chronicle of the invasion by the Count de Ségur, who accompanied Napoleon on his Russian campaign, which relates the same fall and sudden sounding of a sentence.[55] Yet the wording of the French phrase in *The Psychopathology of Everyday Life* indicates that it is to Scott's biography that Freud is alluding. The French translation of the work contains the exact expression that he quotes: "'A bad omen!' said a voice. A Roman would turn back'" (*Mauvais présage, s'écria une voix; un Romain retournerait sur ses pas*).[56]

What in Freud's book may seem a reference to the superstitious customs of "pre-scientific ages" points, therefore, to an incident that is anything but premodern. Quoting Scott without naming him, Freud repeats that "a Roman would turn back" to underline the fact that the nineteenth-century "Emperor of the French" did no such thing. By his act, Napoleon thereby entered into the ranks of a long line of misfortunate invaders. One thinks of Crassus, who, according to Cicero, may or may not have perceived the fateful words *Cauneas, Cauneas!* shouted by a fruit seller as he and his soldiers departed to wage an unjust war against the Parthians. Yet Scott, by contrast, gives no clear indication that the modern sovereign may have failed to hear the words that sounded as he fell. The *Life* even suggests that the voice that sounded could have been his own. Considering the sudden fall, one may also think of Scipio, as Benjamin recalls him, who stumbled as he set foot on a territory that he meant to conquer. Unlike that commander, however, Scott's Napoleon makes nothing of his mishap. Undaunted by the sudden motion of his steed, untouched by the warning uttered as he falls, he proceeds on his campaign to suffer a spectacular defeat.

Yet there is still more than is new in the scene of this modern military mishap. Not only does Napoleon tumble to the ground and infer nothing from the accident. The event is complicated by the fact that the two "bad presages" that are the stumble and the fall are followed by the sounding of a voice. It is an unanticipated auditory portent: a fragment of speech in which a summary judgment makes itself heard. Might it be a modern *klēdōn*? No divinity seems to stand behind the oracular monition. Yet it also cannot be attributed with any certainty to any human being present at the scene. The *Life* is on this point explicit: whether the "voice" was that of the sovereign or a member of his army could not be determined. The words "A bad omen! A Roman would turn back" may be read as revelatory or as redundant. In any case, their source eludes identification. The unexpected utterance also raises the question of a psychic phenomenon that could not have failed to attract Freud's attention. Might the sound of the warning have been a delusion, or more exactly what nineteenth-century medicine called an "auditory hallucination"? Such a possibility raises another. If the utterance was a hallucination rather than a physical event susceptible to perception, a further query can hardly be avoided: Who was its subject?

The fact that the writer presents the voice as either "that of the emperor or one of his suite" is suggestive and implies two accounts of the discursive event. According to the first, it was the rider who grasped the meaning of his fall. According to the second, it was some unidentified observer who inferred it. An indication of the event followed by a remark about the customs of an ancient people, the words "A bad omen! A Roman would turn back" could be read in both ways. Either a first person or a third person names the event, declaring it to be portentous. In that ambiguity, however, a difference that is crucial to the Freudian treatment of the "faulty performance" gives way. It is impossible to distinguish the mishap as it is experienced by its subject from the mishap as it is merely observed by some third party. At the same time, the terms of the Benjaminian opposition between "interpretation" and "use" are also shaken. The words "A bad omen! A Roman would turn back" are a commentary on the event. They may reveal its sense. No "fortune-teller," however, states them, and they hardly arrive "too late." They seem simultaneous with the occurrence to which they refer. In short, the scene of this happening appears to admit of neither "interpretation" nor "use." "Miracles" — whether "telepathic" or otherwise — are as absent as the gods. That Napoleon consults no "Madame Ariane" is all too clear, yet nothing in his *Life* gives suggests that in falling, he succeeded in laying his "hands on the future." The calamitous aftermath of the event strongly suggests that he did not.

In the passage in which he elliptically recalls this scene, Freud lauds the people of "pre-scientific ages" for their sensibility to seemingly insignificant phenomena, chiding the moderns for their unfounded faith in their own rationality. Alluding to the hapless commander, however, Freud loses no time on reproaches or justifications. He merely draws an abbreviated outline. Like the linguists whom he challenges, he limits himself in this case to pointing to some rules legible in mishaps. A major event may occur in what seems no more than a slip; a "determinate" process can show itself in an apparent accident; errors and mistakes, one must conclude, demand the greatest of attention. At each point in his argument, Freud renews an ancient sensibility, even as he proposes his new doctrine of the unconscious. After the chroniclers of *klēdones* and the exponents of variously modern presages, Freud sets forth a new theory of the hidden sense that comes to legibility in apparent coincidence. One might call it a logic of stumbling. Yet the best frame is the doubtless one that its author devises. The psychopathology of everyday life is an elucidation of the many "ghostly beings" that haunt the air. As Dr. Faust knew well, no one can avoid them there.

CHAPTER FOURTEEN

Truth Details

In one of the early evocations of the "distant voice" machine known as the telephone, the narrator of Proust's *In Search of Lost Time* hears the sound of his lover's voice and catches more. Indistinct noises crowd in on the words that he perceives, and it is they that are to him most precious. Returning from an evening at the Princess of Guermantes's, he expected to find Albertine in his apartment. Learning that she has not arrived, he feels the first pangs of a painful longing and begins to wonder "where, and with whom" she may be. It is too late to go out in search of her. To make his room "a little more attractive" in case she should still come, he takes out a turquoise-studded book cover given to him by the love of his youth, Gilberte, putting it on the bedside table. It is the prettiest of his possessions, he muses, and likely to please Albertine. Then he turns the telephone receptor's switch, establishing a direct connexion between the post office and his bedroom. "So that it might not disturb my parents," he explains, "a whirring noise had been substituted for the bell. I did not move, for fear of not hearing it." He recalls the scene in the second part of *Sodom and Gomorrah*: "I settled down . . . to listen, to suffer; for when we are waiting, from the ear which takes in sounds to the mind which dissects and analyzes them, and from the mind to the heart to which it transmits its results, the double journey is so rapid that we cannot even perceive its duration, and imagine that we have been listening directly with our heart."[1]

When the narrator suddenly hears the "top-like whirr of the telephone," "like the fluttering scarf of the shepherd's pipe in *Tristan*," he springs to the instrument:

> It was Albertine. "I'm not disturbing you, ringing you up at this hour?" "Not at all . . . " I said, restraining my joy, for her remark about the lateness of the hour was doubtless meant as an apology for coming round in a moment, so late, and not that she was not coming. "Are you coming round?" I asked in a tone of indifference. "Well . . . no, unless you absolutely must see me."[2]

The narrator is of course feigning. To him "it was essential that she should come." "But," he adds, "I did not tell her so at first; now that we were in communication, I said to myself that I could always oblige her at the last moment either to come to me or to let me rush round to her." She explains that she is near where she lives and is therefore far from him. "I felt sure that she was lying, and now, in my fury, it was from a desire not so much to see her as to inconvenience her that I was determined to make her come." More immediately, however, his attention is drawn to a different matter. "Where was she?"

The narrator intuits that he will glean the answer to that question solely by listening attentively—not to her words, but to the "other sounds" that accompany them:

> With her words were blended other sounds [*À ses paroles se mêlaient d'autres sons*]: a cyclist's horn, a woman's voice singing, a brass band in the distance, rang out as distinctly as the beloved voice, as though to show me that it was indeed Albertine in her actual surroundings who was beside me at that moment, like a clod of earth together with which we have carried away all the grass that was growing from it. The same noises [*les mêmes bruits*] that I heard were striking her ear also, and were distracting her attention: true-to-life details, extraneous to the subject, valueless in themselves, all the more necessary to our perception of the miracle for what it was; simple,

> charming features descriptive of some Parisian street, bitter, cruel features, too, of some unknown festivity which, after she had come away from *Phèdre*, had prevented Albertine from coming to me.[3]

Thanks to technology, the narrator is virtually transported to the unknown place of his beloved. There, unseeing, he is all ears. What "distracts" Albertine from the conversation is what is to him most worthy of his attention. The sonorous circumstances that are "extraneous to the subject" and "valueless in themselves" are not merely "true-to-life details," as the English translation has it. More literally, they are for him "truth details" (*détails de verité*): ordinary indices capable of disclosing to him the "miraculous" evidence that he seeks.

In the long "apprenticeship" on which the narrator embarks in the remembered past of his book, attention to such details plays a major role.[4] It allows him to catch the meaning of utterances that, without corresponding to what they state, provide him with the most crucial of revelations.[5] To perceive such disclosures, however, the narrator must learn to listen closely to the multiform "accidents" of speech: coincidences, errors, inconsistencies, and unexpected lies.[6] His illuminations come to him not from what Albertine explicitly tells him, but from what, by design or chance, she either withholds or distorts. He soon grasps that her "words" (*paroles*) will not satisfy him in themselves. They "never contained an atom of truth." The "truth" was, rather,

> something she let slip only in spite of herself, as a result of a sudden mixing together in her mind of the facts which she had previously been determined to conceal with the belief that one had got wind of them (*la verité, elle ne la laissait échapper que malgré elle, comme un brusque mélange qui se faisait en elle, entre les faits qu'elle était jusque-là décidée à cacher et la croyance qu'on en avait eu connaissance*).[7]

Like other experts in the errors of speaking, the narrator distinguishes among the conditions in which such slips occur. He treats circumstantial utterances as sequences of signs capable of sustaining a subtle analysis. Even in the absence of literal writing, "reading," in his word, proves essential. It submits its sequenced object to several varieties of rearrangement. At some times, it reverses the flow of what it catches; at other times, it consists in a more complex reordering of letters. "Sometimes the script from which I deciphered Albertine's lies, without being ideographic, needed simply to be read backwards," the narrator recalls,

> Thus this evening she had tossed at me casually the message, intended to pass almost unnoticed: "I may go and see the Verdurins tomorrow. I don't really know whether I will go, I don't particularly want to." A childish anagram of the admission: "I shall go to the Verdurins' tomorrow, it's absolutely certain, I attach the utmost importance to it." This apparent hesitation indicated a firm resolution and was intended to diminish the importance of the visit while informing me of it. Albertine always adopted a dubitative tone for irrevocable decisions.[8]

At other moments, the crucial evidence would be discernible in logical inconsistencies. "Strange how the things that are probably most insignificant suddenly assume an extraordinary value when a person whom we love (or who has lacked only this duplicity to make us love her) conceals them from us!" the narrator exclaims a few pages later in *The Captive*.[9] Meaning to assure "us that such and such a man is no more to her than a friend," she may shatter us "by informing us — something we never suspected — that he has been her friend." When she admits that he would indeed have wished her to be more and that she declined his advances, a doubt is born from a moment in her argument: "there is wanting, between the different things that she said to us, that logical and necessary connexion which, more than the facts related, is the sign of truth."[10] Yet the lack of "that logical and necessary connection" may also be perceptible in grammar. Albertine, for one, "employed, not by way of stylistic refinement, but in order to correct her imprudences, abrupt breaches of syntax not unlike that figure which the grammarians call anacoluthon or some such name," the narrator remarks. "Having allowed herself, while discussing women, to say: 'I remember, the other day, I . . . ,' she would suddenly, after a 'semi-quaver rest,' change the 'I' to a 'she': it was something that she had witnessed as an innocent spectator, not a thing that she herself had done."[11] An extreme syntactic convolution — "I remember that I — she . . . " — would then be the surest seal of truth.

Like the author of *The Psychopathology of Everyday Life*, Proust's narrator takes such mishaps to be more consequential than accurate statements of fact. Imprecisions, errors, and lies, for him, can all shelter an unwilled truth. To perceive it, words and gestures must be grasped as the elements of what Freud termed a "rebus or pictorial puzzle." If the narrator's experience teaches him anything, it is that what seems to be a series of signifying sounds may consist of various symbols, some of which resemble those integrated into the "ideograms" that he evokes. "I had in the course of my life followed a progression which was the opposite of that adopted by peoples who make use of phonetic writing only after having considered the characters as a set of symbols," he explains:

> Having, for so many years, looked for the real life and thought of other people only in the direct statements about them which they supplied me with of their own free will, in the absence of these I had come to attach importance, on the contrary, only to disclosures that are not a rational and analytical expression of the truth; the words themselves did not enlighten me unless they were interpreted in the same way as a rush of blood to the cheeks of a person who is embarrassed, or as a sudden silence.[12]

Such nonrational, nonanalytical "disclosures" take time to occur. The narrator suggests that they also require an interval to be combined and fully parsed. Yet the moment of their comprehension seems as instantaneous as the feeling of an electric charge, "the truth" being, as he writes, "a current which flows from what people say to us, and which we pick up, invisible though it is."[13]

In drawing such conclusions, the narrator follows in the steps of the man whose story he places before his own. "It occurred to me, as I thought about it, that the raw material of my experience, which would also be the raw material of my book, came to me from Swann," he notes in *Time Regained*.[14] Long before the narrator confronts Albertine with his anxious desire for knowledge, Swann caught a "truthful detail" (*détail véritable*) in the weave of Odette's lies.[15] He glimpsed that a disturbing truth lies concealed in apparently insignificant sounds. The narrator recalls this instructive incident in the second part of *Swann's Way*:

> One day when Swann had gone out early in the afternoon to pay a call, and had failed to find the person he wished to see, it occurred to him to go to see Odette instead, at an hour when, although he never called on her then as a rule, he knew that she was always at home resting or writing letters until tea-time, and would enjoy seeing her for a moment without disturbing her. The porter told him that he believed Odette to be in; he rang, thought he heard some noise, the sound of footsteps, but no one came to the door [*il sonna, crut entendre du bruit, entendre marcher, mais on n'ouvrit pas*].[16]

"Anxious and irritated," Swann goes round to the other side of the building, in front of the bedroom window, hoping to learn more. The curtains being drawn, he sees nothing. He calls out loudly, knocking on the windowpane, but it is to no avail. When he pays Odette a second visit an hour later, she welcomes him explains herself: "She had been in the house when he rang, but had been asleep; the bell had awakened her, she had guessed that it must be Swann, and had run to meet him, but he had already gone. She had, of course, heard him knocking at the window."[17]

Swann immediately discerns in her words a sign of untruth, not despite the plausibility of her account, but because of it. "At once he detected in her speech [literally, "in this saying," *dans ce dire*] one of those fragments of an exact fact that liars, when caught off guard, console themselves by introducing into the composition of the false fact that they are inventing, thinking that it will play its part and conceal its resemblance to the Truth."[18] The sliver of the "true fact" strikes Swann as the index of the false totality of which it is a part. In the narrative, the situation soon recurs. Swann's jealousy incites Odette to provide him with false confessions whose true details present him with the evidence that he seeks:

> As soon as she found herself face to face with the man to whom she was obliged to lie, she became uneasy, all her ideas melted like wax before a flame, her inventive and her reasoning faculties were paralysed, she might ransack her brain but could find only a void; yet she must say something, and there lay within her reach precisely the fact which she had wished to conceal and which, being true, was the one thing that had remained.[19]

Breaking off from the truth "a small piece, of no importance in itself" (*un petit morceau, sans importance par lui-même*), Odette would insert it into a fraudulent picture, convinced that it "was the better thing to do, since it was a truthful detail [*un détail veritable*], which did not present the same dangers as a false detail."[20] His eye trained in the arts of forgery and authentication, Swann would then catch it: "this fragmentary true detail had sharp edges which could not be made to fit in, except with those contiguous fragments of the truth from which she had arbitrarily detached it."[21] The narrator comments that at such moments, Swann would neither interrupt nor contradict Odette, anticipating that, "left to herself," she would "perhaps produce a lie that would be a faint index of the truth. She would speak."[22] Sometimes it would be enough for her to indicate, with a gesture, that a certain charge was false. Then Swann "understood that it was possibly true."[23]

Even in the absence of his lover and her voice, certain details torment Swann. Soon after she mysteriously refuses and then agrees to receive him, Odette gives him several letters lying on her table, asking him to post them for her. Swann takes them and, arriving at home, suddenly "realises that they were still in his pocket."[24] Is his error an oversight or a parapraxis in the Freudian sense, which betrays some unconscious wish? And is his retention of the missives itself a response, in turn, to a conscious or unconscious provocation on Odette's part? Without pausing to reflect at any length on what he has done or failed to do, Swann intuits that she has put in his hands a letter destined for another lover. Bringing it close to a flame, he makes out the writing on the page that it contains. First he discerns a few words and a phrase; soon he deciphers more. Taking "a firm hold of the card which was sliding to and fro, the envelope being too large for it, and then, by moving it with his finger and thumb," bringing "one line after another beneath the part of the envelope where the paper was not doubled, through which alone it was possible to read," he makes out its contents.[25] Swann's jealous suspicions are confirmed, yet he is also comforted. Odette's words suggest that she is more attached to him than he might have feared.

Alone and apparently untroubled by the evidence of Odette's infidelity, Swann remains susceptible to the power of written and spoken words detached from their contexts. "One day, during the longest period of calm through which he had yet been able to exist without being overtaken by an access of jealousy," he undergoes an unexpected experience of what might be called involuntary bibliomancy. Leafing through the newspaper, his eyes fall on the title of a theatrical performance, *Les Filles du Marbre*, by Théodore Barrière. Its letters strike "him so cruel a blow" that he recoils "instinctively," averting his gaze. The phrase reminds him of a painful incident: "the story which Odette had told him long ago of a visit which she had paid to the Salon at the Palais de l'Industrie with Mme Verdurin, who had said to her, 'Take care, now! I know how to melt you, all right. You're not made of marble.'"[26] Odette had dismissed Mme Verdurin's flirtatious remark as "only a joke [*plaisanterie*]," but Swann cannot believe her. Having encountered a word, *marbre*, that recalls the quip, he tries to distract himself. "Without daring to lift his eyes towards the newspaper," he turns the page so as not to see Barrière's title. "Mechanically," he reads "the news from the provinces": "There had been a storm in the Channel, and damage was reported from Dieppe, Cabourg, Beuzeval. . . . Suddenly he recoiled again."[27]

Once again, a single word strikes Swann with a force irreducible to any of its meanings in its context. This time it is a proper name that overcomes him—not in itself, as the narrator adds, but in its likeness to another. "The name Beuzeval had reminded him of another place in the same area, Beuzeville, which carried also, bound to it by a hyphen, a second name, to wit Bréauté, which he had often seen on maps, but without ever previously remarking that it was the same as that of his friend M. de Bréauté," whom the author of an anonymous letter he once received had identified as Odette's erstwhile lover.[28] Swann's train of thought illustrates the relations of condensation and association, metaphor and metonymy, that Freud detected in his inability to retrieve the name "Signorelli." The place name "Beuzeval" recalls to Swann another place name, "Beuzeville," the principle of the resemblance between them being the identity of the first syllable, *Beuze-*, and the minimal variation of the second (*val/ville*). Such links are metonymic and are examples of a process of displacement. Yet no sooner has his mind passed from "Beuzeval" to "Beuzeville" than it seizes hold of the different name with which "Beuzeville" is tied by a hyphen: "Bréauté." That place-name is linked by homonymy to the name of Swann's friend. In this case, the painful substitution that Swann confronts is based on a fact of phonic identity; one "Bréauté" is "condensed" into another. What seems at first little more than a distracted association exhibits the patterns that define the regular processes of the unconscious. They bring Swann unexpectedly and painfully before his obsession.

That a scrap of speech, even a "tiny word" long forgotten, might entail momentous consequences is a circumstance on which the narrator lingers elsewhere. In *The Guermantes Way*, he observes,

> Each of our actions, our words, our attitudes is cut off from the "world," from the people who have not directly perceived it, by a medium the permeability of which is infinitely variable and remains unknown to ourselves. Having learned from experience that some important utterance which we

> eagerly hoped would be disseminated . . . has at once, often because of our very anxiety, been hidden under a bushel, how immeasurably less do we suppose that some tiny word which we ourselves have forgotten, which may not even have been uttered by us but formed along its way by the imperfect refraction of a different word, could be transported, without ever being halted in its progress, infinite distances . . . and succeed in diverting at our expense the banquet of the gods! What we remember of our conduct remains unknown to our nearest neighbour; what we have forgotten that we ever said, or indeed what we never did say, flies to provoke hilarity on another planet.[29]

In the universe of the Proust's work, words composed and recomposed in transmission move along unknown itineraries among the most diverse of speaking beings. The course of their motions recalls that of the Babylonian *egirrû*. Once "placed," as if by accident, in a certain setting, such a word passes from mortals to mortals, from immortals to mortals, and from mortals to immortals, reaching "the banquet of the gods."

The intuition into the form of such trajectories pervades the artist's practice as Proust presents it in *Time Regained*. "Impelled by the instinct that was in him," the writer omits "to look at a great many things which other people notice," being all too often "accused by others of being absent-minded and by himself of not knowing how to listen or look." That allegation, the reader learns, is utterly unfounded. The truth is that the writer has been "instructing his eyes and his ears to retain for ever what seemed to others puerile trivialities, the tone of voice in which a certain remark had been made, or the facial expression and the movement of the shoulders which he had seen at a certain moment, many years ago, in somebody of whom perhaps he knows nothing else whatsoever." Like the Roman augur whom Proust's narrator explicitly evokes, the writer catches portents in slight and fleeting motions: "There is a feeling for generality which, in the future writer, itself picks out what is general and can for that reason one day enter into a work of art. And this has made him listen to people only when, stupid or absurd though they may have been, they have turned themselves, by repeating like parrots what other people of similar character are in the habit of saying, into birds of augury, mouthpieces of a psychological law."[30]

In the last volumes of the work, such profane birds of augury abound. Their place is in speech acts too numerous and too minimal to be noticed in the instant of their utterance. In retrospect, however, the narrator understands that however imperfect or circumstantial, misleading, and even mendacious their form may have been, they contained hidden prophecies:

> How often we had expressed them, those painful, those ineluctable truths which dominated us and to which we were blind, the truth of our feelings, the truth of our destiny, how often we had expressed them without knowing it, without meaning it, in words which doubtless we ourselves thought mendacious but the prophetic force of which had been established by subsequent events. I remembered many words that each of us had uttered without knowing at the time the truth that they contained, which indeed we had said thinking that we were play-acting and yet the falseness of which was very slight, very uninteresting, wholly confined within our pitiable insincerity, compared with what they contained unbeknown to us—lies and errors falling short of the profound reality which neither of us perceived, truth extending beyond it, the truth of our natures, the essential laws of which escape us and require Time before they reveal themselves, the truth of our destinies also.[31]

Just as with the passing of the years, falsehoods are revealed as truths, the most trivial of pronouncements in time acquires the power of a fateful word: "Often, meeting years later some friend of our youth whom we never particularly liked, we scarcely trouble to shake hands with him, and yet, did we but think of it, it is from a casual remark which he made to us, 'You ought to come to Balbec' or something of the kind, that our whole life and our work have originated."[32]

It is not only in voices of others, however, that unexpected oracles are lodged. The narrator's own speech is no exception to the rules that he sets out for "those painful, those ineluctable truths" that are spoken without distinct awareness. He recalls how, in the time during which Albertine lived with him, he would deprive himself of sleep, rising early so as not to miss the "street cries, which render perceptible to us the peripatetic life of the tradesmen, the victuallers of Paris." "In addition to the pleasure of knowing how fond Albertine was of them and of being out of doors myself without leaving my bed," he explains, "I heard in them as it were the symbol of the atmosphere of the world outside, of the dangerous stirring life through the midst of which I did not allow her to move save under my tutelage, in an external prolongation of her seclusion, and from which I withdrew her at the hour of my choosing to make her return home to my side." He remembers relaying those street cries to Albertine: "Prawns, lovely prawns, alive, alive-o . . . skate, nice fresh skate . . . whiting to fry, to fry . . . here comes the mackerel, freshly caught mackerel, my ladies, beautiful mackerel [*Il arrive le maquereau, maquereau frais, maquereau nouveau. Voilà le maquereau, Mesdames, il est beau le maquereau*] . . . who'll buy my mussels, fine fat mussels!"[33]

In repetition, one element in that series suddenly acquires a new and sinister meaning for the narrator. *Maquereau*, the French word for "mackerel," is homonymous. It signifies both the striped member of the Scombridae fish family and the criminal human known as the "pimp." Reiterating the phrase that he happened to perceive, the narrator suddenly wonders whether, in naming the *maquereau*, he has not unwittingly alluded to the role that his chauffeur may be playing in accompanying Albertine on her outings. "In spite of myself, the announcement [or "warning," *l'avertissement*]: 'Here comes the mackerel' made me shudder. But as it could not, I felt, apply to our chauffeur, I thought only of the fish of that name, which I detested, and my uneasiness did not last."[34] Too late, the narrator learns that he was wrong not to accord more attention to the accidental ambiguity that he perceived. The equivocation in the fishmonger's words was no less portentous than were the words *Cauneas, Cauneas* in the voice of the fabled fruit seller in Brindisium. The narrator's chauffeur was the *beau maquereau* that he unwittingly evoked.[35]

Yet in Proust's work, discourse is not the only locus of such audible revelations. Inhuman sounds are also charged with an oracular force. The narrator recalls how, on the night before Albertine escaped her "seclusion," leaving his apartment without warning and without his knowledge, he might have foreseen what she would do. He had only to trust his sense of a fleeting noise. A sound had struck him: "Suddenly, in the silence of the night, I was startled by a noise which, though apparently insignificant, filled me with terror, the noise of Albertine's window being violently opened."[36] That the sound was obscurely significant was a fact of which he had been certain: "I wondered why this noise had caused me such alarm." Perhaps, he mused, it indicated that Albertine had decided to disregard his fear of draughts, which she had respected till that point. Perhaps her gesture was the substitute of an unuttered sentence: "The noise had been violent, almost rude, as though she had flung the window open, crimson with rage, saying to herself: 'This life is stifling me. I don't care, I must have air!'" For a reason he could not identify, the narrator could not keep himself from thinking of the sound as a portent: "as a presage [*comme à un présage*] more mysterious and more funereal than the hoot of an owl."[37]

That such an intuition defies the inferences dictated by "intelligence" is a point stressed by the narrator.[38] The "panicked fear" that gripped him on the night when he "heard the noise of her window being opened" was not "based on any reason."[39] He comments, "It is life that, little by little, case by case, enables us to observe that what is most important to our hearts or to our minds is taught us not by reasoning but by other powers." Among such "other powers" is the ability to read presages inscribed, as if in an "invisible ink," in discourse, in bodily movements, and in accidental sounds:

> It seemed to me that the unforeseen calamity with which I found myself grappling was also something that I had already known (as I had known of Albertine's friendship with a pair of lesbians), from having read it in so many signs in which (notwithstanding the contrary affirmations of my reason, based upon Albertine's own statements) I had discerned the weariness, the loathing that she felt at having to live in that state of slavery, signs that had so often seemed to me to be written as though in invisible ink behind her sad, submissive eyes, upon her cheeks suddenly inflamed with an unaccountable blush, in the sound of the window that had suddenly been flung open.[40]

Sensitive to the unexpected resonances of sentences and noises, attentive to the meanings implicit in errors, inconsistencies, and apparent accidents, Proust's narrator leads his readers toward an activity that intimately concerns their own practice: the decipherment of truth details in reading and misreading. The most striking example of such an event is to be found in the book's penultimate volume. By this point, Albertine has died. Long in mourning, the narrator has left Paris for Venice in the company of his mother. One evening, as he disembarks from a gondola before his hotel, a porter hands him an envelope. It contains a telegram that has been brought three times already to the hotel for him, but because of "the inaccurate rendering of the addressee's name," the post office has demanded a receipt certifying its delivery. The narrator accepts the missive, brings it to his room and opens it. "Glancing through the message that was filled with inaccurately transmitted words," as he recalls, he succeeds in making out a salutation, a few phrases, and a signature: "MY FRIEND, YOU THINK ME DEAD, FORGIVE ME, I AM VERY MUCH ALIVE, I WOULD LIKE TO SEE YOU, TO TALK WITH YOU OF MARRIAGE, WHEN DO YOU RETURN? AFFECTIONATELY, ALBERTINE."[41]

In his rendition of the incident, the narrator insists first of all on the reaction that the reading provoked in him. It was one of near indifference. "The news that she was alive did not cause me the joy that I might have expected.... Albertine did not rise again for me with the resurrection of her body."[42] Just as the initial news of his beloved grandmother's death had had no effect on him, so, he recalls, the idea of Albertine's unimagined survival hardly touched him. Yet the narrator does not merely note that fact. He also strives to explain it. He reasons that if the news of Albertine's continued life does not count for him as it once would have done, it is because he himself has undergone a metamorphosis:

> Life, in accordance with its habit which is, by unceasing, infinitesimal labours, to change the face of the world, had not said to me on the morrow of Albertine's death: "Become another person," but, by changes too imperceptible for me to be conscious even that I was changing, had altered almost everything in me, with the result that my mind was already accustomed to its new master — my new self — when it became aware that it had changed; it was to this new master that it was attached . . . . As soon as oblivion had taken hold of certain dominant points of suffering and pleasure, the resistance offered by my love was overcome, I no longer loved Albertine.[43]

At this point, Albertine is to him as little as Gilberte had been after the end of their relations. If both women are now, even in life, as dead, it is because the self that loved them is no more: "I would have been incapable of resuscitating Albertine because I would have been just as incapable of resuscitating myself, of resuscitating the self of those days."[44]

Readers of the *Recherche* may recall that however true in principle, those reflections are in their prompting dramatically unfounded. Their sole basis is an error. On the morning after he has perused the telegram, the narrator returns it to the hotel porter, adding that it has reached him "by mistake" (*par erreur*).[45] The following pages evoke his long walks through the Venetian *calli* and his extended reflections on the paintings that he saw in the city's churches and *palazzi*. In the next chapter, he recalls how, at last on the train back to Paris, he read a different letter brought to him. As his mother busies herself with her correspondence, he extracts from his pocketbook an envelope that the porter gave him before his departure. He recognizes the hand that wrote it as Gilberte's. Opening it, he learns that she has already sent him a telegram to Venice but has "had no reply." He comments, "I remembered that I had been told that the telegraphic service there was inefficient. I had never received her telegram. Perhaps she would refuse to believe this."[46] Yet suddenly a different thought occurs to him: "The telegram that I had received a few days earlier, and had supposed to be from Albertine, was from Gilberte."

Details of a graphological variety account for the circumstance:

> As the somewhat laboured originality of Gilberte's handwriting consisted chiefly, when she wrote a line, in introducing into the line above it the strokes of her t's which appeared to be underlining the words, or the dots over her t's which appeared to be punctuating the sentence above them, and on the other hand in interspersing the line below with the tails and flourishes of the words immediately above, it was quite natural that the clerk who dispatched the telegram should have read the loops of s's or y's in the line above as an "-ine" attached to the word "Gilberte." The dot over the i of Gilberte had climbed up to make a suspension point. As for her capital G, it resembled a Gothic A.[47]

Committing a handwritten text to a printed form, the telegraphist misread the signature and effectively forged a new name, belonging to a person unknown in the *Recherche*. The narrator omits to render that proper name its full form, but even in its absence from the text, it is distinctly legible. It can only be "Gilbertine." In that linguistic malformation, "Albertine" fades into "Gilberte," even as it marks it with the original suffix *-ine*. Once again, Freudian condensation and displacement, Jakobsonian selection and combination, or Lacanian metaphor and metonymy are discernible.

Setting out the conditions for his own misreading, the narrator corrects an error. In the passage from the obscurely distorted telegram to the recognizably handwritten letter and from an act of distracted perusal to one of concentrated reading, the first mistaken message is revised by the second. As Sharon Willis remarks, "the name that the telegraph operator has read into the text is now read out of it by the narrator."[48] Long after Albertine replaced Gilberte in the narrator's "intermittencies of the heart," an inverse nominal substitution occurs: "Gilberte" takes the place, in the messages, of "Albertine." Yet the faulty transcription and decryption point beyond themselves; the mistakes lead, in Akane Kawakami's phrase, "to a truth."[49] The superposition of names and the confusion of women that the narrator's misreading implies appears now as the index of an unexpected commonality—not in the letter writers, to be sure, but in their single reader. Now the narrator learns that his past selves, those once devoted to Gilberte and to Albertine, are both irretrievably past: equally resistant to "resuscitation."

Yet the narrator also draws a further conclusion from his faulty performance. Even as he is brought before the difference and the likeness between the two presumed authors from his point of view, and even as he ponders the transience of his own past selves, he infers a general principle, which he introduces by two rhetorical questions:

> How many letters are actually read into a word by a careless person who knows what to expect, who sets out with the idea that the message is from a certain person? How many words into the sentence? We guess as we read, we create [*On devine en lisant, on crée*]; everything starts from an initial error; those that follow (and this applies not only to the reading of letters and telegrams, not only to all reading), extraordinary as they may appear to a person who has not begun at the same place, are all quite natural. A large part of what we believe to be true (and this applies even to our final conclusions) with an obstinacy equalled only by our good faith, springs from an original mistake in our premises.[50]

Error, which is not the exception but the rule, affects the combinations of signifying elements, determining the sequences of letters in words and sentences. If the reception of discourse involves more than a stop along the course of a "communication," if readers participate in the genesis of what they read, it is by virtue of their imperfect acts of decipherment: "We guess as we read, we create." "As for the inner book of unknown signs . . . ," the narrator explains in similar terms in *Time Regained*, "if I tried to read them no one could help me with any rules, for to read them was an act of creation [*un acte de création*] in which no one can do our work for us or even collaborate with us."[51] Given the semantic strata from which the French word for "guessing" (*deviner*) emerged, and given Proust's own vocabulary of augurs and prophets, one might paraphrase, albeit with some forcing, "we *divine* as we read, we create." Without the help of any rules and without any possible "collaboration," we make out the signs of what was never written.

That such an inference should be drawn from a mistyped and misread telegram is not the least of the details in the scene. Just as the precious call that the narrator receives is that of a voice "from afar," the revelatory news that reaches him in distortion is a written mark or *grammē* "from afar," to be deciphered and to be rewritten in error. Each time, confronted by the telephone and by the telegram, the narrator suffers the experience of an uncannily proximate distance. One might characterize both encounters as auratic, according to Benjamin's definition of aura as "the unique appearance of a distance, no matter how close it may be."[52] Yet Proust affords terms of his own for such events of perception and cognition. They are the expressions by which the narrator defines the use to which his work is to be put. In *Time Regained*, he recalls how, when he was at last able to show his friends some fragments of his book, "no one understood anything of them" (*personne n'y comprit rien*). He continues,

> Even those who commended my perception of the truths which I wanted eventually to engrave within the temple, congratulated me on having discovered them "with a microscope," when on the contrary it was a telescope that I had used to observe things which were indeed very small to the naked eye, but only because they were situated at a great distance, and which were each one of them in itself a world.[53]

That passage sets the truth details that occupy the narrator in a striking frame. They may be "very small to the naked eye," but their magnitude is neither intrinsic nor essential. It is merely a function of their distance from the observer.[54] If they elude immediate perception, it is because of the time that removes them from the narrator: the time that Proust's work renders in its vertiginous extension.

Yet the author does not write solely for himself. Guessing and divining in reading, in misreading and "creating," the one who refers to himself as "I" in his book draws his readers into the literary and cognitive process that he reconstitutes. They are to play an unexpected part in the project that he conceives. As the narrator makes clear in the final pages of *Time Regained*, what he calls the "fortuitous and inevitable" impressions from which he has gleaned unexpected insights are but examples pointing to the objects of a new method, which now awaits a further use.[55] Proust's future readers are to find in the pages of the book the "magnifying glass" of their own experience. For that reason, the narrator adds, he can hardly claim such readers to be his own: "For it seemed to me that they would not be 'my' readers but the readers of their own selves." The work that the narrator means one day to write and that the readers of *In Search of Lost Time* may find that they have already read is to be the means of detections and decipherments that are to come. Anticipating itself in its finished form and finding completion in the announcement of its future, the book is to be a divinatory instrument without precedent: a telephone and a telescope by which others, "reading what lies inside themselves,"[56] may learn to listen and to look.

CHAPTER FIFTEEN

Gropings of a Spiritual Ear

Communication, it has often been said, involves the coordination of several elements. Drawing on twentieth-century research in information theory, Roman Jakobson argued that they are six in number: six "factors," as he put it, that must be kept in mind "in any speech event." The first is the context; the second is the addresser; the third is the message; the fourth is the addressee; the fifth is the code (or language); the sixth is the contact or "physical channel and psychological connection between the addresser and the addressee."[1] Jakobson's model is instructive in its clarity. In real speech events, however, the elements of communication are often difficult to identify. Each of the six factors is susceptible to distortion, and some may be lacking. The context may be unclear, the addresser unidentified, the addressee unknown. Depending on the words chosen or perceived, the message may also be uncertain. Signals may be mispronounced or misheard. They may be run together, by chance or by design, and overlaid in many ways upon each other. At times, the identity of the code itself can become a matter of doubt; one language may resemble another to the point that the two seem, if only for a moment, indistinguishable. The supposition of a secure physical or psychological "connection," finally, sometimes proves unfounded. The results of such complications in the communication chain are necessarily diverse. Yet it may be safely surmised that where the links grow unsteady, confusions, redundancies, puns, and misunderstandings are difficult to avoid.

In the same years in which he identified the six factors in the speech event, Jakobson proposed an analysis of aphasia that he linked to general disturbances in communication. He drew on the distinction between two basic modes of arrangement—selection and combination—that he took to be fundamental to the language faculty. Their perturbation, he argued, gives rise to two types of impairment. Where selection is troubled, expressions in messages elude the speaker. "Key words may be dropped or superseded by abstract anaphoric substitutes," such as "this" or "that one," and by the most semantically indefinite of nouns, such as "thing."[2] Where the function of combination is affected, by contrast, "word order becomes chaotic; the ties of grammatical coordination and subordination, whether concord or government, are dissolved."[3] The result is "infantile one-sentence utterances and one-word sentences"; "only a few longer, stereotyped, 'ready made' sentences manage to survive."[4] As the reader will recall, Lacan observed that Jakobson's linguistic distinction between two types of arrangement mirrored the account that Freud had proposed, half a century earlier, in his theory of unconscious processes: condensation and displacement. In condensation, words are exchanged and confused; in displacement, syntax is rearranged. "Similarity disorder" may therefore be taken to illustrate the principle of "condensation," while "contiguity disorder" exhibits that of "displacement."

Yet there are also disturbances of communication that defy the Jakobsonian bipartition. When one or more of the six "factors" fails to be instantiated or appears in a shape that challenges analysis, the regular exchange of meaningful signals between speakers can only falter. In the most extreme cases, in place of the orderly transfer of messages, one witnesses a different event: the irruption of impenetrable signs related to indefinite contexts, committed to indeterminable codes, emitted by unknown addressers, and directed to unidentified addressees.

In his early works, James Joyce called such irruptions "epiphanies." A passage of *Ulysses* contains a sure, but ironic allusion to their place in his literary development. In his silent, yet articulate reflections, Stephen Daedalus issues a command to himself: "Remember your epiphanies written on green oval leaves, deeply deep, copies to be sent if you died to all the great libraries of the world, including Alexandria? Someone was to read them there after a few thousand years, a mahamanvantara. Pico della Mirandola like."[5] When *Ulysses* was published in 1922, readers had no means of understanding which "epiphanies" Stephen thus enjoined himself not to forget. The situation changed in 1944, after Joyce's death in 1941, when *Stephen Hero*, the early version of *A Portrait of the Artist as a Young Man*, appeared in print. In a scene at the center of that posthumously published work, the "hero" is walking along the road when he is struck by a "trivial incident." It is a scrap of dialogue and the first epiphany in Joyce's fiction.

"He was passing through Eccles' St one evening, one misty evening," the reader learns,

> when a trivial incident set him composing some ardent verses which he entitled a "Villanelle of the Temptress." A young lady was standing on the steps of one of those brown brick houses which seem the very incarnation of Irish paralysis. A young gentleman was leaning on the rusty railings of the area. Stephen as he passed on his quest heard the following fragment of colloquy out of which he received an impression keen enough to afflict his sensitiveness very severely.
>
> The Young Lady—(drawling discreetly) . . . O, yes . . . I was . . . at the . . . cha . . . pel . . .
>
> The Young Gentleman—(inaudibly) . . . I . . . (again inaudibly) . . . I . . .
>
> The Young Lady—(softly) . . . O . . . but you're . . . ve . . . ry . . . wick . . . ed . . .

That the recorded exchange involves some variety of flirtation is evident. The context, however, is unexplained. The "messages" are repeatedly interrupted and in large part inaudible. Stephen nonetheless receives a "keen impression" from what he overhears. "Very severely" impressed by the banality of the incident, he is moved to devise a project:

> This triviality made him think of collecting many such moments together in a book of epiphanies. By an epiphany he meant a sudden spiritual manifestation, whether in the vulgarity of speech or of gesture or in a memorable phase of the mind itself. He believed that it was for the man of letters to record these epiphanies with extreme care, seeing that they themselves are the most delicate and evanescent of moments.[6]

The result was to be the poem mentioned in the novel, which bears the title of a text that the young Joyce himself also composed.[7]

In his memoir of his brother's youth, Stanislaus Joyce related that the author of *Stephen Hero* himself developed the practice represented in his unpublished novel. Starting around 1900, James Joyce recorded "what he called 'epiphanies'—manifestations or revelations." His notes, Stanislaus Joyce added, "were in the beginning ironical observations of slips, and little errors and gestures—mere straws in the wind—by which people betrayed the very things they were most careful to conceal. Epiphanies were always brief sketches, hardly ever more than some dozen lines in length, but always very accurately observed and noted, the matter being so slight."[8] Their "collection" was to serve him "as a sketch-book serves an artist."[9]

For several years, Joyce continued to transcribe such fugitive revelations.[10] Today, scholars estimate that he recorded at least seventy-one "epiphanies."[11] Forty of their number survive on pages written in the author's hand and in Stanislaus's transcriptions. Like Stephen adapting snatches of the conversation near Saint Eccles's into his "Villanelle of the Temptress," Joyce wove these "epiphanies" into almost all his later works. From *Stephen Hero* to *A Portrait of the Artist as a Young Man*, which appeared in 1916, to *Ulysses*, published in 1922, and *Finnegans Wake*, which was published in 1939, Joyce drew on his "deeply deep" notations, transforming them in incorporating them into the works of his maturity.[12]

As suggested by the passage in which it is introduced in *Stephen Hero*, the Joycean "epiphany" in each case constitutes a "sudden spiritual manifestation." That characterization recalls the sense of the ancient Greek word *epiphaneia*, which denotes an appearance so luminous as to reveal gods and goddesses. Joyce's description simultaneously alludes to the specifically Christian use of the term for Jesus's birth and rebirth in baptism in the Gospels.[13] It is clear that Joyce subjects the theological notion of epiphany to a redefinition in applying it to profane occurrences. What is perhaps less obvious is that the events that Daedalus takes to be "epiphanic" are of two kinds. They are perceptible either in discourse or in reflection, being discernible "in the vulgarity of speech or of gesture or in a memorable phase of the mind." As the most recent editors of these brief texts remark, "the two kinds of epiphanies represent, therefore, the twin poles of Joyce's art: dramatic irony and lyric sentiment."[14]

Among the "sudden spiritual manifestations" contained in unexpectedly overheard discourse, many are not only brief, but also elliptical and therefore equivocal. The earliest attested example is in this respect exemplary. It consists of two parts, the first of which is a four-part dialogue set "in the parlour of the house in Martello Terrace":

> Mr Vance — (comes in with a stick) . . . O, you know,
> he'll have to apologise, Mrs Joyce.
> Mrs Joyce — O yes . . . Do you hear that, Jim?
> Mr Vance — Or else — if he doesn't — the eagles'll
> come and pull out his eyes.
> Mrs Joyce — O, but I'm sure he will apologise.[15]

Here there is no trace of the dramatic conditions of exchange: neither the deed for which "he'll have to apologise" nor the setting of the dialogue are specified. The second half of the episode indicates, however, that the one whom Mr Vance refers to as "him" and whom Mrs Joyce addresses by name ("Jim") is present at the scene of the exchange: "Do you hear that, Jim"?

The future author is "under the table." He is repeating words "to himself" that, as in an echolalia, recall a four-syllable segment of the exchange that he has just heard:

—Pull out his eyes,
Apologise,
Apologise,
Pull out his eyes.
Apologise,
Pull out his eyes,
Pull out his eyes,
Apologise.[16]

In the insistent recollection of the end of one sentence ("the eagles'll come and pull out his eyes") and the end of another, ("O, but I'm sure he will apologise"), a sonorous coincidence resounds. It is the partial identity of *apologise* and *eyes*: a rhyme without reason. Joyce folded that infantile refrain into the end of the first section of *A Portrait of the Artist as a Young Man*.[17] Commenting on the passage, Hugh Kenner writes that "the eagles, eagles of Rome, are a transformation of the god with the hairy face, the punisher. They are associated with Prometheus, and with gnawing unrelenting conscience." Evoking "the dawning conscience in Stephen" and suggesting the incipience of sin and "the development of Stephen Dedalus from a bundle of sensations to a matured, self-conscious, dedicated, fallen being," the moment announces the itinerary of the *Bildungsroman*, if not "every theme in the entire life-work of James Joyce."[18]

Another "epiphany" consists in a snatch of dialogue that is scarcely more extended. It is recorded in the absence of any context other than the place of its occurrence, "Dublin: on Mountjoy Square":

Joyce — (*concludes*) . . . That'll be forty thousand pounds.
Aunt Lillie — (*titters*) — O, laus ! . . . I was like that too . . . .
. . . When I was a girl I was sure I'd marry a
lord . . . or something . . .
Joyce — (*thinks*) — Is it possible she's comparing
herself with me?[19]

What is "that," the unnamed thing whose cost amounts to "forty thousand pounds"? Jakobson's "abstract anaphoric substitute" is in this case strictly unidentifiable. To what, moreover, does tittering Aunt Lillie remember herself as having once been similar? And why does "Joyce" wonder whether she may be comparing herself with him? Addresser, addressee, code, and contact are discernible, but the context defies reconstruction. The signals relayed in the medium of speech are too fragmentary to lend themselves to paraphrase.

In a further epiphany recorded as having occurred in "Dublin: at the corner of Connaught St, Phibsborough," two young ladies pose an insistent question to an unnamed "Little Male Child," who seems hardly able to respond to them. The context is elusive, the individual utterances elliptical, and the code itself begins to give way as the English of the queries meets an infantile response at the edge of any language:

The Little Male Child — (*at the garden gate*) . . . Na . . . o.
The First Young Lady — (*half kneeling, takes his
hand*) — Well, is Mabie
your sweetheart?
The Little Male Child — Na . . . o.
The Second Young Lady — (*bending over him, looks
up*) — Who is your
sweetheart?[20]

The abbreviated exchange between the ladies and the inarticulate, if obstinately repetitive "little male child" is rewritten in *Ulysses*'s

"Nausicaa" chapter. To the commands of Edy Boardman and Cissy, "Tell us who is your sweetheart," a "tearful Tommy" responds three times with an utterance that bespeaks his understanding of their demand and his refusal to acquiesce to it: "Nao."[21]

In *Stephen Hero*, the definition of the epiphany as "a sudden spiritual manifestation, whether in the vulgarity of speech or of gesture or in a memorable phase of the mind itself" is but the beginning of an elaborate theory of revelations. To expound it to Cranly, Stephen draws on the Thomistic doctrine of the beautiful. He cites "what Aquinas says: The three things requisite for beauty are, integrity, a wholeness, symmetry and radiance," promising "some day" to "expand that sentence into a treatise."[22] The homonymous protagonist of *A Portrait of the Artist as a Young Man* evokes like terms, without making use of the term "epiphany." "The most satisfying relations of the sensible must... correspond to the necessary phases of artistic apprehension," Stephen declares to Lynch. "Find these and you find the qualities of universal beauty. Aquinas says: *ad pulchritudinem tria requiruntur, integritas, consonantia, claritas.* I translate it so: '*Three things are needed for beauty, wholeness, harmony and radiance.*'"[23]

Stephen glosses each term in that Scholastic proposition in *A Portrait of the Artist as a Young Man*. Something is beautiful when it is conceived "as *one* thing," that is "one whole," which implies *integritas*, when it is, moreover, grasped a "*thing*," which involves *consonantia*, and, finally, when, becoming the object of "the only synthesis which is logically and esthetically permissible," it appears as "that thing which it is and no other thing." Then it is felt in its *claritas*, that is, in a "radiance" that Stephen identifies with *quidditas*, "the *whatness* of a thing." "This supreme quality is felt by the artist when the esthetic image is first conceived in his imagination," he specifies:

> The mind in that mysterious instant Shelley likened beautifully to a fading coal. The instant wherein that supreme quality of beauty, the clear radiance of the esthetic image, is apprehended luminously by the mind which has

> been arrested by its wholeness and fascinated by its harmony is the luminous silent stasis of esthetic pleasure, a spiritual state very like to that cardiac condition which the Italian physiologist Luigi Galvani, using a phrase almost as beautiful as Shelley's, called the enchantment of the heart.[24]

In *Stephen Hero*, that "instant" coincides with the moment of epiphany. Stephen presents the "third quality" of the beautiful as the fruit of a long labor to "solve" a difficulty of interpretation. "*Claritas*," he explains, "is *quidditas*." He continues:

> After the analysis which discovers the second quality the mind makes the only logically possible synthesis and discovers the third quality. This is the moment which I call epiphany. First we recognise that the object is one integral thing, then we recognise that it is an organised composite structure, a thing in fact: finally, when the relation of the parts is exquisite, when the parts are adjusted to the special point, we recognise that it is that thing which it is. Its soul, its whatness, leaps to us from the vestment of its appearance. The soul of the commonest object, the structure of which is so adjusted, seems to us radiant. The object achieves its epiphany.[25]

Such words indicate that however theological the doctrine of beauty on which Stephen draws, the "sudden spiritual manifestation" may concern beings of no particular religious significance. As he goes on to explain, a thing such as the clock of Ballast Office is "capable of an epiphany": "I will pass it time after time, allude to it, refer to it, catch a glimpse of it. It is only an item in the catalogue of Dublin's street furniture. Then all at once I see it and I know at once what it is: epiphany." To dispel the perplexity of his interlocutor, Stephen adds, "Imagine my glimpses at that clock as the gropings of a spiritual eye which seeks to adjust its vision to an exact focus. The moment the focus is reached the object is epiphanised. It is just in this epiphany that I find the third, the supreme quality of beauty."[26]

As a term of poetic theory, Joyce's "epiphany" has lent itself to diverse uses. Florence L. Walzl argued that it furnishes the principle for the narratives of *Dubliners* and *A Portrait of the Artist as a*

Young Man.[27] Harry Levin, one of the first interpreters of *Stephen Hero*, took the epiphany to be a crucial element in the "doctrine" informing "all of Joyce's work—the muffled climaxes of *Portrait of the Artist*, the alcoholic apparitions of *Ulysses*, and the protracted nightmare of *Finnegans Wake*."[28] Morris Beja viewed the "moment of illumination" that Joyce named as a constitutive element of the modern novel.[29] Robert Langbaum argued that the Joycean "epiphanic mode" "is to a large extent the Romantic and modern mode."[30] Critics have identified such a mode with other privileged moments in the European literatures of the early twentieth century—not least the sudden visions of Rainer Maria Rilke's Malte Lauridds Brigge, the involuntary memories that assail the narrator of *In Search of Lost Time*, and the "evanescent reality" evoked by Virginia Woolf in *A Room of One's Own:*

> something very erratic, very undependable—now to be found in a dusty road, now in a scrap of newspaper in the street, now a daffodil in the sun. It lights up a group in a room and stamps some casual saying. It overwhelms one walking home beneath the stars and makes the silent world more real than the world of speech—and then there it is again in an omnibus in the uproar of Piccadilly.[31]

To those familiar with older strata in the archeology of unexpected encounters with revelatory words, however, a different conclusion may also be drawn. Perceptible on unrepeatable occasions, intelligible solely in being detached from the contexts in which they might convey information between present speakers, the revelatory "slips, and little errors and gestures" are modern verbal presages, *klēdones* lodged in the soundscapes of Joyce's fiction. In their sounding, Jakobson's six communication factors may be implicit, but they undergo diverse forms of distortion. The context may be unknown to the hearer or familiar while irrelevant to the sense of the disclosure. In the instant that a "vulgarity of speech" is charged with the force of a "sudden spiritual manifestation," participants in conversation may fade from view, either because of the limits of subjective perception or because of the fact that with respect to the fleeting revelation, speakers and their intentions are of no consequence. For words to reach the hearer or overhearer, there must be a contact between the source of the emission and the one who receives it, but the connection may be frayed. The message, finally, may be perforated, its elements missing or even indecipherable. To hold as oracular and to be the medium of a "spiritual manifestation," voices need be neither fully identified nor understood.

Joyce never ceased to probe the power of encounters with scraps of speech. Beyond the seventy-one recorded epiphanies, events of unexpected hearing and overhearing at once unexpected and revelatory are woven into his works. The opening of *Ulysses* presents the occurrence of one *klēdōn* that is all the more striking for being unanticipated in the instances recorded in the early notebook. In the second episode in the novel, Stephen, a history teacher in Dalkey, is conversing with Mr Garrett Deasy, the school headmaster. Boys are noisily playing outside. Stephen utters the novel's most well-known pronouncement on the subject that he is to impart, "History is a nightmare from which I am trying to awake." His statement and the reply that it occasions are immediately caught in a sequence of coincidences in which the most varied of human sounds acquires a startling sense:

> —History, Stephen said, is a nightmare from which I am trying to awake.
> From the playfield the boys raised a shout. A whirring whistle: goal. What if that nightmare gave you a back kick?
> —The ways of the Creator are not our ways, Mr Deasy said. All history moves towards one great goal, the manifestation of God.
> Stephen jerked his thumb towards the window, saying:
> —That is God.
> Hooray! Ay! Whirrwhee!
> —What? Mr Deasy asked.
> —A shout in the street, Stephen answered, shrugging his shoulders.[32]

As the sounds of the game intrude on the learned exchange, cries and statements, exclamations and gestures, compose a single fabric. The answer is the echo of the question that it ostensibly resolves. To Stephen's wish to be woken from the nightmare that is history, the children respond with a shout and "whirring whistle," which, in the idiom of their game, means "goal." That indication spurs Mr Deasy to evoke the metaphoric "goal" that is theophany, which Stephen, prompted by the exclamations outside, reduces to the call that they have just heard. Suddenly, yet surely, the goal on the playing field and the goal of history converge.

It is an inverted *tolle lege,* which recalls and reverses the scene of Augustine's conversion. Rather than summoning a man outside to go into his dwelling to "pick up and read," the boys' cry on the field interrupts discourse on theology in the school.[33] The circumstances dictate the most mundane of substitutions: a score in the game for the end of history, a "shout in the street" for the supreme "spiritual manifestation." What the teachers say, hear, and overhear falls into place like parts of a single score. Discourse is formulated in a code, tied to a context, and delivered by means of a contact, yet it is lacking in any addresser and therefore any addressee. Beyond or before "communication," it is an irreducibly profane revelation. To be recorded, it demands a uniquely sensitive organ: not the "spiritual eye which seeks to adjust its vision to an exact focus," as in Stephen's account of the illumination of the Ballast Office clock, but what one might call a "spiritual ear," whose "gropings" alone can register a divine manifestation in many voices. In the sudden relays of question, exclamation, and answer, what becomes perceptible is a fleeting constellation. Although grasped in a flash, it is irreducible to any instant. It eludes, therefore, even the keenest faculty of sight. It can only be read.

CHAPTER SIXTEEN

The Chain Breaks

Placing the experience of unexpectedly overheard speech at the origin of their work, modern writers pursue the project formulated by Mallarmé's "Demon of Analogy" in diverse, yet consonant ways. Joyce, Proust, and Valéry, Breton, Yeats, and Spicer are caught in the "haunting and harassing" echo of phrases unexpectedly perceived, even as they draw their inspiration from the sound chambers of such captivity. Yet in their fascination with words disjoined from the conditions of their utterance and in their fidelity to the experience of discourse perceived without clear knowledge of its source and setting, such writers also implicitly evoke a variety of auditory perception that cuts across historical periods. Such "epiphanies" of intercepted discourse involve the experiences by which individuals are struck—in exaltation, trepidation, or anxiety—by speech that is inaudible to all but them.

Today that experience is clinically known as "voice hearing." Recalling Jakobson's account of the communication chain, one may say that in such auditory experiences, the words of messages are perceived in a code, yet in the absence of any ostensible addresser, sometimes without an addressee, and in a context that is often strictly unintelligible.[1] The oldest corpus of recorded texts already contains witnesses to such experiences. An ancient Mesopotamian inscription refers to the case of the one to whom "a mournful cry" becomes perceptible without its being heard by any other person: "If a mournful cry [*ikkillu*] cries out to him and he continually answers it [and] when it cries out to him, he says, 'Who are you?,' a *muttillu* bird has touched him."[2] The contemporary editors of those lines treat them as specifying conditions for a diagnosis of mental illness. The Mesopotamian pronouncement seems thus to set out the "abnormal behavioral patterns and mental responses" that bespeak auditory and verbal hallucination.[3] Yet the perception of words in the absence of visible speakers has also been understood to indicate the presence of something other than sensorial or cognitive infirmity.

Voice hearing played fundamental roles in the premodern world. As may be recalled, the major revelations of Hebrew scripture are almost exclusively auditory and verbal. According to the Bible, Isaiah, Jeremiah, and Ezekiel all encounter their God in perceiving discourse at once audible, yet unattributable to any visible person. Early Christian literature is familiar with speech situations that recall such revelatory configurations, even as they invert their sense. In his *Life of Anthony*, Athanasius presents the early Egyptian ascetic as assailed in his solitude by sounds and sentences produced by unseen demonic speakers: "Very often also without appearing, they imitated the music of harp and voice, and recalled the words of Scripture."[4] In the Middle Ages, the hearing of divine speech is a recurrent motif in the biographies of Christian holy women: Hildegard of Bingen, Joan of Arc, and Julian of Norwich, to name but three among them, all make out sacred words without perceiving the persons from whom they emanate.[5]

Many authors of the modern period contested the testimonies of such experience, questioning the reverence shown to them. Even as the theologians of the Reformation cast doubt on claims to the perception of the invisible, thinkers from Bacon and Burton to Descartes and Kant warned against the perils of fanaticism and "enthusiasm." In time, modern medicine took it upon itself to treat such states through a theory of aberrant auditory perceptions.

Introducing a new term into the study of maladies, Jean-Étienne Dominique Esquirol declared in 1817 that people who claim to be aware of sensible phenomena where none are observable suffer from a particular disturbance: "A man who has the inward conviction of a sensation perceived in the present when no external object capable of arousing the sensation is within the field of his senses is," as Esquirol wrote, "in a state of hallucination [*dans un état d'hallucination*]."[6]

The word "hallucination" is attested in medical discourse as early as 1674. It is a reworking of Latin words of several meanings: *allucinor* and *allucinatio* refer at once to madness, rambling, and fabulation.[7] Esquirol ascribed a new sense to the word when he opposed it to expressions pointing to sensory errors. As he would explain in a paper read before the Institut de France in 1832, the misidentification and misinterpretation of perception gleaned from the external world results in "illusion" and no more. By contrast, "in hallucinations, everything takes place within the brain. Visionaries and ecstatics are hallucinators [*des hallucinés*]; they are dreamers who are wide awake. The activity of the brain is so intense that the visionary or the hallucinator bestows a body and substance onto images reproduced by memory without the participation of the senses."[8]

Evoking "visionaries" and their imaginings, Esquirol suggested that hallucinations consist above all in delusions of sight.[9] It would soon become apparent that such a supposition is unfounded. In 1846, Jules Baillarger showed that hearing plays a crucial role among those who dream while "wide awake." "The most frequent and complicated hallucinations affect hearing," he declared in a paper, "On Hallucinations," read before the Royal Academy of Medicine. "Invisible interlocutors address the patient in the third person, so that he is the passive listener in a conversation; the number of voices varies, they come from all directions, and can even be heard only in one ear." Baillarger followed Esquirol in taking such impressions to be irreducible to "sensation," but he observed that, from the patient's perspective, auditory verbal hallucinations may nonetheless be localizable. "Sometimes the voice is heard in the head, or throat, or chest," he explained. Such phenomena exceed sensation as commonly defined, as may be inferred, he argued, from the fact that the deaf are "more prone to hear voices."[10]

Seeking to order the varieties of such experiences, Baillarger divided hallucinations into the "psychosensorial," in which a perceptual faculty is involved in their occurrence, albeit in a diminished form, and the purely "psychical."[11] That distinction became the basis for a theory proposed by Jean-Pierre Falret in 1864. Taking the paradigmatic type of hallucination to be the "psychical," Falret defined such impressions as "perceptions that are not the result of the senses and that arise in the absence of the external objects that are likely to provoke them."[12] According to his account, hallucinations are therefore "perceptions without objects." In the neo-Scholastic terms that Lacan would evoke in the mid-twentieth century, hallucinations are for Falret experiences in which a *percipiens* is detectable in the absence of any *perceptum*.[13]

That hallucinatory "delusions" possess a structure more complex than such terms allow was a point established by Jules Séglas by means of a study of voice hearing. Starting in 1888, Séglas suggested a new explanation of the causes and varieties of speech troubles, which he presented in elaborated form in his 1895 book, *Language Disturbances among the Alienated*.[14] Following Jean-Marie Charcot, who had been his teacher, Séglas argued that to each unit of language, such as a word, there correspond at least four types of associations. In the mind, the word "bell," for instance, is linked to the sound of the term, the sight of the object that it signifies, the motor-articulatory experience of pronouncing it, and the motor-graphic experience of writing it.[15] A specific "hallucinatory" disturbance may be related to each of these associations. Without hearing or uttering a given word, ailing persons may believe that they have heard its sound, that they have seen the object that it signifies, or that they have sensed the articulatory movement necessary for uttering or writing it. Séglas showed a particularly keen interest in the third of those cases, in which patients, as if despite themselves, feel the effort of uttering a word. Séglas noted that such persons are frequently correct in their intuition. Even when they do not intend to speak, articulate sounds or "voices" may nonetheless escape them. Almost inaudible or distinctly perceptible, such utterances constitute incontrovertibly linguistic phenomena. Yet they defy the communication model, belonging to no identifiable addresser and being directed toward no discernible addressee.

Such phenomena are difficult to reconcile with the account of hallucinations as "perceptions without objects" for they imply that the hallucinating *percipiens* does register a *perceptum*, albeit according to a structure that remains to be defined. Baillarger, Séglas notes, provided evidence of such cases, observing that some ailing persons "have an auditory sensation that is at once very real, yet utterly different from the sensory perceptions of patients who hallucinate." Baillarger evoked "those alienated subjects who, even as they believe they hear speech in their epigastrium, themselves utter words, with their mouths closed, after the manner of ventriloquists." He continued,

> As a rule, the sounds are so soft that the sick patient alone perceives them . . . . In analogous cases, there can be no doubt. The hallucination clearly consists in hearing words that the sick utter very softly, without awareness, and with their mouth closed, and which seem, in effect, to arise from the chest or the epigastrium. The alienated then misrecognize their own voice, just as one mistakes it in dreams.[16]

Séglas argues that in such cases, patients' impressions of hearing voices are due neither to a disorder of the senses, as in "psychosensorial hallucination," nor to a delusion lacking in physical symptoms, as in allegedly "psychical hallucination." What is at issue is a "psychomotor verbal hallucination," which involves "the center of articulated language."[17]

At the end of the nineteenth century, Pierre Janet offered further evidence in support of Séglas's thesis. In his *Psychological Automatism* of 1889, Janet notes that some patients who hear voices also feel the "muscular sense" necessary for the articulation of the words that they alone perceive. He goes into greater detail in an essay, "On a Case of Aboulia and *Idées Fixes*," published in 1891: "Often one observes real movements of the mouth or the tongue and even the real uttering of words that subjects believe themselves mysteriously to perceive."[18] Gilbert Ballet reported the case of one "Monsieur X," who "heard voices" whose soundings coincided with the movement of his tongue.[19] Janet himself recalls an "excited and semimaniacal individual" whom he once treated. That man claimed "to be in long-distance communication with counts and marquises in Paris": "I asked him to send my regards to Monsieur the Marquis. He rubbed his head on one side (it was his Cabbalistic sign for transporting himself to the Marquis) and said aloud: 'Monsieur the Marquis, I have been asked to greet you.' Then he lowered his head on one side, as if to listen attentively; but his mouth spoke softly and murmured, 'You will tell that man that. . . .'" "I did not hear what followed," Janet comments, "but the patient straightened himself and said at full voice: 'Monsieur the Marquis asked me to thank you. . . . I heard him perfectly.' Clearly, it was his own speech that suggested to him his hallucination of hearing."[20] To such cases, Janet adds further clinical evidence: a patient named "T.," who, whenever she heard voices, could not speak. She would explain that "There is 'something in my cheeks that keeps me from talking at that moment.'" Like Charcot and Séglas, Janet holds that language presupposes motor articulation. In this case, the hearing of discourse also implies it. Since "two images of the muscular sense of the tongue" cannot occur at once, the patient is incapable of speaking while listening.[21]

As a psychiatrist in training, Lacan encountered such phenomena early in his studies. Between 1927 and 1931, he worked in Parisian medical institutions where many of the major figures of French psychology, from Falret, Charcot, and Séglas to Lacan's own teachers, Henri Claude and Gaëtan Gatian de Clérambault, also practiced.

In the same years, he became well acquainted with the surrealists and their keen interest in the symptomatology of madness and the experience of "automatic" speech. Lacan himself published some of his first papers in the surrealist journal *Minotaure*.[22] In 1931, Lacan and two of his colleagues published an article in the *Année medico-psychologique* that focused on "forced" language in the case of a "writing disturbance" suffered by one "Marcelle C, aged 34," "'Inspired Writing': Schizography."[23] The first major fruit of Lacan's own research, however, was his 1932 doctoral thesis, "On Paranoiac Psychosis and Its Relation to Personality," where he proposed a new interpretation of both delusion and hallucination.[24] Two decades later, he approached madness from a different perspective. In the volume of his *Seminar* that collects his teaching from 1955 to 1956, Lacan set forth his first psychoanalytic account of a phenomenon that he called by a plural noun, "psychoses."[25] His research and teaching were to lead to the essay that he published in 1958 and collected in 1966 in his *Écrits*: "On a Question Prior to Any Possible Treatment of Psychosis."[26]

Lacan begins that article just as he opened his 1955–1956 seminar: by acknowledging the scarce attention that Freud and his school accord to psychoses. When psychoanalytic literature takes such phenomena into account, Lacan notes, it is the theory of paranoia that predominates, Freud having been "initially and essentially interested in paranoia," as his reading of Daniel Paul Schreber's *Memoirs of My Nervous Illness* indicates.[27] Lacan follows Freud in according such a priority to paranoia, but he frames his inquiry in terms that are entirely his own. Asserting that the most characteristic form of psychosis is verbal hallucination, Lacan argues that a single question must dominate the "entire subject": "Who is speaking?"[28] To orient the ensuing discussion, he draws on the French tradition, singling out Jules Séglas. It was Séglas, he states, who first perceived "what is nonetheless sometimes quite visible, which is that the subject himself utters what he says he hears." "By a sort of brilliant stroke at the beginning of his career," Séglas

> pointed out that verbal hallucinations occurred in people who could be observed, by quite obvious signs, in some cases, by looking slightly more closely in others, to be themselves uttering the words they accused their voices of having spoken to them, whether or not they were aware of it, or did not want to know. This constituted a small revolution: observing that the source of auditory hallucination was not external.[29]

Yet Lacan does not limit himself to restating Séglas's discovery, for he also wagers that its validity may be extended to the entire field of verbal hallucinations. "Strictly speaking," he asks, "are there psychical verbal hallucinations? Are they not always, more or less, psychomotor hallucinations?" Rapidly, Lacan recalls an "essential dimension of the phenomenon of speech" to which the theory of information developed in the years of his seminar had hardly granted any importance. It is the apparently simple fact that "when the subject speaks, he hears himself." "The phenomenon of speech can't be schematized by the image that serves a number of what are called communication theories — sender, receiver, and something takes place in between," Lacan asserts. "It seems to have been forgotten that among many other things in human speech, the sender is always a receiver at the same time, that one hears the sounds of one's own words. It's possible not to pay attention to it, but it's certain that one hears it."[30]

Lacan argues that there are circumstances in which that apparently negligible redundancy in the event of discourse proves "essential." In his seminar, as in his later prolegomenon to "any possible treatment of psychosis," he illustrates his thesis by drawing an example from his own experience as a psychiatrist. The example concerns the hallucination of a fragment of speech: a word charged with an extraordinary force, yet disjoined from any communication exchange. Lacan recalls how, "presenting" patients before an audience at a hospital, he once examined "two people and one single delusion, which is known as a *délire à deux*."[31] The two were mother and daughter. It was the younger who related to Lacan the experience on which he focuses. She recounted to him how, one day, "as she was leaving her home, she had a run-in in the hallway with an ill-mannered sort of chap, which came as no surprise to her, since this shameful man was the steady lover of one her neighbors, someone of loose morals."[32] The "run-in" had been the occasion for the hearing of a voice: a hallucination that she could not banish from her mind.

Lacan recalls the daughter's account. "On passing her — she could not hide this from me, it still weighed upon her chest — he had said a dirty word to her, a dirty word that she was disinclined to repeat to me because, as she put it, it devalued her."[33] When Lacan asks her about the circumstance of the exchange, she mentions that "she was not completely innocent in the matter." "She herself had said something in passing," something that, as he puts it, she "confesses . . . more easily than what she had heard." The words that she uttered to the man made up a sentence about herself: "I've just been to the pork butcher's" (*je viens de chez le charcutier*). Lacan's initial response is to suggest to the young woman that in her evocation of swine, she may have been alluding to the "ill-mannered fellow" carrying on an affair with her neighbor. Yet Lacan proceeds cautiously. Holding to his patient's terms, he does not ask her if she had evoked a "dirty *pig*" (*cochon*); he merely wonders about a possible reference to "pork" (*porc*).[34] The woman understands him well and assures him that she called the man by no such names. Striving to reconstruct what happened, Lacan then repeats to her the phrase, "I've just been to the pork butcher's." His echo of her speech incites her to disclose the unsaid word. "She blurts it out to us": "What did *he* say? He said — *Sow* [*Truie*]."[35]

That is the insult (*injure*) that has cut, so to speak, into the young woman's mind. To frame the scene of its sounding, Lacan provides his audience with further details. The man in the hallway is "a married man, the lover of a girl who is herself the friend of our patient and heavily implicated in the desire of which our patient is a victim." The woman and her mother have had a complex relation to the neighbor and her married lover. The two women considered the two "persecutory and hostile characters," even if they never openly argued with them, a circumstance that, Lacan adds, "surprised those present at the interview." The patient herself cannot grasp how, "through malicious gossip, no doubt through taking legal action," the couple managed to have her committed to a hospital. Yet Lacan also adds a further element to his account of the women suffering from a *délire à deux*. Long before the incident in the hallway, the two had been "unable to separate" when the daughter married. Later, they fled the home in the countryside that they shared with the woman's husband. "According to the medical certificates," he had threatened his wife, making it clear that "he wanted nothing less than to slice her up."[36]

Once they were living on their own, the two women felt endangered by their neighbor. Mother and daughter both saw her as "primordially invading": "She would always come and knock at their door while they were at the toilet or just as they were dining or reading."[37] Their "feeling of being intruded upon" developed, Lacan explains, into "a delusion of being watched." The women's principal concern became "distancing this person who was essentially taken to be intrusive."[38] Yet once they had succeeded in their shared undertaking, the situation became unbearable. "Things . . . started to become problematic when this expulsion, this refusal, this rejection, took full effect, I mean when they actually threw her [the neighbor] out."

The encounter in the building's common space occurred after that expulsion. Lacan is well aware that psychoanalysts would be tempted to explain the altercation and the hallucination by various means. They might avail themselves of the theory of projection. They might argue that the woman's paranoid impressions were the result of a defense mechanism. They might suggest that their feeling of being persecuted was linked to "that homosexual fixation, in the widest sense of the term, that is at the base, as Freud says, of social relations." Yet Lacan sets aside such interpretations. He insists that what stands in need of explanation is the perception of a single utterance. "The important thing is that *Sow* has been heard." The daughter, for her part, does not doubt its reality: "She didn't say *I had the feeling that he answered me — 'Sow!'* She said — *I said, 'I've just been to the pork butcher's,' and he said, 'Sow!' to me.*"[39]

Instead of dismissing the woman's impression as a delusion, Lacan proposes a theory of psychotic experience to account for its intelligibility. He contrasts two experiences of speech. He begins with ordinary discourse. In "true speech," he explains, "the Other [*l'Autre*] is that before which you make yourself recognized. But you can only make yourself recognized because it is already recognized." In this case, in order for communication to occur, a dimension must be instituted: that of reciprocity. Lacan offers several examples. When a man says to a woman, "You are my woman," he is implicitly saying to her, "I am your man"; in other words, he recognizes her in such a way that she, in turn, may recognize him. Before making either statement, however, the man has presupposed that he and the woman encounter each other in a dimension that Lacan names "the big Other," the "absolute Other." In that dimension, speakers may hold to their words or break them, committing themselves, in either case, to "complying with many things that are within the rules of the game."[40] In the discourse of the patient whom Lacan examined, by contrast, psychosis bars the way of such "true speech." Paranoia consists precisely in the exclusion of "the big Other." Meeting her neighbor in the corridor, the woman, therefore, can address no one except another individual, an "other with a small *o*.'" "The circuit closes on two small others," Lacan remarks. In the exchange, there is room only for the man whom she sees and herself. That closed circuit is the condition of the word that she suddenly perceives.

Lacan argues that the insult is in truth a fragment of the woman's own discourse that has returned to her, assailing her from a source that she cannot identify. He points out that in saying "*I've just been to the pork butcher's*," the woman utters a sentence that may be interpreted in several senses. In a first meaning, the phrase points to the circumstances of the woman's presence in the building; she has fled her husband, a butcher, who wanted "nothing less than to slice her up." In a second meaning, the sentence expresses the woman's intense preoccupation about the state of psychic disarray in which she finds herself. Lacan proposes the following prolix paraphrase: "*I, the sow, have just been to the butcher's, I am already disjoined, a fragmented body,* membra disjecta*, delusional, and my world is fragmenting, like me.*"[41] The apparently anodyne sentence that the woman utters is in this sense ominous. Like a slip or parapraxis, "I have just been to the pork butcher's" reveals more than it explicitly states; it discloses a truth about its subject that its speaker herself does not know.[42] When examined closely, the statement reveals itself implicitly to contain a riddle that may also be phrased as a question: "Now, who has just been to the pork butcher's?"[43] The solution is the hallucinated invective: *Sow!*

The insult is therefore a sign that the hearer has anticipated and yet also a word of which she can make no sense. Irreducible to the messages exchanged between addresser and addressee, it is an expression in which the seeming continuity of a dialogic exchange comes apart as "normal interlocution," in Lacan's phrase, gives way to "delusional interlocution."[44] In the terms of Lacan's seminar on psychoses, it is an "unchained signifier," which confronts the speaker with the "sudden emergence of total strangeness."[45] Developing Freud's categories, Lacan argues in *Écrits* that what the patient hears in the hallucinated word constitutes the return of what, in her paranoia, she has absolutely rejected (*verworfen*) and "forclosed": "the unsayable object, the object that has no name." The exclamation is for her intolerable and yet incontrovertible, an "irruption in the real" that "presents itself in the form of a broken chain."[46]

In the presentations that he offers of that "signifier in the real" or "symbol in the real," Lacan suggests two accounts of the timing of the injurious event. In *Seminar 3*, he recalls that when the woman heard the man say, *Sow!* she "whispered between her teeth, 'I've just been to the pork butcher's.'"[47] In that reconstruction, the insult incites her own discourse, prompting her allusion to the "pork butcher." Lacan comments, "She receives her speech from him; her own speech is in the other who is herself, the little other, her reflection in the mirror, her counterpart."[48] In "On a Question Prior to Any Possible Treatment of Psychosis" in *Écrits*, however, Lacan presents a different sequence. In that later version, the woman avows that before hearing the man speak, she spoke softly. She "conceded with a smile that, upon seeing the man, she had murmured the following words which, if she is to be believed here, gave no cause for offense: 'I've just been to the pork butcher's. . . .'"[49] In the *Écrits*, the insult therefore reaches her as the response to her own speech. The shifting reconstructions suggest the changes that Lacan's doctrine undergo from the seminar to the *Écrits*.[50] Yet in a sense, Lacan already had announced such a hesitation in his course, noting that "*Sow!* gives tit for tat, and one no longer knows whether the tit or the tat comes first."[51]

Séglas's intuition informs both Lacanian treatments of the incident. In each presentation, the analysis of the scene reveals that the hearer is obscurely but surely implicated in the discourse that she apprehends. The "perceiver" (*percipiens*), in other words, is delivered over to a real "perception" (*perceptum*) in such a way as to provoke a state of extreme psychic disarray. To Séglas's model, Lacan adds that in such a circumstance, in which "addresser" and "addressee" become indistinguishable, there is no room for reciprocity. The "big Other" being excluded, the woman is remitted to her own discourse, which returns to her in its most extreme alienation. It is striking, for this reason, that the sole "message" that the woman claims as her own obliquely announces—or recalls—the monosyllabic invective to which it is indistinctly bound. As Damien Guyonnet notes, in French, the last five letters of "pork butcher" (*charcutier*) are precisely those that, in a different order, spell "sow" (*truie*).[52] The "signifier in the real" is an anagram of the chain from which it is broken.

Recalling Joyce, whom Lacan knew well, one might call the revelatory sounding of such a fragment an "epiphany."[53] Yet premodern sources also furnish terms and examples by which to conceive of occurrences of such a structure. In particular, the possibility that words heard suddenly and in solitude might disclose a truth is one with which cultures of far earlier ages were familiar. An incident from the historiography of ancient Rome is in this regard worth recalling. Livy relates that late one day in 390 BCE, a man named Marcus Caedicius became the witness to a striking phenomenon. "In the silence of the night," the historian writes, "he heard a voice more distinct than that of any human [*vocem noctis silentio audisse clariorem humana*] bidding the magistrates be told that Gauls were approaching."[54] In his dialogue on divination, Cicero renders the exact words that the plebeian perceived: "The walls and gates must be repaired; unless this is done the city will be taken."[55] As Livy informs his readers, the warning went unheeded: "No notice was taken of this, partly owing to the humble rank of the informant, and partly because the Gauls were a distant and therefore an unknown nation."[56] Yet the voice spoke truly. The Gauls soon invaded Rome and, encountering little resistance, sacked the capital.

After the barbarians' departure, the citizens sought to expiate the sin of their indifference to the unknown speaker. Orders were given for a temple to be built on the Nova Via, where the monition had sounded.[57] Since nothing was known of the identity of the divine voice, the temple was consecrated to a being whom the Romans called "Aius Locutius" or "Aius Loquens," "Utterance God," or, to employ a more literal, if ungainly translation, "Speaker Sayer." This was a divinity whose revelation coincided with a single act of speech. Like all sonorous epiphanies, it defied the conventions of communication. The words heard were delivered in an intelligible code and through a contact. They also composed an unequivocal message. The "context," however, was as impenetrable as was the night of its sudden sounding. The addresser and addressee or addressees were no less mysterious. Was Marcus Caedicius the intended recipient of the warning? Perhaps the otherwise undistinguished plebeian had been selected to hear the "voice more distinct than that of any human" and to relay it to his fellow Roman citizens. Perhaps, however, his perception was no more than a coincidence, the overhearing of words meant for another.

One might go further in wondering about the scene of the sudden revelation. How exactly did Marcus Caedicius perceive the great voice? By all accounts, he was alone at the moment of its sounding. Certain questions are difficult for a modern reader to avoid. Could the event have been an invention? Could it have been an auditory verbal hallucination? Without openly contesting the veracity of the report, the Romans seem to have been struck by the obscurity of the subject who thus manifested himself. Whether the divine "Speaker Sayer" had revealed himself before his nocturnal apparition was a matter about which there could scarcely be any certainty. The people of the city, however, had no doubts about the divinity's subsequent taciturnity. Cicero stresses that the god spoke to the Romans when he was unknown to them. Then, he pointedly remarks, "after he had secured a seat, an altar and a name," Speaker Sayer fell silent and never addressed the Roman people again.[58] Having ignored the advice of Aius Locutius and suffered the dire consequences of their negligence, the Romans, aware of their past fault, piously continued to worship at the shrine of the obstinately silent "Sayer."

The name given to the god of the unexpected speech act raises questions of its own. The designation "Aius Locutius" or "Aius Loquens" seems patently redundant. Would it not suffice, one wonders, to call him "Speaker" or "Sayer," but not both? Linguists have established that *aio* is a verb signifying "authoritative speaking." The term, Émile Benveniste explains, "has the value of categorical and positive affirmation."[59] Sometimes the Romans called the god who revealed himself by a voice "more distinct than that of any human" "Aius" and no more. When added to the name "Aius," "Locutius" or "Loquens" rendered explicit what "Aius" denoted, as the grammarian Varro explained.[60] That the double title was the cause of persistent perplexity is suggested by a curious detail in the transmission of his fame. Certain modern authors silently alter the god's name, even as they retain its bipartite form. The change, to be sure, is minimal. Some writers merely add one letter to the first portion of his name. In Andrew Tooke's 1698 translation of François Pomey's 1658 *Pantheum mysticum seu fabulosa deorum historia*, long known in English as *Tooke's Pantheon of the Heathen Gods and Illustrious Heroes*, the deity thus appears in a list of lesser immortals not as "Aius Locutius" but as "*Alius* Locutius."[61] However minute it might appear, that modification is significant. In the passage from "Aius" to "Alius," "the Speaker Sayer" becomes another. He becomes "alien," and more exactly, "the Other Sayer."

The change doubtless bespeaks an error of typography or transcription, if not both. In some editions of the compendium, the divine name appears in both the modified modern form and in its classical shape, mitigating the effects of the slip.[62] Once effected, the deformation, however, was to be repeatedly reaffirmed. In the 1826 English rendition of the Baron de Théis's *Travels of Polycletes*, to cite but one example, "Alius Locutius," "the Other Sayer," again appears in passing.[63] The likelihood that the alteration is a misprision, in any case, hardly excludes the possibility that it is susceptible to interpretation. What Freud would call a "failure to remember the proper name" conceals a fundamental insight. A voice "more distinct than that of any human" may possess "the value of categorical and positive affirmation," as Benveniste states, being therefore worthy of the title "Aius." Insofar as it is audible once and only once, however, it cannot but be the occasion for the appearance of an alterity, which one may rightly name "Alius." The slip in naming and the slide in meaning are in this sense revelatory. A Sayer perceived in a single evanescent moment must be an "Other," if not "the big Other": a speaker who, however distinctly audible, remains essentially unidentifiable. To perceive the voice of a such an alterity is to be the witness of an unexpected epiphany. In terror or in stupor, in piety or in madness, it is to confront the "emergence of a sudden strangeness" that will not sound again.

CHAPTER SEVENTEEN

Something Demonic

Syllables, words, and sentences can acquire an unexpected sense in the moment of their utterance, but sudden blanks in articulation are at times no less significant. When speakers linger on a word or phrase, deliberately or by accident, the sense of what they say may shift. They can find that in the space of no more than a pause, they have suggested something other than what they had meant to state. In the exchange of messages between emitters and receivers, however, it is not only "addressers" whose perception may a change the contents of communication. "Addressees" can also take in what they perceive in unforeseen periods and rhythms. Yet one can also go further. Even those who have merely caught a piece of a sentence spoken by someone to someone else can grasp its elements in unexpected groupings, effectively reordering their constituents. In all such cases, what is said undergoes a change in the interval that separates an utterance from its understanding. The acoustic medium of such an alteration is, each time, a being lacking in any sound of its own: a fleeting pause.

That the placing of silences in the flow of discourse is of major consequence for understanding speech is a fact familiar to readers and editors alike. Since antiquity, punctuation, the art of marking rests in discourse, has played a major role in the establishment and interpretation of texts. The history of biblical interpretation is in this sense instructive. Keenly aware of the differences that phrasal divisions might make in the reading of Hebrew scripture, the Rabbis of late antiquity devoted considerable attention to such stops as commas and periods, which were unmarked in the ancient texts transmitted to them. On a page of the Babylonian Talmud, the Rabbis thus discuss a verse attributed to the prophet Amos: *Nafla lo tossif koum betoulat Israel.* Depending on the segmentation of those six words, the line can be understood in two opposing senses. In a first sounding, the verse falls into two units, with a first pause after *Nafla*. It then states an irrevocable fall: *Nafla* ("she fell"); *lo tossif koum betoulat Israel* ("she will not rise, the bride of Israel"). The King James Version represents the prophetic utterance in that form: "The virgin of Israel is fallen; she shall no more rise."[1] Yet the Talmudic tractate records that "in the West," the Rabbis place a pause elsewhere. According to its Palestinian interpretation, the pronouncement consists of a negation of the "fall" and a command to rise: *Nafla lo tossif* ("She will fall no more"); *koum betoulat Israel* ("arise, bride of Israel")![2]

The fathers of the church were no less sensitive to the effects that pauses in their holy books might entail. Discussing the nature of linguistic signs and the rules for their interpretation in *On Christian Doctrine*, Augustine, therefore stresses the role that punctuation must play in the recitation and the understanding of the testaments. Even a single misplaced silence, he warns, can distort divine revelation beyond repair. As an exemplary illustration, he recalls the opening of the Gospel according to John, "In the beginning was the Word, and the Word was with God, and God was the Word." Few statements in the Gospels seem more firmly established. Yet Augustine cautions that even that sentence is susceptible to being subjected to a "heretical punctuation." Readers known to him partitioned the Evangelist's words according to an aberrant form: "In the beginning was the Word, and the Word was with God, and there was God." "The Word," then, is relegated to the beginning of the next scriptural verse. Such a phrasing implies nothing less than sacrilege: the "refusal to believe that the Word was God."[3] Introducing a pause into the rhythm of John's assertion, the misplaced period after "God" denies the identity of God and Word, defying Christian dogma. It entails the ruin of the Trinity.

Readers, editors, and theologians, however, are not alone in their sensitivity to the effects of punctuation. Rhetoricians are familiar with the crucial role of rhythmic periods and pauses in oratory. Jurists know of countless cases where the resolution of controversies of interpretation ultimately depends on syntactic structures. One might extend almost indefinitely the list of the people for whom punctuation plays a critical role. In the twentieth century, a new set of practitioners would be added to their hallowed company: psychoanalysts. As Raymond de Saussure observed in 1925, one of the major novelties of "Freudian technique" is its "treatment of silence." In what Freud's Anna O. dubbed "the talking cure," patients are to speak, even as psychoanalysts refrain, as much as possible, from judgment, weighing the pauses that mark their patients' discourse.[4] Building on Saussure's remark in a paper presented to the Vienna Psychoanalytic Society in 1926, Theodor Reik noted that the psychoanalyst's taciturnity is for this reason "passive" only in appearance. In truth it is "active," possessing "a stronger effect than words." Reik argued that the psychoanalyst's silence is a "soundingboard" that drives patients forward, allowing them to surprise themselves in catching what they have said or failed to say.[5]

In the second half of the twentieth century, Lacan's clinical experience led him to accord no less importance to the perception of pauses in analytic discourse. He taught that in responding to the "analysand," the analyst must strive not to identify a sense, but to order a series of signifiers in speech, that is, to employ the customary word, to "punctuate." In his 1956 essay "The Function and Field of Speech in Psychoanalysis," Lacan goes so far as to claim that the entire psychoanalytic endeavor depends on such a segmentation of language: "It is a propitious punctuation [*une punctuation heureuse*]," he writes, "that gives sense to the discourse of the subject."[6] Lacan suggests that the work that the psychoanalyst performs on the patient's discourse is therefore analogous to the process by which a philologist defines the meter of a poem. He calls that work a "scansion."[7] Yet since psychoanalysis elucidates a discourse that is unspoken, as well as spoken, its "scanning" plays a role at once more consequential and more obscure than that familiar to adepts of literary and linguistic study. Metrics is concerned with the establishment of feet, accents, and pauses in lines that have been expressly uttered. By contrast, "Freudian technique" must decipher the traces of the unsaid. Lacan draws the startling conclusion that such a circumstance entails. Psychoanalysis implies nothing less than the "pointing" of the unwritten: "a punctuation without a text" (*une ponctuation sans texte*).[8]

Lacan's formula reverses the relationship between sentences and pauses, text and annotation, that is familiar to editors and readers. According to the common representation, punctuation consists in the insertion of marks of breathing into a discursive sequence that is articulated as a series of elements. The indication of stops is in such cases secondary in time and structure with respect to the identification of words. Simply put, punctuation follows discourse. Lacan suggests that in psychoanalysis, the order is the reverse. It is punctuation that is primary, and the "text" at issue emerges from a work of "scansion." That Lacan's claim applies to the singular object that is the psychoanalytic session, with its pauses and interruptions, is clear. Yet the notion of a "punctuation without a text" may also be fruitful beyond the field of clinical practice. It may be brought to bear on a domain that exceeds the phenomena proper to psychoanalysis. A question can be raised about the particular experience of auditory attention—or inattention—that sustains the unexpected hearing of prophetic signs in bits of speech. Might such a perception also involve a "propitious punctuation"? In other words, might there be such a thing as a silent *klēdōn*, an omen lodged in not sounds, but their pauses, even their interruptions?

Martin Heidegger's *Being and Time* suggests an affirmative answer to those questions, an answer formulated in a conceptual vocabulary irreducible both to psychoanalysis and to divination. To reconstruct his argument, the outline of the book's project must be briefly recalled. In his attempt to pose anew the "question of being," Heidegger aims to elucidate the nature of "Da-sein," "the being that we are," beginning not from its abstract structure and properties, but from a phenomenological analysis of its "average everydayness." Heidegger argues that ours is a being whose "essence" or "whatness" lies in "its having to be" (*in seinem Zu-sein*). It can therefore only be understood "in terms of its being (*existentia*)."[9] As a rule, however, Da-sein is inadequate to its "to be" (*Zu-sein*). Da-sein unreflectively understands itself after the fashion of entities that it is not, living in a condition of "*subservience* [*Botmässigkeit*] to others." In that modality, Da-sein itself "is not itself." Heidegger explains that "the others have taken its being away from it. The everyday possibilities of being of Da-Sein are at the disposal of the whims of the others." It would be an error to take such "others" to be any discernible individuals. "The others," Heidegger specifies, "are not *definite* others." They are "not this one and not that one, not oneself [*man selbst*] and not some and not the sum of them all." Heidegger designates such "others" by a new philosophical term, built from an indefinite pronoun. They are, he writes, "the neuter, *the they*" (*das Neutrum*, das Man).[10]

"The they" is no less dominant for being structurally unidentifiable. In its "inconspicuousness and unascertainability," "the they" exerts a "true" or even "authentic dictatorship" (*eigentliche Diktatur*) over the being that we are. In our average everydayness, we exist only as "the they" does. "We enjoy ourselves and have fun the way *they* enjoy themselves. We read, see, and judge literature the way *they* see and judge. But we also withdraw from the 'great mass' the way *they* withdraw, we find 'shocking' the way *they* find shocking. The they, which is nothing definite and which all are, though not as a sum, prescribes the kind of being of everydayness."[11] In such a condition, Da-sein, captivated by the voices of others, "fails to hear its own self." To designate that consistently missed encounter, Heidegger uses the word *überhören*, literally, "overhearing," which in its German construction, unlike in English, relates to "hearing" (*hören*) as the verb "to overlook," in English, relates to "to look." Subjected to others in being remitted to the "they-self," Da-sein "fails to hear [literally, it 'overhears'] its own self in listening to the they-self" (*überhört es im Hören auf das Man-selbst das eigene Selbst*).[12]

Nonetheless, in the "noise" (*Lärm*) of many indistinct voices, Da-sein is summoned. "From afar unto afar" (*aus der Ferne in die Ferne*), a "call" reaches it, "arousing another kind of hearing." Heidegger identifies that call as the sudden manifestation of "the voice of conscience" (*die Stimme des Gewissens*). Unexpectedly and momentarily, it punctures the "listening" (or more exactly, "listening-away" (*Hinhören*) in which Da-sein has lost itself in its captivation by "the they."[13] Lest his argument be misunderstood, Heidegger specifies that the "own self" to which the call summons Da-sein is not to be conceived as an "object" that might be judged. It must be understood neither as "the self that unrestrainedly dissects its 'inner life' with excited curiosity, and not the self that stares 'analytically' at states of the soul and their backgrounds."[14] The self to which Da-sein is called by the voice of conscience is in short inaccessible to sociology, anthropology, and psychology. Only the "fundamental ontology" of the being that we are — only the "existential analytic" that takes Dasein as its subject and object — can adequately define it.

Yet the most striking feature of Heidegger's "call of conscience" lies elsewhere. It may be simply stated: in *Being and Time*, the decisive summons is strictly soundless. "The call is lacking any kind of utterance [*Der Ruf entbehrt jeglicher Verlautbarung*]. It does not even come to words [*Es bringt sich gar nicht erzt zu Worten*], yet it is not at all obscure and indefinite. *Conscience speaks solely and constantly in the mode of silence* [*Das Gewissen redet einzig und ständig im Modus des Schweigens*]."[15] Heidegger admits that such a "call" may seem to evoke a doctrine familiar to the moral, religious, and philosophical tradition: that of "the vulgar interpretation of conscience." "We call this interpretation of conscience vulgar," he explains, "because in characterizing this phenomenon and describing its 'function' it keeps to what *they* know as conscience, how they follow it or fail to follow it."[16] Such an "everyday interpretation" reflects the common representation of "life" as a "'business,' whether or not it covers the costs." Conscience in its "vulgar interpretation" is essentially "bad conscience." It arises after some action has been performed or been omitted, "chastening" human beings so that, having atoned for what they have done or failed to do, they may accede to the goodness of "good conscience," allowing them "to say of themselves: 'I am good.'"[17]

The "call of conscience" as it is defined in *Being of Time* is of a different structure. Insofar as it is a "call," it partakes of what Heidegger names the "mode of discourse" (*Modus der Rede*). It therefore presupposes at once voice, speech, and intelligibility. Yet this call admits of no material form. As Heidegger noted in a handwritten remark added at this point to his own copy of his book, "we don't 'hear' it with the senses."[18] In the expression "voice of conscience," "voice," therefore, is to be conceived not as the physical medium of the sounding of a word or phrase, but as an aphonic yet intelligible event: a "giving to understand" (*Zu-verstehen-geben*) in the form of a "jolt" or "abrupt arousal" (*des Stoßes, des abgesetzten Aufrüttelns*).[19] Conscience appears in a sudden pause and no more, confronting Da-sein with a message that is void of content. "*What* does conscience call to the one summoned?" Heidegger asks, before answering, "Strictly speaking—nothing. The call does not say anything, does not give any information about events of the world, has nothing to tell." Conscience "speaks solely and constantly in the mode of silence." More exactly, it is perceptible in a muteness that belongs to speaking beings alone: "falling silent" (*Schweigen*).[20]

In his analysis, Heidegger insists at once on the necessity of asking "*Who* is calling?" and on the impossibility of replying by means of any simple answer. At one level, "*Da-sein calls itself in conscience*" since the call issues from no one but Da-sein. At another level, however, the one who calls and the one who is called do not coincide. Da-sein's absorption in the world of others is broken by a summons from a "neutrality" that is irreducible to "the they," a neutrality that Heidegger evokes by means of the most impersonal of terms: as the pronoun "It" or "There" (*es*) in a sentence such as "It is . . ." or "There is. . . ." "The call is precisely something that *we ourselves* have neither planned nor prepared for nor willfully brought about. 'It' calls [*'Es' ruft*], against our expectations and even against our will. . . . The call calls *from* me, and yet *over* me [*Der Ruf kommt* aus *mir und doch* über *mich*]."[21] In its silent summons, "it" wrests Da-sein from its unreflective absorption in the affairs of "the they," bringing it before the intimate yet "particularly indefinite" experience of "not-being-at-home" (*Nicht-zuhause-sein*) that Heidegger calls "uncanniness" (*Unheimlichkeit*).[22] "The call does not report any facts; it calls without uttering anything. The call speaks in the uncanny mode of *silence*. And it does this only because in calling the one summoned, it does not call him into the public idle chatter of the they, but *calls* him *back* from that *to the reticence of his existent potentiality-of being*."[23] In the catching of such a "call," Da-sein, released from the "dictatorship" of the no one that is "the they," is remitted to its own blankness. "The call discloses nothing that could be positive or negative as *something to be taken care of*" because it involves a "completely different being": human existence in its irreducibly indeterminate "potentiality-of-being" (*Seinskönnen*).[24]

In the silence of its summons, Heidegger's "call of conscience" echoes one of the most famous experiences in the history of philosophy: that of Socrates's intermittent hearing of a "demonic" sign or voice that he alone perceived. To be sure, nowhere in *Being and Time* does Heidegger evoke that ancient experience. Nowhere in his book, in fact, does Heidegger mention the name of Socrates. That Heidegger was aware of the pertinence of the Socratic perception to the phenomenology of conscience, however, may be inferred from a footnote to *Being and Time*. In that remark, Heidegger summarily recalls "Kant's, Hegel's, Schopenhauer's, and Nietzsche's interpretations of conscience" before drawing the reader's attention to an 1876 essay by Albrecht Ritschl. Finally, he singles out a "monograph just published" in 1925 by Hendrik Gerhardus Stoker to which he dedicates the rest of his paragraph. Heidegger judges Stoker's phenomenological study, *Conscience: Phenomena and Theory*, to constitute "considerable progress as compared to traditional interpretations of conscience."[25] Heidegger's praise is brief and partial, but unmistakable. Only by consultation of the mentioned work would a reader grasp the extent of Heidegger's borrowing from Stoker. In his final chapter, Stoker sets out an account of what he calls "warning conscience" (*warnendes Gewissen*) that is unmistakably similar to Heidegger's theory of the "call."[26] For Stoker, "warning conscience" appears in the mode of a "voice" (*Stimme*) that "tells us what we are not to do, never what we ought to do." It is to be heard at decisive moments, yet it neither reveals nor relates any definite tidings. No sooner does Stoker introduce the voice of such a conscience than he poses, in parentheses, a rhetorical question: "Who does not think here necessarily of Socrates's *daimonion*?"[27]

That enigmatic being is well attested in the works of the classical philosophers. Both Plato and Xenophon recount that Socrates evoked it by various means. Depending on the setting, the ancient thinker dubbed it "something divine" (*theion ti*) or, employing a word derived from the term *daimōn*, which in ancient Greek meant "spirit," "something demonic" (*ti daimonion*), or a "sign of the demonic" (*daimoniou sēmeion*). In Plato's *Apology*, Socrates alludes to that "something" as a matter familiar to many people in Athens—not least his own accusers to whom he addresses himself in his monologue. Socrates recalls that from time to time, "there comes to me a something spiritual or something demonic [*moi theion ti kai daimonion gignetai*]." Socrates presents it as an acoustical phenomenon that impels him to refrain from acting: "It is a voice [*phōnē*] which from childhood has frequently come to me, and which makes itself heard only to turn me back from what I am about to do, but never to impel me forward."[28]

The Platonic dialogues suggest both that Socrates perceived that voice repeatedly and that each time, it was to him unexpected. In a passage in the *Phaedrus*, the philosopher is walking with his young companion outside Athens when he discerns an indistinct sign that appears to him to be a kind of "voice." "Just as I was about to cross the river," he avows to his friend, "the familiar demonic sign [*to daimonion te kai to eiōthos sēmeion*] came to me which, whenever it occurs, holds me back from something I am about to do. I thought I heard a voice coming from this very spot [*tina phōnēn edoxa autothen akousai*], forbidding me to leave."[29] In the *Euthydemus* and the *Republic*, Socrates relates other experiences of perceiving an unanticipated, yet "familiar" "divine," "spiritual," or "demonic" sign (*eōthos sēmeion to daimonion*).[30] In the *Euthyphro* and the *Theatetus*, Socrates presents himself as having been witness to a more indefinite apparition, shorn even of the qualities of being a "voice" or "sign." In those dialogues, he claims to have perceived merely "something demonic" (*daimonion ti*).[31]

Socrates's remarks on those impressions aroused great interest in antiquity. They were sufficiently legendary that when the unknown authors of the *Theages* and the *Alcibiades Major* composed their pseudo-Platonica in the style of the authentic dialogues, they included scenes in which Socrates lingers on his experiences of such signs. In the *Theages*, which dwells at length on the "demonic something," Socrates tells his interlocutor of "a voice [*phōnē*] which, when it comes, always points out to me something to dissuade me from what I am about to do, but never to urge me on."[32] The Socrates of the *Alcibades Major*, by contrast, mentions a "certain demonic opposition" (*ti daimonion enantiōma*) that kept him from conversing with Alcibiades.[33] By the classical age of Rome, if not earlier, such experiences had become for ancient readers inseparable from the figure of the thinker. In his dialogue on divination, Cicero thus refers to a circumstance that he takes to be common knowledge and for which he hesitates to offer any single Latin translation: "what we have heard about Socrates and what is often said by him in the works of his disciples—namely, that there is a certain kind of divinity which he calls his *daimonion* [*esse divinum quiddam, quod* daimonion *appellat*], which he always obeyed, as it never forced him on but often held him back."[34]

Over the course of the next centuries, Greek and Roman commentators sought to elucidate the fleeting evocations of that "demonic something" in the Platonic corpus. As Cicero notes, in Plato's dialogues Socrates never speaks of a "spirit" or "god"; he limits himself to evoking "something spiritual" or "demonic," alluding to his "kind of divinity" (*divinum quiddam*) as a *daimonion* and no more. Before long, however, readers conceived of it as "a personal, tutelary, allotted and active *daimōn*."[35] In the second century AD, Apuleius dedicates a brief work, *The God of Socrates*, to the question. He argues that Socrates perceived "a certain kind of voice" (*quampiam vox*) distinct in nature both from mortal voices and the sonorous presages and omens that superstitious people evoke.[36] Two centuries later, Calcidius removes the *daimonion* further from the domain of sensible phenomena. In his commentary on the *Timaeus*, he recalls that sound, as the Stoics teach, is "struck air" (*aer ictus*). He argues that the "something demonic" that appeared to Socrates was of a different nature, reaching him without the mediation of sensation.[37] In the fifth century AD, Hermeias of Alexandria proposes a similar explanation in his scholia on the *Phaedrus*. Socrates, he writes, was prone to perceive a "nonsensible voice," which his soul apprehended immaterially.[38]

Modern readers were to be no less fascinated by the sign familiar to Socrates. Some grappled with the question of its nature more than once. In his essay "Of Prognostications," Michel de Montaigne suggests that one might explain it without referring to either demons or divinities: "The demon of Socrates was perhaps a certain impulse of the will," he wagers, "that came to him without awaiting the advice of his reason [*sans le conseil de son discours*]."[39] Yet in "Of Experience," Montaigne admits the difficulties that he encountered when seeking to affirm such an "impulse": "Nothing is so hard for me to stomach in the life of Socrates as his ecstasies and possessions by his daemon" [*ses ecstases et ses demoneries*]."[40] Nietzsche, who discusses Socrates repeatedly, accords particular importance to his customary sign. "We are offered a key to the essence of Socrates by that wonderful phenomenon known as the 'daimonion of Socrates,'" he writes in *The Birth of Tragedy*, referring to Plato's *Euthyphro* and *Apology*:

> In particular situations, when his enormous mind began to sway uncertainly, he was able to get a firm hold on things again thanks to a divine voice which made itself heard at such moments. Whenever it appears, this voice always *warns* him to *desist*. In this utterly abnormal nature the wisdom of instinct only manifests itself in order to *block* conscious understanding from time to time. Whereas in the case of all productive people instinct is precisely the creative-affirmative force and consciousness makes critical and warning gestures, in the case of Socrates, by contrast, instinct becomes the critic and consciousness the creator—a true monstrosity *per defectum*![41]

In his later works, Nietzsche evokes the diagnostic categories of modern medicine to elucidate what he calls "the problem of Socrates." Identifying "all visions, frights, extenuations, raptures of the holy" as the "well-known conditions of sickness" in *Human, All-Too-Human*, he suggests that the Socratic experience illustrates such infirmities. "The daimonion of Socrates," he writes, is "perhaps an aliment of the ear [*ein Ohrenleiden*] that he, according to his predominantly moral way of thinking, simply *interprets* otherwise than we would today."[42] In one of his last works, *Twilight of the Idols, or How to Philosophize with a Hammer*, Nietzsche takes a further step, giving the fabled impression a properly modern scientific name. Alluding to Esquirol and the science of alienation, Nietzsche refers to the Socratic impressions by a technical term of psychology: they are, he notes, "auditory hallucinations" (*Gehörs-Hallucinationen*).[43]

In its time, Nietzsche's remark was less provocative than it may appear today. Half a century earlier, Louis Francisque Lélut, physician and philosopher, methodically reached the conclusion that

Nietzsche proclaimed. In 1836, only a few years after Esquirol's introduction of "hallucination" into the modern medical vocabulary, Lélut published a well-documented study, which he revised and augmented for a second edition in 1856, a work pointedly titled *The Demon of Socrates: Specimen of An Application of the Science of Psychology to That of History.*[44] Lélut opened his book by recalling how the ancient sources present Socrates as susceptible to the power of "supernatural forces," a *daimōn*, tutelary spirit or "genius." Lélut proceeded to pose a simple question: What are the "visions" that such a "force" imposes, if not the "false perceptions" familiar to modern physicians? "To say that Socrates was a visionary was, in a more exact language, to say that he was a hallucinator [*un halluciné*]," Lélut wrote in 1856, summarizing his claims. "Moreover, since, in the vocabulary, or better, the realities of science, a hallucinator, insofar as he hallucinates and in the moment of his hallucination — that is, of his false sensation that he judges to be true — is alienated and mad, to say that Socrates had false perceptions, that he was a visionary, a hallucinator, was to say that he was alienated and mad." A "brutally" crystalline reasoning subtended Lélut's argument. "Forgetting that it was a question of Socrates; setting aside the grandeur of the name, to see only the reality of the fact; imperturbably traversing the sequence of my deductions; moving from one term to the other," the man of science followed "this altogether algebraic procedure: a = b; b = c; c = d," thus reaching "this definitive equation: Socrates = mad."[45]

In 1856, Lélut stresses the temerity that he showed two decades earlier. As "a young man, a physician, in the most modest of positions," he dared to bring the categories of medicine to bear on the mythic initiator of philosophy.[46] Recalling the famous account given by Alcibiades in the *Symposium* of the twenty-four hours in which Socrates once stood still, lost in thought at the battle of Potidea, Lélut argued that the thinker was susceptible to states of stupor. "He had ecstatic moments, almost bouts of catalepsy. . . . Soon those ecstatic moments took on the character of more definite hallucinations, which were shorter, but more frequent: hallucinations of the general touch, both internal and external; above all, hallucinations of hearing, and probably also of sight."[47] According to Lélut, such disturbances "only increased as he grew older." Alluding perhaps to the *Theages*, Lélut wrote that Socrates "ended by convincing himself that by means of that divine assistance, he could exert a favorable influence on the young people who kept him company, leading them, by a kind of moral magnetism, toward the goal of his efforts at reform." Lélut took the repeated perception of a "voice" in the absence of any observable sound as the crucial symptom of Socrates's state of mental alienation. "As a criterion of madness, there is nothing more extraordinary, but there is also nothing more irrefutable, than such hallucinations; by their directedness to a single object, by their consequences, by their reasonableness, so to speak, and above all by the fact that they can last a lifetime, without entailing a true maniacal delirium, they constitute a kind of madness that one may term *sensorial* or *perceptive*."[48]

Lélut's claims were widely discussed in medical circles in the nineteenth century. In 1864, the *Journal de médécine mentale* contained an essay by Désiré-Magloire Bourneville—"Was Socrates Mad?"—that was entirely dedicated to the debate incited by "Monsieur Lélut's very famous book." Bourneville noted that some physicians doubted that anyone suffering from insanity could live fifty years as an adult, as Socrates did, without succumbing to total madness. François-Victor Bally, member of the Academy of Medicine, declared himself "scandalized" that a physician would dare to "transform the first sage, not only of Greece, but of the world, into a madman," reducing "sublime moral inspirations and precepts" to "pathological anomalies."[49] Citing clinical evidence, however, Bourneville concluded that Lélut's position was sound: "Mental distress can at times be indefinitely perpetuated without radically compromising physical and psychic forces." The philosopher may therefore have been "truly mad, while preserving, in appearance, the double attribute of a virile health and brilliant faculties."[50]

Lélut was perhaps the first modern physician to consider Socrates from a psychological perspective. He was certainly not to be the last. In the 1960s and 1970s, Lacan repeatedly suggested that psychoanalytic categories might be brought to bear on Plato's Socrates. In the 1970s, Lacan evoked "Socrates the hysteric," who had exhibited the "pathognomonic symptoms," and in his late paper, "Joyce the Symptom," Lacan judged Socrates to be "the perfect hysteric." Given his long-standing clinical and theoretical commitment to the study of psychosis, it is not surprising that Lacan should have shown a particular interest in the "kind of voice" that Socrates claimed to have perceived. In *Seminar 12*, Lacan characterized it as a voice "that is not at all a metaphor," adding that, because of it, Socrates "stopped speaking" to "hear what it had to say to him, just as our hallucinators [*comme un de nos hallucinés*] do."[51] An allusion to Lélut can be found as early as *Seminar 8*, held in 1960–1961, even if Lacan did not cite the nineteenth-century physician by name.[52] Evoking Socrates's characteristic *atopia* or being "out of place" in the order of the city state, Lacan remarked, "Nothing tragic, no tragic sense of life, as we say nowadays, sustains Socrates' *atopia*, only a daemon. Don't forget this *daimon*, for Socrates talks about it incessantly. This daemon seems to haunt him [*l'hallucine*] in order to allow him to survive in space, warning him of possible pitfalls. . . . He is, in a word, a madman who believes himself in the god's ordained service."[53]

Yet Socrates's experience may also be considered from a perspective neither spiritual nor medical, as one of the first works on the subject, Plutarch's *On the Genius of Socrates*, indicates. In that dialogue, a man named Galaxidorus offers an account of the "demonic something" that is worth recalling. His interlocutor, Theocritus, puts the essential question to him: "What, my dear friend, are we to make of Socrates's *daimonion*? Are we to call it a fiction, or what?"[54] Galaxidorus responds that it is a thing of little value in itself, which in some conditions proves to be of major consequence. He proposes an analogy drawn from the fields of physics:

> A single weight by itself does not by itself turn the scale. But if it is added to an evenly-balanced load, it pulls the whole thing down. Likewise, a sneeze or an omen contained in an unexpected word [*klēdōn*] or some such sign [*houtō ptarmos ē klēdōn ē ti toiouton symbolon*], <being small> and light, <cannot> determine a weighty mind to action; but, added to one of two opposing calculations, it resolves the doubt by destroying the equipoise. Movement and impulse follow.[55]

In other words, Galaxidorus grants that the "sign" or "voice" that Socrates perceives is as fleeting as a "sneeze" (*ptarmos*) or *klēdōn*.[56] Yet he adds that it nevertheless bears a sense in a sequence of signifying elements. Joined "to one of two opposing reasons," it can tip the scale of deliberation in one direction or another, deciding on a matter that cannot otherwise be resolved.

In the dialogue, Galaxidorus's argument meets with incredulity and astonishment. Pheidolaus, one of his interlocutors, objects that to admit such an account is to reduce the mightiest of divinations "to sneezes and *klēdones*." Yet Galaxidorus pleads his case:

> In medicine, a throbbing pulse or a blister is a small thing in itself, but the symptom of something serious. For the pilot of a ship, the cry of a sea-bird or the passing over of a thin wisp of cloud is a sign of wind and the sea turning rough. Similarly, for the prophetic mind, a sneeze or a *klēdōn* is a small thing in itself, but <a sign of some important> occurrence. In no art is the prediction of great things by small or many things by few regarded with contempt.[57]

Yet Galaxidorus also offers a further example of an analogous kind of occurrence. After mentioning medicine and seafaring, he evokes a different technique of reasoned inference. It involves an art in which the smallest unit, being in itself not so much of little significance as purely insignificant, yields the most indubitable of meanings.

That art is reading. Galaxidorus explains,

> If a man ignorant of the power of letters [*grammatōn dynamis*], seeing a few unimpressive marks, could not believe that a scholar could read from them

> great wars that befell men of old, foundations of cities, and the deeds and sufferings of kings, and therefore declared that it was "something *daemonic*" that disclosed and related these things to the scholar, you would have a good laugh, my friend, at the fellow's ignorance![58]

From Galaxidorus's perspective, the "voice" that Socrates alone perceives is neither more nor less than the unit of a system of writing, which the thinker alone knows how to read. It is, in short, a kind of letter. Since, however, it never belongs to a word, and since it is rigorously soundless, it might be better represented as the sign of a different nature: a pause. The Galaxidorean idea, in short, is that the "demonic something" is a soundless omen that can be read. Like the sneeze, such a sign interrupts the discourse in which it occurs, giving Socrates a sudden jolt and rendering possible an unexpected, if discouraging intuition. Anticipating Heidegger, one might define such a shock as the appearance of the voice of conscience and its silent call. Summoning Socrates in drawing him from his absorption in matters external to his most proper "potentiality-of-being," it brusquely stops him short. Yet one may also define the "sign," following Galaxidorus, according to the Lacanian formula. A pause that frames what has been said, the unheard voice suggests a "punctuation without a text."

If Socrates constitutes a model for philosophers, it is perhaps not only in his obstinate pursuit of recurrent questions, in his commitment to articulating fundamental concepts, and in his elaboration of the doctrines for which he is still remembered today. It is also in his unmatched susceptibility to the persistent power of such punctuation. For like philology, rhetoric, the law, and psychoanalysis, albeit after a manner all its own, philosophy involves the perception of portentous signs in discourse—not only in arguments and their formal elaborations, but also in ordinary speech and its often unruly elements. Philosophers, for this reason, may not be as far removed as one might imagine from Stephen Daedalus "passing through Eccles' St" when struck by a transient and profane epiphany or from Proust's narrator, straining to detect truths perceptible in the "abrupt breaches of syntax" that mark Albertine's apparently innocuous assertions. Whereas the chronicler of lost time, however, attends in trepidation to the words of a single woman, seeking to glean from their inconsistencies revelations that he cannot foresee, philosophers concern themselves with varieties of discourse that are unlimited in extension, that relate habits and beliefs, theses and arguments, fictions and inventions, and that consist of myth as well as theory, literature no less than the sciences, theologies, and history. Such domains are certainly too vast and too diverse to admit of study by means of any single method. Each time, the practices of reading and listening must be defined anew. Yet the Socratic experience points to one ineliminable possibility. Wherever words are spoken and transcribed and wherever they fall into ordered sequences, a sudden silence may become audible. A "small thing in itself," it can seem little more than a momentary hesitation in the advancement of an inquiry. The pause, however, may also be propitious. Like a sneeze, it can be at once a break in speech and an unexpected breath of air.

Notes

CHAPTER ONE: THE INTERVAL

1. For a classic account, see Roman Jakobson, "Linguistics and Poetics," in *Selected Writings*, 8 vols. (The Hague: Mouton, 1962–1988), vol. 3: *The Poetry of Grammar and Grammar of Poetry*, pp. 18–51. First published in Thomas A. Sebeok, ed., *Style and Language* (Cambridge, MA: MIT Press, 1960), pp. 350–77.

2. Cicero, *De divinatione* 1.9; Latin in *Della divinazione*, ed. and trans. Sebastiano Timpanaro (Milan: Garzanti, 1988), p. 8; English in *On Divination: Book 1*, trans. David Wardle (Oxford: Clarendon Press of Oxford University Press, 2006), p. 48.

3. Sextus Empiricus, *Adv. Math.* 9,132 = *SVF* 2 1018; English in *Against the Physicists*, trans. Richard Bett (Cambridge: Cambridge University Press, 2019), p. 29. Translation modified.

4. Hippocrates, *On Regimen* 1.12, in Hippocrates, *De diaeta / Du régime*, ed. and trans. Robert Joly with Simon Byl (Berlin: Akademie Verlag, 2003), p. 136, quoted in Peter T. Struck, *Divination and Human Nature: A Cognitive History of Intuition in Classical Antiquity* (Princeton: Princeton University Press, 2016), p. 1. Joly (p. 5) dates the treatise to "around 400 C.E."

5. The scholarly literature on divination is immense. Exemplary studies include E. E. Evans-Prichard, *Witchcraft, Oracles, and Magic among the Azande* (Oxford: Clarendon Press of Oxford University Press, 1937); George K. Park, "Divination and Its Social Contexts," *Journal of the Royal Anthropological Institute of Great Britain and Ireland* 93.2 (1963), pp. 195–209; Jean-Pierre Vernant et al., *Divination et rationalité* (Paris: Éditions du Seuil, 1974).

6. Carlo Ginzburg, "Spie: Radici di un paradigma indiziario," in Aldo Gargani, ed., *Crisi della ragione* (Turin: Einaudi, 1979), pp. 59–106, reprinted in *Miti emblemi spie: Morfologia e storia* (Turin: Einaudi, 1986), pp. 158–209; an English translation can be found in Carlo Ginzburg, "Clues: Roots of an Evidential Paradigm," in *Clues, Myths and the Historical Method*, trans. John Tedeschi and Anne C. Tedeschi (Baltimore: Johns Hopkins University Press, 1989), pp. 96–125.

7. Struck, *Divination and Human Nature*, p. 15.

8. Stéphane Mallarmé, "Ballets," in *Oeuvres complètes*, ed. Bertrand Marchal, 2 vols. (Paris: Gallimard, 1998–2003), vol. 2, pp. 170–74; Paul Valéry, "L'âme et la danse," in *Oeuvres*, ed. Jean Hytier, 2 vols. (Paris: Gallimard, 1960), vol. 2, pp. 148–76, esp. p. 164.

9. Walter Benjamin, "Lehre vom Ähnlichen," in *Gesammelte Schriften*, 7 vols., eds. Rolf Tiedemann and Hermann Schweppenhäuser (Frankfurt an Main: Suhrkamp, 1972–1991), vol. 2, p. 209; English in "Doctrine of the Similar," trans. Michael Jennings, in *Selected Writings, Volume 2, 1931–1934*, eds. Michael W. Jennings, Howard Eiland, and Gary Smith (Cambridge, MA: Harvard University Press, 1996–), p. 697. Translation slightly modified.

10. Benjamin, "Lehre vom Ähnlichen," p. 206; English in "Doctrine of the Similar," p. 695.

11. Walter Benjamin, "Über das mimetische Vermögen," in *Gesammelte Schriften*, vol. 2, p. 213; English in "On the Mimetic Faculty," trans. Edmund Jephcott, in *Selected Writings, Volume 2, Part 2, 1931–1934*, p. 722. Translation modified. The citation is from Hofmannsthal's 1893 play, *Der Tor und der Tod*: see Hugo von Hofmannsthal, *Gesammelte Werke*, ed. Herbert Steiner, 14 vols. (Stockholm: Bermann-Fischer, 1945–), vol. 1: *Gedichte und lyrische Dramen*, p. 292. Benjamin quotes the phrase in two other texts: see *Gesammelte Schriften*, vol. 1, part 3, p. 1238, and vol. 5, p. 524. On Benjamin's account of reading and the mimetic faculty, see Werner Hamacher, "The Word *Wolke*—If It Is One," trans. Peter Fenves, in Rainer Nägele, ed., *Benjamin's Ground: New Readings of Walter Benjamin* (Detroit: Wayne State University Press, 1988), pp. 147–76; Irving Wohlfarhth, "'Was nie geschrieben wurde, lesen': Walter Benjamins Theorie des Lesens," in Uwe Steiner, ed., *Walter Benjamin 1892–1940, Zum 100. Geburtstag* (New York: Peter Lang, 1992), pp. 297–344; Eric Downing, "Magic Reading," in Eric Downing, Jonathan M. Hess, and Richard V. Benson, eds., *Literary Studies and the Pursuits of Reading* (Rochester: Camden House, 2012), pp. 189–215. On Benjamin's appropriation of Hofmannsthal's phrase, see Kevin McLaughlin, *The Philology of Life: Walter Benjamin's Critical Program* (New York: Fordham University Press, 2023), pp. 109–11.

CHAPTER TWO: HERMES AT DUSK

1. Homer, "Hymn to Hermes," lines 14–15 and 5–6; Greek and English in *Homeric Hymns, Homeric Apocrypha, Lives of Homer*, ed. and trans. Martin L. West (Cambridge, MA: Harvard University Press, 2003), pp. 112–15.

2. Jenny Strauss Clay, *The Politics of Olympus: Form and Meaning in the Homeric Hymns*, 2nd. ed. (Bristol: Bristol Classical Press, 2006), p. 96.

3. Henry George Liddell and Robert Scott, *A Greek-English Lexicon*, 8th ed. (New York: American Book Company, 1901), s.v. "hermaion."

4. Claudine Leduc, "Une théologie du signe en pays grec: L'hymne homérique à Hermès (I) — Commentaire des vers 1–181," *Revue de l'histoire des religions* 212.1 (1995), p. 12.

5. Homer, "Hymn to Hermes," line 30; Greek and English in West, *Homeric Hymns*, pp. 114–15. Translation slightly modified.

6. Peter Struck, *Birth of the Symbol: Ancient Readers at the Limits of Their Texts* (Princeton: Princeton University Press, 2004), p. 90. See Struck's discussion of "the symbol as interpretable riddle," in ibid., pp. 90–94. On the term *symbolon*, see Walter Müri, "ΣΥΜΒΟΛΟΝ: Wort- und sachgeshichtliche Studie," in Eduard Vischer, ed., *Griechische Studien: Ausgewählte wort- und sachgeschichtliche Forschungen zur Antike* (Basel: Friedrich Reinhardt, 1976), pp. 1–44; Philippe Gauthier, *Symbola: Les étrangers et la justice dans les cités grecques* (Nancy: Univesité de Nancy II, 1972), pp. 62–106; and, for the history of the "symbol" as a term in reading practices, Struck, *Birth of the Symbol*, pp. 111–203.

7. Homer, "Hymn to Hermes," lines 36–40; Greek and English in West, *Homeric Hymns*, pp. 114–17.

8. Homer, "Hymn to Hermes," lines 41–48; Greek and English in West, *Homeric Hymns*, pp. 116–17.

9. Leduc points out that the hymn employs three terms for this instrument: it is at once *khelys* (242), *phorminx* (64, 506), and *kithara* (425, 433, 475, 499, 509). See "Une théologie du signe en pays grec," p. 19.

10. See Laurence Kahn, *Hermès passe: Ou, les ambiguïtés de la communication* (Paris: François Maspero, 1978), p. 123; Clay, *The Politics of Olympus*, p. 106.

11. See Clay, *The Politics of Olympus*, p. 108.

12. Homer, "Hymn to Hermes," line 57; Greek and English in West, *Homeric Hymns*, pp. 116–17.

13. Homer, "Hymn to Hermes," line 59; Greek and English in West, *Homeric Hymns*, pp. 116–17.

14. Susan C. Shelmedrine, "Hermes and the Tortoise: A Prelude to Cult," *Greek, Roman and Byzantine Studies* 25 (1974), p. 208.

15. Clay, *The Politics of Olympus*, p. 102.

16. Homer, "Hymn to Hermes," line 64; Greek and English in West, *Homeric Hymns*, pp. 118–19. As Clay notes (*Politics of Olympus*, p. 111), the phrase is used elsewhere in the Homeric corpus for lions: see *Iliad* 11.551 and 17.660. For a commentary, see Henk Versnel, "A God: Why Is Hermes Hungry?," in *Coping with the Gods: Wayward Readings in Greek Theology* (Leiden: Brill, 2011), pp. 309–77, esp. pp. 322–26.

17. On Hermes and the sacrifice, see Kahn, *Hermès passe*, pp. 56–68; Walter Burkert, "Sacrificio-sacrilegio: Il 'trickster' fondatore," *Studi storici* 25.4 (1984), pp. 835–45; Sarah Iles Johnston, "Myth, Festival, and Poet: The 'The Homeric Hymn to Hermes' and Its Performative Context," *Classical Philology* 97.2 (2002), pp. 124–27. On the meal as not sacrifice, but *dais*, "feast," see Clay, *The Politics of Olympus*, pp. 119–27. See also Versnel, *Coping with the Gods*, pp. 352–64.

18. Homer, "Hymn to Hermes," lines 145–47; Greek and English in West, *Homeric Hymns*, pp. 124–25.

19. Clay, *The Politics of Olympus*, p. 113.

20. Homer, "Hymn to Hermes," line 219; Greek and English in West, *Homeric Hymns*, pp. 130–31.

21. Dominique Jaillard, "Hermès et la mantique grecque," in Stelle Georgoudi, Renée Koch Piettre, and Francis Schmidt, eds., *La raison des signes: Présages, rites, destin dans les sociétés de la méditerranée ancienne* (Leiden: Brill, 2012), p. 92.

22. Ibid., p. 92.

23. Homer, "Hymn to Hermes," lines 235–42; Greek and English in West, *Homeric Hymns*, pp. 130–32.

24. Homer, "Hymn to Hermes," lines 305–306; Greek and English in West, *Homeric Hymns*, pp. 136–37. Cf. the translation by Hugh G. Evelyn-White in *Homerica and the Homeric Hymns* (Cambridge, MA: Harvard University Press, 1914). For an analysis of the gesture, see Maurizio Bettini, "Le orecchie di Hermes: Luoghi e simboli della comunicazione nella cultura antica," in *Le orecchie di Hermes: Studi di antropologia e letteratura classiche* (Turin: Einaudi, 2000), p. 13.

25. Clay judges it the "most difficult" passage in the Homeric corpus (*The Politics of Olympus*, p. 144). At least since 1786, scholars have considered it an addition to the poem: see Hans Herter, "Hermes: Ursprung und Wesen eines griechischen Gottes," *Rheinisches Museum für Philologie* 119.3 (1976), pp. 238–39.

26. Homer, "Hymn to Hermes," line 533; Greek and English in West, *Homeric Hymns*, pp. 154–55.

27. Homer, "Hymn to Hermes," lines 535–38; Greek and English in West, *Homeric Hymns*, pp. 154–55.

28. Homer, "Hymn to Hermes," lines 532–57; Greek and English in West, *Homeric Hymns*, pp. 156–57.

29. See in particular Susan Scheinberg, "The Bee Maidens of the Homeric Hymn to Hermes," *Harvard Studies in Classical Philology* 83 (1979), pp. 1–28, and Jennifer Larson, "The Corycian Nymphs and the Bee Maidens of the Homeric *Hymn to Hermes*," *Greek, Roman and Byzantine Studies* 36.4 (1995), pp. 341–57.

30. Norman O. Brown, *Hermes the Thief: The Evolution of a Myth* (New York: Vintage Books, 1948), p. 104.

31. Clay, *The Politics of Olympus*, p. 147.

32. Homer, "Hymn to Hermes," lines 560–63; Greek and English in West, *Homeric Hymns*, pp. 156–57.

33. See Jaillard, "Hermès et la mantique grecque," pp. 92–96.

34. Pausanias, *Ellados Periēgēsis* 7.22–24; Greek and English in Pausanias, *Description of Greece*, trans. W. H. S. Jones, 5 vols. (Cambridge, MA: Harvard University Press, 1918–1935), vol. 2, pp. 299–301. Translation slightly modified.

35. Jaillard, "Hermès et la mantique grecque," p. 93.

36. See Jean-Pierre Vernant, in *Mythe et pensée chez les Grecs: Études de psychologie historique*, new ed. (Paris: La Découverte, 1988), p. 197. On Hermes and the ears more generally, see Bettini, "Le orecchie di Hermes." On the shrine in Pharae, see also A. D. Rizakis *Achaie I: Sources textuelles et histoire régionale* (Athens: Kentron Hellēnikēs kai Rōmaïkēs Archaiotētos tou Ethnikou Hdrymatos Ereunōn, 1995), pp. 186–88, and Massimo Osanna, *Santuari e culti dell'Acaia antica* (Naples: Edizioni scientifiche italiane, 1996), pp. 151–67; Kenneth Lapatin, "Pharaian Kledomancy," in Jitse Dijkstra, Justin Kroesen, and Yme Kuiper, eds., *Myths, Martyrs, and Modernity: Studies in the History of Religions in Honour of Jan N. Bremmer* (Leiden: Brill, 2010), pp. 135–43.

37. Liddel-Scott, *A Greek-English Lexicon*, s.v. "Klēdōn."

38. W. R. Halliday, *Greek Divination: A Study of Its Methods and Principles* (London: Macmillan, 1913), p. 229. For "kledonomancy," see pp. 229–34.

39. Lisa Maurizio, "Interpretative Strategies for Delphic Oracles and Kledons: Prophecy Falsification and Individualism," in Veit Rosenberger, ed., *Divination in*

the Ancient World: Religious Options and the Individual (Sttutgart: Franz Steiner, 2013), p. 70.

40. Auguste Bouché-Leclercq, *Histoire de la divination en antiquité*, 4 vols. (Paris: E. Leroux, 1879–1882), vol. 1, p. 155. For his treatment of "kledonomancy," see pp. 115–20.

41. Pausanias, *Ellados Periēgēsis* 7.22.4 and 9.11.7. On the Smyrnan institution, see Maurice Holleaux, "ΑΠΟΛΛΩΝ ΣΠΟΔΙΟΣ," in *Mélanges Henri Weil* (Paris: A. Fontemoing, 1898), pp. 193–206, esp. pp. 194–95.

42. See Bouché-Leclerq, *Histoire de la divination en antiquité*, vol. 2, p. 400.

43. Herodotus, *Histories* 9.90. Greek and English in *Histories*, trans. A. D. Godley (Cambridge, MA: Harvard University Press, 1920), pp. 264–65.

44. Herodotus, *Histories* 9.91; Greek and English in Godley, *Histories*, pp. 266–67. Translation slightly modified.

45. On Hermes and whispering, see Hermann Usener, *Götternamen: Versuch einer Lehre von der religiösen Begriffsbildung* (Bonn: Friedrich Cohen, 1896), pp. 267–68, and "PSITHYROS," *Rheinisches Museum für Philologie* 59 (1904), pp. 623–34; Luca Soverini, "ΨΙΘΥΡΟΣ": Hermes, Afrodite e il sussurro nella Grecia antica," in Salvatore Alessandrì, ed., *Ἱστορίη: Studi offerti dagli allievi a Giuseppe Nenci in occasione del suo settantesimo compleanno* (Galatina: Congedo, 1994), pp. 433–60.

46. Jaillard, "Hermès et la mantique grecque," p. 103.

47. Aristophanes, *Peace* 394. On the passage, see Walter F. Otto, *Die Götter Griechenlands: Das Bild des Göttlichen im Spiegel des griechischen Geistes* (1929; Frankfurt am Main: Klostermann, 1987), pp. 108–11.

CHAPTER THREE: THE SUMMONS

1. Henry George Liddell and Robert Scott, *A Greek-English Lexicon*, 8th ed. (New York: American Book Company, 1901), s.v. "Klēdōn."

2. Pierre Chantraine, *La formation des noms en grec ancien* (Paris: Klincksieck, 1933), section 293, pp. 360–62.

3. Homer, *Odyssey* 18.112–15; English in *The Odyssey of Homer: A Modern Translation*, trans. Richard Lattimore (New York: Harper Torchbooks, 1967), p. 273.

4. See Anthony J. Podlecki, "Omens in the *Odyssey*," *Greece and Rome* 14.1 (1967), p. 16; Donald Lateiner, "Telemakhos' One Sneeze and Penelope's Two Laughs (*Odyssey* 17.541–50, 18. 158–168)," in Robert J. Rabel, ed., *Approaches to Homer: Ancient and Modern* (Swansea: Classical Press of Wales, 2005), p. 95.

5. Homer, *Odyssey* 18.117; English in Lattimore, *The Odyssey of Homer*, p. 273.

6. Herodotus, *Histories* 9.91; English in *The Histories*, trans. Aubrey de Sélincourt, rev. John Marincola (New York: Penguin Books, 2003), p. 591.

7. Scol. Ar. *Eq.* 1056a; For the Greek text and translation, see Martin L. West, ed. and trans., *Greek Epic Fragments: From the Seventh to the Fifth Centuries BC* (Cambridge, MA: Harvard University Press, 2003), pp. 124–27.

8. Aristotle, *Poetics* 4.1449a15–18; Greek in Dimitri Gutas and Leonardo Tarán, *Poetics: Editio Maior of the Greek Text with Historical Introductions and Philological Commentaries* (Leiden: E. J. Brill, 2012), p. 171; English in *On Poetics*, trans. Seth Benardete and Michael Davis (South Bend: St. Augustine's Press, 2002), pp. 13–14.

9. Aeschylus, *Choerophoi* 896–98; Greek text in the Oxford Classical Text edited by D. L. Page, *Aeschyli: Septem Quae Supersunt* (Oxford: Oxford University Press, 1972), p. 237; English in *Aeschylus II: The Oresteia*, ed, and trans. David Grene, Richmond Lattimore, Mark Griffith, and Glenn W. Most, 3rd ed. (Chicago: University of Chicago Press, 2013), p. 115. On the passage, see Sheila Murnaghan, "Body and Voice in Greek Tragedy," *Yale Journal of Criticism* 1.2 (1988), pp. 23–43, esp. pp. 32–33.

10. See C. W. Marshall, "Casting the Oresteia," *Classical Journal* 98.3 (2003), pp. 257–74, esp. pp. 261–63.

11. Aeschylus, *Choerophoi* 899, in Page, *Aeschyli: Septem Quae Supersunt*, p. 237; English in Greene and Lattimore, *Aeschylus II*, p. 115.

12. Aeschylus, *Choerophoi* 900–902, in Page, *Aeschyli: Septem Quae Supersunt*, p. 237; English in Greene and Lattimore, *Aeschylus II*, p. 115.

13. Aeschylus, *Choerophoi* 903, in Page, *Aeschyli: Septem Quae Supersunt*, p. 237; English in Greene and Lattimore, *Aeschylus II*, p. 115.

14. Karl Otfried Müller, *Aischylos Eumeniden, griechisch und deutsch, mit erläuternden Abhandlungen* (Göttingen: Dieterich, 1833), p. 47. See the discussion in Marshall, "Casting the Oresteia," pp. 261–63.

15. Bernard Knox, "Aeschylus and the Third Actor," in *Word and Action: Essays on the Ancient Theater* (Baltimore: Johns Hopkins University Press, 1979), p. 42. Cf. Garvie's remarks in his edition of Aeschylus, *Choephori*, ed. A. F. Garvie (Oxford: Oxford University Press, 1986), p. l; H. D. F. Kitto, *Greek Tragedy: A Literary Study*, 3rd. ed. (London: Routledge, 1966), p. 86.

16. Sarah Nooter, *The Mortal Voice in the Tragedies of Aeschylus* (Cambridge: Cambridge University Press, 2017), p. 233. Cf. Deborah H. Roberts, "Apollo and his Oracle in the Oresteia," *Hypomnemata* 78 (1984), p. 46.

17. Aeschylus, *Agamemnon* 34–37, in Page, *Aeschyli: Septem Quae Supersunt*, p. 140; English in Greene and Lattimore, *Aeschylus II*, p. 22. On speaking well and staying silent in the *Oresteia*, see Susanne Göddies, *euphêmia: Die gute Rede in Kult und Literatur der griechischen Antike* (Heidelberg: Winter, 2006), pp. 95–148.

18. Aeschylus, *Agamemnon* 636–37, in Page, *Aeschyli: Septem Quae Supersunt*, p. 161; English in Greene and Lattimore, *Aeschylus II*, p. 42. Simon Goldhill remarks that here, as in Claude Lévi-Strauss's account of the Malay Peninsula in *The Elementary Structures of Kinship*, "it is a misuse of language that leads to disaster": see *Language, Sexuality, Narrative: The Oresteia* (Cambridge: Cambridge University Press, 1984), p. 58.

19. John J. Peradotto, "Cledonomancy in the *Oresteia*," *American Journal of Philology* 90.1 (1969), p. 11.

20. Aeschylus, *Agamemnon* 861–65, in Page, *Aeschyli: Septem Quae Supersunt*, p. 168; English in Greene and Lattimore, *Aeschylus II*, p. 49.

21. On the two, see Peradotto, "Cledonomancy in the *Oresteia*." The first occurrence (863) may be an interpolation. See Eduard Fraenkel, in *Agamemnon, Edited with a Commentary*, ed. Eduard Fraenkel, 3 vols. (Oxford: Clarendon Press of Oxford University Press, 1950), vol., 2, pp. 390–91.

22. David Raeburn and Oliver Thomas, *The Agamemnon of Aeschylus: A Commentary for Students* (Oxford: Oxford University Press, 2011), p. liii.

23. Aeschylus, *Agamemnon* 1382–83, in Page, *Aeschyli: Septem Quae Supersunt*, p. 187; English in Greene and Lattimore, *Aeschylus II*, p. 68.

24. Aeschylus, *Agamemnon*, 926–27, in Page, *Aeschyli: Septem Quae Supersunt*, p. 170; English in Greene and Lattimore, *Aeschylus II*, p. 51. Translation modified. On this scene, see Charles Segal, *Tragedy and Civilization: An Interpretation of Sophocles* (Norman: Oklahoma University Press, 1981), pp. 55–56.

25. Peradotto has observed a further "kledonism" in Agamemnon and Clytemnestra's allusions to the "wealth" of robes and the possibility of their being spoiled: see *Agamemnon* 948–950, 962, 1043, and 1383. "Cledonomancy in the *Oresteia*," p. 14.

26. W. R. Halliday, *Greek Divination: A Study of Its Methods and Principles* (London: Macmillan, 1913), p. 47.

27. Froma I. Zeitlin *Under the Sign of the Shield: Semiotics and Aeschylus' Seven against Thebes* (Rome: Edizioni dell'Ateneo, 1982), p. 47. Cf. H. D. Cameron, "The Power of Words in *Seven against Thebes*," *Transactions and Proceedings of the American Philological Association* 101 (1970), pp. 95–118.

28. Aeschylus, *Agamemnon* 1652–35, in Page, *Aeschyli: Septem Quae Supersunt*, p. 197; English in Greene and Lattimore, *Aeschylus II*, p. 78. See Fraenkel, *Agamemnon*, vol. 3, pp. 787–90.

29. Fraenkel, *Agamemnon*, vol. 3, p. 787. Cf. Goldhill, *Language, Sexuality, Narrative*, pp. 97–98.

30. See Fraenkel, *Agamemnon*, vol. 3, pp. 781–86, and Gary Wills, "*Agamemnon* 1346–71, 1659–53," *Harvard Studies in Classical Philology* 67 (1963), pp. 262–64.

31. Peradotto, "Cledonomancy in the *Oresteia*," p. 7.

32. See Froma I. Zeitlin, "The Motif of the Corrupted Sacrifice in Aeschylus's *Oresteia*," *Transactions and Proceedings of the American Philological Association* 96 (1965), p. 466.

33. Jacqueline de Romilly, "À propos d'Iphigénie dans l'*Agamemnon* d'Eschyle," *Illinois Classical Studies* 19 (1994), p.19.

34. Aeschylus, *Agamemnon* 220–25, in Page, *Aeschyli: Septem Quae Supersunt*, p. 146; English in Greene and Lattimore, *Aeschylus II*, p. 28.

35. Aeschylus, *Agamemnon* 234–38, in Page, *Aeschyli: Septem Quae Supersunt*, p. 147; English in Greene and Lattimore, *Aeschylus II*, p. 28.

36. Peradotto, "Cledonomancy in the *Oresteia*," p. 12.

37. Aeschylus, *Agamemnon* 234–37, in Page, *Aeschyli: Septem Quae Supersunt*, p. 147; English in Greene and Lattimore, *Aeschylus II*, p. 28. The translation quoted is that of Nooter, *The Mortal Voice in the Tragedies of Aeschylus*, p. 158. The editions of the Greek text vary significantly at this crucial point. For a discussion, see Sean Alexander Gurd, *Iphigenias at Aulis: Textual Multiplicity, Radical Philology* (Ithaca: Cornell University Press, 2005), pp. 13–21.

38. Paul Mazon, in *Echyle: Tragédies*, ed. and trans. Paul Mazon, 2nd ed., 2 vols. (Paris: Les Belles Lettres, 1935), vol. 2, p. 18 n. 1.

39. Nooter, *The Mortal Voice in the Tragedies of Aeschylus*, p. 158.

40. Aeschylus, *Agamemnon* 227–30, in Page, *Aeschyli: Septem Quae Supersunt*, pp. 146–47; English in Greene and Lattimore, *Aeschylus II*, p. 28.

41. This is the solution adopted by Gurd: see *Iphigenias at Aulis*, p. 14.

42. Aeschylus, *Libation Bearers* 500–502, in Page, *Aeschyli: Septem Quae Supersunt*, p. 221; English in Greene and Lattimore, *Aeschylus II*, p. 100.

43. See note to lines 503–509 in Green and Lattimore, *Aeschylus II*, p. 169.

44. Aeschylus *Libation Bearers* 505–506, in Page, *Aeschyli: Septem Quae Supersunt*, p. 221; English in Greene and Lattimore, *Aeschylus II*, p. 100.

45. Aeschylus, *Libation Bearers* 853, in Page, *Aeschyli: Septem Quae Supersunt*, p. 235; English in Greene and Lattimore, *Aeschylus II*, p. 113.

46. Aeschylus, *Libation Bearers* 1042–43, in Page, *Aeschyli: Septem Quae Supersunt*, p. 243; English in Greene and Lattimore, *Aeschylus II*, p. 121.

47. It may also be an augur: *klēdones* "are almost to be read as omens" (*quasi omina interpretatur*), notes Christian Gottfried Schütz: see *Aeschyli tragoediae quae supersunt*, 3 vols. (London: G. and W. B. Whittaker, 1823), vol. 2, p. 262, citing Thomas Stanley's 1663 edition. Stanley had translated the line into Latin as *liberi enim hominis mortui famam et nomen servant* ("for the children of the dead man guard the fame and the name").

48. See Carl Ausfeld, *De Graecorum precationibus quaestionis* (Leipzig: B. G. Teubner, 1903), and Henk S. Versnel, "Religious Mentality in Ancient Prayer," in Henk S. Versnel, ed., *Faith, Hope and Worship: Aspects of Religious Mentality in the Ancient World* (Leiden: E. J. Brill, 1981), pp. 26–37.

49. Homer, *Iliad* 16.514–16; in English *The Iliad of Homer*, trans. Richmond Lattimore (Chicago: University of Chicago Press, 1951), p. 344.

50. Homer, *Iliad* 16.527; English in Lattimore, *The Iliad of Homer*, p. 344.

51. Silvia Montiglio, *Silence in the Land of Logos* (Princeton: Princeton University Press, 2000), pp. 10–11.

52. Yopie Prins, "The Power of the Speech Act: Aeschylus' Furies and their Binding Song," *Arethusa* 24.2 (1991), pp. 177–95.

53. Aeschylus, *Eumenides* 224, in Page, *Aeschyli: Septem Quae Supersunt*, p. 255; English in Greene and Lattimore, *Aeschylus II*, p. 131.

54. Aeschylus, *Eumenides* 80–81, in Page, *Aeschyli: Septem Quae Supersunt*, p. 250; English in Greene and Lattimore, *Aeschylus II*, p. 126.

55. Aeschylus, *Eumenides* 235–36, in Page, *Aeschyli: Septem Quae Supersunt*, pp. 255–56; English in Greene and Lattimore, *Aeschylus II*, p. 132.

56. On the binding song, see Prins, "The Power of the Speech Act," and Goldhill, *Language, Sexuality, Narrative*, pp. 228–33.

57. Aeschylus, *Eumenides* 397–98, in Page, *Aeschyli: Septem Quae Supersunt*, p. 262; English in Greene and Lattimore, *Aeschylus II*, p. 138.

58. Peradotto, "Cledonomancy in the *Oresteia*," p. 20.

59. Robert J. Rabel, "Cledonomancy in the *Eumenides*," *Rivista di studi classici* 27.1 (1979), p. 16.

60. Fraenkel, *Agamemnon*, vol. 2, p. 129.

61. For a discussion of the staging of Athena's entrance, see Oliver Taplin, *The Stagecraft of Aeschylus: The Dramatic Use of Exits and Entrances in Greek Tragedy* (Oxford: Clarendon Pres of Oxford University Press, 1977), pp. 388–90; cf. Rabel, "Cledonomancy in the *Eumenides*," pp. 18–19.

62. Rabel, "Cledonomancy in the *Eumenides*," p. 19.

63. Aeschylus, *Eumenides* 299–300; Greek in Page, *Aeschyli: Septem Quae Supersunt*, p. 258; English in Greene and Lattimore, *Aeschylus II*, p. 134.

64. Rabel, "Cledonomancy in the *Eumenides*," p. 20.

65. Aeschylus, *Eumenides* 304–305, in Page, *Aeschyli: Septem Quae Supersunt*, p. 258; English in Greene and Lattimore, *Aeschylus II*, p. 134.

66. Aeschylus, *Eumenides* 834–36; Greek in Page, *Aeschyli: Septem Quae Supersunt*, p. 278; English in Greene and Lattimore, *Aeschylus II*, p. 154. On *sphagē* and *sphazō*, see Zeitlin, "The Motif of the Corrupted Sacrifice," esp. pp. 468–69 n. 13.

67. Aeschylus, *Eumenides* 383–84; Greek in Page, *Aeschyli: Septem Quae Supersunt*, p. 261; English in Greene and Lattimore, *Aeschylus II*, p. 137.

68. Rabel, "Cledonomancy in the *Eumenides*," p. 21.

CHAPTER FOUR: DAWN IN ITHACA

1. Hesiod, *Theogony* 535–57; the Greek text and an English translation can be found in *Hesiod: Theogony, Works and Days, Testimonia*, ed. and trans. Glenn W. Most (Cambridge, MA: Harvard University Press, 2006), pp. 47–49.

2. Hesiod, *Theogony* 588–89; English in Most, *Hesiod*, pp. 50–51.

3. For the Hesiodic accounts of Pandora, see *Theogony* 561–612; Greek in Most, *Hesiod*, pp. 49–53 and English in ibid, pp. 92–95.

4. See Jean-Pierre Vernant, "La cuisine du sacrifice en pays grec," in *Oeuvres: Religions, rationalités, politique*, 2 vols. (Paris: Seuil, 2008), vol. 1, p. 944; cf. the treatment of Prometheus in his *Mythe et pensée en Grèce ancienne* (Paris: Seuil, 1990) now in ibid., vol. 1, esp. pp. 857–59.

5. Hesiod, *Theogony* 567, pp. 48–49; English in Most, *Hesiod*, pp. 90–91.

6. Martin L. West, *Theogony: Edited with Prolegomena and Commentary* (Oxford: Clarendon Press of Oxford University Press, 1971), pp. 324–25.

7. See Jean-Pierre Vernant, *L'univers, les dieux, les hommes: Récits grecs des origines* (Paris: Seuil, 2001), in *Oeuvres*, vol. 1, p. 53.

8. Pliny the Elder, *Naturalis historia* 7.57.198.

9. See D. J. Conacher, "Prometheus as Founder of the Arts," *Greek, Roman, and Byzantine Studies* 18 (1977), p. 191.

10. Aeschylus, *Prometheus Bound* 477. Greek in D. L. Page, *Aeschyli: Septem Quae Supersunt* (Oxford: Oxford University Press, 1972), p. 307; English in *The Complete Greek Tragedies: Aeschylus*, eds. David Grene and Richmond Lattimore, 3rd ed., 2 vols. (Chicago: University of Chicago Press, 2013), vol. 1, p. 192.

11. Aeschylus, *Prometheus Bound* 478–83, in Page, *Aeschyli: Septem Quae Supersunt*, p. 307; English in Grene and Lattimore, *Aeschylus*, p. 192.

12. Aeschylus, *Prometheus Bound* 484, in Page, *Aeschyli: Septem Quae Supersunt*, p. 307; English in Grene and Lattimore, *Aeschylus*, p. 192.

13. Aeschylus, *Prometheus Bound* 484–99, in Page, *Aeschyli: Septem Quae Supersunt*, p. 307; English in Grene and Lattimore, *Aeschylus*, pp. 192–93.

14. Aeschylus, *Prometheus Bound* 487, in Page, *Aeschyli: Septem Quae Supersunt*, p. 307; English in Grene and Lattimore, *Aeschylus*, p. 193.

15. Aeschylus, *Prometheus Bound*, in *Aeschylus*, trans. Herbert Weir Smyth, 2 vols. (Cambridge, MA: Harvard University Press, 1952), vol. 1, p. 259; Henry David Thoreau, "The Prometheus Bound of Aeschylus," in *The Writings of Henry David Thoreau*, vol. 5, *Excursions and Poems*, ed. Bradford Torrey, 20 vols. (Boston: Houghton Mifflin, 1906), p. 354.

16. Aristotle, *Nicomachean Ethics* 6.4.1140a9–10; English in Jonathan Barnes, ed., *The Complete Works of Aristotle: The Revised Oxford Translation*, 2 vols. (Princeton: Princeton University Press, 1984), vol. 2, p. 88.

17. Aristotle, *Nicomachean Ethics* 6.4.1140a5–6; English in Barnes, *The Complete Works of Aristotle*, vol. 2, p. 88.

18. Karl Kerényi, *Prometheus: Die menschliche Existenz in griechischer Deutung* (Hamburg: Rowohlt, 1959), p. 56.

19. Homer, *Odyssey* 11.409–11; English in *The Odyssey of Homer, A Modern Translation*, trans. Richard Lattimore (New York: Harper Torchbooks, 1967), p. 178.

20. Homer, *Odyssey* 11.455–56; English in Lattimore, *The Odyssey of Homer*, p. 180.

21. Homer, *Odyssey* 13.116–19; English in Lattimore, *The Odyssey of Homer*, p. 201.

22. See Jean-Pierre Vernant, "Odysseus in Person," *Representations* 67 (1999), p. 3.

23. Homer, *Odyssey* 4.317.

24. Homer, *Odyssey* 4.244–47; English in Lattimore, *The Odyssey of Homer*, p. 71.

25. Homer, *Odyssey* 4.244–50; English in Lattimore, *The Odyssey of Homer*, p. 71.

26. Homer, *Odyssey* 13.429–38; English in Lattimore, *The Odyssey of Homer*, p. 209.

27. Homer, *Odyssey* 19.357–475; English in Lattimore, *The Odyssey of Homer*, pp. 291–94.

28. Homer, *Odyssey* 19.478–79; English in Lattimore, *The Odyssey of Homer*, p. 294.

29. Homer, *Odyssey* 19.535–53; English in Lattimore, *The Odyssey of Homer*, p. 296.

30. See Peter T. Struck, *Divination and Human Nature: A Cognitive History of Intuition in Classical Antiquity* (Princeton: Princeton University Press, 2016), p. 255. On the dream, cf. Scott B. Noegl, *Nocturnal Ciphers: The Allusive Language of Dreams in the Ancient Near East* (New Haven: American Oriental Society, 2007), p. 199; Anthony J. Podlecki, "Omens in the *Odyssey*," *Greece and Rome* 14.1 (1967), pp. 21–22; Louise Pratt, "*Odyssey* 19.535–50: On the Interpretation of Dreams and Signs in Homer," *Classical Philology* 89.2 (1994), pp. 147–52.

31. "This is the only dream in the Homeric poems that contains its own explanation," as Alexandra Rozokoki observes: "Penelope's Dream in Book 19 of the *Odyssey*," *Classical Quarterly* 51.1 (2001), p. 4.

32. Struck, *Divination and Human Nature*, p. 255.

33. Homer, *Odyssey* 19.555–57; English in Lattimore, *The Odyssey of Homer*, p. 296.

34. Homer, *Odyssey* 19.600–605; English in Lattimore, *The Odyssey of Homer*, p. 297.

35. Homer, *Odyssey* 20.56–58; English in Lattimore, *The Odyssey of Homer*, p. 299.

36. Homer, *Odyssey* 20.91; English in Lattimore, *The Odyssey of Homer*, p. 300.

37. John Russo, in John Russo, Manuel Fernández-Galiano, and Alfred Heubeck, eds., *A Commentary on Homer's Odyssey, Vol. 3: Books XVII–XXIV* (Oxford: Clarendon Press of Oxford University Press, 1992), p. 114. Russo is drawing on Graham Reed, *The Psychology of Anomalous Experience: A Cognitive Approach* (London: Hutchinson, 1972). Cf. Anne Amory, "The Reunion of Odysseus and Penelope," in Charles H. Taylor, Jr., ed., *Essays on the Odyssey: Selected Modern Criticism* (Bloomington: Indiana University Press, 1963), pp. 107–108.

38. Homer, *Odyssey* 20.93–94; English in Lattimore, *The Odyssey of Homer*, p. 300. Translation slightly modified.

39. Homer, *Odyssey* 20.95–101; English in Lattimore, *The Odyssey of Homer*, p. 300.

40. Homer, *Odyssey* 20.102; English in Lattimore, *The Odyssey of Homer*, p. 300.

41. On the milling in Homer and this scene in particular, see Kaarle Hirvonen, "Cledonomancy and the Grinding Slave, Od. XX 91–121," *Acta Philologica Fennica* 6 (1969), pp. 5–20. Cf. Hildebrandt Stockinger, *Die Vorzeichen im homerischen Epos: Ihre Typik und ihre Bedeutung* (St. Ottilien: EOS Verlag, 1959), pp. 75–76.

42. Homer, *Odyssey* 20.111–19; English in Lattimore, *The Odyssey of Homer*, p. 301.

43. Homer, *Odyssey* 20.120–21; English in Lattimore, *The Odyssey of Homer*, p. 301.

44. Pseudo-Plutarch, *Essay on the Life and Poetry of Homer*, eds. J. J. Keaney and Robert Lamberton (Atlanta: Scholars Press, 1996), pp. 212 and 300–301.

45. Aeschylus, *Prometheus Bound* 447–48, in Page, *Aeschyli: Septem Quae Supersunt*, p. 306; English in Grene and Lattimore, *Aeschylus*, p. 191. On "seeing without seeing," see Jesper Svenbro, "Voir en voyant: La perception visuelle chez Empédocle," *Métis* n.s. 2 (2004), pp. 47–70.

46. Aeschylus, *Prometheus Bound* 450, in Page, *Aeschyli: Septem Quae Supersunt*, p. 306; English in Grene and Lattimore, *Aeschylus*, p. 191.

47. Aeschylus, *Prometheus Bound* 456–60, in Page, *Aeschyli: Septem Quae Supersunt*, p. 306; English in Grene and Lattimore, *Aeschylus*, p. 192. Translation slightly modified.

48. The series bears evident affinities to the inventories of goods that other Greek sources attribute to Palamedes. See Joshua Billings, *The Philosophical Stage: Drama and Dialectic in Classical Athens* (Princeton: Princeton University Press, 2021), pp. 36–64. On Prometheus's lists of gifts to men in the play, see also Seth Benardete, "The Crimes and Arts of Prometheus," *Rheinisches Museum für Philologie* 107.2 (1964), pp. 126–39, and D. J. Conacher, *Aeschylus' Prometheus Bound: A Literary Commentary* (Toronto: University of Toronto Press, 1980), pp. 48–52.

49. Aeschylus, *Prometheus Bound* 459–61, in Page, *Aeschyli: Septem Quae Supersunt*, p. 307; English in Grene and Lattimore, *Aeschylus*, p. 192.

50. Filippo Ferlauto, "Prometeo e le γραμμάτων συνθέσεις (Aesch. Prom. Vinct. vv 460–461)," *Bollettino dei classici* 11 (1990), 164–68.

51. See ibid., pp. 170–75.

52. Plato, *Protagoras* 325e.

53. See Aristotle, *De interpretatione* 16a.

54. See Athenaeus 10.453–54, in G. Kaibel, ed., *Athenaei Dipnosophistarum libri XV* (Leipzig: in aedibus B. G. Teubneri, 1887–1890). On Callias, see Jesper Svenbro, *Phrasikleia: An Anthropology of Reading in Ancient Greece*, trans. Janet Lloyd (Ithaca: Cornell University Press, 1993), pp. 182–86.

55. Ferlauto, "Prometeo e le γραμμάτων συνθέσεις," p. 175. For an account of some of the historical ambiguities of the notion of "letter," see David Abercrombie, "What Is a 'Letter'?," *Lingua* 2 (1949), pp. 54–63. On the Greek vocabulary of *gramma* and *stoikheion*, see Jesper Svenbro, *Le tombeau de la cigale: Figures de l'écriture et de la lecture en Grèce ancienne* (Paris: Les Belles Lettres, 2021), pp. 149–64.

56. On ancient notions of the letter, see the texts collected in Martin Irvine, *The Making of Textual Culture: "Grammatica" and Literary Theory 350–1100* (Cambridge: Cambridge University Press, 1994), pp. 97–103.

57. Walter Benjamin, "Über das mimetische Vermögen," in *Gesammelte Schriften*, eds. Rolf Tiedemann and Hermann Schweppenhäuser, 7 vols. (Frankfurt an Main: Suhrkamp, 1972–1991), vol. 2, part 1, p. 213; English in "On the Mimetic Faculty," trans. Edmund Jephcott, in *Selected Writings, Volume 2: 1927–1934*, eds. Michael W. Jennings, Howard Eiland, and Gary Smith (Cambridge, MA: Belknap Press of Harvard University Press, 1999), p. 722. Translation modified.

CHAPTER FIVE: CRASSUS AT THE CROSSING

1. On Crassus and the Parthians, see K. Regling, "Crassus' Partherkrieg," *Klio* 7 (1907), pp. 357–94; Allen Mason Ward, *Marcus Crassus and the Late Roman Republic* (Columbia: University of Missouri Press, 1977); A. N. Sherwin-White, *Roman Foreign Policy in the East, 168 B.C. to 1 A.D.* (London: Duckworth, 1984), pp. 279–90.

2. See Cicero, *De divinatione* 1.29–30; Latin in *Della divinazione*, ed. and trans. Sebastiano Timpanaro (Milan: Garzanti, 1988), pp. 24–26; English in *On Divination: Book 1*, trans. David Wardle (Oxford: Clarendon Press of Oxford University Press, 2006), pp. 54–55. The study of the alleged signs is complicated by the variety of the reports of the portents associated with Crassus's departure. The principal sources, in addition to Cicero, are Plutarch, *Life of Crassus* 16.5–6; Cassius Dio, *Roman History* 40.12–28; Appian, *Civil War* 2.18; and Velleius Paterculus, *Roman History* 2.46.3. The critical discussions are numerous. Among others, see M. Valenton, "De modis auspicandi Romanorum," *Mnemosyne* 17 (1889), pp. 275–325 and 418–52 and *Mnemosyne* 18 (1890), pp. 208–63 and 406–56; *M. Tulli Ciceronis De Divinatione, liber primus*, ed. Arthur Stanley Pease (Urbana: The University of Illinois, 1920–23), pp. 137–38; Jean Bayet, "Les malédictions du tribun C. Ateius Capito," in *Croyances et rites dans la Rome antique* (Rome: Payot, 1971), pp. 353–65; Jerzy Linderski, "The Augural Law," *Aufstieg und Niedergang der römischen Welt* II 16.3 (1986), pp. 2146–312, esp. pp. 2200–2203; C. F. Konrad, "Vellere Signa," in C. F. Konrad, ed., *Augusto Augurio: Rerum humanarum et divinarum commentationes in honorem Jerzy Linderski* (Stuttgart: Fritz Steiner, 2004), pp. 169–203, esp. pp. 181–85; José Kany-Turpin, "Fonction de la verité dans un énoncé augural: Le paradoxe du menteur Ateius Capito," in Marc Baratin and Claude Moussy, eds., *Conceptions latines du sens et de la signification: Colloque du centre Alfred Ernout* (Paris: Presses de l'université Paris-Sorbonne, 1999), pp. 255–66.

3. Sherwin-White, *Roman Foreign Policy in the East*, p. 279. For a summary and analysis, see commentary in Wardle, *On Divination*, pp. 181–83.

4. According to a rule of synalepha, the terminal *e* of *ne* and the initial *e* of *eas* would be pronounced as one, and the bilabial or labiodental consonant *u* of *Caue* would be spoken as was the vowel *u* in *Cauneas*. For an analysis, see Timpanaro, *Della divinazione*, pp. 378–79.

5. See Sherwin-White, *Roman Foreign Policy in the East*, pp. 289–90.

6. Cicero, *De divinatione* 1.9, in Timpanaro, *Della divinazione*, pp. 8–10; English in Wardle, *On Divination*, p. 48. Cf. Sextus Empiricus's definition of *mantikē* as "a theoretical and interpretative knowledge of messages sent by gods to men" (*Adv. Math.* 9.132= *SVF* 2.1018).

7. The implications of Cicero's responses to his brother have been much debated. For some readers, they represent the author's own position; such a reading has been proposed by Pease and Timpanaro in their editions of the dialogue. For influential other perspectives, see Malcolm Schofield, "Cicero for and against Divination," *Journal of Roman Studies* 76 (1986), pp. 47–65; Mary Beard, "Cicero and Divination: The Formation of a Latin Discourse," *Journal of Roman Studies* 76 (1986), pp. 33–46.

8. Cicero, *De divinatione* 2.84; Latin in Timpanaro, *Della divinazione*, pp. 176–78; English in Cicero, *De senectute, De amicitia, De divinatione*, trans. W. A. Falconer (Cambridge, MA: Harvard University Press, 1923), p. 467.

9. Cicero, *De divinatione* 1.11–13; Latin in Timpanaro, *Della divinazione*, pp. 10–12; English in Wardle, *On Divination*, p. 49. Cf. *De divinatione* 2. 11.26–28, in Falconer, *De senectute, De amicitia, De divinatione*, pp. 399–401.

10. Plato, *Timaeus* 71e–72b; Plato, *Phaedrus*, 244a–b.

11. See Robert Flacelière, *Devins et oracles grecs* (Paris: Presses universitaires de France, 1961), pp. 11–12.

12. Auguste Bouché-Leclercq, *Histoire de la divination en antiquité*, 4 vols. (Paris: E. Leroux, 1879–1882), vol. 1, p. 109.

13. For a discussion, see Michael Attyah Flower, *The Seer in Ancient Greece* (Berkeley: University of California Press, 2008), pp. 84–91, and Yulia Ustinova, "Modes of Prophecy, or Modern Arguments in Support of the Ancient Approach," *Kernos: Revue international et pluridisciplinaire de religion grecque antique* 26 (2013), pp. 25–44.

14. Cicero, *De divinatione* 1.103; Latin in Timpanaro, *Della divinazione*, p. 82; English in Wardle, *On Divination*, p. 78.

15. Cicero, *De divinatione* 1.104; Latin in Timpanaro, *Della divinazione*, p. 82; English

in Wardle, *On Divination*, pp. 78–79.

16. Greek text in Rudolf Pfeiffer, ed., *Callimachus* (Oxford: Clarendon Press of Oxford University Press, 1949–1953), p. 80; English in P. M. Fraser, *Ptolemaic Alexandria*, 3 vols. (Oxford: Clarendon Press of Oxford University Press, 1972), vol. 1, p. 593. Translation slightly modified.

17. Virgil, *Aeneid* 7.96–99; English in *Aeneid*, trans. Frederick Ahl (Oxford: Oxford University Press, 2007), p. 160–61.

18. Virgil, *Aeneid* 7.113–15; English in Ahl, *Aeneid*, p. 161.

19. Virgil, *Aeneid* 7.116; English in Ahl, *Aeneid*, p. 161. Translation slightly modified.

20. Virgil, *Aeneid* 7.128–29; English in Ahl, *Aeneid*, p. 162.

21. Cicero, *De divinatione* 1.102; Latin in Timpanaro, *Della divinazione*, p. 80; English in Wardle, *On Divination*, p. 78. Translation modified.

22. Varro 7.76, in Varro, *On the Latin Language*, trans. Roland G. Kent, 2 vols. (Cambridge, MA: Harvard University Press, 1938), vol. 1, pp. 242–43.

23. Sextus Pompeius Festus, *De verborum significatu quae supersunt cum Pauli epitome*, ed. Wallace M. Lindsay (Leipzig: B. G. Teubner, 1913), 226, p. 213.

24. See Ernst Riess, s.v. "Omen," in *Paulys Real-Encyclopädie der classischen Altertumswissenschaft*, 50 vols. (Stuttgart, J. B. Metzler, 1894–1963), vol. 18, pp. 350–78.

25. François Guillaumont, *Philosophie et augure: Recherches sur la théorie cicéronienne de la divination* (Brussels: Latomus, 1984), p. 191. Guillaumont refers the reader to *De divinatione* 1.29, 1.103, 1.104, 2.26.2, 2.83, 2.149. For his entry on *omen*, see ibid., pp. 190–93.

26. Charles T. Lewis and Charles Short, *A Latin Dictionary, Founded on Andrews' Edition of Freund's Latin Dictionary* (Oxford: Clarendon Press of Oxford University Press, 1879), s.v. "Omen."

27. See M. D. Petruševski, "De etymo vocis lat. *omen*," *Živa antika / Antiquité vivante* 3.1–2 (1953), p. 144; see also David Engels, *Das römische Vorzeichenwesen (753–27 v. Chr.): Quellen, Terminologie, Kommentar, historische Entwicklung* (Stuttgart: Franz Steiner, 2007), pp. 279–82.

28. Émile Benveniste, *Hittite et indo-européen: Études comparatives* (Paris: Maisonneuve, 1962), p. 5.

29. Ibid., p. 10.

30. Ibid., p. 11.

31. Émile Benveniste, *Le vocabulaire des institutions indo-européennes*, 2 vols. (Paris: Seuil, 1969), vol. 2: *Pouvoir, droit, religion*, p. 256.

32. Benveniste, *Hittite et indo-européen*, p. 11. Italics in the original. Benveniste refers to Livy 5.55.

33. Cicero, *De divinatione* 1.103: Latin in Timpanaro, *Della divinazione*, p. 82; English in Wardle, *On Divination*, p. 78.

34. Livy 1.7.9–11; English in Livy, *The Early History of Rome: Books I–V of The History of Rome from Its Foundations*, trans. Aubrey de Sélincourt (London: Penguin Books, 2002), p. 38. Translation slightly modified. Cf. Livy 1.55.4, 5.55.2, 8.14.8, 10.11.2, 21.63.15, 22.37.11, 38.18.10.

35. See Ovid, *Met.* 7.620–21; Tacitus, *Ann.* 1.28 and 2.13; *Hist.* 1.62; Pliny, *Pan.* 5.4.

36. Jean Bayet, *Histoire politique et psychologique de la religion romaine* (Paris: Payot, 1973), p. 53.

37. Ibid.

38. Georges Dumézil, *La religion romaine archäique, avec un appendice sur la religion des Étrusques* (Paris: Payot, 1974), p. 133.

39. Raymond Bloch, "Liberté et déterminisme dans la divination romaine," in Marcel Renard and Robert Schilling, eds., *Hommages à Jean Bayet* (Brussels-Berchem: Latomus, revue d'études latines,1964), p. 95.

40. See Ovid, *Fasti* 3.277–374; Plutarch, *Life of Numa* 15; Arnobius, *Against the Gentiles* 5.1–4. For an analysis that also takes into account other classical attestations of the story, see Lindsay G. Driediger-Murphy, "Numa and Jupiter: Whose Smile Is It, Anyway?" *Classical Quarterly* 71.1 (2021), pp. 259–75. Cf. Francesca Presendi, *Décrire et comprendre le sacrifice: Les réflexions des Romains sur leur propre religion à partir de la littérature antique* (Stuttgart: Fritz Steiner, 2007), pp. 189–95; T. P. Wiesman, "Summoning Jupiter: Magic in the Roman Republic," in *Unwritten Rome* (Exeter: Exeter University Press, 2008), pp. 155–66.

41. Ovid, *Fasti* 3.339–44.

42. Driediger-Murphy, "Numa and Jupiter," p. 259.

43. See ibid., p. 260.

44. On the distinction between *auspicia impetrativa* and *oblativa*, see Dumézil, *La religion romaine*, pp. 132–34.

CHAPTER SIX: NOISE THAT ANSWERS

1. On Babylonia and Etruria, see Jean Nougayrol, "Les rapports des haruspiciens étrusque et assyro-babylonienne, et le foie d'argile de *Falerii Veteres* (Villa Giulia

3786)," *Comptes rendus des séances de l'Académie des Inscriptions et Belles-Lettres* 99.4 (1955), pp. 509–19.

2. Jean Bottéro, "Symptômes, signes, écritures en Mésopotamie ancienne," in Jean-Pierre Vernant et al., *Divination et rationalité* (Paris: Éditions du Seuil, 1974), p. 71.

3. Marc Van De Mieroop, *Philosophy before the Greeks: The Pursuit of Truth in Ancient Babylonia* (Princeton: Princeton University Press, 2016), pp. 25 and p. 97.

4. A. Leo Oppenheim, *Ancient Mesopotamia: Portrait of a Dead Civilization*, revised edition by Erica Reiner (1964, Chicago: University of Chicago Press, 1977), p. 206.

5. Van De Mieroop, *Philosophy before the Greeks*, p. 188.

6. Jean Bottéro, *Mésopotamie: L'écriture, la raison et les dieux* (Paris: Gallimard, 1987), p. 197. Marc Van De Mieroop makes a similar point in *Philosophy before the Greeks*, p. 188.

7. Oppenheim, *Ancient Mesopotamia*, p. 207.

8. David B. Weisberg, "An Old Babylonian Forerunner to *šumma ālu*," *Hebrew Union College Annual* 40–41 (1969–1970), pp. 87–104.

9. Sally M. Freedman, *If a City Is Set on a Height: The Akkadian Omen Series* Šumma Alu ina Mēlē Šakin, *Volume 1, Tablets 1–21* (Philadelphia: University of Pennsylvania Museum, 1998), p. 1.

10. For that traditional rendition, see Freedman, *If a City Is Set on a Height*, p. 2; for Freedman's own reading of the cuneiform, which is different, see ibid., p. 19.

11. Ibid., p. 19.

12. Jean Bottéro, *Mésopotamie*, p. 237. Cf. the similar formulation in Bottéro, "Symptômes, signes, écritures," pp. 82–83.

13. Francesca Rochberg, "'If P then Q': Form and Reasoning in Babylonian Divination," in Amar Annus, ed., *Divination and Interpretation of Signs in the Ancient World* (Chicago: University of Chicago Press, 2010), p. 19.

14. E. A. Speiser, "The Idea of History in Ancient Mesopotamia," in J. J. Finkelstein and Moshe Greenberg, eds., *Oriental and Biblical Studies: Collected Writings of E. A. Speiser* (Philadelphia: University of Pennsylvania Press, 1967), p. 298.

15. Hermann Hunger and David Pingree, *Astral Science in Mesopotamia* (Leiden: E. J. Brill. 1999), p. 5.

16. For a similar view, see Bottéro, *Mésopotamie*, p. 239.

17. Francesca Rochberg, *The Heavenly Writing: Divination, Horoscopy, and Astronomy in Mesopotamian Culture* (Cambridge: Cambridge University Press, 2004), p. 58.

18. Ibid.

19. Van De Mieroop, *Philosophy before the Greeks*, p. 126.

20. Rochberg, *The Heavenly Writing*, p. 56.

21. Ivan Starr, *Rituals of the Diviner* (Malibu: Undena Publications, 1983), p. 10.

22. Ibid.

23. Rochberg, *The Heavenly Writing*, p. 56. On Mesopotamian paronomasia, particularly in the interpretation of dreams, see Claudio Saporetti, "Paronomasia nell'oniromanzia assira," *Egitto e vicino Oriente* 18 (1995), pp. 183–91, and Nicla De Zorzi, "The Omen Series *Šumma Izbu*: Internal Structure and Hermeneutic Strategies," *Kaskal* 8 (2011), pp. 43–75, esp. pp. 67–71. Paronomasia is also a recurrent feature of Egyptian oneiromancy. See Scott B. Noegl, "On Puns and Divination: Egyptian Dream Exegesis from a Comparative Perspective," in Kasia Szpakowska, ed., *Through a Glass Darkly: Magic, Dreams and Prophecy in Ancient Egypt* (Swansea: Classical Press of Wales, 2006), pp. 95–119, and more generally for the ancient Near East, *Nocturnal Ciphers: The Allusive Language of Dreams in the Ancient Near East* (New Haven: American Oriental Society, 2007).

24. Francesca Rochberg, *Before Nature: Cuneiform Knowledge and the History of Science* (Chicago: University of Chicago Press, 2016), p. 168. This example is also discussed by Van De Mieroop in *Philosophy before the Greeks*, p. 120.

25. Van De Mieroop, *Philosophy before the Greeks*, p. 120.

26. A. L. Oppenheim, "Sumerian: inim.gar, Akkadian: egirrû=Greek: klēdōn," *Archiv für Orientforschung* 17 (1954–1956), p. 49.

27. Anne-Caroline Rendu Loisel, *Les chants du monde: Le paysage sonore de l'ancienne Mésopotamie*, with an appendix by Ariane Thomas (Toulouse: Presses universitaires du Midi, 2016), p. 44. For a fuller account of the expression, see Anne-Caroline Rendu-Loisel's doctoral dissertation, "Bruit et émotion dans la littérature akkadienne: Archéologie et Préhistoire," University of Geneva (2011), pp. 455–56.

28. Oppenheim, "Sumerian: inim.gar, Akkadian: egirrû," p. 51.

29. Ibid., p. 52.

30. Bottéro, "Symptômes, signes, écritures," p. 98.

31. Ibid., p. 99.

32. André Finet, "Un cas de clédonomancie à Mari," in G. van Driel, T. J. H. Krispijn, M. Stol, and K. R. Veenhof, eds., *Zikir Šumim: Assyriological Studies Presented to F. R. Kraus on the Occasion of His Seventieth Birthday* (Leiden: E. J. Brill, 1982), p. 54.

33. Rendu-Loisel, "Bruit et émotion dans la littérature akkadienne," p. 461.

34. This translation follows Rendu-Loisel, "Bruit et émotion dans la littérature akkadienne," p. 466. Cf. the discussions and renditions in Rendu-Loisel *Les chants du monde*, p. 44; Oppenheim, "Sumerian: inim.gar, Akkadian: egirrû," p. 54; Bottéro, "Symptômes, signes, écritures," p. 98.

35. Oppenheim, "Sumerian: inim.gar, Akkadian: egirrû," p. 54.

36. Ibid., p. 55.

37. Rendu-Loisel, *Les chants du monde*, p. 44. For a detailed account of the series, see Rendu-Loisel, "Bruit et émotion dans la littérature akkadienne," pp. 464–71.

38. Oppenheim, "Sumerian: inim.gar, Akkadian: egirrû," p. 53.

39. Ibid.

40. *Oxford Editions of Cuneiform Texts* (Oxford: Clarendon Press of Oxford University Press, 1923–), vol. 6, p. 84, as cited and translated by Oppenheim, "Sumerian: inim.gar, Akkadian: egirrû," p. 53.

41. *Šurpu* 2.98, in Oppenheim, "Sumerian: inim.gar, Akkadian: egirrû," p. 53.

42. See Rendu-Loisel, "Bruit et émotion dans la littérature akkadienne," pp. 467–68.

CHAPTER SEVEN: A LESSER PROPHESY

1. Leviticus 19:26. English in Robert Alter, trans., *The Hebrew Bible*, 3 vols. (New York: W. W. Norton, 2019), vol. 1, pp. 433–34.

2. See Francis Brown, S. R. Driver, and Charles A. Briggs, eds. *A Hebrew and English Lexicon of the Old Testament, Based on the Lexicon of William Gesenius*, trans. Edward Robinson (Oxford: Clarendon Press of Oxford University Press, 1906), s.v. "Nakhash." For a discussion of the Hebrew term and its cognates in related Semitic languages, see Frederick Cryer, *Divination in Ancient Israel and Its Near Eastern Environment: A Socio-Historical Investigation* (Sheffield: Sheffield Academic Press, 1994), pp. 257–58.

3. *A Hebrew and English Lexicon of the Old Testament, Based on the Lexicon of William Gesenius*, s.v. "'Anan." For a discussion, see Cryer, *Divination in Ancient Israel*, pp. 260–61.

4. Deuteronomy 18:9–14, in Alter, *The Hebrew Bible*, vol. 1, p. 680.

5. See, for instance, Genesis 20:3–7; Genesis 31:24; Genesis 37:5–7 and 9–10; Genesis 41:32.

6. The Hebrew Bible mentions Urim and Thummim seven times: Exodus 28:30, Leviticus 8:8, Numbers 27:21, Deuteronomy 33:8, 1 Samuel 28:6, and Ezra 2:63 and 7:6. On the nature of the Urim and Thummim, see Ingold Friedrich, *Ephod und Chosen im Lichte des Alten Orients* (Vienna: Herder, 1968); Johan Maier, "Urim und Thummim: Recht und Bund in der Spannung zwischen konigstum und Priestertum in Alten Israel," *Kairos* 11

(1969), pp. 22–38; Anne Marie Kitz, "The Plural Forms of 'Ûrîm and Tummîm," *Journal of Biblical Literature* 116.3 (1997), pp. 401–10. For a more recent account of scholarship on the subject, see Victor Avigdor Hurowitz, "True Light on the Urim and Thummim," *Jewish Quarterly Review* 88.3–4 (1998), pp. 263–74, and Cornelis van Dam, *Urim and Thummim: A Means of Revelation in Ancient Israel* (Winona Lake: Eisenbrauns, 1997).

7. For an overview, see Anne Marie Kitz, "The Terminology of Hebrew Lot Casting and Its Ancient Near Eastern Context," *Catholic Biblical Quarterly* 62.2 (2000), pp. 207–14; Cryer, *Divination in Ancient Israel*, pp. 276–77.

8. See Shmuel Ahituv, s.v. "Divination," in Fred Skolnik and Michael Berenbaum, eds., *Encyclopedia Judaica*, 22 vols. (New York: Macmillan, 2007).

9. See Anne Marie Kitz, "Prophecy as Divination," *Catholic Biblical Quarterly* 65.1 (2003), pp. 22–42.

10. Deuteronomy 18:14–15; English in Alter, *The Hebrew Bible*, pp. 680–81.

11. A. L. Oppenheim, "Sumerian: inim.gar, Akkadian: egirrû = Greek: klēdōn," *Archiv für Orientforschung* 17 (1954–1956), pp. 52–53.

12. 1 Samuel 14:6; English in Alter, *The Hebrew Bible*, vol. 2, p. 227.

13. 1 Samuel 14:8–11; English in Alter, *The Hebrew Bible*, vol. 2, p. 227.

14. 1 Samuel 14: 1–12; English in Alter, *The Hebrew Bible*, vol. 2, pp. 227–28.

15. 1 Samuel 14:12; English in Alter, *The Hebrew Bible*, vol. 2, p. 228.

16. 1 Samuel 14:15; English in Alter, *The Hebrew Bible*, vol. 2, p. 228.

17. 1 Kings 20:33; English in Alter, *The Hebrew Bible*, p. 517. Translation modified.

18. Oppenheim, "Sumerian: inim.gar, Akkadian: egirrû=Greek: klēdōn," p. 53.

19. W. R. Halliday, *Greek Divination: A Study of Its Methods and Principles* (London: Macmillan, 1913), p. 229.

20. Psalms 74:9.

21. Amos 8:11.

22. Micah 3:6.

23. See the helpful anthology, to which this account is indebted, in L. Stephen Cook, *On the Question of the Cessation of Prophecy* (Tübingen: Mohr Siebeck, 2011), pp. 5–7.

24. Flavius Josephus, *Against Apion* 1.8.41, in *The Life and Against Apion*, trans. H. St. J. Thackeray (Cambridge, MA: Harvard University Press, 1926), p. 179.

25. Babylonian Talmud, Tractate Sanhedrin 11. Cf. Palestinian Talmud, Tractate Sota 9:13; Babylonian Talmud, Tractate Sota 48b; Babylonian Talmud, Tractate Yoma 9b. For occurrences outside the Talmud, see Tosefta Sota 13:3 and Shir ha-Shirim Rabbah 8:9.

For a selection of texts in English translation, see Cook, *On the Question of the Cessation of Prophecy*, p. 8. On the passage, see Benjamin D. Sommer, "Did Prophecy Cease? Evaluating a Reevaluation," *Journal of Biblical Literature* 115.1 (1996), pp. 33–34, and, at greater length, Peter Kuhn, *Offenbarungsstimmen im antiken Judentum* (Tübingen: J. C. B. Mohr, 1989), pp. 306–29.

26. Kuhn, *Offenbarungsstimmen*, pp. 273–74.

27. L. Blau, s.v. "Bat Ḳol," in Cyrus Adler et al., eds., *The Jewish Encyclopedia*, 12 vols. (New York: Funk and Wagnells, 1901–1906).

28. Babylonian Talmud, Tractate Megilla 32a, quoted in Blau, s.v. "Bat Ḳol."

29. David Sperling, "Akkadian *egerrû* and Hebrew *bt qwl*," *Journal of the Near Eastern Society of Columbia University* 4 (1972), p. 66. For a useful annotated anthology of occurrences, see Peter Kuhn, *Bat Qol: Die Offenbarungsstimme in der rabbinischen Literatur, Sammlung, Übersetzung und Kurzkommentierung der Texte* (Regensburg: Friedrich Pustet, 1989).

30. Palestinian Talmud, Tractate Shabbat 6:9,8c. The translation is by Moulie Vidas, who has helped me with the analysis of this passage. For Sperling's rendition, see "Akkadian *egerrû* and Hebrew *bt qwl*," p. 71.

31. Saul Liebermann, *Hellenism in Jewish Palestine: Studies in the Literary Transmission, Beliefs and Manners of Palestine in the 1st century B.C.E.–4th Century C.E.* (New York: Jewish Theological Society of America, 1950), p. 194.

32. Sperling, "Akkadian *egerrû* and Hebrew *bt qwl*," p. 68.

33. Ibid., p. 71.

34. Ibid., pp. 72–73.

35. José Costa, "Littérature apocalyptique et judaïsme rabbinique: Le problème de la *bat qol*," *Revue des études juives* 169.1–2 (2010), p. 61.

36. Babylonian Talmud, Tractate Berakhot 57b.

37. See Kuhn, *Offenbarungsstimmen im antiken Judentum*, pp. 281–85.

38. Palestinian Talmud, Tractate Shabbat 6:9,8c. Translation by Moulie Vidas (unpublished). For Sperling's English version of the passage, see, "Akkadian *egerrû* and Hebrew *bt qwl*," p. 66.

39. Palestinian Talmud, Tractate Shabbat 6:9.

40. Lieberman, *Hellenism in Jewish Palestine*, p. 195.

41. For the distinction between these two modes of "consultation," I am indebted to Moulie Vidas, who points out that in the second case, the Babylonian Talmud avoids the expression *bat qol*.

42. See, for instance, Babylonian Talmud, Tractate Gittin 68a, and Babylonian Talmud Tractate Gittin 56a, where it is the Emperor Nero who practices such an art of divination, by which he is converted.

43. Babylonian Talmud, Tractate Chagiga 15a,13–15b1.

44. Pieter W. van der Horst, "Ancient Jewish Bibliomancy," *Journal of Greco-Roman Christianity and Judaism* 1 (2000), p. 9. On the notion of the "holy book" in Second Temple Judaism, see Oda Wischmeyer, "Das heilige Buch im Judentum des Zweiten Tempels," *Zeitschrfit für neutestamentliche Wissenschaft* 86 (1995), pp. 218–42.

45. 1 Maccabees 3:48. Cf. 2 Maccabees 8:23. Both passages are commented in Wischmeyer, "Das heilige Buch im Judentum des Zweiten Tempels," pp. 226–27.

46. Van der Horst, "Ancient Jewish Bibliomancy," p. 11.

47. 2 Maccabees 8:23. Horst comments that "we do not find the expression 'help of God' anywhere in the Torah": see "Ancient Jewish Bibliomancy," p. 12.

48. Pirkei avot 5:22.

CHAPTER EIGHT: IN THE GARDEN

1. Goulven Madec, "La conversion et les Confessions," in *Augustin, le message et la foi: Causeries à Radio Notre-Dame* (Paris: Desclée de Brouwer, 1987), p. 18.

2. Augustine, *Confessions* 5.14.25; Latin text in *Confessions*, ed. James J. O'Donnell, 3 vols. (Oxford: Oxford University Press, 1992), vol. 1, p. 57. All subsequent references to the Latin text are to the first volume of this edition. English translation in *Confessions*, trans. Henry Chadwick (Oxford: Oxford University Press, 1991), p. 89.

3. Augustine, *Confessions* 8.1.1, p. 88; English in Chadwick, *Confessions*, p. 133.

4. Ibid.

5. Augustine, *Confessions* 8.5.11, p. 93; English in Chadwick, *Confessions*, p. 140.

6. Augustine, *Confessions* 8.6.14, p. 94; English in Chadwick, *Confessions*, p. 142.

7. See Chadwick, *Confessions,* p. 143 n. 11, where the translation is dated to 371 AD.

8. Augustine, *Confessions* 8.6.15, pp. 94–95; English in Chadwick, *Confessions*, p. 143. Translation slightly modified.

9. Augustine, *Confessions* 8.6.15, p. 95; English in Chadwick, *Confessions*, p. 144.

10. Augustine, *Confessions* 8.6.16, pp. 95–96; English in Chadwick, *Confessions*, p. 144.

11. Augustine, *Confessions* 8.8.19, pp. 96–97; English in Chadwick, *Confessions*, p. 146.

12. Ibid.

13. Augustine, *Confessions* 8.8.20, p. 97; English in Chadwick, *Confessions*, 147.

14. Augustine, *Confessions* 8.9.21, pp. 97–98; English in Chadwick, *Confessions*, pp. 147—48.

15. Augustine, *Confessions* 8.12.28, p. 101; English in Chadwick, *Confessions*, p. 152.

16. Ibid.

17. Ibid.

18. Augustine, *Confessions* 8.12.29, p. 101; English in Chadwick, *Confessions*, p. 152. Translation slightly modified.

19. Augustine, *Confessions* 8.12.29, p. 101; English in Chadwick, *Confessions*, pp. 152–53.

20. Augustine, *Confessions* 8.12.29, p. 101; English in Chadwick, *Confessions*, p. 153.

21. Ibid. The lives of saint Cyprien of Antioch and Babylas the Mime contain similar episodes: see Pierre Courcelle, "L'enfant et les 'Sorts bibliques,'" *Vigiliae Christianae* 7.4 (1953), pp. 204–206.

22. Athanasius, *The Life of Saint Antony*, trans. Robert T. Meyer (Westminster, MD: The Newman Press, 1950), pp. 19–20.

23. Augustine, *Confessions* 8.12.29, p. 101; English in Chadwick, *Confessions*, p. 153.

24. Ibid. See Letter to the Romans 13:13–14.

25. Augustine, *Confessions* 8.12.30, p. 101; English in Chadwick, *Confessions*, p. 153.

26. It was not always so, as Pierre Courcelle demonstrated. Despite his many allusions to the *Confessions*, Isidore of Seville, for example, does not mention the conversion scene, even if he incorporated the phrase *tolle lege* into a poem. See Pierre Courcelle, *Les Confessions de saint Augustin dans la tradition littéraire: Antécédants et postérité* (Paris: Étudies augustiniennes, 1963), pp. 247–48.

27. See Augustine, *Confessions* 3.4.7, p. 25; English in Chadwick, *Confessions*, pp. 38–39.

28. For a study of the three conversions in book 8, see Brian Stock, *Augustine the Reader: Meditation, Self-Knowledge, and the Ethics of Interpretation* (Cambridge, MA: Harvard University Press, 1996), pp. 75–111.

29. Original in Francesco Petrarca, *Opere* (Florence: Sansoni, 1975), p. 390; English in Ernst Cassirer, Paul Oskar Kristeller, John Herman Randall, Jr., eds., *The Renaissance Philosophy of Man* (Chicago: University of Chicago Press, 1948), p. 44.

30. From Augustine, *Confessions* 10.8.15, pp. 124–25; English in Chadwick, *Confessions*, p. 187.

31. Original in Petrarca, *Opere*, p. 391; English in Cassirer et al., *The Renaissance Philosophy of Man*, pp. 44–45.

32. For readings of the scene, see, among others, Courcelle, *Les Confessions de saint*

Augustin dans la tradition littéraire, pp. 339–44; Jill Robbins, *Prodigal Son / Elder Brother: Interpretation and Alterity in Augustine, Petrarch, Kafka, Levinas* (Chicago: University of Chicago Press, 1991), pp. 49–70; Karlheinz Stierle, "Ein experimentum crucis: Die Besteigerung des Mont Ventoux," in *Francesco Petrarca: Ein Intellektueller im Europa des 14. Jahrhunderts* (Munich: Carl Hanser, 2003), pp. 318–43.

33. Luke 4:16–19, New International Version.

34. Luke 4:20.

35. Pieter Willem Van der Horst, "*Sortes*: Sacred Books as Instant Oracles," in *Japheth in the Tents of Shem: Studies on Jewish Hellenism in Antiquity* (Leuven: Peeters, 2002), p. 175; cf. Franz Heinevetter, *Würfel- und Buchstabenorakel in Griechenland und Kleinasien* (Breslau: Graß, Barth. [W. Friedrich], 1912).

36. See Yves de Kitsch, "Les *sortes vergilianae* dans l'Histoire Auguste," *Mélanges d'archéologie et d'histoire* 82.1 (1970), pp. 321–62.

37. Pierre Courcelle, "Source chrétienne et allusions païennes de l'épisode du 'Tolle, Lege,'" *Revue d'histoire de philosophie religieuse* 32.3 (1952), p. 182.

38. Cicero, *De divinatione* 1.103; English in *On Divination: Book 1*, trans. David Wardle (Oxford: Clarendon Press of Oxford University Press, 2006), p. 78. One might also evoke the example of Metellus's daughter, Caecilia, recounted in Cicero, *De divinatione* 1.104.

39. See the summary in Pierre Courcelle, "L'oracle d'Apis et l'oracle du Jardin de Milan (Augustin, *Conf.*, VIII, 11, 29)," *Revue de l'histoire des religions* 139.2 (1951), pp. 216–231, esp. pp. 216–20. On children and divination more generally, see Cristiano Grottanelli, "Bambini e divinazione," in Ottavia Niccoli, ed., *Infanzie: Funzioni di un gruppo liminale dal mondo classico all'età moderna* (Florence: Ponte alle Grazie, 1993), pp. 23–72.

40. Auguste Bouché-Leclercq, *Histoire de la divination en antiquité*, 4 vols. (Paris: E. Leroux, 1879–1882), vol. 3, p. 387, referring to Dio Chryst. *Orat.* 32:13; Aelian *Hist. An.* 11.10.

41. Plutarch, *Isis and Osiris* 14.356e, trans. Frank Cole Babbitt, in *Moralia*, 16 vols. (Cambridge, MA: Harvard University Press, 1927–2004), vol. 5, pp. 38–39. For the comparison to Jewish customs, see Saul Liebermann, *Hellenism in Jewish Palestine: Studies in the Literary Transmission, Beliefs and Manners of Palestine in the 1st century B.C.E.–4th Century C.E.* (New York: Jewish Theological Society of America, 1950), p. 196.

42. József Balogh, "Zu Augustins 'Konfessionen': Doppeltes *Kledon* in der tolle-lege-Szene," *Zeitschrift für neutestamentliche Wissenschaft und die Kunde der älteren Kirche* 25 (1926), pp. 265–70.

43. The point is made by Balogh: see ibid., pp. 267–68.

44. Courcelle, "L'enfant et les 'Sorts bibliques,'" p. 194.

45. See Johannes Geffcken, "Augustins Tolle-Lege Erlebnis," *Archiv für Religionswissenschaft* 31 (1934), p. 3. For Mark's passage, see Mark the Deacon, *Vie de Porphyre, evêque de Gaza*, eds. Henri Grégoire and Marc-Antoine Kugener (Paris: Les Belles Lettres, 1930), chapter 45, pp. 37–38. An English translation can be found in *The Life of Porphyry, Bishop of Gaza*, trans. G. F. Hill (Oxford: Clarendon Press of Oxford University Press, 1913), p. 55.

46. Grégoire dates this passage of Mark's *Life* to 410: see *Vie de Porphyre*, p. 119. O'Donnell dates the *Confessions* to 397. *Confessions*, vol. 1, p. xli.

47. Grégoire, in *Vie de Porphyre*, p. 119.

48. Geffcken, "Augustins Tolle-Lege Erlebnis," pp. 5–13. Courcelle offers examples of similar phrases in Cicero and Apuleius: see *Les Confessions de saint Augustin dans la tradition littéraire*, p. 157 nn. 4–5. Against Geffcken, Robert Joly, following Grégoire, points to Matthew (26:26): "Jesus took bread, and when he had given thanks, he broke it and gave it to his disciples, saying 'Take and eat' [*labete phagete*]; this is my body." See Robert Joly, "La scene du Jardin de Milan: Saint Augustin, *Confessions*, VIII, XII, 29," *La nouvelle Clio* 7–9 (1955–1957), p. 453.

49. Plato, *Phaedo* 98b. See Jean-G. Préaux, "Du Phédon aux *Confessions* de saint Augustin," *Latomus* 16.2 (1957), pp. 314–25.

50. See Courcelle, *Les Confessions de saint Augustin dans la tradition littéraire*, p. 157.

51. See Julius Boehmer, "Augustins *Tolle lege* in der Bibel," *Biblische Zeitschrift* 23 (1935–1936), pp. 58–61.

52. Courcelle, *Les Confessions de saint Augustin dans la tradition littéraire*, p. 158. Cf. O'Donnell, *Confessions*, vol. 2, pp. 64–66.

53. See Courcelle, "Source chrétienne et allusions païennes de l'épisode du *Tolle, lege*," pp. 176–77.

54. See ibid., pp. 177–79. Cf. his treatment in *Les Confessions de saint Augustin dans la tradition littéraire*, pp. 165–68.

55. Sessorainus 55.f.42r: see Pierre Courcelle, *Recherches sur les Confessions de saint Augustin* (Paris: E. de Boccard, 1968), p. 195. For a fuller presentation, see Courcelle, *Les Confessions de saint Augustin dans la tradition littéraire*, pp. 165–68. For a different account of the implications of the "nearby house," see Leo C. Ferrari, "*Ecce audio vocem de vicina domo (Conf.* 8, 12, 29)," *Augustiniana* 33.3–4 (1983), pp. 232–45.

56. Life of St Augustine, scene 9, in Sant' Agostino, Cappella del Coro, San Gimignano.

57. Courcelle, *Les Confessions de saint Augustin dans la tradition littéraire*, p. 169.

58. For a full analysis of the illustrations of the scene, see Pierre Courcelle and Jeanne

Courcelle-Ladmirant, "Explication des planches et considérations iconographiques," in Courcelle, *Les Confessions de saint Augustin dans la tradition littéraire*, pp. 641–88.

59. Courcelle, *Les Confessions de saint Augustin dans la tradition littéraire*, p. 377.

60. See ibid., p. 176 and pp. 388–89.

61. Augustine, *Confessions* 8.11.27, p. 100; English in Chadwick, *Confessions*, p. 151.

62. Ibid.

63. Courcelle, *Recherches sur les Confessions de saint Augustin*, p. 195. Courcelle refined his reading in several later works: "L'oracle d'Apis et l'oracle du Jardin de Milan"; "Note sur le '*Tolle, lege*,'" *L'Année théologique* 39 (1951), pp. 217–32; "Les 'voix' dans les Confessions de saint Augustin," *Hermes* 80 (1952), pp. 31–46; "Source chrétienne et allusions païennes de l'épisode du *Tolle, lege*"; and above all, *Les Confessions de saint Augustin dans la tradition littéraire*, esp. pp. 155–63. For counterarguments, see Franco Bolgiani, *La conversion di S. Agostino e l'VIII libro delle 'Confessioni'* (Turin: Università di Torino, 1956); John O'Meara, "Arripui, aperui, et legi," *Augustinus Magister: Congrès international augustinien*, 3 vols. (Paris: 1954), vol. 1, pp. 59–64; Fulbert Cayré, "La conversion de saint Augustin: Le '*tolle, lege*' des *Confessions*," *L'Année théologique* 11 (1951), pp. 141–51 and 244–52; Joly, "La scène du Jardin de Milan." For an account of the debate, see Henri-Irénée Marrou, "La querelle autour du *Tolle, lege*," in *Christiana tempora: Mélanges d'histoire, d'archéologie, d'épigraphie et de patristique* (Rome: École française de Rome, 1978), pp. 381–91.

64. See Augustine, *Confessions* 1.1.1, p. 3; English in Chadwick, *Confessions*, p. 3.

65. Augustine, *Soliloquies* 1.1, trans. Rose Elizabeth Cleveland (Boston: Little, Brown, 1910), p. 1. On voices in the *Confessions*, see Courcelle, "Les 'voix' dans les Confessions de saint Augustin."

66. See John Freccero, "Autobiography and Narrative," in Thomas C. Heller, Morton Sosna, and David E. Wellbery, eds., *Reconstructing Individualism: Autonomy, Individuality and the Self in Western Thought* (Stanford: Stanford University Press, 1986), pp. 16–29, esp. pp. 22–26.

67. Micah 4:4.

68. See John 1:45–48. On the fig tree in the scene, see Vinzenz Buchheit, "Augustinus unter dem Feigenbaum (zu Conf. VIII)," *Vigiliae Christianae* 22.4 (1968), pp. 257–71, and Bolgiani, *La conversione di S. Agostino e l'VIII libro delle 'Confessioni,'* pp. 104–10.

CHAPTER NINE: THE KNIGHT GUESSES

1. Psalm 35:22, New International Version.

2. Psalms 119:148, followed by Isaiah 44:2, Galatians 3:13, and Psalms 106:2.

3. Theodor Zahn, *Cyprian von Antiochen und die deutsche Faustsage* (Erlangen: A. Deichert, 1882), pp. 151–52. See Pierre Courcelle, "L'enfant et les 'Sorts bibliques,'" *Vigiliae Christianae* 7.4 (1953), p. 205. For a more recent edition of the Greek text and the translation cited here, see Ryan Bailey, "The Acts of Saint Cypian of Antioch: Critical Editions, Translations, and Commentary," PhD diss., School of Religious Studies, McGill University, 2017, pp. 134–37.

4. John Moschus, *Pratum spirituale*, chapter 32, *Patrologia Graeca* vol. 87, 3.2888C, cited in Courcelle, "L'enfant les 'sorts bibliques,'" pp. 205–206. The verse is Matthew 4:17. For the English translation quoted here, see John Moschos (also known as John Eviratus), *The Spiritual Meadow (Pratum Spirituale)*, ed. and trans. John Wortley (Kalamazoo: Cistercian Publications, 1992), p. 23.

5. Gregory of Tours, *The History of the Franks*, trans. Lewis Thorpe (London: Penguin Books, 1974), 2.37, p. 152.

6. Ibid., 4.16, pp. 212–13

7. Ibid., 5.14, pp. 271–72.

8. Augustine, Letter 55, chapter 20, in Jacques-Paul Migne, ed., *Patrologia cursus completus, series latina*, 223 vols. (Paris: Exudebat Migne, 1844–1864), vol. 33, p. 222: *His qui de paginis evangelicis sortes legunt, et si optandum sit ut id potius faciant quam ad daemonia consulenda concurrant, tamen ista mihi displicet consuetudo, ad negotia saecularia et ad vitae huius vanitatem divina oracula velle convertere.* For the English, see Philip Schaff and Henry Wace, eds., *A Select Library of Nicene and Post-Nicene Fathers, First Series*, 14 vols. (Buffalo: Christian Literature Publishing, 1886–1890), vol. 1, p. 315.

9. Thomas Aquinas, *Summa Theologiae*, 2.2, question 95, article 8.

10. See William E. Klingshirn, "Defining the *Sortes Sanctorum*: Gibbon, Du Cange, and Early Christian Lot Divination," *Journal of Early Christian Studies* 10.1 (2002), pp. 77–130, who reports that they are first mentioned (as "Sanctorum sortes") in the final canon of the council of Vannes, which was convened between 462 and 48.

11. See Fritz Graf, "Rolling the Dice for an Answer," in Sarah Iles Johnston and Peter T. Struck, eds., *Mantikê: Studies in Ancient Divination* (Leiden: Brill, 2005), pp. 59–60. On the *sortes sanctorum*, see also Jacqueline Champeaux, "'Sorts' antiques et médiévaux: Les lettres et les chiffres," in *Au miroir de la culture antique: Mélanges offerts au president René Marache* (Rennes: Presses universitaires de Rennes, 1992), pp. 67–89; and Klingshirn, "Defining the *Sortes Sanctorum*."

12. Graf, "Rolling the Dice for an Answer," p. 79. See also William E. Klingshirn,

"Christian Divination in Late Roman Gaul: The *Sortes Sangallenses*," in Johnston and Struck, eds., *Mantikê*, pp. 99–128.

13. See László Sándor Chardonnens, "Mantic Alphabets in Medieval Western Manuscripts and Early Printed Books," *Modern Philology* 110.3 (2013), pp. 342–43.

14. For these dates, see Poirion's remarks in Chrétien de Troyes, *Oeuvres complètes*, eds. Daniel Poirion, with Anne Berthelot, Peter F. Dembowski, Sylvie Lefèvre, Karl D. Uitti, and Philippe Walter (Paris: Gallimard, 1994), p. 1299.

15. Chrétien de Troyes, *Le Roman de Perceval ou le Conte du Graal*, ed. Keith Busby (Tübingen: Max Niemeyer, 1993), lines 103–141, pp. 6–8; English in *Perceval: The Story of the Grail*, trans. Burton Raffel (New Haven: Yale University Press, 1999), pp. 4–6.

16. Chrétien de Troyes, *Le Roman de Perceval ou le Conte du Graal*, lines 189–276, pp. 10–13; English in *Perceval: The Story of the Grail*, pp. 7–8.

17. Chrétien de Troyes, *Le Roman de Perceval ou le Conte du Graal*, *A* and *L*, lines 343–60, p. 427; English in *Perceval: The Story of the Grail*, p. 12.

18. Reto R. Bezzola, *Le sens de l'aventure et de l'amour (Chrétien de Troyes)* (Paris: Champion, 1968), p. 52.

19. Chrétien de Troyes, *Le Roman de Perceval*, lines 435–70, pp. 19–20; English in *Perceval: The Story of the Grail*, p. 15.

20. Chrétien de Troyes, *Le Roman de Perceval*, lines 527–72, pp. 22–24; English in *Perceval: The Story of the Grail*, pp. 18–19.

21. Chrétien de Troyes, *Le Roman de Perceval*, lines 639–40, p. 27; English in *Perceval: The Story of the Grail*, p. 21.

22. Chrétien de Troyes, *Le Roman de Perceval*, lines 700–704, p. 29; English in *Perceval: The Story of the Grail*, p. 23.

23. Chrétien de Troyes, *Le Roman de Perceval*, lines 71215, p. 30; English in *Perceval: The Story of the Grail*, p. 23.

24. Chrétien de Troyes, *Le Roman de Perceval*, lines 734–35, p. 31; English in *Perceval: The Story of the Grail*, p. 24.

25. Chrétien de Troyes, *Le Roman de Perceval*, line 1352, p. 56; English in *Perceval: The Story of the Grail*, p. 43.

26. Chrétien de Troyes, *Le Roman de Perceval*, lines 1648–54, p. 68; English in *Perceval: The Story of the Grail*, p. 53.

27. Chrétien de Troyes, *Le Roman de Perceval*, lines 1675–83, p. 70; English in *Perceval: The Story of the Grail*, pp. 53–54.

28. Chrétien de Troyes, *Le Roman de Perceval*, lines 1686–88, p. 70; English in *Perceval: The Story of the Grail*, p. 54.

29. See Charles Méla, *Blanchefleur et le saint homme ou la semblance des réliques: Étude comparée de littérature médiévale* (Paris: Éditions du Seuil, 1979), p. 29.

30. Chrétien de Troyes, *Le Roman de Perceval*, lines 3052–53, p. 130; English in *Perceval: The Story of the Grail*, p. 97.

31. Chrétien de Troyes, *Le Roman de Perceval*, lines 3213–42, pp. 137–38; English in *Perceval: The Story of the Grail*, pp. 102–103.

32. Chrétien de Troyes, *Le Roman de Perceval*, lines 3202–3209, p. 136; English in *Perceval: The Story of the Grail*, p. 102.

33. Chrétien de Troyes, *Le Roman de Perceval*, lines 3243–47, p. 138; English in *Perceval: The Story of the Grail*, p. 103.

34. Chrétien de Troyes, *Le Roman de Perceval*, lines 3290–97, p. 140; English in *Perceval: The Story of the Grail*, pp. 104–105.

35. Chrétien de Troyes, *Le Roman de Perceval*, lines 3248–51, p. 138; English in *Perceval: The Story of the Grail*, p. 103.

36. Chrétien de Troyes, *Le Roman de Perceval*, lines 3304–3309, p. 141; English in *Perceval: The Story of the Grail*, p. 105.

37. Renaud de Beaujeu, *Le Bel Inconnu*, ed. Michèle Perret, trans. Michèle Perret and Isabelle Weill (Paris: Champion, 2003), lines 99–100, p. 8; English in Renaut de Bâgé, *Le Bel Inconnu (Li Biaus Descouneüs; The Fair Unknown)*, eds. Karen Fresco and Margaret P. Hasselman, trans. Colleen P. Donagher (New York: Garland, 1992), p. 9.

38. Renaud de Beaujeu, *Le Bel Inconnu*, lines 115–16, p. 8; English in Renaut de Bâgé, *Le Bel Inconnu (Li Biaus Descouneüs; The Fair Unknown)*, p. 11.

39. Renaud de Beaujeu, *Le Bel Inconnu*, lines 126–32, p. 10; English in Renaut de Bâgé, *Le Bel Inconnu (Li Biaus Descouneüs; The Fair Unknown)*, p. 11.

40. Renaud de Beaujeu, *Le Bel Inconnu*, lines 3133–50, pp. 186–88; English in Renaut de Bâgé, *Le Bel Inconnu (Li Biaus Descouneüs; The Fair Unknown)*, pp. 186–87.

41. Renaud de Beaujeu, *Le Bel Inconnu*, line 3170, p. 188; English in Renaut de Bâgé, *Le Bel Inconnu (Li Biaus Descouneüs; The Fair Unknown)*, p. 187.

42. Renaud de Beaujeu, *Le Bel Inconnu*, line 3174–77, p. 190; English in Renaut de Bâgé, *Le Bel Inconnu (Li Biaus Descouneüs; The Fair Unknown)*, p. 188.

43. Renaud de Beaujeu, *Le Bel Inconnu*, 3178–84, p. 190; English in Renaut de Bâgé, *Le Bel Inconnu (Li Biaus Descouneüs; The Fair Unknown)*, p. 189.

44. Alice Colby-Hall, "The Lips of the Serpent," in David Feldman, ed., *Homenaje a Robert A. Hall, Jr.: Ensayos lingüísticos e filológicos para su sexagésimo aniversario* (Madrid: Playor, 1977), p. 113, referring to lines 3134–35.

45. *Lybeaus Desconus*, eds. Eve Salisbury and James Weldon (Kalamazoo: Medieval Institute Publications, Western Michigan University, 2013), line 2068, p. 79.

46. Renaud de Beaujeu, *Le Bel Inconnu*, lines 3185–86, p. 190; English in Renaut de Bâgé, *Le Bel Inconnu (Li Biaus Descouneüs; The Fair Unknown)*, p. 189.

47. Renaud de Beaujeu, *Le Bel Inconnu*, lines 3189–92, p. 190; English in Renaut de Bâgé, *Le Bel Inconnu (Li Biaus Descouneüs; The Fair Unknown)*, p. 189.

48. Renaud de Beaujeu, *Le Bel Inconnu*, lined 3232–37, p. 192; English in Renaut de Bâgé, *Le Bel Inconnu (Li Biaus Descouneüs; The Fair Unknown)*, p. 193.

49. Renaud de Beaujeu, *Le Bel Inconnu*, lines 3249–52, p. 194; English in Renaut de Bâgé, *Le Bel Inconnu (Li Biaus Descouneüs; The Fair Unknown)*, p. 193.

50. Wolfram von Eschenbach, *Parzival*, ed. Karl Lachmann (Berlin: De Gruyter, 1952), 3.140.6; English in *Parzival*, trans. A. T. Hatto (New York: Penguin Books, 1980), p. 81.

51. *Parzival*, 3.140.16; English in *Parzival*, p. 81.

52. On the scene, its relation to Chrétien de Troyes, and its importance for Wolfram's poem, see Bodo von Mergell, *Wolfram von Eschenbach und seine französischen Quellen*, 2 vols. (Münster: Aschendorffschen Verlagsbuchhandlung, 1936), vol. 2, pp. 141–48; Christa Ortmann, *Die Selbstaussagen im Parzival: Zur Frage nach der Persongestaltung bei Wolfram von Eschenbach* (Stutgart: W. Kohlhammer, 1972), pp. 25–28.

53. Chrétien de Troyes, *Le Roman de Perceval*, lines 3466–83, pp. 148–49; English in *Perceval: The Story of the Grail*, p. 110.

54. Chrétien de Troyes, *Le Roman de Perceval*, lines 3548–55, p. 152; English in *Perceval: The Story of the Grail*, p. 113.

55. Chrétien de Troyes, *Le Roman de Perceval*, lines 3556–71, p. 152; English in *Perceval: The Story of the Grail*, p. 113.

56. Chrétien de Troyes, *Le Roman de Perceval*, line 3572, p. 152; English in *Perceval: The Story of the Grail*, pp. 112–13.

57. Chrétien de Troyes, *Le Roman de Perceval*, lines, 3573–77, pp. 152–53; English in *Perceval: The Story of the Grail*, p. 113.

58. For a summary, see Jane H. M. Taylor, "Perceval/Perceforest: Naming as Hermeneutic in the *Roman de Perceforest*," *Romance Quarterly* 44.4 (1987), pp. 201–14, esp. pp. 203–205.

59. For the judgment of "absurdity," see Jean Fourquet, *Wolfram d'Eschenbach et le Conte del grail* (Paris: Les Belles Lettres, 1938), p. 43; for that of ineptness, see Maurice Wilmotte, *Le Roman du Gral, d'après les versions les plus anciennes* (Paris: La Renaissance du livre, 1930), p. 139 n. 1. For more nuanced accounts of the scene, as well as its reception, see Jean Frappier, *Chrétien de Troyes et le mythe du Graal: Étude sur 'Perceval ou le Conte du Graal'* (Paris: Société d'édition d'enseignement supérieur, 1972), pp. 120–26; Philippe Ménard, "La révélation du nom pour le héros du *Conte du Graal*," in Danielle Queruel, ed., *Amour et chevalerie dans les romans de Chrétien de Troyes: Actes du Colloque de Troyes (27–29 mars 1992)* (Paris: Les Belles Lettres, 1995), pp. 47–59.

60. Manuscript *S*, in *Le Roman de Perceval*, note to line 3574, p 153: Here the boy "dist a la dame que il avoit / Perchevax li Galois a non."

61. William Albert Nitze, *Perceval and the Holy Grail: An Essay on the Romance of Chrétien de Troyes* (Berkeley: University of California Press, 1949), p. 297 n. 9.

62. See Alfons Hilka, in *Der Percevalroman von Chrétien de Troyes (Li Contes del Graal)*, p. 695, note to line 3574.

63. See the summary in Ménard, "La révélation du nom," pp. 50–51.

64. Frappier, *Chrétien de Troyes et le mythe du Graal*, pp. 124–26.

65. Bezzola, *Le sens de l'aventure et de l'amour*, p. 56.

66. Tajiro Amazawa, "La devineuse du nom de Perceval," in J. Claude Faucon, Alain Labbé, and Danielle Quéruel, eds., *Miscellanea Mediaevalia: Mélanges offerts à Philippe Ménard*, 2 vols. (Paris: Champion, 1998), vol. 1, pp. 33–36.

67. Chrétien de Troyes, *Le Roman de Perceval*, lines 3578–90, p. 153; English in *Perceval: The Story of the Grail*, pp. 113–14.

68. Amazawa, "La devineuse du nom de Perceval," p. 34.

69. On *non* and *sornom* in *Perceval*, see Douglas Kelly, "Le nom de Perceval," in Danielle Buschunger and Wolfgang Spiewok, eds., *Perceval-Parzival, hier et aujourd'hui, et autres essais sur la littérature allemande du Moyen Âge et de la Renaissance* (Greifswald: Reineke, 1994), pp. 123–29; Barbara N. Sargent-Baur, *La destre et la senestre: Étude sur le Conte du Graal de Chrétien de Troyes* (Amsterdam: Rodopi, 2000), pp. 119–38; Jane Bliss, *Naming and Namelessness in Medieval Romance* (Rochester: D. S. Brewer, 2008), p. 34.

70. Frappier, *Chrétien de Troyes et le mythe du Graal*, p. 122 n. 44, quoting *Le Roman de Perceval*, lines 242–44, p. 12; English in *Perceval: The Story of the Grail*, p. 9. Rey-Flaud

has noted that *galois* can also be seen in relation to *galois*, "gay," "joyous": see Henri Ray-Flaud, *Le Sphinx et le graal: Le secret et l'énigme* (Paris: Payot & Rivages, 1998), p. 135.

CHAPTER TEN: OF PROVERBS

1. Alfonso X, *Las Siete Partidas*, Partida 7, Title 2, preamble; English in *Underworlds: The Dead, the Criminal, and the Marginalized*, vol. 5 of *Las Siete Partidas*, ed. Robert I. Burns, trans. Samuel Parsons Scott, 5 vols. (Philadelphia: University of Pennsylvania Press, 2001), p. 1318.

2. *Las Siete Partidas*, Partida 7, Title 23, preamble; English in *Underworlds*, p. 1431.

3. *Las Siete Partidas* Partida 7, Title 23, Law 1; English in *Underworlds*, p. 1431.

4. See Charles T. Lewis and Charles Short, *A Latin Dictionary, Founded on Andrews' Edition of Freund's Latin Dictionary* (Oxford: Clarendon Press of Oxford University Press, 1879), s.v. "Proverbium."

5. See Heinrich Lausberg, *Handbuch der literarischen Rhetorik: Eine Grundlegung der Literaturwissenschaft*, 2 vols. (Munich: Hueber, 1973), vol. 1, paragraph 202.

6. Toufic Fahd, *La divination arabe: Études religieuses, sociologiques et folkloriques sur le milieu natif de l'Islam* (Leiden: E. J. Brill, 1966), p. 451.

7. Real Academia Española, *Diccionario de autoridades*, 3 vols. (1726; facsimile edition, Madrid: Gredos, 1969), s.v. "Alfil."

8. Antonio de Nebrija, *Vocabulario español-latino* (1494; facsimile edition Madrid: Real Academia Espaõla, 1951), s.v. "Alfil."

9. Pedro Ciruelo, *Reprouación de las supersticiones y hechizerías*, ed. Alva V. Ebersole (Valencia: Albatros Hispaniola, 1978), pp. 62–63.

10. Ibid., p. 63.

11. C. E. Aníbal, "Another Note on the Voces del Cielo," *Romanic Review* 18 (1927), p. 250.

12. *Celestina, or the Tragicke-Comedy of Calisto and Melibea, Englished from the Spanish of Fernando de Rojas by James Mabbe*, ed. James Fitzmaurice-Kelly (New York: AMS Press, 1969), p. 79.

13. Mateo Alemán, *Guzmán de Alfarache*, ed. Benito Brancaforte, 2 vols. (Madrid: Ediciones Cátedra, 1979), vol. 2, p. 347; English in *The Rogue; or the Life of Guzman de Alfarache*, 2 vols., trans. John Mabbe (London: Edward Blount, 1622), vol. 2, p. 255.

14. C. E. Aníbal, "*Voces del cielo* — A Note on Mira de Amescua," *Romanic Review* 16 (1925), p. 57.

15. Ibid., p. 58.

16. Ibid., pp. 59–60.

17. Aníbal, "Another Note on the *Voces del cielo*," pp. 251–52. For the text, see Tirso de Molina, *La elección por la virtud: Edición critica, estudio y notas*, ed. Miguel Galindo Abellán (Murcia: Universidad de Murcia, 2012), p. 9.

18. Aníbal, "Another Note on the *Voces del cielo*," p. 252.

19. Sonia Jones, "Two Cases of Kledonomancy in Lope's Theater," *Revista de estudios hispanicos* 9 (1982), p. 139.

20. Miguel de Cervantes, *El ingenioso hidalgo Don Quixote de la Mancha*, ed. Luis Andrés Murillo, 3 vols. (Madrid: Editorial Castilia, 1978), vol. 2, p. 581; English in *Don Quijote: A New Translation*, trans. Burton Raffel (New York: Norton, 1999), pp. 737–38. Translation modified.

21. Cervantes, *El ingenioso hidalgo Don Quixote*, p. 581; English in *Don Quijote*, p. 738.

22. Ibid. Translation modified.

23. Ibid.

24. Cervantes, *El ingenioso hidalgo Don Quixote*, p. 582; English in *Don Quijote*, p. 738.

25. On the scene and Ciruelo, see Ana García Chichester, "Don Quijote y Sancho en El Toboso: Superstición y simbolismo," *Bulletin of the Cervantes Society of America* 3.2 (1983), pp. 121–33.

26. E. C. Riley, "Symbolism in *Don Quixote*, part II, chapter 73," *Journal of Hispanic Philology* 3.2 (1979), p. 163.

27. Ibid.

28. Ibid., p. 165.

29. Ibid., p. 169.

30. Otis H. Green, *Spain and the Western Tradition: The Castilian Mind in Literature from El Cid to Calderón* (Madison: University of Wisconsin Press, 1963), p. 328.

31. Francisco Layna Ranz, "La liebre y la jaula de grillos (*Quijote*, II, 73): El confessor Diego de Yepes y la salvación del alma," in Emilio Martínez Mata and María Fernández Ferreiro, eds., *Comentarios a Cervantes: Actas selectas del VIII Congreso Internacional de la Asociación de Cervantistas, Oviedo, 11–15 de junio de 2012* (Madrid: Fundación María Cristina Masaveu Peterson, 2014), pp. 415–24. On the scene, see also Manuel Simón Viola, "El regreso a la aldea (*Quijote*, II, 73)," *Philologia hispalensis* 182.2 (2014), pp. 211–25; Alan S. Trueblood, "La jaula de grillos (*Don Quijote*, II, 73)," in Marta Cristina Carbonell and Adolfo Sotelo Vázquez, eds., *Homenaje al professor Antonio Vilanova*, 2 vols. (Barcelona:

Universidad de Barcelona, 1989), vol. 1, pp. 699–708; Arturo Marasso, "La adivinación por las palabras," in *Cervantes: La Invención del Quijote* (Buenos Aires: Hachette, 1954), pp. 192–93.

32. François Rabelais, *Le Tiers Livre des dicts heroïques du bon Pantagruel*, in *Oeuvres complètes*, eds. Mireille Huchon with François Moreau (Paris: Gallimard, 1994), p. 380; English in *The Third Book of the Heroic Deeds and Sayings of the Good Pantagruel*, in *The Complete Works of François Rabelais*, trans. Donald M. Frame (Berkeley: University of California Press, 1991), p. 284.

33. Rabelais, *Oeuvres complètes*, p. 388; English in *Complete Works of François Rabelais*, p. 292. Translation slightly modified.

34. René Descartes, "Discours de la méthode pour bien conduire sa raison & chercher la verité dans les sciences," in *Oeuvres complètes*, eds. Charles Adam and Paul Tannery, 11 vols. (Paris: Vrin, 1996), vol. 6, p. 3; English in *A Discourse on the Method*, trans. Ian Maclean (Oxford: Oxford University Press, 2006), p. 6.

35. On the place of Descartes's German stay, see Geneviève Rodis-Lewis, *Descartes: His Life and Thought*, trans. Jane Marie Todd (Ithaca: Cornell University Press, 1998), pp. 35–38.

36. Descartes, "Discours de la méthode," p. 11; English in *A Discourse on Method*, p. 12.

37. On the notebook, see Geneviève Rodis-Lewis, "Le premier registre de Descartes," *Archives de philosophie* 54 (1991), pp. 353–77.

38. Descartes, "Olympica," in *Oeuvres complètes*, vol. 10, p. 179. My translation. On "enthusiasm" as "divine inspiration," see Michael H. Keefer, "The Dreamer's Path: Descartes and the Sixteenth Century," *Renaissance Quarterly* 49.1 (1996), p. 34.

39. Descartes, "Olympica," p. 181; English in John R. Cole, *The Olympian Dreams and Youthful Rebellion of René Descartes* (Urbana: University of Illinois Press, 1992), pp. 32–33.

40. Descartes, "Olympica," p. 181; English in *The Olympian Dreams*, p. 33.

41. Descartes, "Olympica," p. 181; English in *The Olympian Dreams*, pp. 33–34.

42. Descartes, "Olympica," p. 182; English in *The Olympian Dreams*, pp. 34–35.

43. Descartes, "Olympica," p. 182; English in *The Olympian Dreams*, p. 35.

44. Ibid. Translation slightly modified. For a modern edition of these texts, see P. H. Green, ed., *The Works of Ausonius* (Oxford: Oxford University Press, 1991), pp. 104–105 and pp. 106–107.

45. Descartes, "Olympica," pp. 183–84; English in *The Olympian Dreams*, pp. 35–36.

46. Descartes, "Olympica," p. 184; English in *The Olympian Dreams*, p. 36.

47. Descartes, "Olympica," p. 184; English in *The Olympian Dreams*, pp. 36–37.

48. Descartes, "Olympica," p. 184; English in *The Olympian Dreams*, p. 37.

49. Jean-Luc Marion, "Les trois songes, ou L'éveil du philosophe," in Jean-Luc Marion, ed., with Jean Deprun, *La passion de la raison: Hommage à Ferdinand Alquié* (Paris: Presses universitaires de France, 1983), pp. 72–73.

50. Ibid., p. 74.

51. Cole, *The Olympian Dreams*, p. 7. For an account of Leibniz's use of the notebook, see ibid., pp. 1–6. For the text of Leibniz's transcription, see "Cartesii cogitationes privatae," in René Descartes, *Oeuvres inédites de Descartes*, ed. Alexandre Foucher de Careil, 2 vols. (Paris: Auguste Durand, 1859), vol. 1, pp. 2–17. The text is reproduced in Descartes, *Oeuvres complètes*, vol. 10, pp. 213–48.

52. Cole, *The Olympian Dreams*, p. 7.

53. In Foucher, ed., *Oeuvres inédites de Descartes*, pp. 8–9. On the difference between this formulation and the one evoked by Baillet, see Rodis-Lewis, "Le premier registre de Descartes," pp. 363–64. Cf. Gottfried Wilhelm Leibniz, "Notata quaedam G. G. L. circa vitam et doctrima Cartesii," in Gottfried Wilhelm Leibniz, *Die philosophischen Schriften*, ed. C. J. Gerhardt, 7 vols. (1875–1890; Hildesheim: Olms, 1978), vol. 4, p. 310. In Leibniz's transcription, the dream is dated to 1619, not 1610.

54. Leibniz, "Notata quaedam G. G. L. circa vitam et doctrinam Cartesii," in C. Thomasius, *Historia sapientiae et stultitiae*, 2 vols. (Halle: Typis & Sumptibus Christophori Salfeldii, 1693), vol. 2, pp. 113–22; for a modern edition, see Gottfried Wilhelm Leibniz, *Sämtliche Schriften und Briefe* (Berlin: Akademie Verlag, 1998–2017), series 6, vol. 4: *Philosophische Schriften*, number 376, p. 2057. The translation quoted is that of Alice Browne, "Descartes' Dreams," *Journal of the Warburg and Courtauld Institutes* 40 (1977), p. 265.

55. Gottfried Wilhelm Leibniz, *Essais de Théodicée*, preface, in *Die philosophischen Schriften*, vol. 6, p. 31; English in Gottfried Wilhelm Leibniz, *Theodicy*, ed. Austin Farrer, trans. E. M. Huggard (La Salle: Open Court, 1985), p. 55. Translation slightly modified.

56. Exodus 7:3, 8:15, 9:12.

57. Leibniz, *Essais de Théodicée*, section 99, in *Die philosophischen Schriften*, vol. 6, p. 158; English in *Theodicy*, p. 178.

58. Leibniz, *Essais de Théodicée*, section 100, in *Die philosophischen Schriften*, vol. 6, p. 158; English in *Theodicy*, p. 178.

59. See Morgens Lærke, "Leibniz and Steno, 1675–1680)," in Morgens Lærke and Raphaele Andrault, eds., *Steno and the Philosophers* (Leiden: Brill, 2018), p. 67.

60. Leibniz, *Essais de Théodicée*, section 100, in *Die philosophischen Schriften*, vol. 6, pp. 158–59; English in *Theodicy*, pp. 178–79.

61. Leibniz, *Essais de Théodicée*, section 100, in *Die philosophischen Schriften*, vol. 6, p. 178.

62. Christopher Wild, "Apertio Libri: Codex and Conversion," in Eric Downing, Jonathan M. Hess, and Richard V. Benson, eds., *Literary Studies and the Pursuits of Reading* (Rochester: Camden House, 2012), p. 18.

63. Leibniz, *Essais de Théodicée*, preface, in *Die philosophischen Schriften*, vol. 6, p. 26; English in *Theodicy*, p. 50.

64. Leibniz, *Essais de Théodicée*, preface, in *Die philosophischen Schriften*, vol. 6, p. 29; English in *Theodicy*, p. 53.

65. On Leibniz's doctrine of "small perceptions," see Daniel Heller-Roazen, *The Inner Touch: Archaeology of a Sensation* (New York: Zone Books, 2007), pp. 179–209.

66. Leibniz, *Nouveaux essais,* preface, in *Die philosophischen Schriften*, vol. 5, p. 49.

67. Gottfried Wilhelm Leibniz, "Principes de la Nature et de la Grace, fondés en raison," in *Die philosophischen Schriften*, vol. 6, p. 604; English in Gottfried Wilhelm Leibniz, "Principles of Nature and Grace, Based on Reason," in *Philosophical Essays*, ed. and trans. Robert Ariew and Daniel Garber (Indianapolis: Hackett, 1989), p. 211.

CHAPTER ELEVEN: LINES AND SENTENCES

1. Johann Peter Hebel, "Kannitverstan," in *Sämtliche Schriften*, eds. Adrian Braunbehrens, Gustav A. Benrath and Peter Pfaff, 8 vols. (Karlsruhe: C. F. Müller, 1990–2013), vol. 2–3: *Erzählungen und Aufsätze*, pp. 132–35; English in *The Treasure Chest*, trans. John Hibbard (London: Libris, 1994), pp. 40–42.

2. On the tale and its textual history, see Kurt Franz, *Johann Peter Hebel Kannitverstan: Ein Mißverständnis und seine Folgen, Texte, Kommentar, Abbildungen* (Munich: Carl Hanser, 1985).

3. Hebel, "Kannitverstan," p. 133; English in *The Treasure Chest*, p. 40.

4. Hebel, "Kannitverstan," p. 133; English in *The Treasure Chest*, p. 41.

5. Ibid.

6. Hebel, "Kannitverstan," p. 134; English in *The Treasure Chest*, pp. 41–42.

7. Hebel, "Kannitverstan," p. 134; English in *The Treasure Chest*, p. 42.

8. Hebel, "Kannitverstan," p. 132; English in *The Treasure Chest*, p. 40. Translation modified.

9. Hebel, "Kannitverstan," p. 135; English in *The Treasure Chest*, p. 42.

10. Paul Fleming, "'Kannitverstan': The Contingent Understanding of Anecdotes," *Oxford German Studies* 40.1 (2011), p. 77.

11. For a different reading of the senses of the syntagma, see Thomas Schestag, *para-: Titus Lucretius Carus, Johann Peter Hebel, Francis Ponge: Zur literarischen Hermeneutik* (Munich: Boer, 1991), pp. 207–15.

12. Edgar Allan Poe, "The Imp of the Perverse," in *Poetry and Tales* (New York: Literary Classics of the U.S., 1984), p. 826.

13. Ibid., p. 827.

14. Ibid., p. 828.

15. Ibid., p. 829.

16. Ibid., p. 830.

17. Ibid.

18. Ibid., p. 831.

19. Ibid., pp. 830–31.

20. Ibid., p. 831.

21. Ibid.

22. Stanley Cavell, *In Quest of the Ordinary: Lines of Skepticism and Romanticism* (Chicago: University of Chicago Press, 1988), p. 141.

23. Edgar Allan Poe, "Le démon de la perversité," in *Oeuvres en prose*, trans. Charles Baudelaire (Paris: Gallimard, 1951), pp. 283–89.

24. For the details of the publication see Stéphane Mallarmé, "Le démon de l'analogie," in *Oeuvres complètes*, ed. Bertrand Marchal, 2 vols. (Paris: Gallimard, 1998–2003), vol. 1, p. 1335.

25. "The Demon of Analogy," in Stéphane Mallarmé, *Divagations: The Author's 1897 Arrangement*, trans. Barbara Johnson (Cambridge, MA: Harvard University Press, 2007), p. 17.

26. Mallarmé, "Le démon de l'analogie," pp. 86–87.

27. Mallarmé, "Le démon de l'analogie," p. 87; English in "The Demon of Analogy," p. 18. Translation modified.

28. Among others, see Robert Greer Cohn, *Mallarmé's Prose Poems: A Critical Study* (Cambridge: Cambridge University Press, 1987), pp. 8–9; Roger Pearson, *Unfolding Mallarmé: The Development of a Poetic Art* (Oxford: Clarendon Press of Oxford University Press, 2006), pp. 74–82; Éric Benoit, "*Le démon de l'analogie*, ou: La résurrection des mots,"

in Jean-Pierre Saïdeh, ed., *Enchantements: Mélanges offers à Yves Vadé* (Bordeaux: Presses universitaires de Bordeaux, 2002), pp. 97–110; Jan Mieszkowski, *Crises of the Sentence* (Chicago: University of Chicago Press, 2019), pp. 141–49.

29. "Mallarmé, "Le démon de l'analogie," p. 86; English in "The Demon of Analogy," p. 17.

30. Poe, "Le démon de la perversité," p. 288. See Kan Miyabayashi, "Autour d'un poème en prose: Le démon de l'analogie," *Geibun-kenkyu: Journal of Arts and Letters* 91.3 (2016), p. 161.

31. Benoit, "*Le démon de l'analogie*," p. 106.

32. Barbara Johnson, *Défigurations du langage poétique: La seconde révolution baudelerienne* (Paris: Flammarion, 1979), p. 198.

33. Jean-Pierre Richard, *L'univers imaginaire de Stéphane Mallarmé* (Paris: Éditions du Seuil, 1961), p. 61; Cohn, *Mallarmé's Prose Poems*, p. 10.

34. As Pearson observes (*Unfolding Mallarmé*, p. 75), the rules of diaresis require that *ti* not be counted as a metrical syllable.

35. Mallarmé, "Le démon de l'analogie," pp. 1335–36.

36. Johnson, *Défigurations du langage poétique*, p. 193.

37. Stéphane Mallarmé, "Crise de vers," in *Oeuvres complètes*, vol. 1, p. 211; English in "Crisis in Poetry," in Mallarmé, *Divagations*, pp. 201–11 and 208. See Ursula Franklin, *The Prose Poems of Stéphane Mallarmé* (Chapel Hill: University of North Carolina Press, 1976), pp. 60–61, and Cohn, *Mallarmé's Prose Poems*, p. 8.

38. Stéphane Mallarmé, "Un coup de dés," in *Oeuvres complètes*, vol. 2, pp. 376–77; see Cohn, *Mallarmé's Prose Poems*, p. 134 n. 25. On the "Demon of Analogy" as a programmatic text, see A. R. Chisholm, "Le démon de l'analogie," *Essays in French Literature* 1 (1964), p. 5; Norman Paxton, *The Development of Mallarmé's Prose Style* (Geneva: Droz, 1968), p. 16; Johnson, *Défigurations du language poétique*, pp. 200–202; Pearson, *Unfolding Mallarmé*, pp. 81–82.

CHAPTER TWELVE: MAGIC DICTATIONS

1. John Stuart Mill, "Thoughts on Poetry and Its Varieties," in *The Collected Works of John Stuart Mill*, 33 vols. (Toronto: University of Toronto Press, 1963–1991), vol. 1, p. 343.

2. Ibid., p. 344.

3. Ibid., p. 345.

4. Ibid., p. 348.

5. Ibid., pp. 348–49.

6. Gottfried Wilhelm Friedrich Hegel, *Aesthetics: Lectures on Fine Art*, trans. T. M. Knox, 2 vols. (Oxford: Clarendon Press of Oxford University Press, 1975), vol. 2, p. 1113.

7. See, most famously, Northrop Frye, *Anatomy of Criticism: Four Essays* (1957; Princeton: Princeton University Press, 2000), pp. 5–6 and pp. 249–50. Cf. Herbert F. Tucker, "Dramatic Monologue and the Overhearing of Lyric," in Chaviva Hošek and Patricia Parker, eds., *Lyric Poetry: Beyond New Criticism* (Ithaca: Cornell University Press, 1985), pp. 226–43.

8. On the lines and some of the ways in which they have been read and misread, see Anne Janowitz, *Lyric and Labour in the Romantic Tradition* (Cambridge: Cambridge University Press, 1998), p. 19; Virginia Jackson and Yopie Prins, eds., *The Lyric Theory Reader: A Critical Anthology* (Baltimore: Johns Hopkins University Press, 2014), pp. 3–5; Virginia Jackson, *Dickinson's Misery: A Theory of Lyric Reading* (Princeton: Princeton University Press, 2005), pp. 129–33. On J. S. Mill and "lyric address," see also Jonathan Culler, *Theory of the Lyric* (Cambridge, MA: Harvard University Press, 2015), pp. 186–243.

9. Paul Valéry, "Calepin d'un poète," in *Oeuvres*, ed. Jean Hytier, 2 vols. (Paris: Gallimard, 1960), vol. 1, p. 1447.

10. Ibid., p. 1448.

11. Paul Valéry, "Littérature," in *Oeuvres*, vol. 2, p. 547. On Valéry and hearing oneself speak, see Jacques Derrida, "Qual quelle," in *Marges de la philosophie* (Paris: Minuit, 1972), pp. 326–64, esp. pp. 340–45; English in "Qual Quelle: Valéry's Sources," in *Margins of Philosophy*, trans. Alan Bass (Chicago: University of Chicago Press, 1982), pp. 275–306, esp. pp. 286–90.

12. Paul Valéry, *Cahiers*, 29 vols. (Paris: Centre national de la recherche scientifique), vol. 7, p. 615.

13. Valéry, *Cahiers*, vol. 7, p. 643. See Michel Lechantre, "P(h)o(n)étique," *Cahiers Paul Valéry* 1 (1975), pp. 104–105.

14. On Breton and Valéry, see Herbert S. Gershman, "Valéry and Breton," *Yale French Studies* 44 (1970) pp. 199–206.

15. André Breton, "Entrée des médiums," in *Les pas perdus*, in *Oeuvres complètes*, ed. Marguerite Bonnet, 4 vols. (Paris: Gallimard, 1998–2008), vol. 1, p. 274; English in "The Mediums Enter," in *The Lost Steps*, trans. Mark Polizzotti (Lincoln: University of Nebraska Press, 1990), p. 90. Translation slightly modified.

16. Breton, "Entrée des médiums," p. 275; English in "The Mediums Enter," p. 91.

17. Ibid.

18. André Breton, *Manifeste du surréalisme*, in *Oeuvres complètes*, vol. 1, pp. 322–23; English in *Manifestoes of Surrealism*, trans. Richard Seaver and Helen R. Lane (Ann Arbor: University of Michigan Press, 1972), pp. 18–19.

19. Breton, *Manifeste du surréalisme*, p. 324; English in *Manifestoes of Surrealism*, p. 20

20. Breton, "Situation surréaliste de l'objet, situation de l'objet surréaliste," in *Oeuvres complètes*, vol. 2, p. 492; English in *Manifestoes of Surrealism*, p. 275. For Lautréamont's text, see Germain Nouveau Lautréamont, *Maldoror (Les chants de Maldoror)*, in *Oeuvres complètes*, ed. Pierre-Olivier Walzer (Paris: Gallimard, 1980), pp. 224–25. On Breton and this image, see Ora Avni, "Breton et l'idéologie: Machine à coudre—parapluie," *Littérature* 51 (1983), pp. 15–27.

21. Breton, *Manifeste du surréalisme*, pp. 324–25; English in *Manifestoes of Surrealism*, pp. 21–22.

22. Jean-Luc Steinmetz, "Le paradoxe mallarméen: Les poèmes en prose," *Europe* 564–65 (1976), pp. 144–46.

23. Breton, *Manifeste du surréalisme*, p. 325; English in *Manifestoes of Surrealism*, p. 22.

24. Suzanne Guerlac, *Literary Polemics: Bataille, Sartre, Valéry, Breton* (Stanford: Stanford University Press, 1997), pp. 138–41.

25. Pierre Audoin, preface to André Breton and Philippe Soupault, *Les champs magnétiques* (Paris: Gallimard, 1971), p. 20. According to the editor of the Pléiade edition, the passage is by Soupault: see Breton, *Oeuvres completes*, vol. 1, pp. 1133–34.

26. André Breton, *Les champs magnétiques*, in *Oeuvres complètes*, vol. 1, p. 57; English in *The Magnetic Fields*, trans. Charlotte Mandell (New York: New York Review of Books, 2020), p. 8.

27. Breton, *Manifeste du surréalisme*, p. 325; English in *Manifestoes of Surrealism*, p. 21.

28. Hal Foster, "Convulsive Identity," *October* 57 (1991), pp. 22–23.

29. Breton, *Manifeste du surréalisme*, p. 327; English in *Manifestoes of Surrealism*, p. 24.

30. Breton, "Entrée des médiums," p. 274; English in "The Mediums Enter," p. 90.

31. Breton, *Manifeste du surréalisme*, p. 328; English in *Manifestoes of Surrealism*, p. 26.

32. Pierre Janet, *L'automatisme psychologique: Essai de psychologie expérimentale sur les formes inférieures de l'activité humaine* (Paris: Alcan, 1894).

33. Breton, "Entrée des médiums," p. 275; English in "The Mediums Enter," p. 91.

34. Jean Starobinski, "Freud, Breton, Myers," *L'Arc* 34 (1968), pp. 87–96. Cf. Jean-Michel Rabaté, "Loving Freud Madly: Surrealism between Hysterical and Paranoid Modernism," *Journal of Modern Literature* 25.3–4 (2002), pp. 58–74.

35. See F. W. H. Myers's posthumously published study, *Human Personality and Its Survival of Bodily Death* (London: Longmans, Green, 1903), and Théodore Flournoy, *From India to Planet Mars: A Case of Multiple Personality and Imaginary Languages*, ed. Sonu Shamdasani, preface by C. G. Jung (Princeton: Princeton University Press, 1994).

36. Breton, "Le message automatique," vol. 2, p. 379.

37. Starobinski, "Freud, Breton, Myers," p. 95

38. Breton, "Le message automatique," in *Oeuvres*, vol. 2, p. 385

39. Ibid., p. 386.

40. Jean-Louis Houdebine, "Le 'concept' d'écriture automatique: Sa signification et sa function dans le discours idéologique d'André Breton," *Littérature et ideologies: Collqoue de Cluny 2 (2, 3, 4 avril 1970)* (Paris: La Nouvelle Critique, 1971), p. 182

41. Jacques Lacan, *Le séminaire*, vol. 21, *Les non-dupes errent* (1973–1974), 19 March 1974, unpublished. See the discussion in Will Greenshields, "Lacan *contra* the Surrealists," *Nottingham French Studies* 58.1 (2019), p. 72

42. Jacques Lacan, "Une pratique de bavardage," in *Le séminaire*, vol. 25, *Le Temps de conclure* (1977–1978), November 15, 1977, unpublished. The passage appeared in *Ornicar?* 19 (1979), p. 5.

43. Breton, "Activité expérimentale.—Prospection systématique des 'états seconds'.—Pouvoirs de Robert Desnos," in *Oeuvres complètes*, vol. 3, p. 478.

44. William Butler Yeats, *A Vision: An Explanation of Life Founded upon the Writings of Giraldus and upon Certain Doctrines Attributed to Kusta ben Luka* (London: T. Werner Laurie, 1925). For a critical edition, see *A Vision: The Original 1925 Edition*, eds. Catherine E. Paul and Margaret Mills Harper, vol. 13 of *The Collected Works of W. B. Yeats*, ed. Richard J. Finneran and George Mills Harper (New York: Scribner, 1978).

45. Catherine E. Paul and Margaret Mills Harper, "Editors' Introduction," in *A Vision: The Original 1925 Edition*, p. xx.

46. Ibid., p. x.

47. Ibid., pp. x–xi.

48. Ibid., pp. xi.

49. W. B. Yeats, "A Packet for Ezra Pound," in *The Collected Works of W. B. Yeats*, vol. 14: *A Vision, The Revised 1937 Edition*, eds. Margaret Mills Harper and Catherine E. Paul (New York: Scribner, 2015), pp. 3–22.

50. Ibid., p. 7.

51. Ibid., p. 8.

52. Ibid., p. 12.

53. Ibid., p. 13.

54. Ibid., pp. 13–14.

55. Paul and Harper, "Editors' Introduction," in *A Vision, The Original 1925 Edition*, p. xxv.

56. See Margaret Mills Harper, "The Message is the Medium: Identity in the Automatic Script," *Yeats: An Annual of Critical and Textual Studies* 9 (1991), p. 37.

57. Yeats, "A Packet for Ezra Pound," p. 9.

58. Ibid.

59. Ibid., p. 10.

60. Ibid.

61. Ibid., p. 11.

62. Daniel Albright, "Yeats and Modernism," in Marjorie Howes and John Kelly, eds., *The Cambridge Companion to Yeats* (Cambridge: Cambridge University Press, 2007), p. 74.

63. Paul and Harper, "Editors' Introduction," in *A Vision, The Original 1925 Edition,* p. xi.

64. Breton, "Activité expérimentale. — Prospection systématique des 'états seconds'. — Pouvoirs de Robert Desnos," pp. 476–77.

65. Jack Spicer, *The House that Jack Built: The Collected Lectures of Jack Spicer*, ed. Peter Gizzi (Middletown: Wesleyan University Press, 1998), p. 4.

66. Ibid. Peter Gizzi points out that there is no evidence the train was running from San Benardino to Los Angeles: see ibid., p. 42.

67. Ibid., p. 5.

68. Ibid.

69. Ibid.

70. Ibid., p. 7.

71. Jack Spicer, *My Vocabulary Did This to Me*, eds. Peter Gizzi and Kevin Killian (Middletown: Wesleyan University Press, 2008), "Surrealism" (p. 273) and "A Textbook of Poetry" (pp. 299–313). On Spicer and surrealism, see Norman M. Finkelstein, "Jack Spicer's Ghosts and the Gnosis of History," *boundary 2* 9.2 (1981), pp. 81–100.

72. Jean Cocteau, *Orphée* (Paris: Édouard Dermit, 1950), pp. 21–22; English in Jean Cocteau, *Three Screenplays: L'Eternel Retour, Orphée, La Belle et la Bête*, trans. Carol Martin-Sperry (New York: Grossman, 1972), p. 112.

73. Cocteau, *Orphée*, p. 22; English in *Three Screenplays*, p. 112.

74. Cocteau, *Orphée*, p. 41; English in *Three Screenplays*, p. 132.

75. Cocteau, *Orphée*, p. 53; English in *Three Screenplays*, p. 144.

76. Cocteau, *Orphée*, pp. 7–8.

77. Spicer, *The House that Jack Built*, p. 8.

78. Ibid., p. 24.

79. Ibid., p. 9.

80. Ibid., p. 16. Spicer thus revises Cocteau's model, as Daniel Katz notes: see *The Poetry of Jack Spicer* (Edinburgh: Edinburgh University Press, 2013), p. 10.

81. Spicer, *The House that Jack Built*, p. 24

82. See Jacques Lacan, "Position de l'inconscient," in *Écrits* (Paris: Éditions du Seuil, 1966), p. 840. The essay represents a reworked version of a paper delivered in 1960. English in "Position of the Unconscious," *Ecrits*, trans. Bruce Fink in collaboration with Héloïse Fink and Russell Grigg (New York: W. W. Norton, 2002), p. 713.

83. On Spicer and Plato's *Ion*, see Laurie A. Finke and Martin B. Shichtman, "'Can't Get No Satisfaction': Jack Spicer's Medievalism," *Paideuma: Modern and Contemporary Poetics* 46 (2019), pp. 90–91.

84. See Plato, *Ion*, 533e–535a.

85. Dante, *Purgatorio* 24, lines 52–54.

86. Jack Spicer, "Sporting Life," in *My Vocabulary Did This to Me*, p. 373. On the poet as a radio, see also Scott Challener, "Addressing 'Alien Worlds': Publics and Persons in the Poetry of Jack Spicer," *Comparative Literature* 58.4 (2017), pp. 492–525.

CHAPTER THIRTEEN: THE INSIDE OF STUMBLING

1. Walter Benjamin, "Madame Ariane Zweiter Hof Links," in *Einbahnstraße*, in *Gesammelte Schriften*, 7 vols., eds. Rolf Tiedemann and Hermann Schweppenhäuser (Frankfurt am Main: Suhrkamp, 1972–1991), vol. 4, p. 141; English in "Madame Ariane: Second Courtyard on the Left," in *One-Way Street*, trans. Edmund Jephcott, in *Selected Writings, Volume 1, 1913–1926*, eds. Marcus Bullock and Michael W. Jennings (Cambridge, MA: The Belknap Press of Harvard University Press, 1996), p. 483.

2. Benjamin, "Madame Ariane Zweiter Hof Links," p. 141; English in "Madame Ariane: Second Courtyard on the Left," pp. 482–83.

3. Benjamin, "Madame Ariane Zweiter Hof Links," p. 142; English in "Madame Ariane: Second Courtyard on the Left," p. 483.

4. Ibid.

5. On the syntax of the phrase, see Fabio Guidetti, "Tensam non tenuit: Cicerone, Arnobio e il modo di condurre i carri sacri," *Studi Classici e Orientali* 55 (2009), pp. 236–37.

For the sources, see Frontin, *strat.* 1.12.1–2 (*Teneo te, terra mater!*); Suetonius, *Iul* 59 (*Teneo te, Africa!*); Cassius Dio 42.58.2–3 (*Ekhō se, Afrikē*); Nepotian. 1.6, *nov.*1 (*Teneo te, terra Africa!*).

6. Benjamin, "Madame Ariane Zweiter Hof Links," p. 142; English in "Madame Ariane: Second Courtyard on the Left," p. 483. Translation slightly modified.

7. Sigmund Freud, *Zur Psychopathologie des Alltagsleben: Über Vergessen, Versprechen, Vergreifen, Aberglaube und Irrtum* (Frankfurt am Main: Fischer, 2009), p. 61; English in *The Psychopathology of Everyday Life: On Forgetfulness, Slips of the Tongue, Inadvertent Actions, Superstitions and Mistakes*, trans. Anthea Bell (New York: Penguin Books, 2002), p. 1.

8. Freud, *Zur Psychopathologie des Alltagsleben*, p. 303; English in *The Psychopathology of Everyday Life*, p. 229.

9. Ibid.

10. Freud, *Zur Psychopathologie des Alltagsleben*, p. 120; English in *The Psychopathology of Everyday Life*, p. 58.

11. Freud, *Zur Psychopathologie des Alltagsleben*, p. 130; English in *The Psychopathology of Everyday Life*, pp. 67–68.

12. Freud, *Zur Psychopathologie des Alltagsleben*, p. 124; English in *The Psychopathology of Everyday Life*, p. 62.

13. Freud, *Zur Psychopathologie des Alltagsleben*, p. 129; English in *The Psychopathology of Everyday Life*, p. 66.

14. Freud, *Zur Psychopathologie des Alltagsleben*, pp. 162–63; English in *The Psychopathology of Everyday Life*, p. 96.

15. Freud, *Zur Psychopathologie des Alltagsleben*, p. 65; English in *The Psychopathology of Everyday Life*, p. 5.

16. Freud, *Zur Psychopathologie des Alltagsleben*, p. 66; English in *The Psychopathology of Everyday Life*, p. 6.

17. Freud, *Zur Psychopathologie des Alltagsleben*, p. 66; English in *The Psychopathology of Everyday Life*, p. 6

18. Freud, *Zur Psychopathologie des Alltagsleben*, p. 67; English in *The Psychopathology of Everyday Life*, p. 7.

19. Ibid.

20. Ibid.

21. Freud, *Zur Psychopathologie des Alltagsleben*, p. 68; English in *The Psychopathology of Everyday Life*, pp. 7–8.

22. Sigmund Freud, "Zum psychischen Mechanismus der Vergesslichkeit," *Monatsschrift*

für Psychiatrie und Neurologie 4 (1898), pp. 436-443. Freud, *Zur Psychopathologie des Alltagsleben*, p. 70; English in *The Psychopathology of Everyday Life*, p. 9. Translation slightly modified. As the reader will observe, the diagrams from 1898 and from 1901 differ slightly.

23. Among numerous commentaries of the faulty performance, see Michael Billig, "Freud's Different Versions of Forgetting 'Signorelli': Rhetoric and Repression," *International Journal of Pscyho-Analysis* 81.3 (2000), pp. 483–98; Anthony G. Wilden, "Freud, Signorelli, and Lacan: The Repression of the Signifier," *American Imago* 23.4 (1966), pp. 322–66; Johann Georg Reicheneder, "Breuer — Signorelli — Freud: Zur Initial-Fehlleistung der Psychoanalyse," *Jahrbuch der Psychoanalyse* 79 (2019), pp. 157–90; Michael Molnar, "Reading the Look," in Sander Gilman, Jutta Birmele, Jay Geller, and Valerie D. Greenberg, eds., *Reading Freud's Reading* (New York: New York University Press, 1994), pp. 77–90; Didier Anzieu, *Freud's Self-Analysis*, trans. Peter Graham (Madison: International Universities Press, 1986), pp. 359–62; Hubert Damisch, "Le maître, c'est lui," *Savoirs et Clinique* 1.12 (2010), pp. 13–37; Margaret E. Owens, "Forgetting Signorelli: Monstrous Visions of the Resurrection of the Dead," *American Imago* 61.1 (2004), pp. 7–33; R. Karpe and M. Karpe, "The Significance of Freud's Trip to Orvieto," *Israel Annals of Psychiatry and Related Disciplines* 17.1 (1979), pp. 3–20.

24. Sigmund Freud, *Briefe an Wilhelm Fließ, 1887–1904*, ed. Jeffrey Moussaieff Masson, transcription by Michael Schröter (Frankfurt: Fischer, 1986), pp. 35–358; English in *The Complete Letters of Sigmund Freud to Wilhem Fliess, 1887–1904*, ed. and trans. Jeffrey Moussaieff Masson (Cambridge, MA: Harvard University Press, 1985), pp. 326–27.

25. Roman Jakobson, "Linguistics and Poetics," in Jakobson, *Selected Writings*, 8 vols. (The Hague: Mouton, 1962–1988), vol. 3: *The Poetry of Grammar and Grammar of Poetry*, p. 27.

26. Sigmund Freud, *Die Traumdeutung / Über den Traum*, vols. 2–3 in *Gesammelte Werke*, ed. Anna Freud, 18 vols. (London: Imago, 1948–1968). See pp. 284–91 for *Verdichtung*; p. 183, among others, for *Verschiebung*.

27. See Jacques Lacan, *Écrits* (Paris: Éditions du Seuil, 1966), p. 511; English in *Ecrits*, trans. Bruce Fink in collaboration with Héloïse Fink and Russell Grigg (New York: W. W. Norton, 2002), p. 425.

28. Jacques Lacan, *Le séminaire*, vol. 5: *Les formations de l'inconscient*, ed. Jacques-Alain Miller (Paris: Seuil, 1998), pp. 90–91; English in *Formations of the Unconscious: The Seminar of Jacques Lacan, Book 5*, trans. Russell Grigg (Cambridge: Polity, 2017), p. 58. On the claim that "the unconscious is structured like a language," see Jean-Claude Milner, *Le périple structural: Figures et paradigme* (Paris: Seuil, 2002), pp. 144–45.

29. See Jacques Lacan, *Le séminaire*, vol. 3: *Les psychoses*, ed. Jacques-Alain Miller (Paris: Seuil, 1981), pp. 49–57; English in *The Seminar of Jacques Lacan, Book 3: The Psychoses*, trans. Russell Grigg (New York: W. W. Norton, 1993), pp. 29–43.

30. Rudolf Meringer and Karl Meyer, *Versprechen und Verlesen: Eine psychologisch-linguistische Studie* (Stuttgart: G. J. Göschen, 1895).

31. Freud, *Zur Psychopathologie des Alltagsleben*, p. 115; English in *The Psychopathology of Everyday Life*, pp. 53–54.

32. Rudolf Meringer, "Die täglichen Fehler im Sprechen, Lesen und Handeln," *Wörter und Sachen* 8 (1923), p. 141. On Meringer and Freud, see also Sebastiano Timpanaro, *La "fobia romana" e altri scritti su Freud e Meringer* (Pisa: ETS Editrice, 1992), esp. "Postscriptum a Meringer," pp. 142–76. As Timpanaro notes, following Meringer's biting reply, Freud amended his references to Meringer and Mayer in subsequent editions, diminishing the admiration that he had expressed for them.

33. Meringer, "Die täglichen Fehler im Sprechen, Lesen und Handeln," pp. 123–24.

34. Louis Havet, *Manuel de critique verbale appliquée aux textes latins* (Paris: Hachette, 1911), p. xi.

35. Sebastiano Timpanaro, *The Freudian Slip: Psychoanalysis and Textual Criticism*, trans. Kate Soper (London: New Left Books, 1976), p. 19.

36. Ibid., p. 20.

37. Ibid., p. 21.

38. Ibid., p. 64.

39. Ibid., p. 36.

40. Ibid., pp. 143–45.

41. Ibid., p 63. Freud would of course dissent.

42. Ibid., p. 71.

43. For an account of the equal number of letters in the three names that is far more sympathetic to Freud, see Damisch, "Le maître, c'est lui."

44. See Freud, *Zur Psychopathologie des Alltagsleben*, p. 122; English in *The Psychopathology of Everyday Life*, p. 59. Freud refers to Wilhelm Maximilian Wundt, *Völkerpsychologie: Eine Untersuchung der Entwicklungsgesetze von Sprache, Mythus und Sitte*, 2 vols. in 5 parts (Leipzig: W. Engelmann, 1900), vol. 1, part 1, pp. 370–401.

45. Adolf Grünbaum, *The Foundations of Psychoanalysis: A Philosophical Critique* (Berkeley: University of California Press, 1984), p. 74.

46. Sigmund Freud, *Vorlesungen zur Einführung in die Psychoanalyse*, vol. 11 of

Gesammelte Werke, p. 37; English in *Introductory Lectures on Psycho-Analysis*, in *The Standard Edition of the Complete Psychological Works of Sigmund Freud*, trans. James Strachey, with Anna Freud, assisted by Alex Strachey and Alan Tyson, 24 vols. (London: The Hogarth Press, 1953–1974), vol. 15, p. 44. Translation slightly modified.

47. Freud, *Vorlesungen zur Einführung in die Psychoanalyse*, p. 18; English in *Introductory Lectures on Psycho-Analysis*, p. 25.

48. Freud, *Vorlesungen zur Einführung in die Psychoanalyse*, p. 37; English in *Introductory Lectures on Psycho-Analysis*, p. 44.

49. Freud, *Vorlesungen zur Einführung in die Psychoanalyse*, pp. 52–53; English in *Introductory Lectures on Psycho-Analysis*, p. 58. Translation slightly modified.

50. Freud, *Vorlesungen zur Einführung in die Psychoanalyse*, p. 53; English in *Introductory Lectures on Psycho-Analysis*, p. 58.

51. Freud, *Zur Psychopathologie des Alltagsleben*, p. 321; English in *The Psychopathology of Everyday Life*, p. 244. Translation slightly modified.

52. Freud, *Zur Psychopathologie des Alltagsleben*, p. 323; English in *The Psychopathology of Everyday Life*, p. 245.

53. Freud, *Zur Psychopathologie des Alltagsleben*, p. 323; English in *The Psychopathology of Everyday Life*, p. 245.

54. Walter Scott, *The Life of Napoleon Bonaparte*, vol. 6 of *The Prose Works of Sir Walter Scott* (Paris: A. and W. Galignani, 1827), p. 528.

55. Général comte de Ségur, *Histoire de Napoléon et de la Grande-Armée pendant 1812*, 2 vols. (Paris: Baudoin Frères, 1824), vol. 1, pp. 142–43. I owe this reference to Jean-Claude Milner.

56. Walter Scott, *Vie de Napoléon Buonaparte, Empereur des Français*, 9 vols. (Paris: Gosselin, 1827), vol. 7, pp. 237–38.

CHAPTER FOURTEEN: TRUTH DETAILS

1. Marcel Proust, *Sodome et Gomorrhe*, part 2, chapter 1, in vol. 3 of *À la recherche du temps perdu*, ed. Jean-Yves Tadié, 4 vols. (Paris: Gallimard, 1988), pp. 127–28; English in *Sodom and Gomorrah*, in vol. 4 of *In Search of Lost Time*, trans. C. K. Scott Moncrieff, Terence Kilmartin, and Andreas Mayer, revised D. J. Enright, 6 vols. (London: Chatto & Windus, 1992), pp. 176–77.

2. Proust, *Sodome et Gomorrhe*, p. 129; English in *Sodom and Gomorrah*, p. 177.

3. Proust, *Sodome et Gomorrhe*, p. 129; English in *Sodom and Gomorrah*, p. 178. Translation slightly modified. On Proust and "telephony," see John Attridge, "'La vaste rumeur

d'autrefois': Noise, Memory, and Mediation in *À la recherche du temps perdu*," *Modernism/modernity* 26.3 (2019), pp. 617–37, esp. pp. 631–63.

4. On the novel as the itinerary of an "apprenticeship," see Gilles Deleuze, *Proust et le signes* (Paris: Presses universitaires de France, 1964). On Proust's "details," see Sophie Duval, "Le verre grossissant et l'art du tailleur d'images: Un point de détail autoréférentiel au revers du texte proustien," *Poétique* 150.2 (2007), pp. 149–68.

5. On "veridical" and "revelatory" discourse in Proust, see Gérard Genette, *Figures II* (Paris: Seuil, 1969), pp. 250–51.

6. On discursive "accidents" in the *Recherche*, see Genette, *Figures II*, pp. 225–32. For Proust's "ear training," particularly in its relations to sociolinguistics and linguistic anthropology, see Michael Lucey, *What Proust Heard: Novels and the Ethnography of Talk* (Chicago: University of Chicago Press, 2022).

7. Marcel Proust, *La prisonnière*, in vol. 3 of *À la recherche du temps perdu*, pp. 852–53; English in *The Captive*, in *The Captive & The Fugitive*, in vol. 5 of *In Search of Lost Time*, p. 400.

8. Proust, *La prisonnière*, p. 598; English in *The Captive*, p. 95.

9. Proust, *La prisonnière* pp. 601–602; English in *The Captive*, p. 99.

10. Proust, *La prisonnière*, pp. 603–604; English in *The Captive*, pp. 101–102.

11. Proust, *La prisonnière*, p. 659; English in *The Captive*, p. 167. Translation slightly modified. On Proust and anacoluthon, see Gustavo Pellón, "Given the Lie to Liars: A Note on Anacoluthon in *À la recherche du temps perdu*," *MLN* 95.5 (1980), pp. 1347–52.

12. Proust, *La prisonnière*, p. 596; English in *The Captive*, p. 93. On the passage, see Genette, *Figures II*, pp. 271–72, and Malcolm Bowie, *Freud, Proust, and Lacan: Theory as Fiction* (Cambridge: Cambridge University Press, 1997), pp. 51–52.

13. Proust, *Sodome et Gomorrhe*, pp. 482–83; English in *Sodom and Gomorrah*, p. 677.

14. Proust, *Le temps retrouvé*, in vol. 4 of *À la recherche du temps perdu*, p. 494; English in *Time Regained*, in vol. 6 of *In Search of Lost Time*, p. 278.

15. Proust, *Du côté de chez Swann*, part 2, in vol. 1 of *À la recherche du temps perdu*, p. 273; English in *Swann's Way, in* vol. 1 of *In Search of Lost Time*, p. 334.

16. Ibid. Translation slightly modified.

17. Ibid. Translation slightly modified.

18. Proust, *Du côté de chez Swann*, p. 273; English in *Swann's Way*, p. 335. Translation slightly modified.

19. Proust, *Du côté de chez Swann*, p. 273; English in *Swann's Way*, pp. 334–35. Translation slightly modified.

20. Proust, *Du côté de chez Swann*, p. 273; English in *Swann's Way*, pp. 334–35. Translation slightly modified.

21. Proust, *Du côté de chez Swann*, p. 274; English in *Swann's Way*, p. 335. Translation slightly modified.

22. Ibid. Translation modified.

23. Ibid. On the passage, see Lucey, *What Proust Heard*, pp. 30–31.

24. Proust, *Du côté de chez Swann*, p. 277; English in *Swann's Way*, p. 339. Translation modified.

25. Proust, *Du côté de chez Swann*, p. 278; English in *Swann's Way*, p. 340.

26. Proust, *Du côté de chez Swann*, pp. 354–55; English in *Swann's Way*, pp. 433–34.

27. Proust, *Du côté de chez Swann*, p. 354; English in *In Search of Lost Time*, p. 433.

28. Proust, *Du côté de chez Swann*, p. 355; English in *Swann's Way*, p. 434.

29. Proust, *Le côté de Guermantes*, part 1, in vol. 2 of *À la recherche du temps perdu*, p. 568; English in *The Guermantes Way*, in vol. 3 of *In Search of Lost Time*, p. 311. Translation slightly modified.

30. Proust, *Le temps retrouvé*, p. 479; English in *Time Regained*, p. 260.

31. Proust, *Albertine disparue*, part 1, in vol. 4 of *À la recherche du temps perdu*, pp. 88–89; English in *The Fugitive*, in *The Captive & The Fugitive*, in vol. 5 of *In Search of Lost Time*, p. 580.

32. Proust, *Le temps retrouvé*, p. 494; English in *Time Regained*, p. 280.

33. Proust, *La prisonnière*, pp. 632–33; English in *The Captive*, p. 136.

34. Proust, *La prisonnière*, p. 633; English, in *The Captive*, p. 137.

35. See Vincent Clavurier, "Psychopathologie de la vie quotidienne et savoir-faire (*hören*) de l'analyste," *Essaim* 11.1 (2003), p. 230.

36. Proust, *La prisonnière*, p. 903; English in *The Captive*, p. 459.

37. Proust, *La prisonnière*, p. 903; English in *The Captive*, p. 459. Translation slightly modified.

38. On Proust's account of the limits of "intelligence," see Zakir Paul, *Disarming Intelligence: Proust, Valéry, and Modern French Criticism* (Princeton: Princeton University Press, 2024), pp. 52–86.

39. Proust, *La prisonnière*, p. 7; English in *The Captive*, p. 482.

40. Ibid.

41. Proust, *Albertine disparue*, p. 220; English in *The Fugitive*, p. 736. Translation slightly modified.

42. Proust, *Albertine disparue*, p. 220; English in *The Fugitive*, pp. 736–37.

43. Proust, *Albertine disparue*, pp. 221–22; English in *The Fugitive*, pp. 736–37.

44. Proust, *Albertine disparue,* p. 221; English in *The Fugitive*, p. 737. Translation slightly modified.

45. Proust, *Albertine disparue*, p. 223; English in *The Fugitive*, p. 740.

46. Proust, *Albertine disparue*, p. 234; English in *The Fugitive*, p. 753.

47. Proust, *Albertine disparue*, pp. 234–35; English in *The Fugitive*, p. 753.

48. Sharon Willis, "'Gilbertine' apparue," *Romanic Review* 73.3 (1982), p. 342.

49. Akane Kawakami, "Proust and Handwriting," in Nathalie Aubert, ed., *Proust and the Visual* (Cardiff: University of Wales Press, 2012), p. 105. Cf. Mieke Bal, "Faithfully Submitted: The Logic of the Signature in Proust's *À la recherche*," in Sonja Neef, José van Dijck, and Eric Ketelaar, eds., *Sign Here! Handwriting in the Age of New Media* (Amsterdam: Amsterdam University Press, 2006), pp. 150–62.

50. Proust, *Albertine disparue*, p. 235; English in *The Fugitive*, pp. 753–54. On the passage and the Freudian slip, see Jean-Yves Tadié, *Le lac inconnu: Entre Freud et Proust* (Paris: Gallimard, 2012), p. 149.

51. Proust, *Le temps retrouvé*, p. 458; English in *Time Regained*, p. 233.

52. See Walter Benjamin, "Kleine Geschichte der Photographie," in *Gesammelte Schriften*, 7 vols., ed. Rolf Tiedemann and Hermann Schweppenhäuser (Frankfurt am Main: Suhrkamp, 1972–1991), vol. 2, part 1, pp. 368–85, esp. p. 378; English in "Little History of Photography," trans. Edmund Jephcott and Kingsley Shorter, in *Selected Writings, Volume 2: 1927–1934*, ed. Michael W. Jennings, Howard Eiland, and Gary Smith (Cambridge, MA: Belknap Press of Harvard University Press, 1999), pp. 507–30, esp. pp. 518–19; "Das Kunstwerk im Zeitalter seiner technischen Reproduzierbarkeit (Zweiter Fassung)," in *Gesammelte Schriften*, vol. 7, part 1, p. 355. English in "The Work of Art in the Age of its Technological Reproducibility, Second Version," trans. Edmund Jephcott and Harry Zohn, in *Selected Writings, Volume 3, 1935–1938*, ed. Howard Eiland and Michael W. Jennings (Cambridge, MA: Belknap Press of Harvard University Press, 2002), pp. 104–105.

53. Proust, *Le temps retrouvé*, p. 618; English in *Time Regained*, p. 442.

54. On the passage, see Roger Shattuck, *Proust's Binoculars: A Study of Memory, Time, and Recognition in 'À la recherche du temps perdu'* (Princeton: Princeton University Press, 1962), pp. 105–108; Deleuze, *Proust et les signes*, pp. 172–73; Duval, "Le verre grossissant et l'art du tailleur d'images," pp. 158–59.

55. See Proust, *Le temps retrouvé*, p. 457; English in *Time Regained*, p. 233. On Proust's

"impressions," see Christopher Prendergast, *Mirages and Mad Beliefs: Proust the Skeptic* (Princeton: Princeton University Press, 2013), pp. 110–18.

56. Proust, *Le temps retrouvé*, p. 610; English in *Time Regained*, p. 432.

CHAPTER FIFTEEN: GROPINGS OF A SPIRITUAL EAR

1. Roman Jakobson, "Linguistics and Poetics," in *Selected Writings*, 8 vols. (The Hague: Mouton, 1962–1988), vol. 3: *Poetry of Grammar and Grammar of Poetry*, pp. 21–22.

2. Roman Jakobson, "Two Aspects of Language and Two Types of Aphasic Disturbances," in *Selected Writings*, vol. 2: *Word and Language*, p. 245. Here Jakobson relies on Freud's *On Aphasia*.

3. Ibid., p. 251.

4. Ibid.

5. James Joyce, *Ulysses* (New York: Penguin Books, 1992), p. 50.

6. James Joyce, *Stephen Hero* (London: Jonathan Cape, 1956), pp. 210–11.

7. James Joyce, "Epiphanies," in *Poems and Shorter Writings, including* Epiphanies, Giacomo Joyce, *and 'A Portrait of the Artist'*, ed. Richard Ellmann, A. Walton Litz, and John Whittier-Ferguson (London: Faber and Faber, 1991), pp. 161–200.

8. Stanislaus Joyce, *My Brother's Keeper*, ed. Richard Ellmann, preface by T. S. Eliot (London: Faber and Faber, 1958), pp. 124–25.

9. Ibid., p. 125.

10. For the dating of the "Epiphanies," see Joyce, *Poems and Shorter Writings*, p. 157. For different accounts, see Richard Ellmann, *James Joyce* (Oxford: Oxford University Press, 1959), p. 87; Robert Scholes, *The Workshop of Daedalus: James Joyce and the Raw Materials* (Evanston: Northwestern University Press, 1965), p. 5. A. Walton Litz argues for 1901–1902 to 1904: see *The Art of James Joyce: Method and Design in Ulysses and Finnegans Wake* (London: Oxford University Press, 1961), p. 157.

11. Joyce, *Poems and Shorter Writings*, p. 157. Florence L. Walzl put the number at 150: see "The Liturgy of the Epiphany Season and the Epiphanies of Joyce," *PMLA* 80.4 (1965), p. 437.

12. David Hayman, "The Purpose and Permanence of the Joycean Epiphany," *James Joyce Quarterly* (1998), pp. 633–55. The literature of the Joycean epiphany is extensive. For a compellingly comprehensive recent account, see Sangam MacDuff, *Panepiphanal World: James Joyce's Epiphanies* (Gainesville: University Press of Florida, 2020).

13. For a helpful account of the Christian epiphany and Joyce, see Macduff's "brief history of epiphany" in *Panepiphanal World*, pp. 23–50.

14. Introduction to "Epiphanies," in Joyce, *Poems and Shorter Writings*, p. 158.

15. Ibid., p. 161.

16. Ibid.

17. James Joyce, *A Portrait of the Artist as a Young* Man, ed. Seamus Deane (New York: Penguin Books, 1993), p. 4.

18. Hugh Kenner, "The 'Portrait' in Perspective," *Kenyon Review* 10.3 (1948), p. 365. Cf. Hayman, "The Purpose and Permanence of the Joycean Epiphany," pp. 642–43.

19. Joyce, *Poems and Shorter Writings*, p. 164.

20. Ibid., p. 198.

21. Joyce, *Ulysses*, pp. 451–52; on the scene, see MacDuff, *Panepiphanal World*, pp. 155–57.

22. Joyce, *Stephen Hero*, p. 189.

23. Joyce, *A Portrait of the Artist as a Young Man*, p. 196. On the reworking on the epiphany in *A Portrait of the Artist as a Young Man*, see Jean-Michel Rabaté, *James Joyce* (Paris: Hachette, 1993), pp. 11–17.

24. Joyce, *A Portrait of the Artist as a Young Man*, p. 179.

25. Joyce, *Stephen Hero*, p. 213.

26. Ibid., p. 211.

27. See Walzl, "The Liturgy of the Epiphany Season and the Epiphanies of Joyce." MacDuff points out that the evocation of epiphanies in relation to *Dubliners* "has proved controversial," since none of the forty "sketches" transcribed in Joyce's surviving epiphanies reappears in *Dubliners*. *Panepiphanal Joyce*, p. 76.

28. Harry Levin, *James Joyce: A Critical Introduction* (London: Faber and Faber, 1947), p. 29.

29. Morris Beja, *Epiphany in the Modern Novel* (London: Owen, 1971).

30. Robert Langbaum, "The Epiphanic Mode in Wordsworth and Modern Literature," *New Literary History* 14.2 (1983), p. 336.

31. Virginia Woolf, *A Room of One's Own* (London: Grafton, 1977), p. 118. See Shiv K. Kumar, "Joyce's Epiphany and Bergson's 'L'Intuition philosophique,'" *Modern Language Quarterly* 20.1 (1959), p. 29.

32. Joyce, *Ulysses*, p. 42.

33. I owe to Jean-Claude Milner the identification of the scene as that of an inverted *tolle-lege*.

CHAPTER SIXTEEN: THE CHAIN BREAKS

1. For an account of the history of such experiences, see Simon McCarthy-Jones,

Hearing Voices: The Histories, Causes and Meanings of Auditory Verbal Hallucinations (Cambridge: Cambridge University Press, 2012), pp. 9–96.

2. JoAnn Scurlock and Burton R. Anderson, *Diagnoses in Assyrian and Babylonian Medicine: Ancient Sources, Translations, and Modern Medical Analyses* (Champlain: University of Illinois Press, 2005), p. 380.

3. Ibid., p. 367.

4. Athanasius, *The Coptic Life of Anthony*, trans. Tim Vivian (San Francisco: International Scholars Publications, 1994), p. 203.

5. See McCarthy-Jones, *Hearing Voices*, pp. 26–27; see also Corinne Saunders, "Voices and Visions: Mind, Body and Affect in Medieval Writing," in Anne Whitehead and Angela Woods, eds., with Sarah Atkinson, Jane Macnaughton and Jennifer Richards, *The Edinburgh Companion to the Critical Medical Humanities* (Edinburgh: Edinburgh University Press, 2016), pp. 411–27.

6. On the 1817 formulation and its subsequent rewriting see, Tony James, *Dream, Creativity and Madness in Nineteenth-Century France* (Oxford: Clarendon Press of Oxford University Press, 1995), p. 70 n.9.

7. On the history of the term, see *Trésor de la langue française: Dictionnaire de la langue du XIXe et du XXe siècle (1789–1960)*, ed. Paul Imbs, 16 vols. (Paris: Éditions du centre national de la recherche scientifique, 1971–1994), s.v. "Hallucination.". On the Latin cognates, see James, *Dream, Creativity and Madness in Nineteenth-Century France*, pp. 69–73.

8. Jean-Étienne Dominique Esquirol, *Des illusions chez les aliénés: Question médico-légale sur l'isolement des aliénés* (Paris: Crochard, 1832), p. 2.

9. James Berrios, *The History of Mental Symptoms: Descriptive Psychopathology since the Nineteenth Century* (Cambridge: Cambridge University Press, 1996), p. 37.

10. Jules Gabriel François Baillarger, *Des hallucinations, des causes qui les produisent, et des maladies qui les caractérisent*, *Memoires de Academie Royale de Médecine* 12 (Paris: Baillière, 1846), pp. 363–67. Quoted in Berrios, p. 39.

11. On this distinction and the difficulties that it raises, see P. Lefebvre, "De l'aphémie à l'aphasie: Les tribulations d'une dénomination," *L'Information Psychiatrique* 64.7 (1988), pp. 947–54.

12. Jean-Pierre Falret, *Des maladies mentales et des asiles d'aliénés: Leçons cliniques et considérations générales* (Paris: J. B. Baillière et fils, 1864), p. 18; for his treatment of hallucinations, see chapters 4 and 5 of that book.

13. For a modern formulation, see Henri Ey, *Traité des hallucinations*, 2 vols. (Paris:

Masson, 1973), vol. 1, p. 50. For similar recent attempts, see Stijn Vanheule, *The Subject of Psychosis: A Lacanian Perspective* (London: Palgrave Macmillan, 2011), pp. 81–82. For Lacan's terms, see *Écrits* (Paris: Éditions du Seuil, 1966), pp. 532–43; English in *Ecrits*, trans. Bruce Fink in collaboration with Héloïse Fink and Russell Grigg (New York: W. W. Norton, 2002), pp. 446–54.

14. Jules Séglas, *Des troubles du langage chez les aliénes* (Paris: J. Rueff, 1892)

15. For summaries, see Pierre Janet, "Étude sur un cas d'abouie et d'idées fixes," *Revue philosophique de la France et de l'étranger* 31 (1891), pp. 274–75, and Lorraine K. Obler and Martin L. Albert, "Jules Séglas on Language in Dementia," *Brain and Language* 24 (1985), p. 317.

16. Jules Séglas, "L'hallucination dans ses rapports avec la fonction du langage: Les hallucinations psycho-motrices," *Le Progrès Médical*, August 18, 1888, p. 137. Séglas's reference is to Baillarger's *Des hallucinations*, p. 406.

17. Séglas, "L'hallucination dans ses rapports avec la fonction du langage," p. 137. See the corresponding chapter in Séglas, *Des troubles du langage chez les aliénes*, pp. 117–21.

18. Janet, "Étude sur un cas d'aboulie et d'idées fixes," p. 275.

19. Gilbert Ballet, *Le langage intérieur et les diverses formes de l'aphasie*, 2nd ed. (Paris: Félix Alcan, 1888), p. 64.

20. Pierre Janet, *L'automatisme psychologique: Essai de psychologie expérimentale sur les formes inférieures de l'activité humaine* (Paris: Alcan, 1894), p. 432.

21. Janet, "Étude sur un cas d'abouie et d'idées fixes," p. 275.

22. On the historical and biographical conditions of Lacan's encounter with surrealism, see David Macey, *Lacan in Contexts* (London: Verso, 1988), pp. 47–74, and Élisabeth Roudinesco, *Jacques Lacan*, trans. Barbara Bay (New York: Columbia University Press, 1997), pp. 31–34. For Lacan's publications in *Minotaure*, see Jacques Lacan, *Premiers écrits*, ed. Jacques-Alain Miller (Paris: Seuil, 2023), pp. 85–106.

23. J. Lévy-Valensi, Pierre Migault, and Jacques Lacan, "Écrits 'inspirés': Schizographie," *Année médico-psychologiques* 13.89 (1931), pp. 508–22, now in *Premiers écrits*, pp. 61–84.

24. Jacques Lacan, *De la psychose paranoïaque dans ses rapports à la personnalité* (Paris: Seuil, 1932). For an account of the dissertation in the development of Lacan's theory of psychosis, see Vanheule, *The Subject of Psychosis*, pp. 9–32.

25. Jacques Lacan, *Le séminaire*, in vol. 3: *Les psychoses*, ed. Jacques-Alain Miller (Paris: Seuil, 1981); English in *The Seminar of Jacques Lacan, Book 3: The Psychoses*, trans. Russell Grigg (New York: W. W. Norton, 1993) The English translation retains the article (*The*

Psychoses). Perhaps an indefinite English generic plural (simply *Psychoses*) would better render the French.

26. Jacques Lacan, "D'une question préliminaire à tout traîtement possible de la psychose," in *Écrits*, pp. 531–84; English in "On a Question Prior to Any Possible Treatment of Psychosis," *Ecrits*, pp. 445–88. The essay first appeared in *La Psychanalyse* 4 (1959), pp. 1–50.

27. Lacan, *Les psychoses*, p. 12; English in *The Psychoses*, p. 4.

28. Lacan, *Les psychoses*, p. 28; English in *The Psychoses*, p. 23. Translation slightly modified.

29. Lacan, *Les psychoses*, p. 42–43; English in *The Psychoses*, pp. 23–24. Translation slightly modified.

30. Lacan, *Les psychoses*, p. 43; English in *The Psychoses*, p. 24. Translation slightly modified.

31. Lacan, *Les psychoses*, p. 80; English in *The Psychoses*, p. 47.

32. Lacan, *Les psychoses*, p. 81; English in *The Psychoses*, p. 48.

33. Ibid.

34. Lacan, *Les psychoses*, p. 82; English in *The Psychoses*, p. 48. Translation slightly modified.

35. Lacan, *Les psychoses*, p. 83; English in *The Psychoses*, p. 49.

36. Lacan, *Les psychoses*, p. 84; English in *The Psychoses*, p. 49.

37. Lacan, *Les psychoses*, p. 84; English in *The Psychoses*, p. 50.

38. Lacan, "D'une question préliminaire à tout traîtement possible de la psychose," p. 534; English in "On a Question Prior to Any Possible Treatment of Psychosis," p. 447.

39. Lacan, *Les psychoses*, pp. 84–85; English in *The Psychoses*, p. 50. Translation slightly modified.

40. Lacan, *Les psychoses*, p. 86–87; English in *The Psychoses*, pp. 50–51.

41. Lacan, *Les psychoses*, p. 88; English in *The Psychoses*, p. 52.

42. On the sentence as a slip, see Frédéric Pellion, "Six notes à propos de l'hallucination verbale selon Jacques Lacan: Un cas du dialogue psychanalyse/psychiatrie," *Cliniques méditerranéennes* 71.1 (2005), p. 290.

43. Lacan, *Les psychoses*, p. 88; English in *The Psychoses*, p. 52.

44. For "delusional interlocution," see Lacan, *Les psychoses*, p. 205; English in *The Psychoses*, p. 129.

45. Lacan, *Les psychoses*, p. 140; English in *The Psychoses*, p. 86.

46. Lacan, *Les psychoses*, p. 207–27; English in *The Psychoses*, pp. 130–62. Lacan, "D'une question préliminaire à tout traîtement possible de la psychose," p. 536; English in "On a Question Prior to Any Possible Treatment of Psychosis," p. 449.

47. Lacan, *Les psychoses*, p. 196; English in *The Psychoses*, p. 123.

48. Lacan, *Les psychoses*, p. 87; English in *The Psychoses*, p. 51.

49. Lacan, "D'une question préliminaire à tout traîtement possible de la psychose," p. 534; English in "On a Question Prior to Any Possible Treatment of Psychosis," p. 448.

50. See Jacques-Alain Miller, "Forclusion généralisée," *La Cause du désir* 99.2 (2018), pp. 131–35; Damien Guyonnet, "Formalisation lacanienne de l'hallucination verbale 'Truie,'" *L'École de la cause freudienne* 71.1 (2009), pp. 111–18.

51. Lacan, *Les psychoses*, p. 87; English in *The Psychoses*, p. 51.

52. Guyonnet, "Formalisation lacanienne de l'hallucination verbale 'Truie,'" p. 118.

53. On Lacan, the Joycean epiphany, and the theory of psychosis, see Catherine Millot "Épiphanies," in Jacques Aubert, ed. *Joyce avec Lacan* (Paris: Navarin, 1987), pp. 87–95; Jean-Louis Gault, "Two Statuses of the Symptom: 'Let Us Turn to Finn Again,'" in Véronique Voruz and Bogdan Wolf, eds., *The Later Lacan: An Introduction* (Albany: State University of New York Press, 2007), pp. 73–82; Colette Soler, *Lacan, lecteur de Joyce*, 2nd ed. (Paris: Presses universitaires de France, 2019), esp. pp. 148–55.

54. Livy, *Ab urbe condita* 5.32.6–7; English in *Livy in Fourteen Volumes*, vol. 3: *Books V, VI and VII*, trans. B. O. Foster (Cambridge, MA: Harvard University Press, 1924), p. 113. Translation slightly modified.

55. Cicero, *De divinatione* 1.101; Latin in *Della divinazione*, ed. and trans. Sebastiano Timpanaro (Milan: Garzanti, 1988), p. 80; English in *On Divination: Book 1*, trans. David Wardle (Oxford: Clarendon Press of Oxford University Press, 2006), p. 78.

56. Livy, *Ab urbe condita* 5.32.7–8; English in *Livy in Fourteen Volumes*, vol. 3, p. 113. Translation modified.

57. Livy, *Ab urbe condita*, 5.50.5–6; English in *Livy in Fourteen Volumes*, vol. 3, p. 169.

58. Cicero, *De divinatione* 2.69; Latin in Timpanaro, *Della divinazione*, p. 164; English in *De senectute, De amicitia, De divinatione*, trans. W. A. Falconer (Cambridge, MA: Harvard University Press, 1923), p. 449.

59. Émile Benveniste, *Le vocabulaire des institutions indo-européennes*, 2 vols. (Paris: Seuil, 1969), vol. 2: *Pouvoir, droit, religion*, p. 262.

60. Varro's explanation: "Aius deus appellatus araque ei statuta quod eo in loco diuinitus uox edita est." Aulus Gellius, *Noctae Atticae* 16.17.1, quoted in ibid.

61. Andrew Tooke, *The Pantheon, Representing the Fabulous Histories of the Heathen Gods and Most Illustrious Heroes in a Plain and Familiar Method, by Way of Dialogue* (New York: Evert Duyckinck, 1810), p. 261. The original has the ancient name.

62. See, for example, Andrew Tooke, *The Pantheon, Representing the Fabulous History of the Heathen Gods and Most Illustrious Heroes* (London: J. Johnson et al., 1803), p. 261.

63. Alexandre de Théis, *Travels of Polycletes in Letters from Rome* (London: J. Souter, 1826), p. 77.

CHAPTER SEVENTEEN: SOMETHING DEMONIC

1. Amos 5:2.

2. Babylonian Talmud, Tractate Berakhot 4b, in *Hebrew-English Edition of the Babylonian Talmud*, trans. Maurice Simon, ed. I. Epstein, 18 vols. (London: Soncino Press, 1990), vol. 1: Translation modified. On the passage, see James Kugel, "Two Introductions to Midrash," *Prooftexts* 3. 2 (1983), pp. 131–34.

3. Augustine, *On Christian Doctrine*, book 3, chapter 2, in *On Christian Doctrine*, ed. and trans. R. P. H. Green (Oxford: Clarendon Press of Oxford University Press, 1995), pp. 134–35.

4. Raymond de Saussure, "Remarques sur la technique de la psychanalyse freudienne," *L'Évolution psychiatrique* (1925), p. 51.

5. Theodor Reik, "Die psychologische Bedeutung des Scweigens," in *Wie Man Psychologe Wird* (Vienna: Internationaler Psychoanalytischer Verlag, 1927), pp. 101–26; English in "The Psychological Meaning of Silence," *Psychoanalytic Review* 55.2 (1968), pp. 172–86.

6. Jacques Lacan, "Fonction et champ de la parole et du langage en psychanalyse," in *Écrits* (Paris: Éditions du Seuil, 1966), p. 252; English in "The Function and Field of Speech in Psychoanalysis," *Ecrits*, trans. Bruce Fink in collaboration with Héloïse Fink and Russell Grigg (New York: W. W. Norton, 2002), p. 209.

7. On Lacan's uses of the term, see Isabelle Alfandary, "The Function and Field of Scansion in Jacques Lacan's Poetics of Speech," *Paragraph* 40.3 (2017), pp. 386–82.

8. Lacan, "Fonction et champ de la parole et du langage en psychanalyse," p. 388; English in "Function and Field of Speech in Psychoanalysis," p. 324.

9. Martin Heidegger, *Sein und Zeit*, in vol. 2 of *Gesamtausgabe*, 101 vols. (Frankfurt am Main: Vittorio Klostermann, 1977), section 9, p. 42; English in *Being and Time: A Translation of Sein und Zeit*, trans. Joan Stambaugh (Albany: State University of New York Press, 1996), p. 39. Translation slightly modified. Here and in the following notes, the German page numbers refer to the first 1927 edition, which are included in the margins of the 1977 *Gesamtausgabe* volume.

10. Heidegger, *Sein und Zeit*, section 27, p. 126; English in Stambaugh, *Being and Time*, pp. 118–19.

11. Heidegger, *Sein und Zeit*, section 27, pp. 126–27; English in Stambaugh, *Being and Time*, p. 119. Translation slightly modified. Given Heidegger's theory of "authenticity" (*Eigentlichkeit*) in this work, it is striking that, in this passage, the "dictatorship" by "the they" is qualified as "authentic" *(eigentlich)*.

12. Heidegger, *Sein und Zeit*, section 55, p. 271; English in Stambaugh, *Being and Time*, p. 250.

13. For the first appearance of the phrase "voice of conscience" in *Being and Time*, see section 54, p. 268; English in Stambaugh, *Being and Time*, p. 248. For "listening," see section 56, p. 271; English in Stambaugh, *Being and Time*, p. 250. In their translation, Macquarrie and Robinson render *Hinhören* as "listening-away": see *Being and Time*, trans. John Macquarrie and Edward Robinson (New York: Harper & Row, 1962), p. 316.

14. Heidegger, *Sein und Zeit*, section 56, p. 273; English in Stambaugh, *Being and Time*, p. 252.

15. Ibid.

16. Heidegger, *Sein und Zeit*, section 59, p. 289; English in Stambaugh, *Being and Time*, p. 266.

17. Heidegger, *Sein und Zeit*, section 59, pp. 289–91; English in Stambaugh, *Being and Time*, pp. 266–68.

18. The annotation is to Heidegger, *Sein und Zeit*, p. 271 in the *Gesamtausgabe* edition, p. 361 n. a; English in Stambaugh, *Being and Time*, p. 251.

19. Heidegger, *Sein und Zeit*, section 55, p. 271; English in Stambaugh, *Being and Time*, p. 251.

20. Heidegger, *Sein und Zeit*, section 55, p. 273; English in Stambaugh, *Being and Time*, p. 252.

21. Heidegger, *Sein und Zeit*, section 57, p. 275; English in Stambaugh, *Being and Time*, p. 254.

22. For the definition of uncanniness, see Heidegger, *Sein und Zeit*, section 40, p. 188; English in Stambaugh, *Being and Time*, p. 176. For the "uncanniness" of the call of conscience, see *Sein und Zeit*, section 57, pp. 276–78; English in Stambaugh, *Being and Time*, pp. 254–56.

23. Heidegger, *Sein und Zeit*, section 57, p. 277; English in Stambaugh, *Being and Time*, pp. 255–56.

24. Heidegger, *Sein und Zeit*, section 59, p. 294; English in Stambaugh, *Being and Time*, p. 271.

25. Heidegger, *Sein und Zeit*, section 55, p. 272; English in Stambaugh, *Being and Time*, p. 262..

26. See the account of "warning conscience" (*mahnendes Gewissen*) in Hendrik Gerhardus Stoker, *Das Gewissen: Erscheinungsformen und Theorie* (Bonn: F. Cohen, 1925), pp. 206–208; an English edition can be found in Stoker, *Conscience: Phenomena and Theories*, trans. Philip E. Blosser (Notre Dame: University of Notre Dame Press, 2018), pp. 225–27.

27. Stoker, *Das Gewissen*, p. 206; Stoker, *Conscience*, p. 225. Translation slightly modified.

28. Plato, *Apology*, 31c–d, trans. John Ferguson, in John Ferguson, ed., *Socrates: A Source Book* (London: Macmillan for the Open Press, 1970), p. 61. Translation slightly modified.

29. Plato, *Phaedrus*, 242b–c; English in *Phaedrus*, trans. Alexander Nehamas and Paul Woodruff (Indianapolis: Hackett, 1995), p. 24. Translation slightly modified.

30. Plato, *Euthydemus* 272e; *Republic* 6.496c.

31. Plato, *Euthyphro* 272e; *Theatetus* 151a; *Alcibiades I*, 603s.

32. *Theages* 128d. On the *daimonion* of the *Theages*, see Bruno Centrone, "Il *daimonion* di Socrate nello pseudoplatonico *Teage*," in Gabriele Giannantoni and Michel Narcy, eds., *Lezioni socratiche* (Naples: Bibliopolis, 1997), pp. 331–48.

33. Plato, *Alcibades Major* 103a.

34. Cicero, *de Divinatione* 1.122: Latin in *Della divinazione*, ed. and trans. Sebastiano Timpanaro (Milan: Garzanti, 1988), p. 96; English in Wardle, *On Divination*, p. 85.

35. Mark Joyal, "Tradition and Innovation in the Transformation of Socrates' Divine Sign," in Lewis Ayres, ed., *The Passionate Intellect: Essays on the Transformation of Classical Tradition Presented to Professor I. G. Kidd* (London: Routledge, 1995), p. 55. On demonology both in Plato and the Neoplatonists, see Andrei Timotin, *La démonologie platonicienne: Histoire de la notion de* daimōn *de Platon aux derniers néoplatoniciens* (Leiden: Brill, 2012).

36. For a summary and analysis, see Claudio Moreschini, "Le démon de Socrate et son langage dans la philosophie médioplatonicienne," in Luciana Gabriela Soares Santoprete and Philippe Hoffmann, eds., *Langage des dieux, langages des demons, langages des hommes dans l'Antiquité* (Turnhout: Brepols, 2017), pp. 126–29.

37. Calcidius, Commentary on *Timaeus* 255, in *Commentaire au Timée de Platon*, ed. Béatrice Bakhouche, with Luc Brisson, 2 vols. (Paris: Vrin, 2011), vol. 1, p. 484. On

Calcidius's demonology, see J. Den Boeft, *Calcidius on Demons (Commentarius ch. 127–136)* (Leiden: Brill, 1977); Moreschini, "Le demon de Socrate et son langage dans la philosophie médioplatonicienne," pp. 131–32, and Timotin, *Démonologie platonicienne*, pp. 132–41.

38. The most recent edition of the *scholiae* is that by Carlo M. Lucarini and Claudio Moreschini, *In Platonis Phaedrum scholia* (Berlin: De Gruyter, 2012). On Hermeias's account of the Socratic "demon," see Moreschini, "Le démon de Socrate et son langage dans la philosophie médioplatonicienne," pp. 132–35.

39. Michel de Montaigne, *Les essais*, ed. Jean Balsamo, Michel Magnien, and Catherine Magnien-Simonin (Paris: Gallimard, 2007), p. 66; English in *The Complete Essays of Montaigne*, trans. Donald M. Frame (Stanford: Stanford University Press, 1943), p. 29. Translation modified.

40. Montaigne, *Les essais*, p. 1166; English in *Complete Essays of Montaigne*, p. 856. Translation modified.

41. Friedrich Nietzsche, *Die Geburt der Tragödie*, in *Sämtliche Werke*, ed. Giorgio Colli and Mazzino Montinari, 15 vols. (Berlin: De Gruyter, 1967–1977), vol. 1, p. 90; English in *The Birth of Tragedy*, ed. Rayond Geuss and Ronald Speirs, trans. Ronald Speirs (Cambridge: Cambridge University Press, 1999), section 13, p. 66.

42. Nietzsche, *Menschliches, allzumenschliches*, section 126, in *Sämtliche Werke*, vol. 2, p. 122. English in *Human, All Too Human (I)*, trans. Gary Handwerk (Stanford: Stanford University Press, 1995), pp. 97–98.

43. Nietzsche, "Das Problem des Socrates," section 4, *Götzen-Dämmerung*, in *Sämtliche Werke*, vol. 6, p. 69. English in *The Anti-Christ, Ecce Homo, The Twilight of the Idols, and Other Writings*, ed. Aaron Ridkey and Judith Norman, trans, Judith Norman (Cambridge: Cambridge University Press, 2005), p. 163.

44. Louis Francisque Lélut, *Du démon de Socrate: Spécimen d'une application de la science psychologique à celle de l'histoire*, 2nd ed. (1836; Paris: Libraire J.-B. Bailliere et Fils, 1856).

45. Ibid., pp. 6–7.

46. Ibid., p. 8.

47. Ibid., pp. 215–16. For Alcibiades's account of Socrates's immobility at Potidea, see *Symposium* 220d.

48. Lélut, *Du démon de Socrate*, pp. 217–18.

49. Désiré-Magloire Bournveille, "Socrate était-il fou?," *Journal de Médicine mentale* 4 (1864), p. 209.

50. Ibid., p. 212.

51. Jacques Lacan, *Le séminaire*, in vol. 12: *Problèmes cruciaux pour la psychanalyse* (1964–1965), session of January 20, 1965 (unpublished), quoted in Nicolas Brémaud, "Folie de Socrate," *L'Information psychiatrique* 88.5 (2012), p. 386.

52. On Lacan and Lélut, see Brémaud, "Folie de Socrate"; cf. Juan-Pablo Lucchelli, *Métaphores de l'amour: Étude lacanienne sur le Banquet de Platon* (Rennes: Presses universitaires de Rennes, 2012), pp. 137–38.

53. Jacques Lacan, *Le séminaire*, in vol. 8: *Le transfert*, ed. Jacques-Alain Miller (Paris: Éditions du Seuil, 1991), session of December 21, 1960, pp. 104–105; English in *Transference*, trans. Bruce Fink (Cambridge: Polity, 2015), p. 82.

54. Plutarch, *De genio Socratis* 580c. For the text and translation, see *On the Daimonion of Socrates: Human Liberation, Divine Guidance and Philosophy*, ed. Heinz-Günther Nesselrath (Tübingen: Mohr Siebeck, 2010), pp. 32–33. The text and translation are by D. A. Russell.

55. Plutarch, *De genio Socratis* 580f–581a, in *On the Daimonion of Socrates*, pp. 32–33. Translation slightly modified.

56. On Galixidorus's argument and the reception it has received among modern scholars, see Daniel Babut, "La part de rationalisme dans la religion de Plutarque: L'exemple du *De genio Socratis*," *Illinois Classical Studies* 13.2 (1988), pp. 395–403.

57. Plutarch, *De genio Socratis* 581f–582a, in *On the Daimonion of Socrates*, pp. 36–37. Translation slightly modified.

58. Plutarch, *De genio Socratis* 582a–b, in *On the Daimonion of Socrates*, pp. 36–37.

Bibliography

Abercrombie, David. "What is a 'Letter'?" *Lingua* 2 (1949), pp. 54–63.

Aeschylus. *Aeschyli tragoediae quae supersunt*. Ed. Christian Gottfried Schütz. 3 vols. London: G. and W. B. Whittaker, 1823.

——. *Aeschylus*. Trans. Herbert Weir Smyth. 2 vols. Cambridge, MA: Harvard University Press, 1952.

——. *Aeschylus II: The Oresteia*. Ed, and trans. David Grene, Richmond Lattimore, Mark Griffith, and Glenn W. Most. 2 vols. 3rd. ed. Chicago: University of Chicago Press, 2013.

——. *Agamemnon, Edited with a Commentary*. Ed. Eduard Fraenkel. 3 vols. Oxford: Clarendon Press of Oxford University Press, 1950.

——. *Choephori*. Ed. A. F. Garvie. Oxford: Oxford University Press, 1986.

——. *Echyle: Tragédies*. Ed. and trans. Paul Mazon. 2 vols. 2nd ed. Paris: Les Belles Lettres, 1935.

——. *Prometheus Bound*. In *The Complete Greek Tragedies: Aeschylus*. Ed. David Grene and Richmond Lattimore. 3rd ed. 2 vols. Chicago: University of Chicago Press, 2013, vol. 1.

——. *Septem Quae Supersunt*. Ed. D. L. Page. Oxford: Oxford University Press, 1972.

Albright, Daniel. "Yeats and Modernism." In Marjorie Howes and John Kelly, eds., *The Cambridge Companion to Yeats*. Cambridge: Cambridge University Press, 2007, pp. 59–76.

Alemán, Mateo. *Guzmán de Alfarache*. Ed. Benito Brancaforte. 2 vols. Madrid: Ediciones Cátedra, 1979.

———. *The Rogue; or the Life of Guzman de Alfarache*. 2 vols. Trans. John Mabbe. London: Edward Blount, 1622.

Alfandary, Isabelle. "The Function and Field of Scansion in Jacques Lacan's Poetics of Speech." *Paragraph* 40.3 (2017), pp. 386–82.

Alfonso X. *Las Siete Partidas*. Ed. Robert I. Burns. Trans. Samuel Parsons Scott. 5 vols. Volume 5, *Underworlds: The Dead, the Criminal, and the Marginalized*. Philadelphia: University of Pennsylvania Press, 2001.

Amazawa, Tajiro. "La devineuse du nom de Perceval." In J. Claude Faucon, Alain Labbé, and Danielle Quéruel, eds., *Miscellanea Mediaevalia: Mélanges offerts à Philippe Ménard*. 2 vols. Paris: Champion, 1998, vol. 1, pp. 33–36.

Amory, Anne. "The Reunion of Odysseus and Penelope." In Charles H. Taylor, Jr, ed., *Essays on the Odyssey: Selected Modern Criticism*. Bloomington: Indiana University Press, 1963, pp. 100–121.

Aníbal, C. E. "Another Note on the Voces del Cielo." *Romanic Review* 18 (1927), pp. 246–52.

———. "*Voces del cielo*—A Note on Mira de Amescua." *Romanic Review* 16 (1925), pp. 57–70.

Anzieu, Didier. *Freud's Self-Analysis*. Trans. Peter Graham Madison: International Universities Press, 1986.

Aristotle, *Nicomachean Ethics*. In *The Complete Works of Aristotle: The Revised Oxford Translation*. Ed. Jonathan Barnes. 2 vols. Princeton: Princeton University Press, 1984, vol. 2.

———. *On Poetics*. Trans. Seth Benardete and Michael Davis. South Bend: St. Augustine's Press, 2002.

———. *Poetics: Editio Maior of the Greek Text with Historical Introductions and Philological Commentaries*. Ed. Dimitri Gutas and Leonardo Tarán, Leiden: E. J. Brill, 2012.

Athanasius. *The Coptic Life of Anthony*. Trans. Tim Vivian San Francisco: International Scholars Publications, 1994.

———. *The Life of Saint Antony*. Trans. Robert T. Meyer. Westminster: The Newman Press, 1950.

Attridge, John. "'La vaste rumeur d'autrefois': Noise, Memory, and Mediation in *À la recherche du temps perdu*." *Modernism/modernity* 26.3 (2019), pp. 617–37,

Augustine. *Confessions*. Trans. Henry Chadwick. Oxford: Oxford University Press, 1991.

———. *Confessions*. Ed. James J. O'Donnell. 3 vols. Oxford: Oxford University Press, 1992.

———. *On Christian Doctrine*. Ed. and trans. R. P. H. Green. Oxford: Clarendon Press of Oxford University Press, 1995.

———. *Soliloquies*. Trans. Rose Elizabeth Cleveland. Boston: Little, Brown, 1910.

Ausfeld, Carl. *De Graecorum precationibus quaestionis*. Leipzig: B. G. Teubner, 1903.

Ausonius. *The Works of Ausonius*. Ed. P. H. Green. Oxford: Oxford University Press, 1991.

Avni, Ora. "Breton et l'idéologie: Machine à coudre—parapluie." *Littérature* 51 (1983), pp. 15–27.

Babut, Daniel. "La part de rationalisme dans la religion de Plutarque: L'exemple du *De genio Socratis*." *Illinois Classical Studies* 13.2 (1988), pp. 383–408.

Bailey, Ryan. "The Acts of Saint Cypian of Antioch: Critical Editions, Translations, and Commentary." PhD diss., School of Religious Studies, McGill University, 2017.

Baillarger, Jules Gabriel François. *Des hallucinations, Mémoires de Académie Royale de Médecine* 12. Paris: Baillière, 1846, pp. 273–475.

Bal, Mieke. "Faithfully Submitted: The Logic of the Signature in Proust's *À la recherche*." In Sonja Neef, José van Dijck, and Eric Ketelaar, eds., *Sign Here! Handwriting in the Age of New Media* Amsterdam: Amsterdam University Press, 2006, pp. 150–62.

Ballet, Gilbert. *Le langage intérieur et les diverses formes de l'aphasie*. 2nd ed. Paris: Félix Alcan, 1888.

Balogh, József. "Zu Augustins 'Konfessionen'—Doppeltes *Kledon* in der Tolle-lege-Szene." *Zeitschrift für neutestamentliche Wissenschaft und die Kunde der älteren Kirche* 25 (1926), pp. 265–70.

Bayet, Jean. *Histoire politique et psychologique de la religion romaine*. Paris: Payot, 1973.

———. "Les malédictions du tribun C. Ateius Capito." In *Croyances et rites dans la Rome antique*. Rome: Payot, 1971, pp. 353–65.

Beard, Mary. "Cicero and Divination: The Formation of a Latin Discourse." *Journal of Roman Studies* 76 (1986), pp. 33–46.

Beja, Morris. *Epiphany in the Modern Novel*. London: Owen, 1971.

Benardete, Seth. "The Crimes and Arts of Prometheus." *Rheinisches Museum für Philologie* 107.2 (1964), pp. 126–39.

Benjamin, Walter. "Doctrine of the Similar." Trans. Michael Jennings. In *Selected Writings, Volume 2, 1931–1934*. Ed. Michael W. Jennings, Howard Eiland, and Gary Smith. Cambridge, MA: Belknap Press of Harvard University Press, 1996, pp. 694–98.

———. "Kleine Geschichte der Photographie." In *Gesammelte Schriften*. Ed. Rolf Tiedemann and Hermann Schweppenhäuser. 7 vols. Frankfurt am Main: Suhrkamp, 1972–1991, vol. 2, part 1, pp. 368–85.

——. "Das Kunstwerk im Zeitalter seiner technischen Reproduzierbarkeit (Zweiter Fassung)," in *Gesammelte Schriften*, vol. 7, part 1, pp. 350–84.

——. "Lehre vom Ähnlichen." In *Gesammelte Schriften*, vol. 2, pp. 204–210.

——. "Little History of Photography." Trans. Edmund Jephcott and Kingsley Shorter. In *Selected Writings, Volume 2: 1927–1934*, pp. 507–30.

——. "Madame Ariane: Second Courtyard on the Left." In *One-Way Street*. Trans. Edmund Jephcott. In *Selected Writings, Volume 1, 1913–1926*. Ed. Marcus Bullock and Michael W. Jennings. Cambridge, MA: Belknap Press of Harvard University Press, 1996, pp. 444–88.

——. "Madame Ariane Zweiter Hof Links." In *Einbahnstraße*, in *Gesammelte Schriften*, vol. 4, pp. 83–148.

——. "On the Mimetic Faculty." Trans. Edmund Jephcott. In *Selected Writings*, vol. 2, pp. 720–22.

——. "Über das mimetische Vermögen." In *Gesammelte Schriften*, vol. 2, pp. 210–13.

——. "The Work of Art in the Age of its Technological Reproducibility, Second Version." Trans. Edmund Jephcott and Harry Zohn. In *Selected Writings, Volume 3, 1935–1938*. Ed. Howard Eiland and Michael W. Jennings, Cambridge, MA: Belknap Press of Harvard University Press, 2002, pp. 101–33.

Benoit, Éric. "*Le démon de l'analogie*, ou: La résurrection des mots." In in Jean-Pierre Saïdeh, ed., *Enchantements: Mélanges offers à Yves Vadé*. Bordeaux: Presses universitaires de Bordeaux, 2002, pp. 97–110.

Benveniste, Émile *Hittite et indo-européen: Études comparatives*. Paris: Maisonneuve, 1962.

——. *Le vocabulaire des institutions indo-européennes*. 2 vols. Paris: Seuil, 1969.

Berrios, James. *The History of Mental Symptoms: Descriptive Psychopathology since the Nineteenth Century*. Cambridge: Cambridge University Press, 1996.

Bettini, Maurizio. "Le orecchie di Hermes: Luoghi e simboli della comunicazione nella cultura antica." In *Le orecchie di Hermes: Studi di antropologia e letteratura classiche*. Turin: Einaudi, 2000, pp. 5–51.

Bezzola, Reto R. *Le sens de l'aventure et de l'amour (Chrétien de Troyes)*. Paris: Champion, 1968.

Billig, Michael. "Freud's Different Versions of Forgetting 'Signorelli': Rhetoric and Repression." *International Journal of Pscyho-Analysis* 81.3 (2000), pp. 483–98.

Billings, Joshua. *The Philosophical Stage: Drama and Dialectic in Classical Athens*. Princeton: Princeton University Press, 2021.

Bliss, Jane. *Naming and Namelessness in Medieval Romance*. Rochester: D. S. Brewer, 2008.

Bloch, Raymond. "Liberté et déterminisme dans la divination romaine." In Marcel Renard and Robert Schilling, eds., *Hommages à Jean Bayet*. Brussels-Berchem: Latomus, revue d'études latines, 1964, pp. 89–100.

Boehmer, Julius. "Augustins *Tolle, lege* in der Bibel." *Biblische Zeitschrift* 23 (1935–1936), pp. 58–61.

Bolgiani, Franco. *La conversione di S. Agostino e l'VIII libro delle 'Confessioni.'* Turin: Università di orino, 1956.

Bottéro, Jean. *Mésopotamie: L'écriture, la raison et les dieux*. Paris: Gallimard, 1987.

———. "Symptômes, signes, écritures en Mésopotamie ancienne." In Jean-Pierre Vernant et al., *Divination et rationalité*. Paris: Éditions du Seuil, 1974, pp. 70–196.

Bouché-Leclercq, Auguste. *Histoire de la divination en antiquité*. 4 vols. Paris: E. Leroux, 1879–1882.

Bournveille, Désiré-Magloire. "Socrate était-il fou?" *Journal de Médicine mentale* 4 (1864), pp. 209–22.

Bowie, Malcolm. *Freud, Proust, and Lacan: Theory as Fiction*. Cambridge: Cambridge University Press, 1997.

Brémaud, Nicolas. "Folie de Socrate." *L'Information psychiatrique* 88.5 (2012), pp. 385–91.

Breton, André. "Activité expérimentale.—Prospection systématique des 'états seconds'.—Pouvoirs de Robert Desnos." In *Oeuvres complètes*, ed. Marguerite Bonnet. 4 vols. Paris: Gallimard, 1998–2008, vol. 3, pp. 473–81.

———. "Entrée des médiums." In *Les pas perdus*. In *Oeuvres complètes*, vol. 1, pp. 273–77.

———. *Les champs magnétiques*. In *Oeuvres complètes*, vol. 1, pp. 51–106.

———. *The Magnetic Fields*. Trans. Charlotte Mandell. New York: New York Review of Books, 2020.

———. *Manifeste du surréalisme*. In *Oeuvres complètes*, vol. 1, pp. 309–46.

———. *Manifestoes of Surrealism*. Trans. Richard Seaver and Helen R. Lane. Ann Arbor: University of Michigan Press, 1972.

———. "The Mediums Enter." In *The Lost Steps*. Trans. Mark Polizzotti. Lincoln: University of Nebraska Press, 1990.

———. "Le message automatique." In *Oeuvres complètes*, vol. 2, pp. 375–92.

———. "Situation surréaliste de l'objet, situation de l'objet surréaliste." In *Oeuvres complètes*, vol. 2, pp. 472–96

———, and Philippe Soupault. *Les champs magnétiques*. Preface by Pierre Audoin. Paris: Gallimard, 1971.

Browne, Alice. "Descartes' Dreams." *Journal of the Warburg and Courtauld Institutes* 40 (1977), pp. 256–73.

Brown, Francis, S. R. Driver, and Charles A. Briggs, eds. *A Hebrew and English Lexicon of the Old Testament, Based on the Lexicon of William Gesenius.* Trans. Edward Robinson. Oxford: Clarendon Press of Oxford University Press, 1906.

Brown, Norman O. *Hermes the Thief: The Evolution of a Myth.* New York: Vintage Books, 1948.

Buchheit, Vinzenz. "Augustinus unter dem Feigenbaum (zu Conf. VIII)." *Vigiliae Christianae* 22.4 (1968), pp. 257–71.

Burkert, Walter. "Sacrificio-sacrilegio: Il 'trickster' fondatore." *Studi storici* 25.4 (1984), pp. 835–45.

Calcidius. *Commentaire au Timée de Platon.* Ed. Béatrice Bakhouche, with Luc Brisson. 2 vols. Paris: Vrin, 2011.

Callimachus. *Callimachus.* Ed. Rudolf Pfeiffer. Oxford: Clarendon Press of Oxford University Press, 1949–1953.

Cameron, H. D. "The Power of Words in *Seven against Thebes.*" *Transactions and Proceedings of the American Philological Association* 101 (1970), pp. 95–118.

Cassirer, Ernst, Paul Oskar Kristeller, and John Herman Randall Jr, eds. *The Renaissance Philosophy of Man.* Chicago: University of Chicago Press, 1948.

Cavell, Stanley. *In Quest of the Ordinary: Lines of Skepticism and Romanticism.* Chicago: University of Chicago Press, 1988.

Cayré, Fulbert. "La conversion de saint Augustin: Le '*tolle, lege*' des *Confessions.*" *L'Année théologique* 11 (1951), pp. 141–51 and 244–52.

Celestina, or the Tragicke-Comedy of Calisto and Melibea, Englished from the Spanish of Fernando de Rojas by James Mabbe. Ed. James Fitzmaurice-Kelly. New York: AMS Press, 1969.

Centrone, Bruno. "Il *daimonion* di Socrate nello pseudoplatonico *Teage.*" In Gabriele Giannantoni and Michel Narcy, eds., *Lezioni socratiche* Naples: Bibliopolis, 1997, pp. 331–48.

Cervantes, Miguel de. *Don Quijote: A New Translation.* Trans. Burton Raffel. New York: Norton, 1999.

———. *El ingenioso hidalgo Don Quixote de la Mancha.* Ed. Luis Andrés Murillo. 3 vols. Madrid: Editorial Castilia, 1978.

Challener, Scott. "Addressing 'Alien Worlds': Publics and Persons in the Poetry of Jack Spicer." *Comparative Literature* 58.4 (2017), pp. 492–525.

Champeaux, Jacqueline. "'Sorts' antiques et médiévaux: Les lettres et les chiffres." In *Au miroir de la culture antique: Mélanges offerts au president René Marache*. Rennes: Presses universitaires de Rennes, 1992, pp. 67–89.

Chantraine, Pierre. *La formation des noms en grec ancien*. Paris : Klincksieck, 1933.

Chardonnens, László Sándor. "Mantic Alphabets in Medieval Western Manuscripts and Early Printed Books." *Modern Philology* 110.3 (2013), pp. 340–66.

Chrétien de Troyes. *Le Roman de Perceval ou le Conte du Graal*. Ed. Keith Busby. Tübingen: Max Niemeyer, 1993.

———. *Oeuvres complètes*. Ed. Daniel Poirion, with Anne Berthelot, Peter F. Dembowski, Sylvie Lefèvre, Karl D. Uitti, and Philippe Walter. Paris: Gallimard, 1994.

———. *Der Percevalroman (Li Contes del Graal)*. Ed. Alfons Hilka. Halle: Max Niemeyer, 1932.

———. *Perceval: The Story of the Grail*. Trans. Burton Raffel. New Haven: Yale University Press, 1999.

Chisholm, A. R. "Le démon de l'analogie." *Essays in French Literature* 1 (1964), pp. 1–6.

Cicero. *Della divinazione*. Ed. and trans. Sebastiano Timpanaro. Milan: Garzanti, 1988.

———. *M. Tulli Ciceronis De Divinatione, liber primus*. Ed. Arthur Stanley Pease. Urbana: The University of Illinois, 1920–1923.

———. *On Divination: Book 1*. Trans. David Wardle. Oxford: Clarendon Press of Oxford University Press, 2006.

———. *De senectute, De amicitia, De divinatione*. Trans. W. A. Falconer. Cambridge, MA: Harvard University Press, 1923.

Ciruelo, Pedro. *Reprouación de las supersticiones y hechizerías*. Ed. Alva V. Ebersole. Valencia: Albatros Hispaniola, 1978.

Clavurier, Vincent. "Psychopathologie de la vie quotidienne et savoir-faire (*hören*) de l'analyste." *Essaim* 11.1 (2003), pp. 227–39.

Clay, Jenny Strauss. *The Politics of Olympus: Form and Meaning in the Homeric Hymns*. 2nd ed. Bristol: Bristol Classical Press, 2006.

Cocteau, Jean. *Orphée*. Paris: Édouard Dermit, 1950.

———. *Three Screenplays*: L'Eternel Retour, Orphée, La Belle et la Bête. Trans. Carol Martin-Sperry. New York: Grossman, 1972.

Cohn, Robert Greer. *Mallarmé's Prose Poems: A Critical Study*. Cambridge: Cambridge University Press, 1987.

Colby-Hall, Alice. "The Lips of the Serpent." In David Feldman, ed., *Homenaje a Robert*

A. Hall, Jr.: Ensayos lingüísticos e filológicos para su sexagésimo aniversario. Madrid: Playor, 1977, pp. 111–15.

Cole, John R. *The Olympian Dreams and Youthful Rebellion of René Descartes*. Urbana: University of Illinois Press, 1992.

Conacher, D. J. *Aeschylus'* Prometheus Bound: *A Literary Commentary*. Toronto: University of Toronto Press, 1980.

——. "Prometheus as Founder of the Arts." *Greek, Roman, and Byzantine Studies* 18 (1977), pp. 189–206.

Cook, L. Stephen. *On the Question of the Cessation of Prophecy*. Tübingen: Mohr Siebeck, 2011.

Costa, José. "Littérature apocalyptique et judaïsme rabbinique: Le problème de la *bat qol*." *Revue des études juives* 169.1–2 (2010), pp. 57–96.

Courcelle, Pierre. *Les Confessions de saint Augustin dans la tradition littéraire: Antécédants et postérité*. Paris: Études augustiniennes, 1963.

——. "L'enfant et les 'Sorts bibliques.'" *Vigiliae Christianae* 7.4 (1953), pp. 194–220.

——. "Note sur le '*Tolle, lege*.'" *L'Année théologique* 39 (1951), pp. 217–32.

——. "L'oracle d'Apis et l'oracle du Jardin de Milan (Augustin, *Conf.*, VIII, 11, 29)." *Revue de l'histoire des religions* 139.2 (1951), pp. 216–31.

——. *Recherches sur les Confessions de saint Augustin*. Paris: E. de Boccard, 1968.

——. "Source chrétienne et allusions païennes de l'épisode du *Tolle, lege*." *Revue d'histoire de philosophie religieuse* 32.3 (1952), pp. 171–200.

——. "Les 'voix' dans les *Confessions* de saint Augustin." *Hermes* 80 (1952), pp. 31–46.

Cryer, Frederick. *Divination in Ancient Israel and Its Near Eastern Environment: A Socio-Historical Investigation*. Sheffield: Sheffield Academic Press, 1994.

Culler, Jonathan. *Theory of the Lyric*. Cambridge, MA: Harvard University Press, 2015.

Damisch, Hubert. "Le maître, c'est lui." *Savoirs et Clinique* 1.12 (2010), pp. 13–37.

De Kitsch, Yves. "Les *sortes vergilianae* dans l'Histoire Auguste." *Mélanges d'archéologie et d'histoire* 82.1 (1970), pp. 321–62.

Deleuze, Gilles. *Proust et le signes*. Paris: Presses universitaires de France, 1964.

Den Boeft, J. *Calcidius on Demons (Commentarius ch. 127–136)*. Leiden: Brill, 1977.

Derrida, Jacques. "Qual quelle." In *Marges de la philosophie*. Paris: Minuit, 1972, pp. 326–64.

——. "Qual Quelle: Valéry's Sources." In *Margins of Philosophy*. Trans. Alan Bass. Chicago: University of Chicago Press, 1982, pp. 275–306.

Descartes, René. "Discours de la méthode pour bien conduire sa raison & chercher lar verité dans les sciences." In volume 6 of *Oeuvres complètes.* Ed. Charles Adam and Paul Tannery. 11 vols. Paris: Vrin, 1996, pp. 1–78.

———. *A Discourse on the Method.* Trans. Ian Maclean. Oxford: Oxford University Press, 2006.

———. "Cartesii cogitationes privatae." In *Oeuvres inédites de Descartes.* Ed. Alexandre Foucher de Careil. 2 vols. Paris: Auguste Durand, 1859, vol. 1, pp. pp. 2–17. Also in *Oeuvres complètes*, vol. 10, pp. 213–48.

———. "*Olympica.*" In volume 10 of *Oeuvres complètes*, pp. 179–88.

De Zorzi, Nicla. "The Omen Series *Šumma Izbu*: Internal Structure and Hermeneutic Strategies." *Kaskal* 8 (2011), pp. 43–75.

Downing, Eric. "Magic Reading." In Eric Downing, Jonathan M. Hess, and Richard V. Benson, eds., *Literary Studies and the Pursuits of Reading.* Rochester: Camden House, 2012, pp. 189–215.

Driediger-Murphy, Lindsay G. "Numa and Jupiter: Whose Smile Is It, Anyway?" *Classical Quarterly* 71.1 (2021), pp. 259–75.

Dumézil, Georges. *La religion romaine archäique, avec un appendice sur la religion des Étrusques.* Paris: Payot, 1974.

Duval, Sophie. "Le verre grossissant et l'art du tailleur d'images: Un point de détail autoréférentiel au revers du texte proustien." *Poétique* 150.2 (2007), pp. 149–68.

Ellmann, Richard. *James Joyce.* Oxford: Oxford University Press, 1959.

Engels, David. *Das römische Vorzeichenwesen (753–27 v. Chr.): Quellen, Terminologie, Kommentar, historische Entwicklung.* Stuttgart: Franz Steiner, 2007.

Esquirol, Jean-Étienne Dominique. *Des illusions chez les aliénés: Question médico-légale sur l'isolement des aliénés.* Paris: Crochard, 1832.

Evans-Prichard, E. E. *Witchcraft, Oracles, and Magic among the Azande.* Oxford: Clarendon Press of Oxford University Press, 1937.

Ey, Henri. *Traité des hallucinations.* 2 vols. Paris: Masson, 1973.

Fahd, Toufic. *La divination arabe: Études religieuses, sociologiques et folkloriques sur le milieu natif de l'Islam.* Leiden: E. J. Brill, 1966.

Falret, Jean-Pierre. *Des Maladies mentales et des asiles d'aliénés: Leçons cliniques et considérations générales.* Paris: J.-B. Baillière et fils, 1864.

Ferlauto, Filippo. "Prometeo e le γραμμάτων συνθέσεις (Aesch. *Prom.* Vinct. vv 460–461)." *Bollettino dei classici* 11 (1990), pp. 164–77.

Ferrari, Leo C. "*Ecce audio vocem de vicina domo* (*Conf.* 8, 12, 29)." *Augustiniana* 33.3–4 (1983), pp. 232–45.

Festus, Sextus Pompeius. *De verborum significatu quae supersunt cum Pauli epitome.* Ed. Wallace M. Lindsay. Leipzig: B. G. Teubner, 1913.

Finet, André. "Un cas de clédonomancie à Mari." In G. van Driel, T. J. H. Krispijn, M. Stol, and K. R. Veenhof, eds., *Zikir Šumim: Assyriological Studies Presented to F. R. Kraus on the Occasion of His Seventieth Birthday.* Leiden: E. J. Brill, 1982, pp. 48–55.

Finke, Laurie A., and Martin B. Shichtman. "'Can't Get No Satisfaction': Jack Spicer's Medievalism." *Paideuma: Modern and Contemporary Poetics* 46 (2019), pp. 85–108.

Finkelstein, Norman M. "Jack Spicer's Ghosts and the Gnosis of History." *boundary 2* 9.2 (1981), pp. 81–100.

Flacelière, Robert. *Devins et oracles grecs.* Paris: Presses universitaires de France, 1961.

Fleming, Paul. "'Kannitverstan': The Contingent Understanding of Anecdotes." *Oxford German Studies* 40.1 (2011), pp. 72–81.

Flournoy, Théodore. *From India to Planet Mars: A Case of Multiple Personality and Imaginary Languages.* Ed. Sonu Shamdasani. Preface by C. G. Jung. Princeton: Princeton University Press, 1994.

Flower, Michael Attyah. *The Seer in Ancient Greece.* Berkeley: University of California Press, 2008.

Foster, Hal. "Convulsive Identity." *October* 57 (1991), pp. 18–54.

Fourquet, Jean. *Wolfram d'Eschenbach et le Conte del grail.* Paris: Les Belles Lettres, 1938.

Franklin, Ursula. *The Prose Poems of Stéphane Mallarmé.* Chapel Hill: University of North Carolina Press, 1976.

Franz, Kurt. *Johann Peter Hebel Kannitverstan: Ein Mißverständnis und seine Folgen, Texte, Kommentar, Abbildungen.* Munich: Carl Hanser, 1985.

Frappier, Jean. *Chrétien de Troyes et le mythe du Graal: Étude sur 'Perceval ou le Conte du Graal.'* Paris: Société d'édition d'enseignement supérieur, 1972.

Fraser, P. M. *Ptolemaic Alexandria.* 3 vols. Oxford: Clarendon Press of Oxford University Press, 1972.

Freccero, John. "Autobiography and Narrative." In Thomas C. Heller, Morton Sosna, and David E. Wellbery, eds., *Reconstructing Individualism: Autonomy, Individuality and the Self in Western Thought.* Stanford: Stanford University Press, 1986, pp. 16–29.

Freedman, Sally M. *If a City Is Set on a Height: The Akkadian Omen Series* Šumma Alu ina Mēlē Šakin, *Volume 1, Tablets 1–21.* Philadelphia: University of Pennsylvania Museum, 1998.

Freud, Sigmund. *Briefe an Wilhelm Fließ, 1887–1904.* Ed. Jeffrey Moussaieff Masson. Transcription Michael Schröter. Frankfurt: Fischer, 1986.

———. *The Complete Letters of Sigmund Freud to Wilhem Fliess, 1887–1904*. Ed. and trans. Jeffrey Moussaieff Masson. Cambridge, MA: Harvard University Press, 1985.

———. *Die Traumdeutung / Über den Traum*. Volume 2–3 of *Gesammelte Werke*. Ed. Anna Freud. 18 vols. London: Imago, 1948–1968.

———. *Introductory Lectures on Psycho-Analysis*. In *The Standard Edition of the Complete Psychological Works of Sigmund Freud*. Trans. James Strachey, with Anna Freud, assisted by Alex Strachey and Alan Tyson. 24 vols. London: The Hogarth Press, 1953–1974.

———. *The Psychopathology of Everyday Life: On Forgetfulness, Slips of the Tongue, Inadvertent Actions, Superstitions and Mistakes*. Trans. Anthea Bell. New York: Penguin Books, 2002.

———. *Vorlesungen zur Einführung in die Psychoanalyse*. In *Gesammelte Werke*, vol. 11.

———. "Zum psychischen Mechanismus der Vergesslichkeit." *Monatsschrift für Psychiatrie und Neurologie* 4 (1898), pp. 436–43.

———. *Zur Psychopathologie des Alltagsleben: Über Vergessen, Versprechen, Vergreifen, Aberglaube und Irrtum*. Frankfurt am Main: Fischer, 2009.

Friedrich, Ingold. *Ephod und Chosen im Lichte des Alten Orients*. Vienna: Herder, 1968.

Frye, Northrop. *Anatomy of Criticism: Four Essays*. 1957; Princeton: Princeton University Press, 2000.

García Chichester, Ana. "Don Quijote y Sancho en El Toboso: Superstición y simbolismo." *Bulletin of the Cervantes Society of America* 3.2 (1983), pp. 121–33.

Gault, Jean-Louis. "Two Statuses of the Symptom: 'Let Us Turn to Finn Again.'" In Véronique Voruz and Bogdan Wolf, eds., *The Later Lacan: An Introduction*. Albany: State University of New York Press, 2007, pp. 73–82.

Gauthier, Philippe. *Symbola: Les étrangers et la justice dans les cites grecques*. Nancy: Univesité de Nancy II, 1972.

Geffcken, Johannes. "Augustins Tolle-lege-Erlebnis." *Archiv für Religionswissenschaft* 31 (1934), pp. 1–13.

Genette, Gérard. *Figures II*, Paris: Seuil, 1969.

Gershman, Herbert S. "Valéry and Breton." *Yale French Studies* 44 (1970) pp. 199–206.

Ginzburg, Carlo. "Clues: Roots of an Evidential Paradigm." In *Clues, Myths, and the Historical Method*. Trans. John Tedeschi and Anne C. Tedeschi. Baltimore: Johns Hopkins University Press, 1989, pp. 96–125.

———. "Spie: Radici di un paradigma indiziario." In Aldo Gargani, ed., *Crisi della ragione*. Turin: Einaudi, 1979, pp. 59–106; reprinted in *Miti emblemi spie: Morfologia e storia* (Turin: Einaudi, 1986), pp. 158–209.

Göddies, Susanne. *euphêmia: Die gute Rede in Kult und Literatur der griechischen Antike.* Heidelberg: Winter, 2006.

Goldhill, Simon. *Language, Sexuality, Narrative: The Oresteia.* Cambridge: Cambridge University Press, 1984.

Graf, Fritz. "Rolling the Dice for an Answer." In Sarah Iles Johnston and Peter T. Struck, eds., *Mantikê: Studies in Ancient Divination.* Leiden: Brill, 2005, pp. 51–98.

Greenshields, Will. "Lacan *contra* the Surrealists." *Nottingham French Studies* 58.1 (2019), pp. 64–81.

Gregory of Tours. *The History of the Franks.* Trans. Lewis Thorpe. London: Penguin Books, 1974.

Green, Otis H. *Spain and the Western Tradition: The Castilian Mind in Literature from El Cid to Calderón.* Madison: University of Wisconsin Press, 1963.

Grottanelli, Cristiano. "Bambini e divinazione." In Ottavia Niccoli, ed., *Infanzie: Funzioni di un gruppo liminale dal mondo classico all'età moderna.* Florence: Ponte alle Grazie, 1993, pp. 23–72.

Grünbaum, Adolf. *The Foundations of Psychoanalysis: A Philosophical Critique.* Berkeley: University of California Press, 1984.

Guerlac, Suzanne. *Literary Polemics: Bataille, Sartre, Valéry, Breton.* Stanford: Stanford University Press, 1997.

Guidetti, Fabio. "Tensam non tenuit: Cicerone, Arnobio e il modo di condurre i carri sacri." *Studi Classici e Orientali* 55 (2009), pp. 233–48.

Guillaumont, François. *Philosophie et augure: Recherches sur la théorie cicéronienne de la divination.* Brussels: Latomus, 1984.

Gurd, Alexander. *Iphigenias at Aulis: Textual Multiplicity, Radical Philology.* Ithaca: Cornell University Press, 2005.

Guyonnet, Damien. "Formalisation lacanienne de l'hallucination verbale 'Truie.'" *L'École de la cause freudienne* 71.1 (2009), pp. 111–18.

Halliday, W. R. *Greek Divination: A Study of Its Methods and Principles.* London: Macmillan, 1913.

Hamacher, Werner. "The Word *Wolke*—If It Is One." Trans. Peter Fenves. In Rainer Nägele, ed., *Benjamin's Ground: New Readings of Walter Benjamin.* Detroit: Wayne State University Press, 1988, pp. 147–76.

Harper, Margaret Mills. "The Message is the Medium: Identity in the Automatic Script." *Yeats: An Annual of Critical and Textual Studies* 9 (1991), pp. 35–54.

Havet, Louis. *Manuel de critique verbale appliquée aux textes latins.* Paris: Hachette, 1911.

Hayman, David. "The Purpose and Permanence of the Joycean Epiphany." *James Joyce Quarterly* 34.5–36.1 (1998), pp. 633–55.

Hebel, Johann Peter. "Kannitverstan." In *Sämtliche Schriften*, ed. Adrian Braunbehrens, Gustav A. Benrath, and Peter Pfaff. 8 vols. Karlsruhe: C. F. Müller, 1990–2013, vols. 2–3, pp. 132–35.

———. "Kannitverstan." In *The Treasure Chest*. Trans. John Hibbard. London: Libris, 1994, pp. 40–42.

The Hebrew Bible. Trans. Robert Alter. 3 vols. New York: W.W. Norton, 2019.

Hegel, Gottfried Wilhelm Friedrich. *Aesthetics: Lectures on Fine Art*. Trans. T. M. Knox. 2 vols. Oxford: Clarendon Press of Oxford University Press , 1975.

Heidegger, Martin. *Being and Time: A Translation of Sein und Zeit*. Trans. Joan Stambaugh. Albany: State University of New York Press, 1996.

———. *Being and Time*. Trans. John Macquarrie and Edward Robinson. New York: Harper & Row, 1962.

———. *Sein und Zeit*. Volume 2 of *Gesamtausgabe*. 101 vols. Frankfurt am Main: Vittorio Klostermann, 1977.

Heinevetter, Franz. *Würfel- und Buchstabenorakel in Griechenland und Kleinasien*. Breslau: Graß, Barth [W. Friedrich], 1912.

Heller-Roazen, Daniel. *The Inner Touch: Archaeology of a Sensation*. New York: Zone Books, 2007.

Herodotus. *Histories*. Trans. A. D. Godley. Cambridge, MA: Harvard University Press, 1920.

———. *The Histories*. Trans. Aubrey de Sélincourt, rev. John Marincola. New York: Penguin Books, 2003.

Hesiod, *Theogony: Edited with Prolegomena and Commentary*. Ed. Martin L. West. Oxford: Clarendon Press of Oxford University Press, 1971.

———. *Theogony, Works and Days, Testimonia*. Ed. Glenn W. Most. Cambridge, MA: Harvard University Press, 2006.

Herter, Hans. "Hermes: Ursprung und Wesen eines griechischen Gottes." *Rheinisches Museum für Philologie* 119.3 (1976), pp. 193–241.

Hippocrates. *De diaeta / Du régime*. Ed. and trans. Robert Joly, with Simon Byl. Berlin: Akademie Verlag, 2003.

Hirvonen, Kaarle. "Cledonomancy and the Grinding Slave, *Od*. XX 91–121" *Acta Philologica Fennica* 6 (1969), pp. 5–20.

Hofmannsthal, Hugo von. *Der Tor und der Tod*. In *Gesammelte Werke*. Ed. Herbert Steiner. 14 vols. Stockholm: Bermann-Fischer, 1945–. *Gedichte und lyrische Dramen*, pp. 269–92.

Hollaux, Maurice. "ΑΠΟΛΛΩΝ ΣΠΟΔΙΟΣ." In *Mélanges Henri Weil*. Paris: A. Fontemoing, 1898, pp. 193–206.

Homer. *Homeric Hymns, Homeric Apocrypha, Lives of Homer*. Ed. and trans. Martin L. West. Cambridge, MA: Harvard University Press, 2003.

———. *Homerica and the Homeric Hymns*. Ed. and trans. Hugh G. Evelyn-White. Cambridge, MA: Harvard University Press, 1914.

———. *The Iliad of Homer*. Trans. Richmond Lattimore. Chicago: University of Chicago Press, 1951.

———. *The Odyssey of Homer: A Modern Translation*. Trans. Richard Lattimore. New York: Harper Torchbooks, 1967.

Houdebine, Jean-Louis. "Le 'concept' d'écriture automatique: Sa signification et sa function dans le discours idéologique d'André Breton." *Littérature et ideologies: Collqoue de Cluny 2 (2, 3, 4 avril 1970)*. Paris: La Nouvelle Critique, 1971, pp. 178–85.

Hunger, Hermann, and David Pingree. *Astral Science in Mesopotamia*. Leiden: E. J. Brill. 1999.

Hurowitz, Victor Avigdor. "True Light on the Urim and Thummim." *Jewish Quarterly Review* 88.3–4 (1998), 263–74.

Imbs, Paul, ed. *Trésor de la langue française: Dictionnaire de la langue du XIXe et du XXe siècle (1789–1960)*. 16 vols. Paris: Éditions du centre national de la recherche scientifique, 1971–1994.

Irvine, Martin. *The Making of Textual Culture: 'Grammatica' and Literary Theory 350–1100*. Cambridge: Cambridge University Press, 1994.

Jackson, Virginia. *Dickinson's Misery: A Theory of Lyric Reading*. Princeton: Princeton University Press, 2005.

———, and Yopie Prins, eds. *The Lyric Theory Reader: A Critical Anthology*. Baltimore: Johns Hopkins University Press, 2014.

Jaillard, Dominique. "Hermès et la mantique grecque." In Stelle Georgoudi, Renée Koch Piettre, and Francis Schmidt, eds., *La raison des signes: Présages, rites, destin dans les sociétés de la méditerranée ancienne*. Leiden: Brill, 2012, pp. 91–107.

Jakobson, Roman. "Linguistics and Poetics." In *Selected Writings*. 8 vols. The Hague: Mouton, 1962–1988. Volume 3: *Poetry of Grammar and Grammar of Poetry*, pp. 18–51.

———. "Two Aspects of Language and Two Types of Aphasic Disturbances." In *Selected Writings*, vol. 2: *Word and Language*, pp. 239–59.

James, Tony. *Dream, Creativity and Madness in Nineteenth-Century France.* Oxford: Clarendon Press of Oxford University Press, 1995.

Janet, Pierre. *L'automatisme psychologique: Essai de psychologie expérimentale sur les formes inférieures de l'activité humaine.* Paris: Alcan, 1894.

———. "Étude sur un cas d'aboulie et d'idées fixes." *Revue philosophique de la France et de l'étranger* 31 (1891), pp. 258–87.

Janowitz, Anne. *Lyric and Labour in the Romantic Tradition.* Cambridge: Cambridge University Press, 1998.

Johnson, Barbara. *Défigurations du langage poétique: La seconde révolution baudelerienne.* Paris: Flammarion, 1979.

Johnston, Sarah Iles. "Myth, Festival, and Poet: The 'The Homeric Hymn to Hermes' and Its Performative Context." *Classical Philology* 97.2 (2002), pp. 109–32.

Joly, Robert. "La scène du Jardin de Milan: Saint Augustin, *Confessions*, VIII, XII, 29." *La nouvelle Clio* 7–9 (1955–1957), pp. 443–64.

Jones, Sonia. "Two Cases of Kledonomancy in Lope's Theater." *Revista de estudios hispanicos* 9 (1982), pp. 137–42.

Josephus, Flavius. *Against Apion.* In *The Life and Against Apion.* Trans. H. St. J. Thackeray. Cambridge, MA: Harvard University Press, 1926.

Joyal, Mark. "Tradition and Innovation in the Transformation of Socrates' Divine Sign." In Lewis Ayres, ed., *The Passionate Intellect: Essays on the Transformation of Classical Tradition Presented to Professor I. G. Kidd.* London: Routledge, 1995, pp. 39–56.

Joyce, James. *Poems and Shorter Writings, including* Epiphanies, Giacomo Joyce, *and 'A Portrait of the Artist'.* Ed. Richard Ellmann, A. Walton Litz, and John Whittier-Ferguson. London: Faber and Faber, 1991.

———. *A Portrait of the Artist as a Young Man.* Ed. Seamus Deane. New York: Penguin Books, 1993.

———. *Stephen Hero.* London: Jonathan Cape, 1956.

———. *Ulysses.* New York: Penguin Books, 1992.

Joyce, Stanislaus. *My Brother's Keeper.* Ed. Richard Ellmann. Preface by T. S. Eliot. London: Faber and Faber, 1958.

Kahn, Laurence. *Hermès passe: Ou, les ambiguïtés de la communication.* Paris: François Maspero, 1978.

Kaibel, G., ed. *Athenaei Dipnosophistarum libri XV.* Leipzig: in aedibus B. G. Teubneri, 1887–1890.

Kany-Turpin, José. "Fonction de la verité dans un énoncé augural: Le paradoxe du menteur Ateius Capito." In Marc Baratin and Claude Moussy, eds., *Conceptions latines du sens et de la signification: Colloque du centre Alfred Ernout*. Paris: Presses de l'université Paris-Sorbonne, 1999, pp. 255–66.

Karpe, R., and M. Karpe. "The Significance of Freud's Trip to Orvieto." *Israel Annals of Psychiatry and Related Disciplines* 17.1 (1979), pp. 3–20.

Katz, Daniel. *The Poetry of Jack Spicer*. Edinburgh: Edinburgh University Press, 2013.

Kawakami, Akane. "Proust and Handwriting." In Nathalie Aubert, ed., *Proust and the Visual*. Cardiff: University of Wales Press, 2012, pp. 95–114.

Keefer, Michael H. "The Dreamer's Path: Descartes and the Sixteenth Century." *Renaissance Quarterly* 49.1 (1996), pp. 30–76.

Kelly, Douglas. "Le nom de Perceval." In Danielle Buschunger and Wolfgang Spiewok, eds., *Perceval-Parzival, hier et aujourd'hui, et autres essais sur la littérature allemande du Moyen Âge et de la Renaissance* Greifswald: Reineke, 1994, pp. 123–29.

Kenner, Hugh. "The 'Portrait' in Perspective." *Kenyon Review* 10.3 (1948), pp. 361–81.

Kerényi, Karl. *Prometheus: Die menschliche Existenz in griechischer Deutung*. Hamburg: Rowohlt, 1959.

Kitto, H. D. F. *Greek Tragedy: A Literary Study*. 3rd. ed. London: Routledge, 1966.

Kitz, Anne Marie. "The Plural Forms of 'Ûrîm and Tummîm." *Journal of Biblical Literature* 116.3 (1997), pp. 401–10.

———. "Prophecy as Divination." *Catholic Biblical Quarterly* 65.1 (2003), pp. 22–42.

———. "The Terminology of Hebrew Lot Casting and Its Ancient Near Eastern Context." *Catholic Biblical Quarterly* 62.2 (2000), pp. 207–14.

Klingshirn, William E. "Christian Divination in Late Roman Gaul: The *Sortes Sangallenses*." In Sarah Iles Johnston and Peter T. Struck, eds., *Mantikê: Studies in Ancient Divination*. Leiden: Brill, 2005, pp. 99–128.

———. "Defining the *Sortes Sanctorum*: Gibbon, Du Cange, and Early Christian Lot Divination." *Journal of Early Christian Studies* 10.1 (2002), pp. 77–130.

Konrad, C. F. "Vellere Signa." In C. F. Konrad, ed., *Augusto Augurio: Rerum humanarum et divinarum commentationes in honorem Jerzy Linderski*. Stuttgart: Fritz Steiner, 2004, pp. 169–203.

Knox, Bernard. "Aeschylus and the Third Actor." In *Word and Action: Essays on the Ancient Theater*. Baltimore: Johns Hopkins University Press, 1979, pp. 39–55.

Kugel, James. "Two Introductions to Midrash." *Prooftexts* 3.2 (1983), pp. 131–55.

Kuhn, Peter. *Bat Qol: Die Offenbarungsstimme in der rabbinischen Literatur, Sammlung, Übersetzung und Kurzkommentierung der Texte.* Regensburg: Friedrich Pustet, 1989.

——. *Offenbarungsstimmen im antiken Judentum.* Tübingen: J. C. B. Mohr, 1989.

Kumar, Shiv K. "Joyce's Epiphany and Bergson's 'L'Intuition philosophique.'" *Modern Language Quarterly* 20.1 (1959), pp. 27–30.

Lacan, Jacques. *De la psychose paranoïaque dans ses rapports à la personnalité.* Paris: Seuil, 1932.

——. "D'une question préliminaire à tout traîtement possible de la psychose." In *Écrits.* Paris: Éditions du Seuil, 1966, pp. 531–84.

——. "Fonction et champ de la parole et du langage en psychanalyse." In *Écrits,* pp. 237–322.

——. *Formations of the Unconscious: The Seminar of Jacques Lacan, Book 5.* Trans. Russell Grigg. Cambridge: Polity, 2017

——. "The Function and Field of Speech in Psychoanalysis." In *Ecrits.* Trans. Bruce Fink in collaboration with Héloïse Fink and Russell Grigg. New York: W. W. Norton, 2002, pp. 197–268.

——. "On a Question Prior to Any Possible Treatment of Psychosis." In *Ecrits.* Trans. Bruce Fink, pp. 445–88.

——. "Position de l'inconscient." In *Écrits,* pp. 829–50.

——. "Position of the Unconscious." In *Ecrits.* Trans. Bruce Fink, pp. 703–21.

——. "Une pratique de bavardage." In *Le séminaire,* vol. 25: *Le temps de conclure* (1977–1978), unpublished.

——. *Premiers écrits.* Ed. Jacques-Alain Miller. Paris: Seuil, 2023.

——. "On a Question Prior to Any Possible Treatment of Psychosis." In *Ecrits.* Trans. Bruce Fink, pp. 445–88.

——. *The Seminar of Jacques Lacan, Book 3: The Psychoses.* Trans. Russell Grigg. New York: W. W. Norton, 1993.

——. *Le séminaire,* vol. 3: *Les psychoses.* Ed. Jacques-Alain Miller. Paris: Seuil, 1981.

——.*Le séminaire,* vol. 5: *Les formations de l'inconscient.* Ed. Jacques-Alain Miller. Paris: Seuil, 1998.

——. *Le séminaire,* vol. 8: *Le transfert.* Ed. Jacques-Alain Miller. Paris: Éditions du Seuil, 1991.

——. *Le séminaire,* vol. 12: *Problèmes cruciaux pour la psychanalyse* (1964–1965). Unpublished.

——. *Le séminaire,* vol. 21: *Les non-dupes errent* (1973–1974). Unpublished.

———. *Transference*. Trans. Bruce Fink. Cambridge: Polity, 2015.

———, J. Lévy-Valensi, and Pierre Migault. "Écrits 'inspirés': Schizographie," *Année médico-psychologiques* 13.89 (1931), pp. 508–22. Now in *Premiers écrits*, pp. 61–84.

Laerke, Morgens. "Leibniz and Steno, 1675–1680)." In Morgens Laerke and Raphaele Andrault, eds., *Steno and the Philosophers*. Leiden: Brill, 2018, pp. 63–84.

Langbaum, Robert. "The Epiphanic Mode in Wordsworth and Modern Literature." *New Literary History* 14.2 (1983), pp. 335–58.

Lapatin, Kenneth. "Pharaian Kledomancy." In Jitse Dijkstra, Justin Kroesen, and Yme Kuiper, eds., *Myths, Martyrs, and Modernity: Studies in the History of Religions in Honour of Jan N. Bremmer* Leiden: Brill, 2010, pp. 135–43.

Larson, Jennifer. "The Corycian Nymphs and the Bee Maidens of the Homeric *Hymn to Hermes*." *Greek, Roman and Byzantine Studies* 36.4 (1995), pp. 341–57.

Lateiner, Donald. "Telemakhos' One Sneeze and Penelope's Two Laughs (*Odyssey* 17.541–50, 18. 158–168)." In Robert J. Rabel, ed., *Approaches to Homer: Ancient and Modern*. Swansea: Classical Press of Wales, 2005, pp. 91–104.

Lausberg, Heinrich. *Handbuch der literarischen Rhetorik: Eine Grundlegung der Literaturwissenschaft*. 2 vols. Munich: Hueber, 1973.

Lautréamont, Germain Nouveau. *Maldoror (Les chants de Maldoror)*. In *Oeuvres complètes*, ed. Pierre-Olivier Walzer. Paris: Gallimard, 1980.

Layna Ranz, Francisco. "La liebre y la jaula de grillos (*Quijote*, II, 73): El confessor Diego de Yepes y la salvación del alma." In Emilio Martínez Mata and María Fernández Ferreiro, eds., *Comentarios a Cervantes: Actas selectas del VIII Congreso Internacional de la Asociación de Cervantistas, Oviedo, 11–15 de junio de 2012* Madrid: Fundación María Cristina Masaveu Peterson, 2014, pp. 415–24.

Lechantre, Michel. "P(h)o(n)étique." *Cahiers Paul Valéry* 1 (1975), pp. 91–122.

Leduc, Claudine. "Une théologie du signe en pays grec: L'hymne homérique à Hermès (I)—Commentaire des vers 1–181." *Revue de l'histoire des religions* 212.1 (1995), pp. 5–49.

Lefebvre, P. "De l'aphémie a l'aphasie: Les tribulations d'une dénomination." *L'Information Psychiatrique* 64.7 (1988), pp. 947–54.

Lélut, Louis Francisque. *Du démon de Socrate: Spécimen d'une application de la science psychologique à celle de l'histoire*. 2nd ed. 1836; Paris: Libraire J.-B. Bailliere et Fils, 1856.

Leibniz, Gottfried Wilhelm. "Notata quaedam G. G. L. circa vitam et doctrima Cartesii." In *Die philosophischen Schriften*. Ed. C. J. Gerhardt. 7 vols. 1875–1890:. Hildesheim: Olms, 1978, vol. 4, pp. 310–14. Also in C. Thomasius, *Historia sapientiae et stultitiae*.

2 vols. Halle: Typis & Sumptibus Christophori Salfeldii, 1693, vol. 2, pp. 113–22. In a modern edition: *Sämtliche Schriften und Briefe*. Berlin: Akademie Verlag, 1998–2017, series 6, vol. 4, *Philosophische Schriften*, number 376, pp. 2057–65.

———. "Principes de la Nature et de la Grace, fondés en raison." In *Die philosophischen Schriften*, vol. 6, pp. 598–606.

———. "Principles of Nature and Grace, Based on Reason." In *Philosophical Essays*. Ed. and trans. Robert Ariew and Daniel Garber. Indianapolis: Hackett, 1989.

———. *Theodicy*. Ed. Austin Farrer. Trans. E. M. Huggard. La Salle: Open Court, 1985.

Levin, Harry. *James Joyce: A Critical Introduction*. London: Faber and Faber, 1947.

Lévy-Valensi, Pierre Migault, and Jacques Lacan. "Écrits 'inspirés': Schizographie." *Année médico-psychologiques* 13.89 (1931), pp. 508–22.

Lewis, Charles T., and Charles Short. *A Latin Dictionary, Founded on Andrews' Edition of Freund's Latin Dictionary*. Oxford: Clarendon Press of Oxford University Press 1879).

Liebermann, Saul. *Hellenism in Jewish Palestine: Studies in the Literary Transmission, Beliefs and Manners of Palestine in the 1st century B.C.E.–4th Century C.E.* New York: Jewish Theological Society of America, 1950.

Linderski, Jerzy. "The Augural Law." *Aufstieg und Niedergang der römischen Welt* II 16.3 (1986), pp. 2146–312.

Litz, A. Walton. *The Art of James Joyce: Method and Design in Ulysses and Finnegans Wake*. London: Oxford University Press, 1961.

Livy. *The Early History of Rome: Books I–V of The History of Rome from Its Foundations*. Trans. Aubrey de Sélincourt. London: Penguin Books, 2002.

———. *Livy in Fourteen Volumes*. Trans. B. O. Foster. Cambridge, MA: Harvard University Press, 1924.

———. *The Early History of Rome: Books I–V of The History of Rome from Its Foundations*. Trans. Aubrey de Sélincourt. London: Penguin Books, 2002.

Lucarini, Carlo M., and Claudio Moreschini. *In Platonis Phaedrum scholia*. Berlin: De Gruyter, 2012.

Lucchelli, Juan-Pablo. *Métaphores de l'amour: Étude lacanienne sur le Banquet de Platon*. Rennes: Presses universitaires de Rennes, 2012.

Lucey, Michael. *What Proust Heard: Novels and the Ethnography of Talk*. Chicago: University of Chicago Press, 2022.

MacDuff, Sangam. *Panepiphanal World: James Joyce's Epiphanies*. Gainesville: University Press of Florida, 2020.

Macey, David. *Lacan in Contexts.* London: Verso, 1988.

Madec, Goulven. "La conversion et les Confessions." In *Augustin, le message et la foi: Causeries à Radio Notre-Dame.* Paris: Desclée de Brouwer, 1987, pp. 17–31.

Maier, Johan. "Urim und Tummim: Recht und Bund in der Spannung zwischen konigstum und Priestertum in Alten Israel." *Kairos* 11 (1969), pp. 22–38.

Mallarmé, Stéphane. "Ballets." In *Oeuvres complètes*, ed. Bertrand Marchal, 2 vols. Paris: Gallimard, 1998–2003, vol. 2, pp. 170.

———. "Un coup de dés." In *Oeuvres complètes*, vol. 2, pp. 363–407.

———. "Crise de vers." In *Oeuvres complètes*, vol. 1, pp. 204–13.

———. "Crisis in Verse." In *Divagations: The Author's 1897 Arrangement.* Trans. Barbara Johnson. Cambridge, MA: Harvard University Press, 2007, pp. 201–11.

———. "Le démon de l'analogie." In *Oeuvres complètes*, vol. 1, pp. 86–88.

———. "The Demon of Analogy." In *Divagations: The Author's 1897 Arrangement*, pp. 17–18.

———. "Sonnet en yx." In *Oeuvres complètes*, vol. 1, pp. 1335–36.

Marasso, Arturo. "La adivinación por las palabras." In *Cervantes: La Invención del Quijote.* Buenos Aires: Hachette, 1954, pp. 192–93.

Mark the Deacon. *The Life of Porphyry, Bishop of Gaza.* Trans. G. F. Hill. Oxford: Clarendon Press of Oxford University Press, 1913.

———. *Vie de Porphyre, evêque de Gaza.* Ed. Henri Grégoire and Marc-Antoine Kugener. Paris: Les Belles Lettres, 1930.

Marion, Jean-Luc. "Les trois songes, ou L'éveil du philosophe." In Jean-Luc Marion, ed., with Jean Deprun, *La passion de la raison: Hommage à Ferdinand Alquié.* Paris: Presses universitaires de France, 1983, pp. 55–78.

Marrou, Henri-Irène. "La querelle autour du *Tolle, lege*." *Christiana tempora: Mélanges d'histoire, d'archéologie, d'épigraphie et de patristique.* Rome: École française de Rome, 1978, pp. 381–91.

Marshall, C. W. "Casting the Oresteia." *Classical Journal* 98.3 (2003), pp. 257–74.

Maurizio, Lisa. "Interpretative Strategies for Delphic Oracles and Kledons: Prophecy Falsification and Individualism." In Veit Rosenberger, ed., *Divination in the Ancient World: Religious Options and the Individual.* Stuttgart: Franz Steiner, 2013, pp. 61–79.

McCarthy-Jones, Simon. *Hearing Voices: The Histories, Causes and Meanings of Auditory Verbal Hallucinations.* Cambridge: Cambridge University Press, 2012.

McLaughlin, Kevin. *The Philology of Life: Walter Benjamin's Critical Program.* New York: Fordham University Press, 2023.

Méla, Charles. *Blanchefleur et le saint homme ou la semblance des réliques: Étude comparée de littérature médiévale*. Paris: Éditions du Seuil, 1979.

Ménard, Philippe. "La révélation du nom pour le héros du *Conte du Graal*." In Danielle Queruel, ed., *Amour et chevalerie dans les romans de Chrétien de Troyes: Actes du Colloque de Troyes (27–29 mars 1992)* Paris: Les Belles Lettres, 1995, pp. 47–59.

Meringer, Rudolf. "Die täglichen Fehler im Sprechen, Lesen und Handeln." *Wörter und Sachen* 8 (1923), pp. 122–41.

———, and Karl Meyer. *Versprechen und Verlesen: Eine psychologisch-linguistische Studie*. Stuttgart: G. J. Göschen, 1895.

Mieszkowski, Jan. *Crises of the Sentence*. Chicago: University of Chicago Press, 2019.

Migne, Jacques-Paul, ed. *Patrologia cursus completus, series latina*. 223 vols. Paris: Exudebat Migne, 1844–1864.

Mill, John Stuart. "Thoughts on Poetry and Its Varieties." In *The Collected Works*. 33 vols. Toronto: University of Toronto Press, 1963–1991, vol. 1, pp. 341–66.

Miller, Jacques-Alain. "Forclusion généralisée." *La Cause du désir* 99.2 (2018), pp. 131–35.

Millot, Catherine. "Épiphanies." In Jacques Aubert, ed. *Joyce avec Lacan*. Paris: Navarin, 1987, pp. 87–95.

Milner, Jean-Claude. *Le périple structural: Figures et paradigme*. Paris: Seuil, 2002.

Miyabayashi, Kan. "Autour d'un poème en prose: Le démon de l'analogie." *Geibun-kenkyu: Journal of Arts and Letters* 91.3 (2016), pp. 148–68.

Molina, Tirso de. *La eleccíon por la virtud: Edición critica, estudio y notas*. Ed. Miguel Galindo Abellán. Murcia: Universidad de Murcia, 2012.

Molnar, Michael. "Reading the Look." In Sander Gilman, Jutta Birmele, Jay Geller, and Valerie D. Greenberg, eds., *Reading Freud's Reading*. New York: New York University Press, 1994, pp. 77–90.

Montaigne, Michel de. *The Complete Essays of Montaigne*. Trans. Donald M. Frame. Stanford: Stanford University Press, 1943.

———. *Les essais*. Ed. Jean Balsamo, Michel Magnien, and Catherine Magnien-Simonin. Paris: Gallimard, 2007.

Montiglio, Silvia. *Silence in the Land of Logos*. Princeton: Princeton University Press, 2000.

Moreschini, Claudio. "Le démon de Socrate et son langage dans la philosophie médio-platonicienne." In Luciana Gabriela Soares Santoprete and Philippe Hoffmann, eds., *Langage des dieux, langages des démons, langages des hommes dans l'Antiquité*. Turnhout: Brepols, 2017, pp. 121–35.

Moschos, John [John Eviratus]. *The Spiritual Meadow (Pratum Spirituale)*. Ed. and trans. John Wortley. Kalamazoo: Cistercian Publications, 1992.

Müller, Karl Otfried. *Aischylos Eumeniden, griechisch und deutsch, mit erläuternden Abhandlungen*. Göttingen: Dieterich, 1833.

Müri, Walter. "ΣΥΜΒΟΛΟΝ: Wort- und sachgeshichtliche Studie." In Eduard Vischer, ed., *Griechische Studien: Ausgewählte wort- und sachgeschichtliche Forschungen zur Antike*. Basel: Friedrich Reinhardt, 1976, pp. 1–44.

Murnaghan, Sheila. "Body and Voice in Greek Tragedy." *Yale Journal of Criticism* 1.2 (1988), pp. 23–43.

Myers, F. W. H. *Human Personality and Its Survival of Bodily Death*. London: Longmans, Green, 1903.

Nebrija, Antonio de. *Vocabulario español-latino*. 1494; facsimile edition Madrid: Real Academia Espaõla, 1951.

Nietzsche, Friedrich. *The Anti-Christ, Ecce Homo, The Twilight of the Idols, and Other Writings*. Ed. Aaron Ridkey and Judith Norman. Trans. Judith Norman. Cambridge: Cambridge University Press, 2005.

——. *The Birth of Tragedy*. Ed. Rayond Geuss and Ronald Speirs. Trans. Ronald Speirs. Cambridge: Cambridge University Press, 1999.

——. *Die Geburt der Tragödie*. Volume 1 of *Sämtliche Werke*. Ed. Giorgio Colli and Mazzino Montinari, 15 vols. Berlin: De Gruyter, 1967–1977.

——. *Götzen-Dämmerung*. Volume 6 of *Sämtliche Werke*.

——. *Human, All Too Human (I)*. Trans. Gary Handwerk. Stanford: Stanford University Press, 1995.

——. *Menschliches, allzumenschliches*. Volume 2 of *Sämtliche Werke*.

Nitze, William Albert. *Perceval and the Holy Grail: An Essay on the Romance of Chrétien de Troyes*. Berkeley: University of California Press, 1949.

Noegl, Scott B. *Nocturnal Ciphers: The Allusive Language of Dreams in the Ancient Near East*. New Haven: American Oriental Society, 2007.

——. "On Puns and Divination: Egyptian Dream Exegesis from a Comparative Perspective." In Kasia Szpakowska, ed., *Through a Glass Darkly: Magic, Dreams and Prophecy in Ancient Egypt*. Swansea: Classical Press of Wales, 2006, pp. 95–119.

Nooter, Sarah. *The Mortal Voice in the Tragedies of Aeschylus*. Cambridge: Cambridge University Press, 2017.

Nougayrol, Jean. "Les rapports des haruspiciens étrusque et assyro-babylonienne, et le foie d'argile de *Falerii Veteres* (Villa Giulia 3786)." *Comptes rendus des séances de l'Académie des Inscriptions et Belles-Lettres* 99.4 (1955), p. 509–19.

Obler, Lorraine K., and Martin L. Albert. "Jules Séglas on Language in Dementia." *Brain and Language* 24 (1985), pp. 314–25.

Oppenheim, A. Leo, *Ancient Mesopotamia: Portrait of a Dead Civilization*. Revised edition by Erica Reiner. 1964, Chicago: University of Chicago Press, 1977.

———. "Sumerian: inim.gar, Akkadian: egirrû=Greek: klēdōn." *Archiv für Orientforschung* 17 (1954–1956), pp. 49–55.

Ortmann, Christa. *Die Selbstaussagen im Parzival: Zur Frage nach der Persongestaltung bei Wolfram von Eschenbach*. Stutgart: W. Kohlhammer, 1972.

Osanna, Massimo. *Santuari e culti dell'Acaia antica*. Naples: Edizioni scientifiche italiane, 1996.

Otto, Walter F. *Die Götter Griechenlands: Das Bild des Göttlichen im Spiegel des griechischen Geistes*. 1929; Frankfurt am Main: Klostermann, 1987.

O'Meara, John. "Arripui, aperui, et legi." *Augustinus Magister: Congrès international augustinien*. 3 vols. Paris: 1954), vol. 1, pp. 59–64.

Owens, Margaret E. "Forgetting Signorelli: Monstrous Visions of the Resurrection of the Dead." *American Imago* 61.1 (2004), pp. 7–33.

Park, George K. "Divination and Its Social Contexts." *Journal of the Royal Anthropological Institute of Great Britain and Ireland* 93.2 (1963), pp. 195–209.

Paul, Zakir. *Disarming Intelligence: Proust, Valéry, and Modern French Criticism*. Princeton: Princeton University Press, 2024.

Pausanias. *Description of Greece*. Trans. W. H. S. Jones. 5 vols. Cambridge, MA: Harvard University Press, 1918–1935.

Paxton, Norman. *The Development of Mallarmé's Prose Style*. Geneva: Droz, 1968.

Pearson, Roger. *Unfolding Mallarmé: The Development of a Poetic Art*. Oxford: Clarendon Press of Oxford University Press, 2006.

Pellion, Frédéric. "Six notes à propos de l'hallucination verbale selon Jacques Lacan: Un cas du dialogue psychanalyse/psychiatrie." *Cliniques méditerranéennes* 71.1 (2005), pp. 283–99.

Pellón, Gustavo. "Given the Lie to Liars: A Note on Anacoluthon in *À la recherche du temps perdu*." *MLN* 95.5 (1980), pp. 1347–52.

Peradotto, John J. "Cledonomancy in the *Oresteia*." *The American Journal of Philology* 90.1 (1969), pp. 1–21.

Petrarca, Francesco. *Opere*. Florence: Sansoni, 1975.

Petruševski, M. D. "De etymo vocis lat. *omen*." *Živa antika / Antiquité vivante* 3.1–2 (1953), p. 144.

Plato. *Apology*. Trans. John Ferguson. In John Ferguson, ed., *Socrates: A Source Book*. London: Macmillan for the Open Press, 1970, pp. 50–67.

———. *Phaedrus*. Trans. Alexander Nehamas and Paul Woodruff. Indianapolis: Hackett, 1995.

Plutarch. *Isis and Osiris*. Trans. Frank Cole Babbitt. In *Moralia*. 16 vols. Cambridge, MA: Harvard University Press, 1927–2004, vol. 5.

———. *On the Daimonion of Socrates: Human Liberation, Divine Guidance and Philosophy*. Ed. Heinz-Günther Nesselrath. Trans. D. A. Russell. Tübingen: Mohr Siebeck, 2010.

Podlecki, Anthony J. "Omens in the *Odyssey*." *Greece and Rome* 14.1 (1967), pp. 12–23.

Poe, Edgar Allan. "Le démon de la perversité." In *Oeuvres en prose*. Trans. Charles Baudelaire. Paris: Gallimard, 1951, pp. 283–89.

———. "The Imp of the Perverse." In *Poetry and Tales*. New York: Literary Classics of the U.S., 1984, pp. 826–32.

Pratt, Louise. "*Odyssey* 19.535–50: On the Interpretation of Dreams and Signs in Homer." *Classical Philology* 89.2 (1994), pp. 147–52.

Préaux, Jean-G. "Du Phédon aux *Confessions* de saint Augustin." *Latomus* 16.2 (1957), pp. 314–25.

Prendergast, Christopher. *Mirages and Mad Beliefs: Proust the Skeptic*. Princeton: Princeton University Press, 2013.

Presendi, Francesca. *Décrire et comprendre le sacrifice: Les réflexions des Romains sur leur propre religion à partir de la littérature antique*. Stuttgart: Fritz Steiner, 2007.

Prins, Yopie. "The Power of the Speech Act: Aeschylus' Furies and their Binding Song." *Arethusa* 24.2 (1991), pp. 177–95.

Proust, Marcel. *The Captive*. In *The Captive & The Fugitive*. Volume 5 of *In Search of Lost Time*. Trans. C. K. Scott Moncrieff, Terence Kilmartin, and Andreas Mayer, revised D. J. Enright. 6 vols. London: Chatto and Windus, 1992.

———. *Du côté de chez Swann*. Volume 1 of *À la recherche du temps perdu*. Ed. Jean-Yves Tadié. 4 vols. Paris: Gallimard, 1988.

———. *La prisonnière*. Volume 3 of *À la recherche du temps perdu*.

———. *Sodom and Gomorrah*. Volume 4 of *In Search of Lost Time*.

———. *Sodome et Gomorrhe*. Volume 3 of *À la recherche du temps perdu*.

———. *Swann's Way*. Volume 1 of *In Search of Lost Time*.

———. *Le temps retrouvé*. Volume 4 of *À la recherche du temps perdu*.

———. *Time Regained*. Volume 6 of *In Search of Lost Time*.

Pseudo-Plutarch. *Essay on the Life and Poetry of Homer*. Eds. J. J. Keaney and Robert Lamberton. Atlanta: Scholars Press, 1996.

Rabaté, Jean-Michel. *James Joyce*. Paris: Hachette, 1993.

———. "Loving Freud Madly: Surrealism between Hysterical and Paranoid Modernism." *Journal of Modern Literature* 25.3–4 (2002), pp. 58–74.

Rabel, Robert J. "Cledonomancy in the *Eumenides*." *Rivista di studi classici* 27.1 (1979), pp. 16–21.

Rabelais, François. *The Third Book of the Heroic Deeds and Sayings of the Good Pantagruel*. In *The Complete Works of François Rabelais*. Trans. Donald M. Frame. Berkeley: University of California Press, 1991, pp. 253–414.

———. *Le Tiers Livre des faicts et dicts heroïques du bon Pantagruel*. In *Oeuvres complètes*. Ed. Mireille Huchon, with François Moreau Paris: Gallimard, 1994, pp. 341–515.

Raeburn, David, and Oliver Thomas. *The Agamemnon of Aeschylus: A Commentary for Students*. Oxford: Oxford University Press, 2011.

Ray-Flaud, Henri. *Le Sphinx et le graal: Le secret et l'énigme*. Paris: Payot & Rivages, 1998.

Real Academia Española. *Diccionario de Autoridades*. 3 vols. 1726; facsimile edition, Madrid: Gredos, 1969.

Reed, Graham. *The Psychology of Anomalous Experience: A Cognitive Approach*. London: Hutchinson, 1972.

Regling, K. "Crassus' Partherkrieg." *Klio* 7 (1907), pp. 357–94.

Reicheneder, Johann Georg. "Breuer–Signorelli–Freud: Zur Initial-Fehlleistung der Psychoanalyse." *Jahrbuch der Psychoanalyse* 79 (2019), pp. 157–90.

Reik, Theodor. "The Psychological Meaning of Silence." *Psychoanalytic Review* 55.2 (1968), pp. 172–86.

———. *Wie Man Psychologe Wird*. Vienna: Internationaler Psychoanalytischer Verlag, 1927.

Renaud de Beaujeu. *Le Bel Inconnu*. Ed. Michèle Perret. Trans. Michèle Perret and Isabelle Weill. Paris: Champion, 2003.

Renaut de Bâgé. *Le Bel Inconnu (Li Biaus Descouneüs; The Fair Unknown)*. Eds. Karen Fresco and Margaret P. Hasselman. Trans. Colleen P. Donagher. New York: Garland, 1992.

Rendu Loisel, Anne-Caroline, "Bruit et émotion dans la littérature akkadienne: Archéologie et Préhistoire." PhD diss., University of Geneva, 2011.

———. *Les chants du monde: Le paysage sonore de l'ancienne Mésopotamie*. With an appendix by Ariane Thomas. Toulouse: Presses universitaires du Midi, 2016.

Richard, Jean-Pierre. *L'univers imaginaire de Stéphane Mallarmé*. Paris: Éditions du Seuil, 1961.

Riley, E. C. "Symbolism in *Don Quixote*, part II, chapter 73." *Journal of Hispanic Philology* 3.2 (1979), pp. 161–74.

Rizakis, A. D. *Achaie I: Sources textuelles et histoire régionale*. Athens: Kentron Hellēnikēs kai Rōmaïkēs Archaiotētos tou Ethnikou Hdrymatos Ereunōn, 1995.

Roberts, Deborah H. "Apollo and his Oracle in the Oresteia." *Hypomnemata* 78 (1984), pp. 39–59.

Robbins, Jill. *Prodigal Son / Elder Brother: Interpretation and Alterity in Augustine, Petrarch, Kafka, Levinas*. Chicago: University of Chicago Press, 1991.

Rochberg, Francesca. *Before Nature: Cuneiform Knowledge and the History of Science*. Chicago: University of Chicago Press, 2016.

———. *The Heavenly Writing: Divination, Horoscopy, and Astronomy in Mesopotamian Culture*. Cambridge: Cambridge University Press, 2004.

———. "'If P then Q': Form and Reasoning in Babylonian Divination." In Amar Annus, ed., *Divination and Interpretation of Signs in the Ancient World*. Chicago: University of Chicago Press, 2010.

Rodis-Lewis, Geneviève. "Le premier registre de Descartes." *Archives de philosophie* 54 (1991), pp. 353–77.

———. *Descartes: His Life and Thought*. Trans. Jane Marie Todd. Ithaca: Cornell University Press, 1998.

Roudinesco, Élisabeth. *Jacques Lacan*. Trans. Barbara Bay. New York: Columbia University Press, 1997.

Rozokoki, Alexandra. "Penelope's Dream in Book 19 of the *Odyssey*." *Classical Quarterly* 51.1 (2001), pp. 1–6.

Romilly, Jacqueline de. "À propos d'Iphigénie dans l'*Agamemnon* d'Eschyle." *Illinois Classical Studies* 19 (1994), pp. 19–26.

Russo, John, Manuel Fernández-Galiano, and Alfred Heubeck. *A Commentary on Homer's Odyssey*. In volume 3: *Books XVII–XXIV*. Oxford: Clarendon Press of Oxford University Press, 1992.

Salisbury, Eve., and James Weldon, eds. *Lybeaus Desconus*. Kalamazoo: Medieval Institute Publications, Western Michigan University, 2013.

Saporetti, Claudio. "Paranomasia nell'oniromanzia assira." *Egitto e vicino Oriente* 18 (1995), pp. 183–91.

Sargent-Baur, Barbara N. *La destre et la senestre: Étude sur le Conte du Graal de Chrétien de Troyes.* Amsterdam: Rodopi, 2000.

Saunders, Corinne. "Voices and Visions: Mind, Body and Affect in Medieval Writing." In Anne Whitehead and Angela Woods, eds., with Sarah Atkinson, Jane Macnaughton and Jennifer Richards, *The Edinburgh Companion to the Critical Medical Humanities.* Edinburgh: Edinburgh University Press, 2016, pp. 411–27.

Saussure, Raymond de. "Remarques sur la technique de la psychanalyse freudienne." *L'Évolution psychiatrique* (1925), pp. 37–54.

Schaff, Philip and Henry Wace, eds. *A Select Library of Nicene and Post-Nicene Fathers, First Series.* 14 vols. Buffalo: Christian Literature Publishing, 1886–1890.

Scheinberg, Susan. "The Bee Maidens of the Homeric Hymn to Hermes." *Harvard Studies in Classical Philology* 83 (1979), pp. 1–28.

Schestag, Thomas. *para–: Titus Lucretius Carus, Johann Peter Hebel, Francis Ponge: Zur literarischen Hermeneutik.* Munich: Boer, 1991.

Schofield, Malcolm. "Cicero for and against Divination." *Journal of Roman Studies* 76 (1986), pp. 47–65.

Scholes, Robert. *The Workshop of Daedalus: James Joyce and the Raw Materials.* Evanston: Northwestern University Press, 1965.

Scott, Walter. *The Life of Napoleon Bonaparte.* Volume 6 of *The Prose Works of Sir Walter Scott.* Paris: A. and W. Galignani, 1827.

———. *Vie de Napoléon Buonaparte, Empereur des Français.* 9 vols. Paris: Gosselin, 1827.

Scurlock, JoAnn, and Burton R. Anderson. *Diagnoses in Assyrian and Babylonian Medicine: Ancient Sources, Translations, and Modern Medical Analyses.* Champlain: University of Illinois Press, 2005.

Segal, Charles. *Tragedy and Civilization: An Interpretation of Sophocles.* Norman: Oklahoma University Press, 1981.

Séglas, Jules. "L'hallucination dans ses rapports avec la fonction du langage—Les hallucinations psycho-motrices." *Le Progrès Médical*, August 18, 1888, pp. 124–26 and pp. 137–39.

———. *Des troubles du langage chez les aliénes.* Paris: J. Rueff, 1892.

Ségur, Général comte de. *Histoire de Napoléon et de la Grande-Armée pendant 1812.* 2 vols. Paris: Baudoin Frères, 1824.

Sextus Empiricus. *Against the Physicists*. Trans. Richard Bett. Cambridge: Cambridge University Press, 2019.

Shattuck, Roger. *Proust's Binoculars: A Study of Memory, Time, and Recognition in 'À la recherche du temps perdu'*. Princeton: Princeton University Press, 1962.

Shelmedrine, Susan C. "Hermes and the Tortoise: A Prelude to Cult." *Greek, Roman and Byzantine Studies* 25 (1974), pp. 201–207.

Sherwin-White, A. N. *Roman Foreign Policy in the East, 168 B.C. to 1 A.D.* London: Duckworth, 1984.

Soler, Colette. *Lacan, lecteur de Joyce*. 2nd ed. Paris: Presses universitaires de France, 2019.

Sommer, Benjamin D. "Did Prophecy Cease? Evaluating a Reevaluation." *Journal of Biblical Literature* 115.1 (1996), pp. 31–47.

Soverini, Luca. "ΨΙΘΥΡΟΣ: Hermes, Afrodite e il sussurro nella Grecia antica." In Salvatore Alessandrì, ed., *Ἱστορίη: Studi offerti dagli allievi a Giuseppe Nenci in occasione del suo settantesimo compleanno*. Galatina: Congedo, 1994, pp. 433–60.

Speiser, E. A. "The Idea of History in Ancient Mesopotamia." In J. J. Finkelstein and Moshe Greenberg, eds., *Oriental and Biblical Studies: Collected Writings of E. A. Speiser*. Philadelphia: University of Pennsylvania Press, 1967, pp. 270–312.

Sperling, David. "Akkadian *egerrû* and Hebrew *bt qwl*." *Journal of the Near Eastern Society of Columbia University* 4 (1972), pp. 63–74.

Spicer, Jack. *The House that Jack Built: The Collected Lectures of Jack Spicer*. Ed. Peter Gizzi. Middletown: Wesleyan University Press, 1998.

——. "Sporting Life." In *My Vocabulary Did This to Me*. Eds. Peter Gizzi and Kevin Killian. Middletown: Wesleyan University Press, 2008, pp. 373–74.

——. "Surrealism." In *My Vocabulary Did This to Me*, p. 273.

——. "A Textbook of Poetry." In *My Vocabulary Did This to Me*, pp. 299–313.

Starobinski, Jean. "Freud, Breton, Myers." *L'Arc* 34 (1968), pp. 87–96.

Starr, Ivan. *Rituals of the Diviner*. Malibu: Undena Publications, 1983.

Steinmetz, Jean-Luc. "Le paradoxe mallarméen: Les Poèmes en prose." *Europe* 564–65 (1976), pp. 134–59.

Stierle, Karlheinz. *Francesco Petrarca: Ein Intellektueller im Europa des 14. Jahrhunderts*. Munich: Carl Hanser, 2003.

Stock, Brian. *Augustine the Reader: Meditation, Self-Knowledge, and the Ethics of Interpretation*. Cambridge, MA: Harvard University Press, 1996.

Stoker, Hendrik Gerhardus. *Conscience: Phenomena and Theories.* Trans. Philip E. Blosser. Notre Dame: University of Notre Dame Press, 2018.

———. *Das Gewissen: Erscheinungsformen und Theorie.* Bonn: F. Cohen, 1925.

Stockinger, Hildebrandt. *Die Vorzeichen im homerischen Epos: Ihre Typik und ihre Bedeutung.* St. Ottilien: EOS Verlag, 1959.

Struck, Peter T., *Birth of the Symbol: Ancient Readers at the Limits of Their Texts.* Princeton: Princeton University Press, 2004.

———. *Divination and Human Nature: A Cognitive History of Intuition in Classical Antiquity.* Princeton: Princeton University Press, 2016.

Svenbro, Jesper. *Phrasikleia: An Anthropology of Reading in Ancient Greece.* Trans. Janet Lloyd. Ithaca: Cornell University Press, 1993.

———. *Le tombeau de la cigale: Figures de l'écriture et de la lecture en Grèce ancienne.* Paris: Les Belles Lettres, 2021.

———. "Voir en voyant: La perception visuelle chez Empédocle." *Métis* n.s. 2 (2004), pp. 47–70.

Tadié, Jean-Yves. *Le lac inconnu : Entre Freud et Proust.* Paris: Gallimard, 2012.

Talmud. *Hebrew-English Edition of the Babylonian Talmud.* Ed. I. Epstein. Trans. Maurice Simon. 18 vols. London: Soncino Press, 1990.

Taplin, Oliver *The Stagecraft of Aeschylus: The Dramatic Use of Exits and Entrances in Greek Tragedy.* Oxford: Clarendon Pres of Oxford University Press, 1977.

Taylor, Jane H. M. "Perceval/Perceforest: Naming as Hermeneutic in the *Roman de Perceforest.*" *Romance Quarterly* 44.4 (1987), pp. 201–14.

Théis, Alexandre de. *Travels of Polycletes in Letters from Rome.* London: J. Souter, 1826.

Thoreau, Henry David. "The Prometheus Bound of Aeschylus." In *Excursions and Poems.* Volume 5 of *The Writings of Henry David Thoreau.* Ed. Bradford Torrey. 20 vols. Boston: Houghton Mifflin, 1906, pp. 338–75.

Timotin, Andrei. *La démonologie platonicienne: Histoire de la notion de* daimōn *de Platon aux derniers néoplatoniciens.* Leiden: Brill, 2012.

Timpanaro, Sebastiano. *La "fobia romana" e altri scritti su Freud e Meringer.* Pisa: ETS Editrice, 1992.

———. *The Freudian Slip: Psychoanalysis and Textual Criticism.* Trans. Kate Soper. London: New Left Books, 1976.

Tooke, Andrew. *The Pantheon, Representing the Fabulous History of the Heathen Gods and Most Illustrious Heroes.* London: J. Johnson et al., 1803.

———. *The Pantheon, Representing the Fabulous Histories of the Heathen Gods and Most Illustrious Heroes in a Plain and Familiar Method, by Way of Dialogue.* New York: Evert Duyckinck, 1810.

Trueblood, Alan S. "La jaula de grillos (*Don Quijote*, II, 73)." In in Marta Cristina Carbonell and Adolfo Sotelo Vázquez, eds., *Homenaje al professor Antonio Vilanova.* 2 vols. Barcelona: Universidad de Barcelona, 1989, vol. 1, pp. 699–708.

Tucker, Herbert F. "Dramatic Monologue and the Overhearing of Lyric." In Chaviva Hošek and Patricia Parker, eds., *Lyric Poetry: Beyond New Criticism* Ithaca: Cornell University Press, 1985, pp. 226–43.

Usener, Hermann. *Götternamen: Versuch einer Lehre von der religiösen Begriffsbildung.* Bonn: Friedrich Cohen, 1896.

———. "Psithyros." *Rheinisches Museum für Philologie* 59 (1904), pp. 623–34.

Ustinova, Yulia. "Modes of Prophecy, or Modern Arguments in Support of the Ancient Approach." *Kernos: Revue international et pluridisciplinaire de religion grecque antique* 26 (2013), pp. 25–44.

Valenton, M. "De modis auspicandi Romanorum." *Mnemosyne* 17 (1889), pp. 275–325 and 418–52, and *Mnemosyne* 18 (1890), pp. 208–63 and 406–56.

Valéry, Paul. "L'âme et la danse." In *Oeuvres*, ed. Jean Hytier, 2 vols. Paris: Gallimard, 1960, vol. 2, pp. 148–76.

———. *Cahiers.* 29 vols. Paris: Centre national de la recherche scientifique, 1957–.

———."Calepin d'un poète." In *Oeuvres*, vol, 1, pp. 1447–63.

———. "Littérature." In *Oeuvres*, vol. 2, pp. 546–70.

Van Dam, Cornelis. *Urim and Thummim: A Means of Revelation in Ancient Israel.* Winona Lake: Eisenbrauns, 1997.

Van De Mieroop, Marc. *Philosophy before the Greeks: The Pursuit of Truth in Ancient Babylonia.* Princeton: Princeton University Press, 2016.

Vanheule, Stijn. *The Subject of Psychosis: A Lacanian Perspective.* London: Palgrave Macmillan, 2011.

Van der Horst, Pieter W. "Ancient Jewish Bibliomancy." *Journal of Greco-Roman Christianity and Judaism* 1 (2000), pp. 9–17.

———. "*Sortes:* Sacred Books as Instant Oracles." In *Japheth in the Tents of Shem: Studies on Jewish Hellenism in Antiquity.* Leuven: Peeters, 2002, pp. 159–89.

Varro. *On the Latin Language.* Trans. Roland G. Kent, 2 vols. Cambridge, MA: Harvard University Press, 1938.

Vernant, Jean-Pierre, "La cuisine du sacrifice en pays grec." In *Oeuvres: Religions, rationalités, politique*. 2 vols. Paris: Seuil, 2008, vol. 1, pp. 891–985.

———. *Mythe et pensée chez les Grecs: Études de psychologie historique*. Paris: La Découverte, 1988.

———. "Odysseus in Person." *Representations* 67 (1999), pp. 1–26.

———, et al. *Divination et rationalité*. Paris: Éditions du Seuil, 1974.

Versnel, Henk S. "A God: Why Is Hermes Hungry?" In *Coping with the Gods: Wayward Readings in Greek Theology*. Leiden: Brill, 2011, pp. 309–77.

———. "Religious Mentality in Ancient Prayer." In Henk S. Versnel, ed., *Faith, Hope and Worship: Aspects of Religious Mentality in the Ancient World*. Leiden: E. J. Brill, 1981, pp. 309–77.

Viola, Manuel Simón. "El regreso a la aldea (*Quijote*, II, 73)." *Philologia hispalensis* 182.2 (2014), pp. 211–25.

Virgil. *Aeneid*. Trans. Frederick Ahl. Oxford: Oxford University Press, 2007.

Von Mergell, Bodo. *Wolfram von Eschenbach und seine französischen Quellen*. 2 vols. Münster: Aschendorffschen Verlagsbuchhandlung, 1936.

Walzl, Florence L. "The Liturgy of the Epiphany Season and the Epiphanies of Joyce." *PMLA* 80.4 (1965), pp. 436–50.

Ward, Allen Mason. *Marcus Crassus and the Late Roman Republic*. Columbia : University of Missouri Press, 1977.

Weisberg, David B. "An Old Babylonian Forerunner to *šumma ālu*." *Hebrew Union College Annual* 40–41 (1969–1970), pp. 87–104.

West, Martin L., ed. and trans. *Greek Epic Fragments: From the Seventh to the Fifth Centuries BC*. Cambridge, MA: Harvard University Press, 2003.

Wiesman, T. P., "Summoning Jupiter: Magic in the Roman Republic." In *Unwritten Rome*. Exeter: Exeter University Press, 2008.

Wild, Christopher. "Apertio Libri: Codex and Conversion." In Eric Downing, Jonathan M. Hess, and Richard V. Benson, eds., *Literary Studies and the Pursuits of Reading* Rochester: Camden House, 2012, pp. 17–39.

Wilden, Anthony G. "Freud, Signorelli, and Lacan: The Repression of the Signifier." *American Imago* 23.4 (1966), pp. 322–66.

Willis, Sharon. "'Gilbertine' apparue." *Romanic Review* 73.3 (1982), pp. 331–45.

Wilmotte, Maurice. *Le Roman du Gral, d'après les versions les plus anciennes*. Paris: La Renaissance du livre, 1930.

Wills, Gary. "*Agamemnon* 1346–71, 1659–53." *Harvard Studies in Classical Philology* 67 (1963), pp. 255–67.

Wischmeyer, Oda. "Das heilige Buch im Judentum des Zweiten Tempels." *Zeitschrfit für neutestamentliche Wissenschaft* 86 (1995), pp. 218–42.

Wohlfarhth, Irving. "'Was nie geschrieben wurde, lesen': Walter Benjamins Theorie des Lesens." In Uwe Steiner, ed., *Walter Benjamin 1892–1940, Zum 100. Geburtstag*. New York: Peter Lang, 1992, pp. 297–344.

Wolfram von Eschenbach. *Parzival*. Ed. Karl Lachmann. Berlin: De Gruyter, 1952.

———. *Parzival*. Trans. A. T. Hatto. New York: Penguin Books, 1980.

Woolf, Virginia. *A Room of One's Own*. London: Grafton, 1977.

Wundt, Wilhelm Max. *Völkerpsychologie: Eine Untersuchung der Entwicklungsgesetze von Sprache, Mythus und Sitte*. 2 vols. in 5 parts. Leipzig: W. Engelmann, 1900.

Yeats, William Butler. *A Vision: An Explanation of Life Founded upon the Writings of Giraldus and upon Certain Doctrines Attributed to Kusta ben Luka*. London: T. Werner Laurie, 1925.

———. *A Vision, The Original 1925 Edition*. Eds. Catherine E. Paul and Margaret Mills Harper. Volume 13 of *The Collected Works of W. B. Yeats*, eds. Richard J. Finneran and George Mills Harper (New York: Scribner, 1978).

Zahn, Theodor. *Cyprian von Antiochen und die deutsche Faustsage*. Erlangen: A. Deichert, 1882.

Zeitlin, Froma I. "The Motif of the Corrupted Sacrifice in Aeschylus's *Oresteia*." *Transactions and Proceedings of the American Philological Association* 96 (1965), pp. 463–508.

———. *Under the Sign of the Shield: Semiotics and Aeschylus' Seven against Thebes*. Rome: Edizioni dell'Ateneo, 1982.

Index

Zone Books series design by Bruce Mau
Image placement and production by Julie Fry
Typesetting by Meighan Gale
Printed and bound by Maple Press